For my wife Lesley, our son Thomas, his wife Sarah and our grandson George.

In loving memory of my mother and father Vera and Tommy Hall and to my great uncle Lance Corporal 39649 James Hall 1/9th Battalion Manchester Regiment and 126th Infantry Brigade Machine Gun Company Killed in Action May 11th 1917.

Contents

Illustrations

CHAPTER ONE

1st July to 17th September 1917

Forty Mile March
Live Bomb Practice
Horse Show
King's Declaration
To Flanders
Defence of Nieuport
Mustard Gas and Training
East of Ypres

Bailleulmont

1 July 1917. The battalion was scheduled to leave Boyelles in four trains on the light railway at 7am, 7.05am, 7.10am, and 7.15am, but the trains were forty-five minutes late. 'A' and 'B' Companies caught the first two trains and they arrived at Beaumetz-lès-Loges at 9.45am. They then marched to Bailleulmont and reached their billets at 11am. 'C' Company got the third train and arrived at Beaumetz-lès-Loges at 10.45am. They then marched to Bailleulmont, arriving at the billets at noon. 'D' Company got the last train and arrived at Beaumetz-lès-Loges at 11am, and then marched to Bailleulmont, arriving at 12.15pm.

The battalion transport left Boyelles at 7am and arrived at Bailleulmont at 11.20am. 'A' Company's field kitchen had to be left en route because of a broken axle.

2 July. The battalion remained in billets. 98th Infantry Brigade Order 152 was received at 3.15pm for the move of the battalion the following day.

Arquèves

3 July. The battalion was placed under the command of the 98th Infantry Brigade for the march from Bailleulmont via la Cauchie, Gaudiempré, Hénu, Authie, and Vauchelles-lès-Authie to Arquèves.

This was a real stop-start day. At 5am packs were loaded on three lorries for transportation. The battalion had breakfast between 5am and 6.30am. The march started at 6.37am from Bailleulmont Church. Not long after they had to wait to let past the 4th Battalion King's (Liverpool) Regiment, an infantry battalion of 98th Brigade. The battalion stopped again between 7.50am to 9am while the 98th Infantry Brigade had breakfast. The halt merely wasted an hour of cool weather during which time all the men became stiff.

After 9am the march became difficult because of the very hot weather and miles of loose flint road surface. Hundreds of men, mainly 1/4th Suffolks another infantry battalion of the 98th Brigade, fell out. This set a very bad example and 180 18th Middlesex men failed to march in with the battalion.

The main body of the battalion completed the 14 mile march to Arquèves at 1.30pm. Fifteen of the men who fell out rejoined within half an hour. An officer was detailed to bring in the rest. 143 men were brought in within an hour. 22 men had not rejoined by 4pm. Two men were admitted to hospital suffering from heat exhaustion. The remainder rejoined the battalion by 8.30pm.

Villers-Bocage

4 July. The battalion marched under the orders of the 98th Infantry Brigade leaving Arquèves at 5.30am and went via Raincheval, Puchevillers and Rubempré to Villers-Bocage completing the ten-mile march at 10.15am.

The road between Raincheval and Puchevillers was in very poor condition and flooded in several places by heavy rain during the night.

A lorry carried the packs of N.C.O.s and the 180 men aged over forty. Thirteen men fell out.

St. Sauveur

5 July. Under the orders of the 100th Infantry Brigade the battalion marched the

six miles from Villers-Bocage via Bertangles to St. Sauveur. They marched at 5.25am and arrived 8.30am. Only three men fell out.

Major-General Pinney recorded in his war diary 'Bruised right ankle when taking off boot Jack. Slipped. Sausage (his charger) pecked badly outside le Quesnoy Wood while galloping fast. Went a bit lame walking – old broken thigh a bit stiff in the afternoon'.[1]

Le Mesge

6 July. The battalion marched from St. Sauveur and headed south across the River Somme to Ailly-sur-Somme. It then marched nine miles north-west through Breilly, Picquigny to Soues and le Mesge. 'A' and 'B' Companies were billeted at Souses and H.Q. 'C' Company and 'D' Company were billeted at le Mesge. Five men fell out.

Following Plumer's Second Army success in capturing the Messines – Wyschaete Ridge, the British front in Flanders was rearranged between 10 June and the first week of July. The British Fifth Army, under General Sir Hubert de la Poer Gough, took command of the front from Observation Ridge to Boesinghe. French troops extended the British left flank northwards beyond Boesinghe. British troops relieved French troops holding the coast sector from St. George to the sea. The First French Army, under General Anthoine, relieved Belgium troops holding the front from Boesinghe to Noordschoote.

The British Army in Flanders was then totally engaged in completing preparations for the forthcoming attack. They were engaged in the construction of roads and railways, the provision of adequate water supplies and accommodation for the troops, forming dumps, digging dugouts, subways and trenches and assembling and registering of guns.[2]

7 July. The day was spent in clearing up. Clothing and equipment were then inspected. Over the past four days the battalion had marched 40 miles and they were now safely tucked away from the front in the rest area west of Amiens

8 July. The battalion had church parade at 11.30am. Major Ionides rejoined the battalion from leave.

9 July. 'A' Company and a proportion of 'H.Q.' Company were re-inoculated against typhoid.

'B', 'C' and 'D' Companies carried out platoon training.

10 July. 'A' Company was recovering from inoculation. 'B' Company and more of 'H.Q.' Company were inoculated.

'C' Company together with 'D' Company continued training.

11 July. 'A' and 'D' Companies trained. 'B' Company was recovering from their inoculations. 'C' Company and some of 'H.Q.' Company were inoculated. Capt. Coles rejoined from attachment to divisional H.Q. and resumed command of 'B' Company.

Private Alfred Price was posted back to the battalion having moved to the 41st Infantry Base Depot on 1 December 1916 and then onto 2nd Battalion Middlesex Regiment on 3 December 1916.[3]

The Germans shelled the Nieuport bridgehead using their new yellow cross (Mustard) gas for the first time.[4]

12 July. 'A' and 'B' Companies trained. 'D' Company was inoculated. 'C' Company got a day off training to allow them to recover from the inoculation.

Overnight on 12 /13 July the Germans deluged the town of Ypres with yellow cross mustard gas causing 2,014 casualties, mostly in the 15th Division. This caused severe pains in the head, throat, and eyes, vomiting and bronchial irritation. The affect was in many cases extremely painful, but caused no permanent damage to the eyes.[6]

13 July. 'A', 'B' and 'C' Companies trained. 'D' Company was recovering from inoculation. Officers were instructed in map reading and writing reports from 2.45pm to 4.45pm.

Capt. Simmonds left to join the 19th Battalion Northumberland Fusiliers.

14 July. Bastille Day. Vive la France – Vive la Revolution!

The battalion exercised in close order drill from 8am to 9.30am. This was the first battalion drill for which the opportunity and training ground had been available since they landed in France in November 1915.

15 July. Church parade was held at 9.30am. Lt.-Col. Storr went to Boulogne to

interview the Command Paymaster about additional, working pay and pioneer pay.

16 July. 'A', 'B', 'C' and 'D' Companies trained. The C.O. returned from Boulogne.

17 July. 2nd Lieut. Cotton took charge of a live bomb practice. He was chosen for this because he had gained a little experience using Mills hand grenades in England. The mills bomb was a hand thrown grenade which had a safety lever which self released at the point the bomb left the hand and it exploded four seconds later.

The practice took place in a trench and each man had to throw one live grenade over the top. During the practice a nervous private dropped a bomb and the safety lever was released. It fell amongst the men and near to a box of live bombs. 2nd Lieut. Cotton acted instantly, picked up the bomb and threw it out of the trench two seconds before it exploded. This act of gallantry saved the private and those around him from certain injury and probably death.

Captain Crawford witnessed the incident and reported it to Lt.-Col. Storr. In turn the Commanding Officer asked 2nd Lieut. Cotton if he wished the incident to be reported to Divisional Headquarters but he declined.[6]

The 33rd Division summer horse show was held at Cavillon. Present at the show was the Royal Welch Fusiliers mascot a white ram with huge horns.[7]

The battalion won first and second place in Class IIB. Pack Animals (Mules), second in Class VB. (Teams of Four Mules), and third place in Class I. Single Horse Turnout.[8]

The following notice was posted at Buckingham Palace.

By THE KING

A PROCLAMATION

DECLARING THAT THE NAME OF WINDSOR IS TO BE BORNE BY HIS ROYAL HOUSE AND FAMILY AND RELINQUISHING THE USE OF ALL GERMAN TITLES AND DIGNITIES.

GEORGE R.I.

WHEREAS We, having taken into consideration the Name and Title of Our Royal House and Family, have determined that henceforth Our House and Family shall be styled and known as the House and Family of Windsor:

And whereas We have further determined for Ourselves and for and on behalf of Our descendants and all other the descendants of Our Grandmother Queen Victoria of blessed and glorious memory to relinquish and discontinue the use of all German Titles and Dignities:

And whereas We have declared these Our determinations in Our Privy Council:

Now, therefore We, out of Our Royal Will and Authority, do hereby declare and announce that as from the date of this Our Royal Proclamation Our House and Family shall be styled and known as the House and Family of Windsor, and that all the descendants in the male line of Our said Grandmother Queen Victoria who are subjects of these Realms, other than female descendants who may marry or may have married, shall bear the said Name of Windsor:

And do hereby further declare and announce that We for Ourselves and for and on behalf of Our descendants and all other the descendants of Our said Grandmother Queen Victoria who are subjects of these Realms, relinquish and enjoin the discontinuance of the use of the Degrees, Styles, Dignities, Titles and Honours of the Dukes and Duchesses of Saxony and Princes and Princesses of Saxe-Coburg and Gotha, and all other German Degrees, Styles, Dignities, Titles, Honours and Appellations to Us or to them heretofore belonging or appertaining.

Given at Our Court at Buckingham Palace, this Seventeenth day of July in the year of our Lord One thousand nine hundred and seventeen, and in the Eighth year of Our Reign.

GOD SAVE THE KING.[9]

After 715 days of the bloodiest warfare in the history of the British Army

King George V decided to sever his family's historic links with the German Royal Family and renounce all of his and his family's hereditary claims and titles in Germany.

18 July. The battalion trained in the morning. The divisional horse show continued but the battalion did not win any more prizes.

The supplement to the London Gazette of the 18 July 1917 recorded that His Majesty the KING has been graciously pleased to award the Military Medal for bravery in the Field to P.W/443 Pte. T. McBride, Mdx. R.[10] Sergeant P.W/430 G. Matthews, Sergeant P.W/1296 William Till, and Sergeant P.W/157 Charles Ward were also 'gazetted' for the Military Medal.[11]

19 July. 'C' Company held a sports day.

20 July. Lt.-Col. Storr, Captain C.P. Hinman Adjutant, and Captain (Acting Major) R.W. Cardew M.C., R.E. the Officer commanding the 33rd Divisional Signals and signallers started a divisional exercise without troops. This exercise was scheduled to finish at 9.15am the following day.

'C' Company's sports day continued.

21 July. The battalion exercised in close order drill from 8am to 10am. 'D' Company held a sports day.

22 July. Church parade was held at 11am followed by a celebration of Holy Communion. Company commanders held a conference at 5.30pm.

23 July. Officers were exercised in map reading etc. from 5.30pm to 6.30pm.

24 July. Training.

25 July. 'B' Company held a sports day.

26 July. 'A' Company held a sports day.

27 July. Officers were exercised in map reading from 5.30pm to 6.30pm.

28 July. The battalion exercised in close order drill from 8am to 9.30am. The

battalion received Divisional Order 212 at 12.30pm for the move of the 33rd Division to the Fourth Army area in Belgium.

29 July. Heavy rain caused the cancellation of the morning church parade. A conference of officers was held at 2.30pm to discuss the battalion move. The battalion received Divisional Order 213 at 3.30pm giving transport instructions.

2nd Lieuts. A. Burgoyne and C.R. Pughe, joined the battalion on appointment and were posted to 'B' Company. 2nd Lieut. C.G. Sothers joined on appointment and was posted to 'A' Company.

Liercourt

30 July. A billeting party was sent on by rail to Dunkerque to arrange billets at Coudekerque. Permission was obtained to move to Liercourt on the 31st to avoid the long march to Pont Remy for entrainment. A billeting party was sent to Liercourt to make arrangements. Orders for the move were issued at 2pm.

31st July Third Battle of Ypres

The stated objective of the Flanders offensive was to destroy the German submarine bases and clear the enemy from the Belgian coast. Field Marshal Haig also held the view that 'Germany was within six months of total exhaustion of her available manpower, *if the fighting continues at its present intensity*'.[12]

Following the British success at Messines – Wytschaete Haig sent Sir William Robertson his 'Appreciation of Military Situation, Present Situation and Future Plans'. In this appreciation Haig stated 'if our resources are concentrated in France to the fullest possible extent the British armies are capable and can be relied on to effect great results this summer – results which will make final victory more assured and which may even bring it within reach this year'.[13]

Haig went on to state 'it is possible that the Belgian coast could be cleared this summer, and the defeats on the German troops entailed in doing so might quite possibly lead to their collapse'.[14]

Clearly Haig believed the German Army was at breaking point and the Third Battle of Ypres would provide him with the decisive victory he needed.

The Third Battle of Ypres – The Battle of Pilckem Ridge

For the Battle of Pilckem Ridge Haig assembled 281 heavy guns, 718 medium guns and 2,092 field guns. On 15 July the British guns started a barrage on the enemy positions facing the city of Ypres. Between 15 July and 2 August they poured 4,283,550 shells into the fifteen-mile long German front as the precursor to and during the Battle of Pilckem Ridge.[15]

The front selected for the attack extended from the Lys River opposite Deulemont northwards to beyond Steenstraat. The main area of attack was the seven-and-half mile central front from the Zillebeke – Zandvoorde road and Boesinghe.

Gough's Fifth Army took the centre. Plumer's Second Army covered the right flank of the Fifth Army. The French First Army, under General Anthoine, covered the left flank of the Fifth Army securing them from counter-attacks from the north.[16]

The Fifth Army objectives were to advance three miles and capture the whole of Gheluvelt Ridge, Pilckem Ridge, all the German defensives including their Third Line and then advance on to the main Ypres Ridge at Broodseinde, with the left flank along the Gravenstafel Spur and Langemarck.[17]

Haig observed 'On no previous occasion, not excepting the attack on the Messines – Wytschaete Ridge, had the whole ground for which we had to attack been so completely exposed to the enemy's observation'.[18] This begs the obvious question why did Haig choose to attack from a completely exposed position? Likewise, why did he choose to attack German defences that had been established in great depth over three years of occupation, that were formidable, well defended and in an elevated position?

From midnight on 30 July until 3.50am on 31 July gas shelling was extended over all the known battery positions, a procedure which had proved successful before the Messines assault. By these means, the German initial defence barrage was mostly neutralised; but subsequent events during the day were to reveal that the German artillery still had a great and un-mastered reserve of fire-power, particularly in its concentration of guns about the Gheluvelt Plateau.[19]

At 3.50am on 31 July, without any element of surprise, Sir Hubert Gough's Fifth Army launched the summer offensive to capture Passchendaele Ridge. British and French troops advanced behind a creeping barrage across the shattered German outposts and made early progress.

Sir Douglas Haig recorded in his diary '*The heavy firing near here at 4.15 woke me up.* The whole ground was shaking with the terrific bombardment. During the night the Fifth Army was to discharge 80,000 gas shells! The French also kept up a heavy fire. In the afternoon I visited General Gough with C.G.S. He had been to H.Qrs. of 19th and 2nd Corps. Fighting on our right had been most severe. This I had expected. Our Divisions had made good progress and were on top of the ridge which the Menin road crosses, but had not advanced sufficiently eastwards to have observation into the valley beyond. Further to the west, our troops had established themselves beyond the Steenbeck (Steenbeek) and the French had taken Bixschoote and the Cabaret Kortekeer...This was a fine day's work'.[20]

Sir Douglas Haig gave a more detailed account of the first day of the battle in his fourth despatch 'The Campaign of 1917'. At the end of the day the Fifth Army had carried the German first system of defence south of Westhoek and established themselves on the outskirts of the village. The difficult country east of Ypres, where the Menin Road crossed the crest of the Wytschaete – Passchendaele Ridge was the key to the German position and here the British troops met the most determined opposition. The 24th, 30th and 8th British Divisions fought their way steadily forward and captured Shrewsbury Forest, Sanctuary Wood, Stirling Castle, Hooge and the Bellewaarde Ridge. The German first line system was captured but the advance beyond this was held up in front of Glencorse Wood and Inverness Copse.

The Second Army New Zealand troops attacked on the right front and captured La Basse Ville, the 41st Division captured Hollebeke and the difficult ground north of the bend of the Ypres-Comines Canal and east of Battle Wood.

Further north British and French troops carried the whole of the German trench system and proceeded to attack the German second line of defence. The Scottish troops of the 15th Division took Verlorenhoek and Frezenberg. The Welsh troops of the 38th Division took Pilckem. The West Lancashire Territorials 55th Division took the strong point Pommern Redoubt. The German second line was captured as far as St. Julien. North of St. Julien the German second line was passed with British troops holding the line of the Steenbeek to the junction with the French. On the left flank the French protected the British left flank, advanced to the Steenbeek and took Bixschoote.[21]

Prime Minister David Lloyd George in his War Memoirs points out that

the orders given by Field Marshal Haig to Sir Hubert Gough and his Fifth Army were to capture the Passchendaele – Staden Ridge and the Roulers – Thourout railway to facilitate a landing between the Yser River and Ostend and in combination with a force so landed, to gain possession of the Belgian coast. He further pointed out that on the left the first two lines were reached, but not the green line which was the ultimate objective of the first day's attack. On the right, little progress was made and the casualties were undoubtedly heavy. The failure on the right was serious. It meant that the further we drove the Germans on the left, the more we should be creating a dangerous salient commanded by German artillery planted on the heights to the right.[22]

Field Marshal Haig instructed Gough 'to carry out the original plan; to consolidate ground gained, and to improve his position as he may deem necessary, for facilitating the next advance; the next advance will be made as soon as possible, *but only after adequate bombardment and after dominating the hostile Artillery*'.[23]

The ground conditions were already atrocious due to the low lying nature of the land, the clayey soil, extremely poor drainage, the predictably wet summer and damage caused by artillery bombardment. The persistent rain made the ground conditions markedly worse. Gough's Fifth Army struggled to consolidate the limited gains they had made and found it difficult to make any further advances.

31 July. After twenty-four days away from the front the battalion was now heading for Flanders. 'C' Company was made up of 8 officers, 256 other ranks, one cooker, four G.S. wagons and sixteen horses. The battalion marched six miles from le Mesge at 8.30am via Soues and Hangest-sur-Somme to Longpré-les-Corps-Saints arriving at 11.45am. They had their dinner at Longpré and then got on train No.6 that left at 3.51pm.

'A', 'B' and 'D' Companies marched to Liercourt via Hangest – Condé – Fontaine-sur-Somme, starting from Soues at 5.30am and arriving at 9.45am.

During the ten-mile march 28 men fell out. As a result these companies were refused permission to board any trains for the day. All the men who fell out, except those certified unfit by the medical officer, were given an hour's pack drill from 5pm to 6pm.

A conference of company commanders was held at 11am to arrange for the entrainment at Pont Remy.

Coudekerque

1 August 1917. 'C' Company arrived at Dunkerque at 1.30am, detrained and marched to Coudekerque, arriving at 4am. 'C' Company transport arrived at 6am.

'A', 'B' and 'D' Companies marched from Liercourt to Pont Remy and boarded train No. 17 which left at 8.58am and arrived at Dunkerque at 7.30am. The companies marched to Coudekerque and arrived about 9.30pm. The transport left Dunkerque at 9pm and arrived about 10.45pm.

The battalion was billeted in farms over an area of about three square miles. Steady rain all day welcomed them to Flanders Fields.

2nd August – The Battle of Pilckem Ridge

The battle ended with only modest gains but very heavy casualties. The German observation areas on the highest part of Gheluvelt Plateau near Clapham Junction and along the long rise via Bellewaarde to Pilckem were captured and the general front had been advanced by about 3,000 yards.[24] This fell well short of Gough's planned three mile advance.

The Second and Fifth Armies had 31,850 men killed, missing or wounded. Of the 117 tanks deployed 77 ditched, bellied or broke down mechanically. 42 of these, including those that received direct hits, were completely written off.

The losses for the German Fourth Army for 21-23 July were given as 30,000 in round numbers. Brigadier-General Edmonds calculated that, including the wounded that were expected to recover in a reasonable time, the German total casualties were 40,000.[25]

2 August. The battalion had a day's rest. It threw it down all day and the men were forced to stay in their billets.

The battalion received Divisional Order 216 at 11.55pm for the two battalions of the 98th Infantry Brigade to relieve two battalions of the 147th Infantry Brigade.

3 August. It rained all day again but that did not stop Lt.-Col. Storr from ordering each company on a route march.

Four days of incessant rain followed by stormy and unsettled weather had turned Passchendaele into a succession of vast muddy pools. The valleys of the

choked and overflowing streams were speedily transformed into long stretches of bog, impassable except by a few well defined tracks, which became marks for the German artillery. To leave these tracks was to risk death by drowning and in the course of the subsequent fighting, on several occasions, both men and pack animals were lost in this way. Haig was forced to postpone the resumption of his Flanders summer offensive until the weather allowed the ground to recover.[26]

4 August. Each company went on another route march. Major-General Pinney visited battalion H.Q. at 11.30am.

5 August. Church parade was held at 10.30am. Orders were received at 3.30pm for the battalion to move to camp east of La Panne on the 7th.

6 August. Two platoons of 'A' Company, with one G.S. wagon and one limbered wagon, under Capt. Hill M.C. marched from Coudekerque at 4.30am. They arrived at La Panne at 11.45am. Two men fell out. 'A' Company were ordered to prepare a camp for the battalion. The site for the camp was pointed out. Tents were drawn down and arrangements were made for a small supply of timber to be delivered.

The rest of the battalion trained. Orders for the march on the 7th were issued at 11.30am. Lieut. Baer rejoined the battalion and was posted to 'D' Company.

Thomas McBride's daughter Martha celebrated her fifth birthday.

La Panne Bains (De Panne)

7 August. The battalion marched from Coudekerque via Uxem, Ghyvelde, Adinkerke, and La Panne to camp just east of La Panne Bains. The head of the column passed Boomkens at 7am and arrived at 1.45pm.

Due to a map reading error the battalion ended up trudging through a track of deep sand east of Ghyvelde. They eventually rejoined the main road along the Belgian frontier.

The transport found it tough going and had serious problems getting through the deep sand. One man broke his leg when he was thrown off a G.S. wagon.

Eleven men fell out.

One platoon of 'B' Company left the column at Ghyvelde and proceeded to XV Corps School at La Panne, a mile north-west of Ghyvelde, for work on the training grounds there.

The two platoons of 'A' Company under Capt. Hill pitched the camp and started creating sheds in readiness for the battalion.

8 August. The battalion spent the day improving the camp. Eighteen G.S. wagon loads of material were brought up from XV Corps dump.

At 4pm the battalion paraded for bathing in the sea.

9 August. The battalion worked on camp improvements. Men not working on camp improvements undertook drill exercises on the seashore.

10 August. Work continued on camp improvements.

11 August. Training.

12 August. Church parade was held at 11.45am.

13 August. Major Ionides left to take command of the 10th Battalion, Duke of Cornwall's Light Infantry (Pioneer Battalion 66th Division). Captain George Bernard Stratton the Commanding Officer of the 10th Duke of Cornwall's L.I. was 40 years old and he had been killed in action between 10 and 11 August 1917. He was married to Gladys Stratton (nee Knowles) and lived at 17 Nettlecomb Avenue, Southsea, Hants. He is buried in the Ramscappelle Road Military Cemetery.[27]

14 August. Training.

Fifteen officers attended a lecture on the topography of the corps front line.

2nd Lieuts. A.W. Drage and F.J. Smith joined on appointment and were posted to 'C' Company.

The battalion received Divisional Order 217 at 5pm and 33rd Divisional Royal Engineer Order 8 at 9pm for the relief of 32nd Division by 33rd Division.

15 August. Lt.-Col. Storr and officers commanding 'A', 'C' and 'D' Companies went to Brisbane Camp at Witte Burg one mile south of the North Sea to arrange taking over the quarters and work of the 9th Battalion Seaforth

Highlanders (Pioneers) in respect of operations on the Flanders coast at and around Nieuport. The 9th Seaforth Highlanders were the pioneer battalion of the 9th Division. Nieuport was the northern most point of the Western Front.

Training. One platoon 'D' Company worked by night unloading R.E. stores from a train.

16th August – Third Battle of Ypres – The Battle of Langemarck

The II Corps launched the main attack with the objective of capturing the German Third Line from Polygon Wood (inclusive) along Anzac Farm spur to the Ypres – Roulers railway, an average advance of 1,500 yards; a southern defensive flank was to be formed by capturing and consolidating eight selected strong points at intervals between Stirling Castle and Black Watch Corner at the south-western corner of Polygon Wood.

At 4.45am, under a creeping barrage, Gough's Fifth Army attacked.

The 56th Division advance on their objective to form the southern defensive flank was met and halted by a barrage of high explosives from Zandvoorde and machine gun fire from Inverness Copse.

The 8th Division crossed the muddy bed of the Hanebeek, stormed the eastern slope of the valley, reached Iron Cross and Zonnebeke redoubts in the German Third Line and Anzac Farm. German machine gun fire from Potsdam against their left flank prevented any movement south of the Ypres – Roulers railway. A German counter-attack forced the 8th Division to withdraw from Anzac Farm.

The 16th and 36th Divisions advance to the German Third Line on the Anzac and Zonnebeke spur required them to cross a mile of open ground chequered with pillboxes and strong points. The 16th Division advance was met with machine gun fire from Potsdam, Vampir and Borry farms. They were cut to pieces and only isolated parties got to within 100 yards of the German Third Line.

The 36th Division, likewise, were swept with machine gun fire from Gallipoli and Somme farms. The new and strong wire entanglements set diagonally across these two strong points stopped any further advance by the 36th Division.

The 48th Division captured a strong point in the most northern house in St. Julien but their advance was halted on top of the rise 200 yards east of Steenbeek by machine gun fire.

The 11th Division gained their objective of White House. The 20th Division captured the troublesome strong point Au Bon Gîte and reached the farther side of Langemarck. The 29th Division took the strong point Langemarck – Weidendreft road and the block houses offering resistance near Montmirail Farm were outflanked.[28]

The Fifth Army had 16,056 men killed, wounded or missing.[29]

General Gough advised Sir Douglas Haig 'The state of the ground was by this time frightful. The labour of bringing up supplies and ammunition, of moving or firing the guns, which had often sunk up to their axles, was a fearful strain on the officers and men, even during the daily task of maintaining the battle front. When it came to the advance of infantry for an attack across the water-logged shell-holes, movement was so slow and so fatiguing that only the shortest advances could be contemplated. In consequence I informed the Commander-in-Chief that tactical success was not possible, or would be too costly, under such conditions, and advised that the attack should now be abandoned. I had many talks with Haig during these days and repeated this opinion frequently, but he told me that the attack must be continued'.[30]

Haig's imperative for continuing offensive operations at Passchendaele was his grand plan to break through the German lines and clear the enemy from the coastal ports in a pincer movement involving an amphibious and land attack between the Yser and Ostend.

16 August. One platoon 'D' Company moved to the forward area in relief of a platoon of 9th Seaforth Highlanders working with the 458th Field Company R.E. of the 49th Division.

Brisbane Camp

17 August. The battalion marched from La Panne to Brisbane Camp near Oost Dunkerke. (The 33rd Division War Diary records that the 18th Middlesex marched to Camp Gillimard giving the same map reference as Brisbane Camp.)[31] The transport proceeded via Kerkepanne and Coxyde to Brisbane Camp. The remainder of the battalion went via St. Idesbalde and Coxyde Bains starting at 7am and arrived between 9 and 9.30am.

'D' Company (less one platoon) continued marching to Groot Labeur Farm

(Grote Labeur Farm) where it was billeted. The billet was 300 yards north of the Dunkerque Canal.

One platoon of 'A' Company started work by night on a track for an Anti Aircraft (A.A.) gun at West Cloet Farm east of Square Wood on the Dunkerke Road.

'D' Company worked by night with 458th Field Company R.E. on the bridges just east of Nieuport, over the Canal de Passchendaele and the Crique de Nieuwendamme. The front line ran south of Lombartzyde along the eastern bank of the River Yser opposite Nieuport to the North Sea.

18 August. 'A' Company worked by day on roads in the northern half of the divisional area. 'C' Company worked partly by day and partly by night on roads in the southern area. 'B' Company worked on improvements in camp. 'D' Company worked partly by day and mainly by night with 458th Field Company R.E. on the bridges.

19 August. 'A' Company worked by day on roads. 'B' Company continued on improvements in camp. 'C' Company worked by day and by night on roads. 'D' Company worked partly by day and mainly by night on the bridges. Major Best returned from leave and took over duties of second-in-command.

One man was wounded.

20 August. 'D' Company on completion of day work moved into Brisbane Camp. 'A' and 'C' Companies worked on roads. 'B' Company continued in camp on various improvements.

At 11.45pm a bomb was dropped on the northern edge of the camp from a British aeroplane. Fortunately no damage was done.

21 August. 'A' and 'C' Companies worked on roads.

In the morning a piece of the bomb dropped the previous night was removed from its crater. It had an arrowhead (↑) drawn on. This was meant for Fritz but nearly got the battalion instead.

Major G.S. Hutchison M.C. Argyll and Sutherland Highlanders, the Divisional Machine Gun Officer, was to have met officers of 'B' and 'D' Companies to point out sites for machine gun emplacements to be constructed in the Yellow Line and Western Nieuport Switch. The officer failed to turn up. He sent a message to the rendezvous saying that he was otherwise engaged.

As a result work could not be started that night.

One man was slightly wounded at work.

22 August. Between 12.45am and 1am the enemy fired twenty six-inch calibre shells into the camp. Fortunately very little damage was done. Three animals were slightly cut and one tent was torn.

'A' and 'C' Companies worked on roads.

One platoon 'B' Company worked on New Avenue and one platoon 'D' Company on No Bon Avenue.

Major G.S. Hutchison pointed out the sites for the six machine gun emplacements in the Yellow Line and Western Nieuport Switch and work was started by night by 'B' Company on the former and 'D' Company on the latter.

One platoon 'B' Company and one platoon 'D' Company constructed covered ways in Nieuport and they encountered 'mustard' gas.

This mustard gas attack delayed the work. Most of the men of these platoons suffered sore throats and headaches on return from work and had to be excused work the following day.

Mustard gas was bis (2-chloroethyl) sulphide which was a vesicant blistering agent smelling or tasting of onion, garlic and mustard. Its colour varied from yellow, to light tan, to dark brown. The organs most commonly affected by mustard gas were those that came into direct contact with the gas. The skin with extensive blistering, burning and erythema (reddening of the skin); eyes with lesions, eye lid edema, corneal ulcerations and ultimately blindness; and the airway with inflammation of the respiratory tract causing hoarseness and escalating to severe dyspnea (shortage of breath) and massive pulmonary damage complicated by infection (bronchopneumonia) and sepsis. After significant amounts of mustard gas was absorbed through the skin or inhaled, the hemopoietic system (formation of blood or blood cells) was damaged as was the gastrointestinal tract causing nausea and vomiting. The central nervous system was also damaged causing apathy, depression, intellectual dullness and languor.

Of the 4,167 fatal mustard gas casualties among British troops in World War One 84% took four or more days to die.

The Germans called bis (2-chloroethyl) sulphide 'lost' after the two German chemists, Lommell and Steinkopf, who suggested its use as a chemical weapon or 'yellow cross' which was the identifying mark on the gas shells. The French called it 'Yperite' after its first use at Ypres. The British code-named it 'HS' for 'Hun Stoffe' (German stuff). However the name mustard gas stuck.[32]

Gough's Fifth Army launched another general attack deploying the three corps on the right – the II, XIX and XVIII. The objectives in this attack had been reduced to those within a short distance of British lines. 'As it was impossible for men to go forward over any long distance; (General Gough's) object was to spare the troops to the upmost possible degree, while at the same time complying with (his) orders from G.H.Q. to the effect that the battle must be continued'.[33]

The objective of the attack was to establish a starting line for the larger attack planned for 25 August. The 11th Division, assisted by tanks advanced a few hundred yards and captured one strong point east of the Kerselaere crossroads and another east of Bülow Farm.

The 15th Division attacked the pillboxes at Potsdam, Vampir, Borry and Iberian farms. Their attack was checked in front of these four strong points. They also advanced up Hill 35 but were halted by the Gallipoli Farm strong point.

The 61st Division advanced its line about 600 yards to include Somme Farm and Hindu Cottage.

The attack by the 14th Division further on the right of the Gheluvelt Plateau attempting to capture Inverness Copse was more important. This attack, supported by tanks, penetrated the copse and a line halfway through was taken and consolidated.[34]

For the week ending 24 August the Fifth Army suffered 16,937men killed, wounded or missing.[35]

23 August. 'A' and 'C' Companies worked on roads. One platoon 'B' Company worked on covered ways in Nieuport and two platoons on machine gun emplacements in Yellow Line. One platoon 'D' Company worked on covered ways in Nieuport and two platoons on machine gun emplacements in the Western Nieuport Switch.

24 August. The battalion carried on the same work as the previous day.

Two men were wounded and one man was slightly wounded.

Private P.W.600 Charles Robert West, aged 30 from Queensferry, Fife, who enlisted in Stafford was killed in action. He was son of Susan and Joseph West of 27 Commercial Street, Middlesbrough and a navvy by trade. He married Sarah L. West on 22 March 1913 at the Episcopal Church, Inverkeithing and they had a daughter Susan Elizabeth dob 6 November 1914. Mrs West lived at 3 Guard Crossing, Gretna Green, Cumberland. She received 16 shillings

Separation Allowance and 3 shillings and sixpence Allotment of Pay. On her husband's death she was awarded a pension for herself and her daughter of 18 shillings and 9 pence a week with effect from 11 March 1918. On 26 January 1918 she was sent her late husband's personal effects of his identity disc, photos, pocket book, jet ring, fountain pen, watch and chain. He was the first member of the battalion to be killed in Belgium. He is buried in the Coxyde Military Cemetery, Koksijde, West-Vlaanderen, Belgium.[36]

25 August. 'A' and 'C' Companies worked on roads. 'C' Company also constructed screens along the road near the Pelican Bridge. Two platoons 'B' Company and one platoon of 'D' Company worked on covered ways in Nieuport. The other two platoons of 'B' Company and two platoons of 'D' Company worked on machine gun emplacements. One platoon of 'D' Company worked on roads at western edge of Nieuport.

One man wounded.

26 August. 'A' and 'C' Companies worked on roads. 'B' Company had one platoon working on machine gun emplacements and three platoons on covered ways in Nieuport. 'D' Company was given a day's rest.

One man was wounded.

27 August. The battalion received Divisional order 221 at 7.30am for the relief of the 33rd Division by 32nd Division.[37]

'A' Company was given a day's rest. 'B' Company built machine gun emplacements and covered ways in Nieuport. 'C' Company worked on roads. 'D' Company worked on the roads on which 'A' Company had previously worked.

An officer and twenty-four other ranks of 9th Seaforth Highlanders (Pioneers) arrived at 12.30pm to take over the work and camp.

During the morning an officer was sent to arrange the takeover of the La Panne Camp. He returned about 2pm to report that the 5th Battalion Duke of Wellington's Regiment was still occupying the camp and they were not going to move.

A report was made accordingly to Divisional H.Q. and instructions asked for. At 10.30pm instructions were received for the battalion to move to Coudekerque on 28th instead of La Panne. The battalion transport and men were to go by road to Adinkerke and from there by barge at 1pm to Furnes Gate, Dunkerque and from there by road.

Three limbered G.S. wagons and mules rejoined the battalion from attachment to 19th and 100th Infantry Brigades and D.A.C.

Coudekerque Branche

28 August. One limbered G.S. wagon and mules rejoined from attachment to 98th Infantry Brigade.

The transport marched from Brisbane Camp at 9.45am via Coxyde, La Panne, Adinkerke, and Coudekerque Branche to Coudekerque and arrived at about 6pm.

The battalion marched at 10am and arrived at Adinkerke at 12.55pm. During the march a message was received from 33rd Division to say that the battalion would be convoyed in lorries from Adinkerke instead of barges.

The 9th Seaforth Highlanders arrived at Adinkerke in three barges at 1.15pm and not in lorries. Once they had disembarked the battalion embarked on the barges which started back from Adinkerke at 2pm. Two barges reached Furnes Gate, Dunkerque at 5.15pm and the other at 6pm. The companies disembarked and marched to Coudekerque, to occupy the billets that they had left on 7 August.

On arriving at Coudekerque it was found that the 1st Battalion The Queen's Regiment was occupying the billets intended for the battalion. The battalion remained on the roadside while Lt.-Col. Storr went to the 100th Infantry Brigade H.Q. at Téteghem to telephone the 33rd Division H.Q. He also telephoned the area commandant. He returned at 8.45pm with instructions for the battalion to proceed to billets at Coudekerque Branche.

The battalion arrived there about 10pm. The list of billets given by the area commandant at Téteghem were inaccurate and of little use.

By 2.30am on 29th the battalion was under shelter, but several of the billets were in a very bad condition.

Captain and Adjunct Hinman rejoined for duty and 2nd Lieuts. J. Woodgate, G.M. Lowcock and H. Jones joined on appointment and were posted to 'A', 'D' and 'C' Companies respectively.

It blew a gale all day with rain squalls throughout the morning.

29 August. The day was principally occupied in finding billets for officers and men to replace the highly unsanitary ones occupied the previous night.

30 August. Companies exercised in marching.

The battalion received Divisional Order 222 at 12.30pm for the move of the 33rd Division to Éperlecques training area. The battalion received Divisional Order 223 at 8.45pm and amendment thereto at 11pm giving details of accommodation of units on arrival.

31 August. Companies trained.

1 September 1917. The battalion received Divisional order 224 at 10.30am and Divisional R.E. order 11 at 4pm and amendment at 11pm. Orders for the march of the transport were issued accordingly.

Major-General Pinney had been suffering since the 5 July with an old leg injury aggravated by horse riding. Field Marshal Haig did not want to risk Pinney breaking down during operations and he wanted to see him right, so he ordered him to go to hospital.[38]

2 Sept. The transport with two officers and 114 other ranks left Coudekerque Branche at 7.45am. They marched via Galghoeck, les 5 Chemins, Bambecque, Kruystraete and Houtkerque to Proven where they were billeted for the night. From Galghoeck they marched under the orders of Capt. Balcombe, 11th Field Company Royal Engineers

A church parade was held at 11am.

Major-General Pinney was admitted to 14 General Hospital Boulogne. Brigadier-General Philip Richard Wood C.B. C.M.G. from the 43rd Infantry Brigade took over temporary command of the Division.[39] He was promoted to temporary Major-General with effect from 2 September 1917.[40] Philip Wood was born on 4 February 1868, he was married with one son. He joined the Army in 1887 and was made Captain that year. He was promoted to Major in 1906. He served with the Egyptian Army between 1899 and 1906 and took part in the Nile Expedition of 1899. He was awarded the Egyptian Medal with clasp. He was promoted to Lieutenant-Colonel on 14 March 1913 and took command of the 2nd Battalion Princess Victoria's (Royal Irish Fusiliers). He was mentioned twice in despatches during the Great War.[41]

Ridge Wood north of Vierstraat

3 Sept. Enemy aircraft bombed Coudekerque Branche at midnight and at

12.10am. The bombs caused a few civilian casualties and damage to property but the battalion escaped uninjured.

The transport marched from Proven to near Groote Vierstraat arriving at about 3pm.

The battalion left Coudekerque Branche at 8.45am marched to the embusment point. The buses were an hour late arriving so the column only started to move after 11.30am. It went via Bergues, Rexpoëde, Rousbrougge (Roesbrugge-Haringhe), Proven, Poperinghe, Abeele, Reningelst to between La Clytte and Dickebusch, de-bussed about 3.30pm and marched to the allotted campsite. 17 tents and 120 trench shelters sent by X Corps were pitched.

4 Sept. The floors in the shelters and tents were dug out to one foot below the surface. Five officers were taken by the Field Engineer X Corps to reconnoitre the country around Zillebeke where the battalion was to be employed improving communications and fortifications in advance of attacks on the enemy positions east of Ypres.

Zillebeke is almost a mile south on the road leading from Hellfire Corner on the Menin Road. It is also a mile west of the front line and a mile south-east of Ypres.

5 Sept. Arrangements had been made for eight lorries to take 200 men to work starting at 5am and returning at 1pm and a similar number at 11am to return at 7pm. In both cases the lorries failed to arrive. After some delay, the companies had to march to and from the work.

Companies worked in two shifts. 'A' Company worked on the formation for a slab road from Knoll Road past Battersea Cottage to Valley Cottages.

'B' Company worked on camp improvements and a track near the camp.

'C' Company worked on the Knoll Road from Zillebeke village. 'D' Company worked on the Verbranden Road.

The battalion was repeatedly shelled by the Germans. This caused considerable delays in the work.

Two men were wounded.

Capt. Horace Frederick Hill M.C. dob 23/7/1896 lived at Holly Lea, Wolstanton, Staffordshire and was educated at Newcastle High School where he was a Platoon Sergeant with the Officer Training Corps in April 1910. He

applied for a commission in the Army on 17 February 1915 on the recommendation of Captain John Ward M.P. He was commissioned 5 May 1915 and joined the 18th Battalion Middlesex Regiment.

Captain Hill was evacuated to England on 23 August 1916 with trench fever (pyrexia) with a temperature above 100 Fahrenheit. He made a slow recovery and was passed fit for home service at a medical held at the Military Hospital Chatham on 30 September and he was posted to 5th Battalion Middlesex Regiment. A further medical held on 5 December passed him fit to return to general service.

On 28 December Lt.-Col. Storr wrote to the Officer Commanding XV Corps requesting the return of Captain Hill. Storr stated 'I earnestly hope that this officer may be sent to rejoin the Battalion at the earliest moment that he is fit. He is a most capable company commander and a splendid Pioneer Officer and I badly need his services'.

On 30 December, on behalf of Major-General Pinney Officer Commanding 33rd Division, Brigadier-General Heriot-Maitland agreed. The Officer Commanding XV Corps concurred on 1 January 1917 and passed the request up to the Fourth Army Headquarters. Captain Hill was ordered to rejoin the B.E.F. on 13 January 1917 and he returned to the Western Front on 25 January.

He suffered fatal shell shrapnel wounds to his leg and back and died from shock and haemorrhage at the Larch Wood Collection Post (No. 133rd Field Ambulance).

He was a bachelor and died without leaving a will. His father Captain Alfred Arthur Hill was his next of kin. Captain Hill's net estate was £134. 3s. 4d. The bulk of the estate was made up by the £155 pounds gratuity paid under Article 497 Royal Warrant for Pay. His personal effects included 1 pocket photo case containing pictures, 1 pair of spectacles in case, 1 pair of Pince Nez in case, 1 New Testament, 1 small book 'Chesterfield's Letters', 1 Advance book, 3 Cheque books and a piece of Military Cross Ribbon.[42]

6 Sept. 'B' Company carried on the work begun by 'A' Company on the slab road. 'C' Company worked on Knoll Road. 'D' Company worked on Verbranden Road.

2nd Lieut. Buesst was promoted to be Temporary Lieutenant.[43]

One man was slightly wounded.

'A' Company continued camp improvements in the morning and paraded

for the funeral of Captain Hill M.C. at 3pm. He is buried in the Ridge Wood Military Cemetery, Heuvelland, West-Vlaanderen.

7 Sept. 'A', 'B' and 'D' Companies worked on the formation for the slab road along the northern edge of Armagh Wood along Observation Ridge 500 yards from the front line. 'C' Company worked on Knoll Road.

8 Sept. 'A', 'B' and 'D' Companies continued on the slab road. 'C' Company worked on the road between Zillebeke and Valley Cottages.

9 Sept. All companies worked on the slab road. 'B' and D' Companies laid slabs and 'A' and 'C' Companies worked on the formation.

Six men were wounded, four of them slightly.

10 Sept. The battalion worked on the slab road.

Four men were wounded.

11 Sept. 'A', 'B' and 'D' Companies laid slabs. 'C' Company worked on the formation. The work of the battalion was considerably delayed by enemy action. Gas bombs forced 'A', 'C' and 'D' Companies to stop work for thirty minutes. Artillery fire and German aeroplanes firing at working parties interrupted work at intervals.

Brigadier-General J.A.S. Tulloch the Chief Engineer X Corps inspected some of the work and visited battalion H.Q. at 3.15pm.

One man was wounded.

12 Sept. A', 'B' and 'D' Companies laid slabs.

Major-General Wood was given full command of the 33rd Division.[44]

'C' Company worked on the formation. The battalion made good progress and Fritz did not bother them at all.

13 Sept. All companies laid slabs and good progress was made.

At 9.30am Lieut.-General Sir T.N. Morland, Commanding Officer X Corps, ordered the battalion to send one company, as soon as possible, to relieve a company of 12th Sherwood Foresters working under the Advanced Division Light Railway (A.D.L.R.). The 12th Sherwood Foresters were the pioneer battalion of the 24th Division.

Details of the work were to be arranged with 24th Division. 'B' Company

was selected and on return from work moved to the Matawai Camp north of the Kruisstraathoek to Vijverhoek crossroads. The two platoons of 'B' Company still out at work and not due to return until 7pm were ordered to follow the next morning.

Brigadier-General J.A.S. Tulloch visited battalion H.Q. about noon and arranged for 'B' Company's work to be taken over by the 14th Battalion Northumberland Fusiliers, the pioneer battalion of the 21st Division. He gave further instructions on the continuing construction of the road.

14 Sept. 'B' Company worked in an afternoon shift on a railway formation. 'A', 'C' and 'D' Companies worked on the slab road which had been laid out further east taking it closer still towards the front line.

Three men were wounded, two slightly.

15 Sept. Enemy shelling considerably delayed the work of the battalion.

'B' Company worked on the railway formation. 'A', 'C' and 'D' Companies worked on the slab road.

Two horses were killed.

Private P.W.58 Alexander Cairnie aged 31, born in Dundee and enlisted in Edinburgh, died of his wounds. He was the son of Margaret and Alexander Cairnie of Alyth, Forfarshire. He was married to Rebecca Isabella Cairnie (nee Willis) of 43/4, Dumbredykes Road, Edinburgh. He was only 5´2˝ and weighed 108 lbs. He is buried in the Voormezeele Enclosures No.1 and No.2 – Ieper, West-Vlaanderen, Belgium.[45]

16 Sept. 'B' Company worked on the railway. 'A', 'C' and 'D' Companies worked on the slab road.

Artillery batteries fired practice barrages at German positions on the Gheluvelt Plateau for the attack of the 23rd Division on 20 September.[46] This attracted considerable retaliation from the Germans, which interfered with the work of the battalion.

One man was wounded.

17 Sept. 'B' Company worked on the railway, the rest of the battalion worked on the slab road.

The battalion received 33rd Divisional Royal Engineer Order 12 at 6.20pm for

the move of the Division to the Berthen area. A conference of company commanders and staff was held at 6.45pm when orders for the move of the battalion were issued.

One man was wounded.

1 Private Papers of Major-General Sir Reginald J. Pinney, Imperial War Museum, Book 6 8 April – 2 September 1917, Documents. 20421
2 Boraston (Editor), *Sir Douglas Haig's Despatches (December 1915 – April 1919),* p. 109
3 Private Price British Army WW1 Pensions Records 1914-1920, National Archives, WO 364
4 Edmonds, *Military Operations, France and Belgium, 1917*, Vol. 2, p.137
5 Ibid., p.138
6 Private Papers of Lieutenant G. Cotton, Imperial War Museum, Documents. 14729, p.p.60-61
7 Private Papers of Major-General Pinney
8 Hutchinson, *The Thirty-Third Division in France and Flanders 1915 -1919*, p.p. 56 – 58
9 The London Gazette 17th July 1917, Gazette Issue 30186, p. 7119
10 The Second Supplement to the London Gazette 17th July 1917, Published 18th July 1917, Gazette Issue 30188, p. 7282
11 Ibid., p. 7282 and p. 7286
12 Blake (Editor), *The Private Papers of Douglas Haig 1914 -1919,* p. 240
13 Ibid., p. 238
14 Ibid.
15 Edmonds, *Military Operations, France And Belgium, 1917 Vol. 2*, p.138
16 Borastan (Editor), *Sir Douglas Haig's Despatches (December 1915 – April 1919),* p. p. 112-113
17 Edmonds, *Military Operations, France and Belgium, 1917 Vol. 2*, p.127
18 Borastan (Editor*) Sir Douglas Haig's Despatches (December 1915 – April 1919)*, p. 109
19 Edmonds, *Military Operations, France And Belgium, 1917 Vol. 2*, p.138
20 Blake (Editor), *The Private Papers of Douglas Haig 1914 -1919,* p.p. 249-250
21 Borastan (Editor), *Sir Douglas Haig's Despatches (December 1915 – April 1919),* p. p. 114-115
22 David Lloyd George, *War Memoirs of David Lloyd George, Vol. 2*, Odhams Press Limited, London, 1936, p.p. 1305-1306
23 Blake (Editor), *The Private Papers of Douglas Haig 1914 -1919,* p. 250
24 Edmonds, *Military Operations, France And Belgium, 1917 Vol. 2*, p. 178
25 Ibid., p.p. 178-179
26 Borastan (Editor), *Sir Douglas Haig's Despatches (December 1915 – April 1919),* p. 115
27 *Officers Died In The Great War 1914 -1919*, p. 115

28 Edmonds, *Military Operations, France And Belgium, 1917 Vol. 2*, p.p. 190-191

29 Ibid., p. 364

30 General Sir Hubert Gough, *The Fifth Army*, Hodder and Stoughton, London, 1931, p. 205

31 33rd Division War Diary

32 Frederick R. Sidell, M.D.; John S. Urbanetti, M.D., FRCP (C), FACP, FCCP; William J. Smith, PH.D; and Charles G. Hurst, M.D., in *Textbook of Military Medicine Part 1, Warfare, Weaponry, and the Casualty, Medical Aspects Of Chemical And Biological Warfare*, p.p. 198 – 212

33 General Sir Hubert Gough, *The Fifth Army*, p. 206

34 Edmonds, *Military Operations, France And Belgium, 1917 Vol. 2*, p.p. 202-204

35 Ibid., p. 364

36 *Soldiers Died In The Great War 1914 -1919* p. 105; Commonwealth War Graves Commission casualty details; Private West Army Service Record, National Archives, WO 363

37 33rd Division War Diary

38 Private Papers of Major-General Pinney, Book 6

39 33rd Division War Diary

40 Third Supplement to the London Gazette 9th October 1917, Published 12th October 1917, Gazette Issue 30331, p. 10493

41 Who's Who 1918 An Annual Biography Dictionary with which is incorporated Men and Women of the Seventeenth Year of issue, Published by A & C Black Ltd., London 1918, p. 2603; The London Gazette 22nd April 1913, Gazette Issue 28712, p. 2888

42 Captain Hill Army Service Record, National Archives, WO 339/25089, Commonwealth War Graves Commission casualty details; British Army Lists 1917

43 Lieut. Buesst Army Service Record

44 Order of Battle of Divisions Part 3B – New Army Divisions (30-41) & 63rd, Compiled by Major A.F. Becke, p. 31

45 *Soldiers Died In The Great War 1914 -1919* p. 102; Commonwealth War Graves Commission casualty details

46 33rd Division Commander Royal Artillery War Diary, National Archives, WO 95/2410

CHAPTER TWO

18th September 1917 to 3rd October 1917

Third Battle of Ypres
Battles for Menin Road Ridge and Polygon Wood
Major-General P. Wood Special Order of the Day

One mile north-east of Boeschepe west of Loye

18 Sept. The Area Commandant ordered the camp to be dismantled and the stores were returned to him by lorry at La Clytte. Temporary buildings were the only things left behind.

The battalion (less 'B' Company) marched at 8.10am via Reningelst to the billets and camp at Loye one mile north-east of Boeschepe arriving at 11.30am. The battalion transport went via La Clytte and Westoutre to the camp north-east of Boeschepe. Men over forty years of age were sent in five lorries provided by X Corps.

Lt.-Col. Storr attended a 33rd Divisional conference at Berthen at 2.45pm. The Commander Royal Engineers Corps Troops X Corps visited battalion H.Q. and gave instructions on the erection of twenty-three Nissen huts.

19 Sept. 'A', 'C' and 'D' Companies started constructing Nissen huts 300 yards west of Bangle Farm and a mile south-east of Boeschepe. At about midday the C.R.E. X Corps Troops arrived at the site and said that only five Nissen huts were to be built. Part of the battalion was to be deployed on the construction of similar huts north of Steen Akker, details to be sent to the battalion the following day.

Piles were driven for twenty-two huts south-east of Boeschepe and the superstructure of five huts started.

The battalion received Divisional Order 226 at 8am for the move of Infantry Brigade groups.

The two-hundred men from 'B' Company had a bath and were given a change of underclothes at Boeschepe.

20th September – The Battle for Menin Road Ridge – Third Battle of Ypres

Haig decided that two things had to happen if his Passchendaele offensive was going to succeed; 1) The Gheluvelt Plateau had to be taken; 2) Gough had tried and failed and he needed someone else to do the job.

Haig placed Plumer and his Second Army in charge of the next phase of the Third Battle of Ypres. 'General Plumer's intention was to capture the plateau by four separate steps, with an interval of six days between each to allow time to bring forward artillery and supplies; the distance of each step, governed by the need to meet the strong German counter-attacks with fresh infantry supported by an effective artillery barrage, was to be limited to about fifteen hundred yards. For the first step he considered a thousand yards to be the maximum frontage for each division'.[1]

This approach was known as 'bite and hold'.

The front selected by Haig for the attack 'extended from the Ypres – Comines Canal north of Hollebeke to the Ypres – Staden railway north of Langemarck, a distance of just over eight miles along the line held by us. The average depth of our objectives was 1,000 yards, which increased to a depth of a mile in the neighbourhood of the Menin Road'.[2]

The attack was preceded by artillery bombardment which started on 31 August and daily grew heavier reaching a crescendo on the 18 and 19 September.

At 5.40am General Plumer attacked with four divisions, the 41st, 23rd, 1st Australian and 2nd Australian, along the four-thousand yard frontage of the Gheluvelt Plateau.

The 39th Division had the task of forming the left sector of the southern defensive flank of the X Corps from the Bassevillebeek up the western slope of the valley to near Groenenburg Farm. The 19th Division had the task of extending the flank to the Comines Canal.

Supporting the Second Army was Gough's Fifth Army. The V Corps of the Fifth Army had the task of taking the Gheluvelt – Langemarck Line on its right, In the centre the XVIII Corps was to complete the occupation of Gheluvelt-Langemarck Line from east of Schuler Farm to east of Langemarck and then advance 500 to 800 yards towards Poelcappelle. The XIV Corps was to form a northern flank.[3]

By mid day the Second and Fifth Armies had secured their objectives on the Gheluvelt Plateau and in anticipation of a prompt German counter-attack work was started immediately to consolidate their positions.

Between 10am and 7pm the Germans launched numerous counter-attacks against the new positions held by the Second and Fifth Armies. These were met with accurate artillery and machine gun fire and all were repulsed.[4]

The British Second and Fifth Armies paid a very high price in casualties for their success at Menin Road Ridge. In total the two armies lost 22,441 men killed, missing or wounded.[5]

20 Sept. The C.R.E. X Corps visited battalion H.Q. at 11.30am and ordered the erection of thirteen Nissen huts north of Steen Akker just under a mile north-west of Boeschepe. Two platoons of 'C' Company and 'D' Company started this work in the afternoon. Further material for the twenty-three huts south-east of Boeschepe arrived and 'A' Company and two platoons of 'C' Company continued on these.

Two men of 'B' Company were wounded.

21 Sept. The battalion worked on constructing the huts south-east of Boeschepe and north of Steen Akker.

22 Sept. Work continued on huts south-east of Boeschepe.

When parties of 'C' and 'D' Companies arrived north of Steen Akker they found that another unit had been assigned to do the work and they returned to their billets.

The rest of the battalion who had not bathed on the 19th had a bath and were given a change of underclothing at Boeschepe.

The Rev. H. Ridsdale joined the battalion on attachment as chaplain.

A conference of officers was held at 5.30pm and orders for the move of 'C' and 'D' Companies were issued at 9pm.

Two men from 'B' Company were wounded.

23 Sept. A church parade was held at 10am.

'C' and 'D' Companies marched at 2pm to Railway Dugouts next to the Ypres to Menin railway and arrived at 6.30pm.

At 5pm Lt.-Col. George Farrington Evans, C.R.E. 33rd Division, notified the battalion that the 9th Battalion South Staffordshire Regiment, which was the pioneer battalion of the 23rd Division, had been ordered by X Corps to remain in their present position. The C.R.E 23rd Division was arranging accommodation near Burgomaster Farm for 'H.Q.' Company and one other company.

Near Dickebusch

24 Sept. 'H.Q.' Company and 'A' Company marched at 10am to Dickebusch arriving at 1pm and erected bivouac shelters and tents at the camp 900 yards south-west of Dickebusch past Malplaquet Camp off the road to Locre.

A report was made to the 33rd Division that 'B' Company had not yet been released from working for A.D.L.R.

'C' Company worked by day on track W leading up through the right brigade area.

'D' Company worked partly by day on a track near Stirling Castle in the left brigade area, and partly by night on the Jap Avenue and Northampton Trench both of which were communication trenches in left brigade area.

Two men were wounded.

In the 100th Brigade area a relief was carried out. The 1st Queen's relieved the 8th King's Own Yorkshire Light Infantry at the front trenches on the Menin Road near Veldhoek. The section of the front line taken over ran north from the Menin Road along the road to Polygon Wood.[6] This is now the junction of Polygonestraat and Menenstraat on the N8.

The ground taken over consisted of short lengths of hastily consolidated trench with no wire in front and followed the line of the old Veldhoek Trench. Its defence was considerably handicapped by the occupation by the enemy of the Tower Hamlets Ridge and the continuation of the Veldhoek Spur south of the Menin Road.

The relief itself started at 2pm. It took place over difficult terrain of shell holes interspersed with marshes. The only landmarks were the various German concrete dugouts, what was left of Inverness Copse, numerous discarded tanks and the two-storey, loopholed, round Tower east of Inverness Copse that was used as an observation and signalling station.

The 98th and 100th Infantry Brigades used the Zillebeke Track on their way to the front. There was serious congestion on the track due to the volume of troops moving forward, the unpunctuality of some units and the failure to keep the prescribed distance between platoons.[7]

The relief was observed by German aeroplanes and considerably hampered by German artillery fire. Many casualties were incurred by all the British battalions before the relief was complete.[8]

The effect on the troops going forward of the dead bodies along the Zillebeke track, which should have been a fairly safe one, cannot have been good.[9]

25 Sept. The 33rd Division of Plumer's Second Army held the British front line from the Polygon Wood Road junction on the Menin Road to southern edge of Polygon Wood.

At 5.15am German artillery launched a very heavy bombardment along the whole 33rd Divisional front from the Menin Road to Polygon Wood. Captured German orders show they deployed 27 Batteries of Field Artillery, 17 Field Howitzer Batteries, 15 Heavy Howitzer Batteries and 5 Batteries of long range H.V. guns in this bombardment. In addition the neighbouring German Divisions carried out counter-battery work and subsidiary bombardment.[10] At 5.50am the barrage was followed by a strongly organised German counter-attack along that section of the front line.[11] The Germans timed their attack to take place as the 33rd Division was relieving the 23rd Division at the front.

In the 100th Infantry Brigade sector a message was sent at 7.30am from the companies of 1st Queen's at the front to their Battalion Headquarters that the enemy had penetrated the line. Shortly afterwards 2nd Lieut. Hughes of 'B' Company returned wounded with information that the front line had been practically wiped out by heavy minnies, but 'D' Company was still holding out.[12]

The 1st Queen's were driven out of the front line and forced back to their support line.[13] At 7.49am Company Sergeant Major Tipper arrived at 1st Queen's Battalion Headquarters badly wounded and confirmed that only 'D' Company were holding out. Reinforcements were asked for by pigeon.

Captain and Adjutant L.A. Crook was killed by a shell near the Battalion H.Q.

The heavy German barrage of the front line initially made it impossible for the 1st Queen's to move forward and counter-attack. When the barrage slacked at 8.45am 'C' Company, under Captain Carslake, advanced in good order north of the Menin Road.

By 10am they reached the support line and made contact with the 1/9th Highland Light Infantry on their left and a Sussex battalion of the 39th Division on their right. The 1st Queen's prepared to attack the front line held in strength by the enemy.

At 11.30am one company of the 16th King's Royal Rifles, under Captain Francis, arrived but were too blown to push on. They took over the reserve line and 'A' Company 1st Queen's advanced to support 'C' Company 1st Queen's at the front.

The 1st Queen's counter-attack failed to regain the British front line.

Captain Carslake of 'C' Company and Captain Burrell 'A' Company were wounded. The two companies suffered severe casualties and were reduced to about one hundred rifles.

At 3.10pm one company of King's Royal Rifles moved forward to support the Queen's. However no further advance was possible because the left flank of the Queen's had been thrown back to connect with the 1/9th Highland Light Infantry position.[14]

Captured German orders, issued by the 50th Reserve Division, confirmed that the attacks on the British front line held by the 33rd Division were carried out by the Third Battalion of 229th Regiment and the Third Battalion of the 230th Regiment together with the Assault Battalion of the Fourth German Army. The objectives of the attack were the Veldhoek Trench and Carlisle Farm. The 229th attacked the section between Polygon Wood and the Reutelbeek. The 230th attacked south of the Reutelbeek to the Menin Road. The Assault Battalion attacked dugouts about the Menin Road.[15]

25 Sept. One company of 18th Middlesex was placed at the disposal of the 98th Brigade and one company at the disposal of the 100th Brigade.[16]

The German artillery barrage interfered with the day work on track W by 'C' Company 18th Middlesex.

A lorry load of wire and pickets for use on the strong points to be made by five platoons was sent up to The Culvert opposite Wing House on the Menin Road out of Ypres. A party of 'A' Company was sent to carry the wire and pickets from there to form a dump near Inverness Copse 500 yards south-east of Clapham Junction on the Menin Road.

At 3.30pm a report was received from C.R.E. that the lorry could not get beyond Hellfire Corner and it had been unloaded there. This was one mile short of The Culvert. Hellfire Corner is at the crossroads of the Menin Road and Zillebeke to Zonnebeke road and where the Ypres to Roulers railway line crossed the Menin Road.

The party of 'A' Company under the command of Lieut. Adams had been gone some two hours when the C.R.E. report was received. It was not possible to communicate the contents to Lieut. Adams.

Lieut. Adams found the wire and pickets after some delay and moved them up to The Culvert. This was still 2,350 yards short of Inverness Copse. His working party was unable to get it forward beyond The Culvert because the

ammunition dumps all along the Menin Road were on fire and exploding. He returned with his party at midnight.

At 5pm, Division informed the battalion that the attack ordered in Divisional Order 230 would take place the following day. The Second Army instructed A.D.L.R. to order 'B' Company to rejoin the battalion immediately.

The battalion received Divisional Order 231 at 10.40pm. In response, the Division was asked to confirm this order cancelled the construction of the two southern most of the five strong points the battalion had been ordered to make. Confirmation was received at 11.30pm.

'D' Company worked by night on Jap Avenue. Their work interfered with the assembly of troops for the attack on Polygon Wood the following day.

Despite the Second Army instruction three platoons of 'B' Company remained with the A.D.L.R. for work. One platoon was kept in camp available for making a strong point.

During the work fortifying the gains from the attack on the Menin Road Ridge and in preparations for the attack on Polygon Wood, fourteen men were wounded, four of them slightly.

Private 11610 George Ronald Marley aged 20, born in Paddock Wood, Kent and enlisted in Mill Hill, died of his wounds. He was the son of Minnie Elizabeth and George Marley of 12 Muir Road, Maidstone. He is buried in Bedford House Cemetery – Ieper, West-Vlaanderen.[17]

26th September – Battle of Polygon Wood – Third Battle of Ypres

The Battle for Polygon Wood was the second 'bite' of Plumer's Second Army step by step attempt to capture the Gheluvelt Plateau. The front for this attack was over five miles long and stretched from St. Julien in the north to the Tower Hamlets spur in the south.

The objective was to extend the front line by a further 1,200 yards. Zero hour was at 5.50am. The attack was preceded by heavy artillery barrage.

The I Anzac Corps, under the command of Major-General Sir William Riddell Birdwood, led the main attack. Their objective was to secure the whole of Polygon Wood. In the vanguard of the attack was the Australian 5th Division under Major-General J. Talbot Hobbs.

The 33rd Division, as the left division of the X Corps, under the command of Lieutenant-General Sir Thomas Morland D.S.O., was detailed to cover the

Australian right flank and to occupy a line giving observations to the south and east over the Reutelbeek Valley. The 39th Division was on the right flank of the 33rd Division.[18] Their objective was to secure the Tower Hamlets spur south of the Menin Road.

Initially it was planned that both the 98th and 100th Infantry Brigades of the 33rd Division would cover the left flank of the 5th Australian Division but the 100th Infantry Brigade was deployed instead to regain the section of front line along the Polygon Wood road to the Menin Road lost the previous day.[19]

At 5.50am 'five belts of the barrage, a thousand yards in depth, fell on the German position. The ground was so powdery that the bursts of high-explosive shells raised a dense wall of dust and smoke, which together with the morning mist clouded the battlefield. The advancing troops had to use compass bearings to keep their directions. The Australians closely followed the dust cloud and most of the German machine gun detachments were rushed or outflanked before they could fire a shot'.[20]

The Australian 5th Division attacked Polygon Wood without the support of the 98th Brigade of the 33rd Division whose arrival at the front line was delayed by heavy shelling and thick mist.[21] The 98th Brigade had suffered serious losses the previous day fending off a German counter-attack north of the Reutelbeek.

The 15th Australian Brigade covered the right flank of 5th Australian Division because the 98th Brigade of the 33rd Division had not been able to push forward to carry out this order. The 5th Australian Division took Polygon Wood, including the strategic and heavily fortified elevated 'butte', giving a commanding view over the Gheluvelt Plateau.

The 4th Australian Division advanced their line by 1,200 yards, they crossed the Steenbeek and established a new line along the Tokio spur, a feature parallel to its own line on Anzac House spur.

The 3rd Division of V Corps Fifth Army advanced and kept in touch with the Australians and consolidated a position south of the railway including the western outskirts of Zonnebeke. North of the railway the 3rd Division was held up by heavy machine gun fire 600 yards from their final objective Hill 40.

To the north of Zonnebeke the 59th Division took the Waterend House – Schuler Farm sector including a number of strong points. They were held up a quarter of a mile short of their objective Gravenstafel.

The 39th Division, like the previous attempts, failed to secure the Tower Hamlets spur being held by the 'Quadrilateral'.[22]

Two companies of the 16th King's Royal Rifles and two companies of the 1st Queen's of the 100th Brigade, together with the 14th Battalion Hampshire Regiment, advanced at 5.50am just south of the Menin Road at its junction with Polygon Road. They were held up by a strong point with a machine gun on the north side of the road. They took twenty prisoners and consolidated their position.

At 8.30am one machine gun was sent forward and a German aeroplane was brought down in flames by Lewis gun fire. At 9.30am one company of Cameronians arrived and half of the men were sent forward to support the front line companies. A German bombing attack on the left flank was driven off.

At 3pm the Germans were reported massing for a counter-attack. A small attack developed on the left but was driven off. At 5pm an SOS went up on the left and the right. British artillery responded with a strong barrage which continued for two hours.

At 7pm Lieut. Preston of the Cameronians organised a party of various regiments and rushed the strong point just north of the Menin Road. They captured a machine gun, 26 prisoners and killed 70 Boche.

The front line was advanced to its original position and the 1/9th Highland Light Infantry came up, cleared the dugout and a further 28 prisoners were captured. The original line was consolidated and the rest of the night passed without further incident.[23]

'B' Company and 'D' Company, the two front companies of the 1st Queen's, lost all their officers and most of their men. The battalion had 4 officers killed, 9 wounded and one missing. They had 59 other ranks killed, 169 wounded and 219 missing.[24]

The Battle for Polygon Wood advanced the British front line up to the foot of the Broodseinde Ridge. British and Colonial armies lost 15,375 men killed, missing or wounded in this battle.[25]

The 33rd Division did not tell the 18th Middlesex the time for the attack on Polygon Wood. 98th Infantry Brigade order 170 and amendment thereto confirmed zero hour was 5.50am.

The officer commanding 'A' Company was told to construct three strong points. He was also told to send an officer to report at 98th Brigade H.Q. by zero hour.

'A' Company had only come in at midnight and the platoons constructing strong points were not required to move forward from Railway Dugouts before

dusk. Railway Dugouts were 1,200 yards south of Ypres on the south side of the Ypres to Menin railway line. In view of these facts, the officer commanding 'A' Company reported the position of wire and pickets to the C.R.E.'s office. He also telephoned 98th Brigade to find out if the platoons were required at Railway Dugouts by zero hour.

Message No. G521 from the Division, despatched 'priority' at 10.25pm the night before, but apparently sent in error via 19th Infantry Brigade, was received at 1.30am. It had been delivered at 11.50pm to the officer commanding 'C' Company at Railway Dugouts and was sent by him to the officer commanding 'D' Company as the senior officer of the detachment. The message did not reach the officer commanding 'D' Company until 12.50am because he was still out at work.

He immediately sent it on by brigade orderly. It ordered one company to be placed at the disposal of 98th Infantry Brigade and one company at the disposal of 100th Infantry Brigade. They were to be employed as carrying parties.

'D' Company had been out at work all night and was not available. 'B' Company at Matawai Camp two miles south-west of Ypers near Café Belge and 'C' Company at Railway Dugouts were ordered to proceed to the Advanced Divisional Dump just north of Observation Ridge immediately. 'B' Company was deployed to carry for the 98th Infantry Brigade and 'C' Company for 100th Infantry Brigade.

The officer commanding 'A' Company returned from Divisional H.Q. at 4.30am. He instructed the platoons that were to work on strong points to be at Railway Dugouts by 8.30am. These platoons moved off at 6.30am in G.S. wagons.

At 9.50am Lt.-Col. Storr was ordered to attend Divisional H.Q. After explaining the position of the battalion, he was instructed to establish a temporary headquarters at Bedford House near 19th Infantry Brigade H.Q. He was also instructed to concentrate 'A' and 'D' Companies at the Railway Dugouts, ready to carry out any orders issued at short notice.

Lt.-Col. Storr returned to camp at 10.20am and at 10.45am moved with the 2nd in Command, Adjutant, and a few orderlies to Bedford House. The rest of 'A' Company moved up to Railway Dugouts at 11am.

'B' Company returned to camp from their carrying work between 12.30pm and 4.30pm.

'C' Company remained out in the field under the orders of 100th Infantry Brigade throughout the 26th and up to daylight on the 27th. They spent most of the day in the Tor Top Tunnel on Hill 62 just east of Sanctuary Wood.

Private Thomas McBride MM reported sick with a mild case of what his cockney mates call the 'thre'penny bits' and was admitted to the No. 9 Lakeside U.S.A. General Hospital in Rouen.[26]

At 4.55pm the battalion received orders for 'A' and 'D' Companies to be placed at the disposal of 98th Infantry Brigade. 'D' Company was employed on carrying duties. 'A' Company was employed on the construction of three strong points.

One platoon 'B' Company moved up to Railway Dugouts arriving at 7pm and remainder of 'B' Company arrived there at midnight.

Lieut. Fisher was slightly wounded, thirteen men were wounded, two slightly.

Private G/41416 John Edward Baker aged 28, who enlisted in Luton, was killed in action. He was the husband of Amy Maclaine Baker of 40 Pleasant Road, Southend-on-Sea. He was the son of Mary and William Baker. His name is on the Tyne Cot Memorial – Zonnebeke, West-Vlaanderen.[27]

Private G/597 Isaac Busby aged 38, born in Belfast and enlisted in Woolwich, Kent, on 13 March 1915 and recorded he had no fixed abode. He was killed in action. He was the son of Catherine and Samuel Busby of 88 Henry Street, Belfast. He is buried in the Hooge Crater Cemetery, Ieper, West-Vlaanderen.[28]

27 Sept. At 7.30am, in accordance Divisional Order 232, all companies were instructed to concentrate at Railway Dugouts immediately and to rest during the day and be prepared to carry for 23rd Division overnight on the 27/28th.

Two companies were to work for the 70th Infantry Brigade on the right; two companies were to work for 69th Infantry Brigade on the left. 'A' Company returned at 4.45am and 'D' Company at 5.30am having accomplished their tasks. 'C' Company returned by 8am.

At 4.30pm, 23rd Division sent instructions to the 69th and 70th Infantry Brigades to contact the battalion at Railway Dugouts and let them know what carrying was required.

The battalion received its first request for assistance at 11.10pm. The 70th Brigade reported they urgently required small arms ammunition and water, and

asked for as much as possible to be taken forward from the Divisional Dump on Observation Ridge. Half the supplies were to be taken to right battalion and half to left.

'B' Company carried for the left battalion and 'C' Company carried for right battalion. On arrival at the front line in the left area the troops complained that they already had more small arms ammunition than they knew what to do with.

The 69th Infantry Brigade did not make any requests for assistance from the battalion during the night of 27/28th.

An officer of 'A' Company was sent to reconnoitre the tramway between Battersea Farm and Tor Top Tunnel with a view to repairing it.

'A' and 'B' Companies were ordered to return to their camps on the morning of 28th.

2nd Lieut. Clay was wounded, burnt by chlorine gas. Nine other men were wounded.

Brigadier-General Baird, Officer commanding 100th Infantry Brigade in his report on the Operation of 25, 26, and 27 September 1917 recorded 'A special word of praise is due to the company of the 18th Middlesex (Pioneers) who had been placed at my disposal for carrying purposes. They did two trips with SAA and water over ground, the state of which must be seen to be appreciated. Apart from the fact that the ground had been rendered infinitely more impassable through shell holes than anything I have seen either on the Somme or at Arras, the presence of such marshy ground through which no trace of any tracks remained, made the work of all carrying parties and runners difficult beyond description. In spite of this and the heavy expenditure of Small Arms Ammunition throughout the fighting on the 25th and 26th, sufficient supplies could just be got forward'.[29]

During the Operations between 25 and 28 September 1917 the 100th Infantry Brigade had 9 officers and 236 other ranks killed, 35 officers and 822 other ranks wounded and 4 officers and 463 others ranks missing.[30]

28 Sept. 'A' Company moved back to camp at 6am. 'B' Company returned to Railway Dugouts at 7.30am and moved on at 8.30am to their camp. 'C' Company returned at 6.45am to Railway Dugouts.

Lt.-Col. Storr and the Adjutant moved back to camp at 9.30am. Major Best returned to camp the previous evening.

At 12.45pm the battalion received orders through C.R.E. for 'A' Company to proceed to Tor Top Tunnel by 6pm and to wire the front line immediately north of the Ypres – Menin road. At 3pm, 'A' Company went on G.S. wagons to Valley Cottages 600 yards east of Zillebeke along the road to Observation Ridge. The kit was carried on six pack mules. This work was necessary to secure the ground retaken during the Battle for Polygon Wood.

When 'A' Company arrived at Tor Top Tunnel they found the wire and picket dumps had been blown up so they could not work. This proved to be costly as far as the battalion's animals were concerned. Of the six mules used, three were killed and two wounded.

'B' Company was ordered to the camp vacated by 'A' Company.

'C' and 'D' Companies at Railway Dugouts were ordered to work by night on a communication trench from Clapham Junction via Verbeek Farm to Black Watch Corner. This was north of the Ypres to Menin road to the south-west corner of Polygon Wood. The 11th Field Company Royal Engineers and attached infantry were also deployed to work on the communication trench. They dug 800 yards of trench to depth of four feet deep.

One platoon 'A' Company had to wear gas respirators for two hours whilst wiring the new front line.

Eight men were wounded.

Private G/50629 Thomas William Atkinson born in Acton and enlisted in Hounslow, Middlesex, died of his wounds. He is buried in the Lijssenthoek Military Cemetery – Poperinghe, West-Vlaanderen.[31]

29 Sept. 'A' Company brought forward wire and pickets from Battersea Farm dump by day. By night, two platoons working about twenty yards in advance of the front line, put up a 700 yard long wire fence east of Gheluvelt from the Ypres – Menin road northwards to the Scherriabeek.

'B' Company was given a day's rest.

'C' and 'D' Companies worked at night on the communication trench begun the previous night. They dug out 1,350 yards of trench from Clapham Junction.

Seven men were wounded.

A special order of the day was issued by Major-General Wood on 29 September.

SPECIAL ORDER OF THE DAY

by

MAJOR-GENERAL P. WOOD, C.B., C.M.G.

Commanding 33rd Division.

1. I have received the following messages in connection with the operations in which the 33rd Division took part on September 25th, 26th and 27th, 1917.

I.

From

The Field-Marshal Commanding-in-Chief,
British Armies in FRANCE.

To

General Sir H. C.O. PLUMER,
Commanding 2nd Army.

G.H.Q., 27th September, 1917.

"The ground gained by the 2nd Army yesterday under your command, and the heavy losses inflicted on the enemy in the course of the day, constitute a complete defeat of the German forces opposed to you. Please convey to all Corps and Divisions engaged, my heartist congratulations, and especially to the 33rd Division whose successful attack following a day of hard fighting, is deserving of all praise."

II.

From X Corps.

To 33rd Division.

G.B. 131 26th September 1917.

"Following received from General PLUMER begins AAA Please accept my congratulations on success of to-day's operations, and convey them to the troops engaged. AAA The 33rd Division has done fine work under extraordinarily difficult circumstances, and the 39th Division have carried out their task most successfully AAA message ends AAA

The Corps Commander adds his own congratulations."

2. In circulating the above messages, I wish to congratulate all Officers, Non commissioned Officers and men of the Division, on having gained, by their fine fighting qualities, such marks of appreciation from the Commander-in-Chief, and from Army and Corps Commanders.

Captured enemy documents...show what efforts the enemy made, on 25th September 1917, against the front held by the Division between the Ypres – Menin Road and the southern edge of POLYGON WOOD.

3. I wish this order to be read on parade to all ranks of the Division, as a mark of my appreciation of their gallant conduct in the past and as a proof of my confidence in their being able to maintain their high reputation in the future.

P. Wood
September 29th 1917 Major-General,
Commanding 33rd Division.[32]

30 Sept. By day, 'B' Company worked under instructions from C.R.E. 23rd Division on the northern end of Plumer's Drive near its junction with the Ypres – Menin road, adjacent to Clapham Common. They were driven up to Zillebeke in G.S. wagons. The same wagons brought 'A' Company back from Tor Top Tunnel. 'A' Company returned to camp between 10.30 and 11am.

'C' and 'D' Companies were ordered to march from Railway Dugouts at noon and they arrived in camp between 1.30 and 2pm. Sixty trench shelters were drawn down and the camp enlarged to accommodate them.

The Lewis gunners of 'C' and 'D' Companies, holding four anti-aircraft posts south-east of Ypres near the Etang de Zillebeke, were not relieved by 5th Division owing to a change of divisional areas. X Corps were asked for instructions about how and when they are to be relieved.

Five men were wounded.

Private G/13580 George Martin aged 34, born in Stoke Newington, enlisted in St. Paul's, Middlesex and lived in the New Kent Road, died of his wounds received on 28 September. He was the son of Emma and William Martin. His name is on the Tyne Cot Memorial.[33]

1 October 1917. 'B', 'C' and 'D' Companies worked by day on Plumer's Drive from Sanctuary Wood to the Ypres – Menin road. The first shifts were driven into Zillebeke in G.S. wagons at 6am and the wagons went out again and brought back the second shifts.

'A' Company was given a day off work.

At 11.30am, 33rd Division ordered that the Lewis Gunners of 'C' and 'D' Companies holding four anti–aircraft positions at Zillebeke Lake were to be withdrawn. A limber wagon was dispatched to pick them up and they arrived at 4pm.

A draft of 104 other ranks arrived at 9pm. There should have been 105 in the draft but one fell out on the march from Abeele and was admitted to hospital.

Lt.-Col. Storr went on leave at 8.30pm and Major Best assumed temporary command of the battalion.

Capt. H.H. Pillinger of the United States Medical Corps arrived and relieved Capt. Simon as medical officer, who also went on leave.

Private G/41517 Harry Weller aged 31 died of his wounds. He was born and lived in Hawkhurst, Kent and enlisted in Ashford. He was the son of Maria and

Joseph Weller of Gun Green, Hawkhurst Kent. He is buried in the Longuenesse (St. Omer) Souvenir Cemetery – Pas de Calais.[34]

2 Oct. The battalion finally got a day's rest.

'A', 'B' and 'D' Companies worked on Plumer's Drive from Sanctuary Wood to the Ypres – Menin road.

33rd Division ordered two Lewis guns to report to officer commanding 33rd Divisional Wing, X Corps Musketry and Reinforcement Camp near Abeele by 6pm on 4 Oct. The battalion was also asked to forward the name of one N.C.O. as an instructor in wiring and field engineering.

Six men were wounded.

Private G/32381 John Smith aged 20, born in Thornwood, Essex and enlisted in Epping, was killed in action. He was the son of William Thomas Smith of Hill House, Thornwood Common, Epping, Essex. He is buried in the Railway Dugouts Burial Ground – Ieper, West-Vlaanderen.[35]

3 Oct. As a result of the arrival of the 105 ex-Royal Engineers the 33rd Division ordered 55 men from the battalion to be sent to the 2nd Battalion Middlesex Regiment and 50 to the 4th Middlesex. Orders were therefore issued for a selection of men to be sent to the 2nd and 4th Battalions of the Regiment.

Lt.-Col. E.H. Rooke, C.R.E. 23rd Division, at 3pm issued verbal orders that the battalion would work under the command of Lt.-Col. G.H. Boileau, C.R.E. 7th Division, from 4 Oct. in accordance with X Corps orders.

Major Best called for and received from C.R.E. 7th Division particulars on the continuation of a slab road from Jargon Switch north of Surbiton Villas through Glencorse Wood to the northwest corner of Polygon Wood. The work was to start on 4 October at a time to be notified. Written confirmation of this was received from C.R.E. 23rd Division at 9pm. 'A', 'B' and 'C' Companies worked on Plumer's Drive. 'D' Company was given a day off work.

Seven men were wounded, two slightly.

Sergeant P.W.433 William Burr was killed in action. He was 33 years old, born in Clapham, Middlesex and enlisted in London on 8 March 1915. Burr travelled with the battalion to France on 12 November 1915. He returned to England on 21 April 1917 suffering from myalgia (muscle pain). On 30 July he was posted to 6th Middlesex at Chatham. On 22 August he was found guilty and reprimanded for 'When on active service neglect of duty'. He had

been in charge of an escort when a prisoner escaped. He rejoined the 18th Middlesex in the field on 23 September 1917. Burr was the husband of Mrs Mary Ann Elizabeth Burr of 51 Southwold Road, Clapham, London. He is buried in the Railway Dugouts Burial Ground.[36]

Lance Corporal S.R.6931 James Christopher Jenkins born in Hendon, Middlesex and enlisted in Mill Hill, was killed in action. He is also buried in the Railway Dugouts Burial Ground.[37]

1 Edmonds, *Military Operations, France And Belgium, 1917 Vol. 2*, p. 237
2 Borastan (Editor), *Sir Douglas Haig's Despatches (December 1915 – April 1919)*, p. 121
3 Edmonds, *Military Operations, France And Belgium, 1917 Vol. 2*, p. 253, p. 261 & p. 263
4 Ibid., p.p. 271-276
5 Ibid., p. 279
6 1st Battalion Queen's Royal West Surrey Regiment War Diary, National Archives, WO 95/2430 Image Ref 1/431
7 2nd Battalion Worcestershire Regiment War Diary
8 100th Infantry Brigade War Diary, National Archives, WO 95/2429
9 2nd Battalion Worcestershire Regiment War Diary
10 1st Queen's Battalion War Diary
11 33rd Division War Diary
12 1st Queen's Battalion War Diary
13 33rd Division War Diary
14 1st Queen's Battalion War Diary
15 100th Machine Gun Company War Diary
16 33rd Division War Diary
17 *Soldiers Died In The Great War 1914 -1919* p. 103; Commonwealth War Graves Commission casualty details
18 33rd Division War Diary
19 Ibid.
20 Edmonds, *Military Operations, France And Belgium, 1917 Vol. 2*, p. 284
21 33rd Division War Diary
22 Edmonds, *Military Operations, France And Belgium, 1917 Vol. 2*, p.p. 285-289
23 1st Queen's Battalion War Diary
24 Ibid.
25 Edmonds, *Military Operations, France And Belgium, 1917 Vol. 2*, p. 293
26 McBride Army Service Record
27 *Soldiers Died In The Great War 1914 -1919* p. 102; Commonwealth War Graves Commission casualty details
28 Ibid.; Private Busby Army Service Record, National Archives, WO 363
29 100th Machine Gun Company War Diary

30 Ibid.

31 *Soldiers Died In The Great War 1914 -1919* p. 102; Commonwealth War Graves Commission casualty details

32 1st Queen's Battalion War Diary

33 *Soldiers Died In The Great War 1914 -1919* p. 103; Commonwealth War Graves Commission casualty details

34 Ibid., p. 105; 1911 Census

35 Ibid., p. 104

36 Ibid., p. 102; Sergeant Burr Army Service Record, National Archives, WO 363

37 Ibid., p. 103

CHAPTER THREE

4th October 1917 to 6th November 1917

Third Battle of Ypres
The Front east of Messines
New Cross Street

4th October – The Battle of Broodseinde – Third Battle of Ypres

Having secured Polygon Wood and beaten back counter-attacks by German shock troops the British and Colonial troops launched the 'third step' of the offensive to take Gheluvelt Plateau with an assault on Broodseinde ridge and village.[1]

The front for the attack was eight miles wide. The northern left flank of the attack was just north of Langemarck at the Ypres – Staden railway line. It ran south around the western edge of Zonnebeke and the eastern edge of Polygon Wood to Ypres – Menin road to the west of Gheluvelt Wood and Tower Hamlets forming the right flank.[2]

The main assault was made by the I and II Anzac Corps. The I Corps was to capture the Broodseinde ridge on a frontage of 2,000 yards astride the Moorslede Road from its junctions with Gheluvelt Plateau about Noordemdhoek, northwards to Nieuwemolen. The II Corps, to the north on the left flank of the I Corps, was to attack on a frontage of 3,000 yards. Their objective was to overrun the Zonnebeke and Gravenstafel spurs and hold their position in such strength so that it could be used as the jumping off line for the next 'step' to take the Broodseinde – Passchendaele section of the main ridge.

The Fifth Army was to attack on the left, towards Poelcappelle and have their left resting on the Ypres – Staden railway. The X Corps on the right flank, on a frontage of 1,400 yards, was to advance 1,200 yards to the eastern edge of the Gheluvelt Plateau capturing on the way the dominating observation areas near Reutel and In de Ster Cabaret.

The southern flank of the attack south of the Menin Road was to be established by the IX Corps on a frontage of 1,400 yards.[3]

The Second Army artillery plan was designed to keep the Germans guessing about the time and date of the next 'step'. As well as carrying out normal counter-battery work and the deliberate destruction of strong points, full scale practice barrages, including gas shells were laid down at various hours on several days from 27 September.

The II Anzac Corps left Ypres via the Menin Gate, marched to their positions in front of the Zonnebeke and Gravenstafel spurs and assembled overnight. By 4am they lay crowded on the wet ground behind the jumping off tapes. At 5.20am the Germans appear to have detected the massing of Australian forces and launched an intense barrage against their lines causing heavy casualties. An estimated one-in-seven men were killed or wounded.

At Zero hour 6am the British barrage suddenly crashed down on the whole depth of German positions. The Anzacs surged forward across No Man's Land. The 1st and 2nd Australian Divisions of the I Anzac Corps attacked the slopes of Broodseinde Ridge.

The 1st Australian Division was met by German troops advancing across No Man's Land with fixed bayonets. They overcame these troops and those hiding in every shell hole. Next the Anzacs took out the pillboxes in Flandern I and those near Molenaarelsthoek and the machine gun post at Retaliation Farm. They silenced the machine guns covering the bare open ridge south of Broodseinde and then reached their final objective of Broodsneide village.

The 2nd Australian Division also met and dealt with Germans advancing with fixed bayonets. They then by-passed Zonnebeke 'lake' and overcame the German machine gun detachments in the ruins of Zonnebeke and cleared the village. They thrust onto the ridge and took Broodseinde hamlet. They then encountered further machine gun fire as they topped the crest of the ridge. They dug in two hundred yards short of their final objective line between Dairy Wood and Flinte Farm.

The 3rd Australian Division was held up by machine gun fire from pillboxes in the Flandern I and Abraham Heights. This opposition was overcome and the Anzacs reached the Nieuwemolen crossroads on the main Broodseinde ridge. They reached their final objective after occupying all the pillboxes in the Flandern I in their sector.

The New Zealand Division captured Gravenstafel spur and village and

Boetleer Farm on Hill 32. They then pressed onto the upper Stroombeek valley and reached their final objective near the Ravebeek.

The attack by the Anzacs was supported on their left flank by the Fifth Army. The 48th Division of the Fifth Army attacked on the muddy southern side of the Lekkerboterbeek and was held up in the centre about 300 yards short of their final objective Wallemolen spur. The 11th Division, supported by ten tanks, advanced up the gradual slope of the Poelcappelle spur. They were met by sweeping machine gun fire from a number of strong points and suffered heavy casualties. The tanks played a central part in enabling the 11th Division to take the western half of Poelcappelle.

The 29th Division gained its objective and established themselves overlooking the Broembeek Valley. The 4th Division crossed 19 Metre Hill but was held up a few hundred yards short of its objective north-west of Poelcappelle.

On the right of the Anzacs the X Corps advanced 150 yards onto the eastern edge of Gheluvelt Plateau reaching the area between Noordemdhoek and In de Ster Cabaret. The 7th Division took their first objective the Reutel – Broodseinde track but fell short of the final objective between Reutel and In de Ster. Their position looked over the broad Heulebeek depression between the plateau and Keiberg spur to the north-east.

The 21st Division had the task of establishing the southern flank of the X Corps between Polygon Wood and the Menin Road. With the assistance of four tanks they crossed the slough of Polygonbeek taking out pillboxes on the opposite bank and passed through the edge of the Gheluvelt Plateau. They secured the southern flank of the main Broodseinde battle front but were held up short of their final objective between Reutel and Judge Cross Roads.

The 5th Division of X Corps occupied Cameron Covert at the head of the Reutelbeek re-entrant, advanced 800 yards and with the help of a tank captured the pillboxes within it. For a time they also occupied the strongly defended ruins of Polderhoek Château. However they were forced to withdraw during the night. Their advance north of the Menin Road gained little ground.

The IX Corps south of the Menin Road kept in touch with the 5th Division but failed to capture Gheluvelt Wood and the heavily defended Tower Hamlets spur.[4]

The Fifth Army lost 3,210 men killed, missing or wounded in the week up to 5 October. The Second Army lost 12,256 men in the week up to 4 October.[5]

C.R.E. 7th Division called at the 18th Middlesex H.Q. at 9am and said that in view of the tactical situation caused by the offensive then underway, he only required two companies to work if the conditions allowed.

'A' Company worked on camp improvements and repairs to the overland track from Dickebusch to Valley Cottages.

'B' Company was given a day off of work.

'C' Company and 'D' Companies went out to start the slabbing work ordered the previous day. However, the continuous and heavy 'Alleyman' barrage on Glencorse Way Road made work impossible. They were therefore employed on carrying slabs from Hooge Crater.

Hooge Crater was 120 feet wide and 20 feet deep. It was caused by an underground mine exploded on 19 July 1915 between the western edge of Hooge and Etang de Bellewaarde.[6]

The battalion received 33rd Division Order 236 at 11.50am. The two Lewis guns and instructor were sent to 33rd Divisional Wing, X Corps Musketry and Reinforcement Camp. A draft of 163 other ranks arrived at 2pm.

Seven men were wounded.

Private G/32396 Arthur Dennis Beckett born in Tottenham, enlisted in Mill Hill, aged 32 of 'B' Company died of his wounds. He was the son of Louisa and John Dennis Beckett and the husband of Ellen Edith Beckett of 37A, St. John's Road, Tottenham. He is buried in the Bedford House Cemetery.[7]

Private P.W.1071 Ernest Bentley born in Longton, Staffordshire and enlisted in Stoke-on-Trent, died of his wounds. He is buried in the Lijssenthoek Military Cemetery.[8]

The following three soldiers were killed in action and are buried in the Railway Dugouts Burial Ground.

Sergeant P.W.840 John Thomas Derricott was born and enlisted in Fenton Staffordshire.[9]

Private G/7214 Arthur James Farr aged 24, born and enlisted in Grays, Essex. He was the son of Mr and Mrs Farr of 57 Parker Road, Grays, Essex.[10]

Private G/61174 Reginald Jones, formerly 183114 Royal Engineers born in Newton Abbot, lived in Sandford, and enlisted in Exeter, Devon.[11]

Private T.F.238150 Cecil West, formerly 1415 Devonshire Regiment who enlisted in Plymouth, Devon, died of his wounds. His name is on the Tyne Cot Memorial.[12]

Lt.-Col. P.D. Ionides, the former Second-in-Command of the 18th Battalion Middlesex Regiment, was seriously wounded whilst commanding the 10th Battalion Duke of Cornwall's Light Infantry Regiment. He was hit by a piece of shrapnel which entered over his pubic bone and fractured it. The shrapnel cut his bowel and exited through his right buttock near his coccyx. The wound

left Lt.-Col. Ionides unable to ride and only able walk two to three miles. He was fatigued after mental exercise and suffered mentally for a long time after the wound had healed. He lived at Poplar Tree, Copdock, Ipswich. He relinquished his commission on ill-health grounds on 12 August 1921 and received a pension of £150 from 4 October 1919 to 3 October 1920.[13]

5 Oct. 'A', 'B' and 'D' Companies worked in two shifts on Glencorse Way Road.

'C' Company had a day off work.

The battalion struck camp and moved into the adjoining Sherwood Camp less than a mile south-west of Dickebusch.

Fifty-five other ranks were sent to the 2nd Battalion Middlesex Regiment and fifty other ranks to the 4th Battalion Middlesex Regiment.

Sherwood Camp

6 Oct. 'A', 'B' and 'C' Companies worked in two shifts on Glencorse Way Road. The first shift completing 360 yards of single formation. The second shift carried materials.

Eighty men loaded forty lorries bringing slabs from the La Clytte Dump four miles south-west of Ypres.

'D' Company was given a day off.

The battalion received 33rd Divisional Order 237 at 10.15am and 33rd Divisional Order 238 at 8.45pm. As a result the 33rd Division transferred from X Corps to the VIII Corps commanded by Lieut.-General Sir Aylmer Hunter-Weston. The 33rd Division took over the line held by the 14th Division.

Lieut. Hartley and Lieut. McL.Colvin and three men were wounded.

Private P.W.114 Alfred Barnes aged 33, born and enlisted in Longton, Staffordshire, died of his wounds. He was the son of Emma and Alfred John Barnes and the husband of Elizabeth Barnes of 5 Drewery Court, Longton, Stoke-on-Trent. He is buried in the Lijssenthoek Military Cemetery.[14]

Curragh Camp Westoutre

7 Oct. 'B', 'C' and 'D' Companies solely carried materials. 'A' Company had a day's rest.

The battalion embussed at Withuis Cabaret at 5pm and proceeded via Kruisstraathoek, Kemmel, La Clytte, and Canada Corner to Curragh Camp in No 8 area (Westoutre) south-west of Scherpenberg arriving at 6.15pm.

The transport left at 2pm and arrived at 3.15pm.

Winter time came into force and the clocks put back one hour at 1am.

Three company commanders of the 11th Battalion King's (Liverpool) Regiment, pioneer battalion of the 14th Division called at battalion H.Q. at 10am and were given particulars of the work in hand.

Three men were wounded.

Private G/61131 Henry Samuel Thompson aged 29, born in Walthamstow, Essex and enlisted in Chatham, Kent, died of his wounds. A former Royal Engineer (Army number 204040), he was the son of Sophia and Samuel William Thompson of Leytonstone. He was the husband of Alice Edith Thompson of 44 Queen's Road Leytonstone, London. He is buried in the Godewaersvelde British Cemetery – Nord.[15]

Gable Farm Wulverghem

8 Oct. At 8.30am the battalion marched via Canada Corner, Locre, Dranoutre and Lindenhoek to Gable Farm, Wulverghem arriving at 10.30am and took over the camp of the 11th King's (Liverpool) Regiment (Pioneers). No one fell out.

Gable Farm was 600 yards on the road leading north-west out of Wulverghem and was in the front line prior to the Battle of Messines in June 1917. During the battle the front line was pushed east of Messines towards Warneton and back across the River Lys south of Warneton.

The transport went on to the transport lines at Neuve Église.

Particulars of the work in hand were received from the officer commanding the 11th King's 'leather hats' handing over party. Two officers per company were taken round their company's work during the afternoon.

9th October – The Battle of Poelcappelle – Third Battle of Ypres

The front of the attack for the 'fourth step' was over six miles from a point east of Zonnebeke to the junction with the French north-west of Langemarck. On

the British left the French prolonged the front of the attack to a point opposite Draaibank. Simultaneously the British launched minor operations on the right of the main attack east and south-east of Polygon Wood.[16]

The success of the preceding three phases of the Third Battle of Ypres had been achieved by deadly accurate artillery barrages inflicting serious damage to the German front line defences and providing a 'creeping' barrage to guide and protect the advancing British and Colonial troops.

It had rained persistently since the 4 October and reports showed there was more stormy weather on the way. The roads and tracks across the battle area had gravely deteriorated and in some areas conditions became impossible. The entire valley of the upper Steenbeek and its tributaries behind the II Anzac Corps had become 'a porridge of mud'. This made it impossible to move guns forward along the plank roads.

The field batteries of the II Anzac Corps should have been positioned near the Zonnebeke – Winnipeg road to support the main attack. However the ground conditions meant they had to remain west of the Steenbeek mounted on hurriedly constructed and unstable platforms, making them slower and more difficult to load and less accurate to fire. Their targets in the German lines were 6,000 yards away and at the very extreme margin of their range.

The majority of the I Anzac Corps artillery was also well behind their intended position at Anzac House and Tokio spurs.[17]

Getting the troops forward was just as difficult. The II Anzacs, already assembled behind Frezenberg and Potijze, set off for the front line at 7pm and were expected to cover the two-and-a-half miles to the jumping off tapes by midnight to arrive well in time for Zero hour at 5.20am.

The night was inky dark and it poured with rain. The last mile to the front had men walking through mud above their ankles and often above their knees. They arrived at the front muddy, drenched and exhausted. Many of them were late causing large gaps along the jumping off tapes.

The barrage prior to the attack was a disaster. Large numbers of guns and howitzers failed to participate and the others fired inaccurately from their unstable platforms. The barrage was so weak and erratic that that no edge was apparent or visible to guide the infantry. The high-explosive shells, which formed a high proportion of the total, buried themselves in the mud and soft ground losing most of their effect.[18]

The attack, launched at 5.20am, had a most unfavourable start and things did not get any better as the attempt to advance ran into swollen water courses,

deep mud, barbed wire entanglements twenty-five to forty feet wide, rifle and machine gun fire.

In the main the ground gained had been small and was confined to near Reutel, opposite Passchendaele. The Fifth Army operating on the northern front had better results. On their left they crossed the Broembeek and advanced to the southern edge of Houthulst Forest. On their right they established a line east of the Poelcappelle – Houthulst road. They reached their final objective astride the Staden railway. They also advanced 2,500 yards on the western extremity of the long Veldhoek – Vijwegen spur facing the south edge of the forest. Fifth Army troops also got close to les 5 Chemins crossroads on the summit of the spur and the crossroads 500 yards east of Veldhoek.[19]

The British and Colonial casualties were 6,957 men killed, missing or wounded.[20]

Field Marshal Haig referring to the Battle for Poelcappelle said 'The results were very successful'.[21]

9 Oct. Daily patrols and maintenance parties of one N.C.O. and six men from each company reconnoitred the work allocated to their company.

Two platoons of 'D' Company carried materials by night for work on New Cross Communication Trench in the front line east of Messines. (The Battalion War Diary has this as New Cross Street.)

A party of 21 other ranks was placed under the command of 2nd Lieut. D.B. Evans as a permanent gang in charge of the trench tramway. They took up quarters at Wulverghem Station.

One platoon of 'A' Company worked on the new horse standings in Neuve Église commenced by the 11th King's. One platoon of 'C' Company started making a road in to the battalion headquarters. The rest of the battalion improved the camp.

10 Oct. 2nd Lieut. Bradbury with a party of 24 other ranks took over the divisional workshop at Neuve Église in accordance with instructions received from C.R.E.

The battalion started night work on the front line. 'A' Company worked on Fanny's Avenue which was a communication trench in the left battalion sector. (The Battalion War Diary has this trench as Fanny Street.) They worked backwards along Fanny's Avenue from the reserve line at the northern end of Owl Trench a mile north-east of Messines.

'C' Company worked on the 600 yard section of the reserve line Undulating Trench and on 300 yards of the connected reserve line Undulating Support. This was a mile south-east of Messines. 'B' and 'D' Companies worked on New Cross Communication Trench in the right battalion area.

By day a small party of 'A' Company cleared the Blauwepoortbeek Stream in the vicinity of Delpotre Farm. A party from 'D' Company cleared La Douve River south of Messines.

After 1 year and 332 days active service in France and Belgium Pte. Thomas McBride was sent back to England and admitted to the Bath War Hospital.[22]

11 Oct. The battalion worked on communication trenches, river and stream clearing.

Three men were wounded.

12th October – The First Battle of Passchendaele – Third Battle of Ypres

Despite the failure of the Battle for Poelcappelle, three more days of solid rain, the impossibility of getting sufficient artillery pieces forward and ever deepening mud on the battlefield, Haig decided to 'press on while circumstances still permitted and arrangements were made for the renewal of the attack'. The frontage was from the Ypres – Routlers railway to Houthulst Forest.[23]

As on 9 October and for the same reasons the artillery barrage to support the attack was weak and erratic at the start of the assault and became even thinner and more ragged as the troops advanced. At 5.25am the 3rd Australian Division tried to advance on Passchendaele and the New Zealand Division on the left tried to advance on Bellevue and Goudberg defences on the high ground of Wallemolen spur. Once again they were met by the triple combination of murderous deep mud, uncut barbed wire and concentrated machine gun fire. Once again very little ground was gained.[24]

British and Colonial casualties were 15,429 men killed, missing or wounded.[25]

12 Oct. 'A' Company worked on Fanny's Avenue Communication Trench. 'B' Company worked on New Cross Communication Trench. 'C' Company worked on the reserve line in Undulating Trench and Undulating Support. 'D' Company dug a new communication trench towards the front line by night, continuing New Cross Communication Trench eastwards from Pollard Support.

Private G/29683 Frank Older was killed in action. He is buried in the Tyne Cot Cemetery, Zonnebeke, West-Vlaanderen.[26]

13 Oct. Field Marshal Haig held a conference at Cassel with Generals Plumer, Gough and their Staff Officers. Also present were Haig's Staff Officers, Kiggell, Nash, Birch, Charteris and Davidson. All agreed that mud and bad weather prevented troops getting forward the previous day. They all agreed that a further attack should only be launched when there was a fair prospect of fine weather. They held the view that when the ground was dry no opposition which the enemy had put up had been able to stop their attacks.[27]

13 Oct. The battalion worked on Fanny's Avenue C.T., New Cross C.T. and its extension east towards the front line. Work also continued on Undulating Trench and Support reserve line.

Lt.-Col. Storr returned from leave at 8pm and assumed command of the battalion.

14 Oct. Twenty-five men of 'C' Company worked under the Divisional Drainage Officer. The battalion worked on Undulating Trench and Support reserve line, Fanny's Avenue C.T., New Cross C.T. and extension.

There was no night work because of the brigade relief and because parties had been out five successive nights.

Four Lewis guns of 'B' and 'C' Companies took up position at the Duke of Connaught railway marshalling yard in accordance with orders received from the Division.

15 Oct. The battalion worked on the C.T. trenches and reserve line. 400 men were bathed and given a change of underclothes.

One man was slightly wounded.

16 Oct. Work continued on C.T. trenches and reserve line. A lecture on revetting was given by the Lt.-Col. Storr to all officers.

17 Oct. Work continued on C.T. trenches and reserve line.

18 Oct. 100 N.C.O.s and men were sent to join the 17th Battalion Middlesex Regiment leaving at 4.30am. The 17th Middlesex Regiment was designated the

1st Football Battalion and was raised by the Rt. Hon. W. Joynson-Hicks M.P. Initially the 17th Middlesex was part of the 100th Infantry Brigade of the 33rd Division and was commanded by Col. H.T. Fenwick. It arrived in France on the 18 November 1915.[28] The battalion transferred to 6th Infantry Brigade of the 2nd Division on 8 December 1915 and was disbanded on 10 February 1918.[29]

Part of the battalion worked on C.T. trenches and reserve line. The rest of the battalion bathed and were given a change of underclothing.

Three men were wounded.

19 Oct. Work continued on C.T. trenches and reserve line. 'C' and 'D' Companies did not work by night.

Lt.-Col. Storr attended a conference held by Lieut.-General Sir Aylmer Hunter-Weston Commander VIII Corps at Divisional H.Q. at 3.30pm.

2nd Lieut. H.S. St. John joined on appointment and was posted to 'B' Company.

2nd Lieut. Burgoyne and one man were wounded.

Private P.W.2826 Herbert Ollerhead born and lived in Talke, Staffordshire, enlisted in Stoke-on-Trent, died of his wounds. He was 31 years old and a miner by trade. He attested on 18 May 1915 and was posted to the 18th Middlesex. He transferred to 25th Middlesex on 8 August 1915 and then returned to the 18th Middlesex on 29 September 1915. He received a shell wound to the back on 8 August 1916. He was moved from a Casualty Clearing Station to hospital in Étaples on 10 August 1916 and then transported back to England on H.M.H.S. Newhaven on 16 August and hospitalised in Clandon Park Auxiliary Hospital, Guildford. He was discharged from hospital on 18 September 1916. He returned to service with the 18th Middlesex on 28 November 1916.

Private Ollerhead was wounded again on 28 September 1917 suffering gunshot wounds to the left side of his chest and his left thigh. On 2 October 1917 he was moved from the Casualty Clearing Station to the No. 10 General Hospital in Rouen. On 7 October 1917 he was transported to England and admitted to the 5th Southern Hospital in Portsmouth where he died of the gunshot wound to his left lung at 9.25am. He was the son of Sarah and Samuel Ollerhead who lived at 7 John Street, New Road, Talke, Stoke-on-Trent. He was unmarried and his father was his next of kin. Mr Samuel Ollerhead received the personal effects of his son which included a steel clip, bag, 3 discs, thong (leather), 2 clasp knives, handkerchief, buttons, post cards, L. belt, tin of tobacco, pipe and purse. He is buried in the Portsmouth (Milton) Cemetery, Hampshire.[30]

20 Oct. The battalion worked on C.T. trenches and reserve lines. 'B' Company was given a day's rest.

21 Oct. 'B' Company stopped work on revetting New Cross Communication Trench and commenced laying a Duckboard Track from Pollard Support through to the front line.

'A' Company was given a day's rest.

2nd Lieut. F.S. Mason joined the battalion on appointment and was posted to 'A' Company. 2nd Lieuts. G.W Squier, and E.G. Caprara joined on appointment and were posted to 'B' Company.

22 Oct. 'A' Company work on drains to Fanny's Avenue. Night work on New Cross Communication Trench was suspended owing to the Brigade relief.

A conference of officers was held from 6 to 7.30pm to explain the points raised on 19 October by the Lieut.-General Hunter-Weston.

23 Oct. 'A' Company worked on drains to Fanny's Avenue. 'B' Company continued work on the Duckboard track from Pollard Support to the front line. 'C' Company stopped working on the reserve line and commenced a drain for the portion of New Cross Communication Trench between Pollard Support and the front line. 'D' Company worked on a similar drain.

Parties worked under the Divisional Drainage Officer, the Trench Training Officer and the Divisional Workshop Officer on clearing the River Douve and the River Blauwepoortbeek.

The 98th Machine Gun Company relieved the 100th Machine Gun Company in the front line east of Messines. A Section occupied the Gapaard Group area, two guns of C Section occupied Steignast Farm and deployed one gun in a position on the opposite bank of the Douve River. D Section occupied the support line. B Section, with one gun of C Section was in reserve positions. In total sixteen guns were in the line.[31]

24 Oct. 'A' Company worked on drains. 'B' Company worked on the Duckboard track. 'C' and 'D' Companies continued on the drain in New Cross Communication Trench between Pollard Support and the front line.

Parties cleared the River Douve and the River Blauwepoortbeek.

25 Oct. 'A', 'C' and 'D' Companies continued on drains. 'B' Company worked on the Duckboard track. Parties continued on clearing the two rivers.

Four men were wounded, one slightly.

26th October – Second Battle of Passchendaele – Third Battle of Ypres

Nearly half the area in front of Passchendaele was under water or had been turned into deep mud and the Ravebeek valley was impassable – except for bridging of some sort. Despite this Haig determined to continue with his attack against Passchendaele and the ridge northwards to Westroosebeke.[32]

The Australian Divisions had lost 38,000 men so far in the Third Battle of Ypres. The exhausted and depleted II Anzac Corps was relieved at the front by the Canadian Corps under the command of General Sir Arthur Currie.

Currie planned to take the Passchendaele area in three short advances at three or more days' interval. By the 16 October cutting of the German wire and the bombardment of pillbox strong points had commenced, but the date of his attack was dependant on having artillery protection and the state of the roads.[33]

As part of Currie's preparation for the Second Battle of Passchendaele major works were undertaken to improve the plank roads and battery positions. Two infantry battalions, seven pioneer battalions, ten field companies of R.E., seven tunnelling companies, four Army Troops companies R.E., and two labour companies were employed on a daily basis on the forward roads of the Second Army.[34]

At Zero hour – 5.40am the 4th Canadian Division advanced behind a creeping barrage and attacked a frontage of 1,300 yards south of the Ravebeek. An advance of 400 yards was achieved, but later in the day they were forced back 300 yards. The 3rd Canadian Division also followed close behind the barrage across the broken wire and reached the pillboxes north of Bellevue and when reinforcements arrived they pressed onto the crest of the spur north of Bellevue. They then fought southwards and outflanked the remaining pillboxes near Bellevue and Laamkeek. This in turn enabled the 3rd Canadian Division to consolidate the positions gained. By 3.30pm the Germans had been driven from the Flandern I out of Ravebeek northwards to Wolf Copse.

The Canadians had advanced 500 yards, but were still 500 yards short of their objective including a portion of Flandern I across the Wallemolen spur.

However they were now established on the drier high ground of the main ridge to the south-west and west of Passchendaele village.

On the right flank and to the south of the Canadian attack the X Corps launched a diversionary attack through knee deep mud on the Gheluvelt and Polderhoek spurs and the Tower Hamlets Quadrilateral. Polderhoek Château was captured but a strong German counter-attack retook the strongpoint. The attack was a costly failure with 3,321 men killed, missing or wounded.

On the northern flank of the Canadians, the renewed efforts of the Fifth Army to advance up the Lekkerboterbeek floundered and failed in the mud.[35]

For the week ending the 26 October the Second and Fifth Armies lost 13,133 men killed, missing or wounded.[36]

26 Oct. 'A' Company commenced laying a Duckboard track alongside New Cross Communication Trench from Pollard Trench back to Bethléem Road (The 18th Middlesex War Diary records this as Bethlehem Road), then they followed the tramway to the Petite Douve dump. Bethléem Road ran south from Messines to Tilluel Farm.

'B', 'C' and 'D' Companies stopped work by night, but day parties worked on the Duckboard Track, drains and clearing the two rivers.

One man was wounded.

Private G/29788 Samuel James Pipe aged 28, born in Aldeby and enlisted Beccles, Norfolk, was killed in action. He was the son of Samuel Pipe and the husband of Thirza Louisa Pipe of 3 Fenn Lane, Beccles. He is buried in the La Plus Douve Farm Cemetery – Comines-Warneton, Hainaut.[37]

Private P.W.6397 Walter Woods aged 41, born in Hedling and enlisted in Chichester, Hants, died of his wounds. He was the son of Mary and James Woods of Petersfield. He was the husband of Elizabeth Esther Woods of Copy Hall, Chithurst, Petersfield. He is buried in the Kandahar Farm Cemetery – Heuvelland, West-Vlaanderen.[38]

27 Oct. 'A' and 'B' Companies worked on the Duckboard track. 'C' and 'D' Companies dug drains.

28 Oct. 'A' and 'B' Companies continued on the Duckboard track. 'C' and 'D' Companies dug drains. At 9.45pm 'A' Company's work was suspended whilst the 98th Machine Gun Company fired gas projectors on to the German front line position at Kiwi Farm. The enemy was much disturbed but did little in retaliation.[39]

29 Oct. 'A' Company worked on laying a trench board track. The party from 'A' Company that was working by night was given a night's rest. 'B' Company having completed their Duckboard track commenced digging a drain for New Cross Communication Trench just west of Pollard Support. 'C' and 'D' Companies dug drains.

30th October – Second Battle of Passchendaele – Third Battle of Ypres

The objective of the Currie's 'second step' attack was to take the 500 yards of ground the Canadians failed to take on 26 October, including the portion of Flandern I across the Wallemolen spur and to establish a position on the southern edge of Passchendaele for the final assault.[40]

The frontage for the attack extended from the Ypres – Roulers Railway on the right to the Poelcappelle – Westroosebeke road on the left.[41]

Zero hour was 5.50am and the barrage from British artillery came down exactly on time. The 4th Canadian Division reached the outskirts of Passchendaele either side of the ridge highway. They captured the important German strong point at Crest Farm. The 3rd Canadian Division reached Meetcheele but encountered hard and costly fighting on the narrow summit of Bellevue spur. An advance of 800 yards was made and a footing gained at Vapour Farm on the western tip of Goudberg spur.

During the afternoon the 3rd Canadian Division successfully repelled five German counter-attacks from the north of Passchendaele.

On the left the 63rd and 58th Divisions, up to their knees in mud, once again made very little progress across Lekkerboterbeek.[42]

In the week ending 2 November the Second and Fifth Armies lost 19,381 men killed missing or wounded.[43]

30 Oct. A party of 'A' Company laid a Duckboard track by night. The party of 'A' Company which had been carrying by day was given a day off work.

'B' Company, except the trench maintenance party, was also given a day off work. 'C' Company, except the party working under the Divisional Drainage Officer, was given a day's rest. 'D' Company, except the party clearing the bed of the River Douve, was given a day's rest.

31 Oct. The parties that had worked on 30th, with the exception of 'A'

Company, were given a day off work.

Parties returning from night work came through an area shelled with mustard gas and had to wear respirators but did not suffer any fatalities.

One man was wounded.

Private P.W.468 Richard Hackney aged 34, born in Congleton and enlisted in Chester, Cheshire, died of his wounds. He was the husband of Annie Hackney of 33 Spragg Street, Congleton, Cheshire. He is buried in the Railway Dugouts Burial Ground.[44]

1 November 1917. 'A' Company worked, partly by day and partly by night, laying the Duckboard Track from Pollard Support back to Bethléem Road 330 yards south of Bethléem Farm.

'B' Company worked by night on drain A to New Cross Street communication trench.

'C' Company completed drain C by night.

'D' Company worked on the drain B and commenced work on sloping back the sides of New Cross Street between the reserve line and right battalion H.Q. in places where it was most urgently required.

Trench maintenance patrols worked under the Divisional Drainage Officer and the Trench Training Officer clearing the bed of the River Douve.

The divisional workshop party constructed horse lines and the approaches to horse lines.

2 Nov. 'A' Company worked by day and night laying a trench track. 'B' Company worked by night on drain A. 'C' Company by night started on the urgent work of sloping back the sides of New Cross Street. 'D' Company worked on the drain B and on sloping back the sides of New Cross Street.

3 Nov. 'A' Company worked by day and by night on laying the Duckboard Track. 'B' Company worked by night on drain A. 'C' Company sloped back the sides of New Cross Street. 'D' Company worked on the drain B and on sloping back the sides of New Cross C.T.

4 Nov. Men working by night were given a night's rest. 'A' Company laid the Duckboard Track by day. 'C' Company sloped back the sides of New Cross C.T. 'D' Company worked on the drain B and on sloping back the sides of New Cross C.T.

Private Powell transferred to the Labour Corps.

5 Nov. Lt.-Col. Storr attended a conference at Divisional H.Q. at 10am where arrangements for the forthcoming move of the Division were discussed.

2nd Lieut. Clay rejoined the battalion from the base camp. Hon. Lieut. J.W. Ritchie of the Royal Scots, joined the battalion on attachment for duty as the Quarter Master.

'A' and 'D' Companies commenced work by night on drain D. 'B' Company having completed drain A commenced the trench working either way from the drain. 'C' Company started the construction of a drain to New Cross Street. Major-General Wood visited battalion H.Q. in the afternoon and inspected part of the line.

Two men were wounded.

The officer strength of the 18th Battalion Middlesex Regiment was Lt.-Col. H. Storr in command, Major F.M. Best, Captains W.H. Coles, J.W. Young, H.K. Banks, C.P. Hinman Adjutant, F.S. Crawford (3rd Battalion Monmouth Regiment), A.S. Hands, A. Shaw M.C., Lieutenants E.H. Bennett, C. Taaffe, A.W. Hills, A.M. Baer, E.S. Hartley, C.H. Tollemache, L.H. White, J.F. Chapman, N.W.P. Walsh, W.T. Bowen, H.C. Fisher, F.N.M. Buesst, S. McL.Colvin, 2nd Lieutenants R.G. Bineham, G. Prior, R.M. Lester (Employed with the Ministry of Munitions) H.C. Bradbury, P. Clay, R.C. Ballard, C.H. Wight M.C., F.C. Wright, L.B. Wright, H.P. Boreham, F.A. Roger, G. Cotton, A. Payton, T. Tye, A.W. Drage, F.J. Smith, A. Burgoyne, C.R. Pughe, C.G. Sothers, J.A. Woodgate, H.C.B. Jones, G.M. Lowcock, E.G. Caprara, F.S. Mason, G.W. Squier, H.S. St. John and Quarter-Master Hon J. Ritchie 9th Royal Scots.[45]

6th November – Second Battle of Passchendaele – Third battle of Ypres

The objective of the Canadian attack was a wide arc east and north-east of Passchendaele.

The 2nd Canadian Division, following a well delivered artillery barrage, attacked at Zero hour 6am along a 750 yard frontage. By 7.10am they were streaming through and past either side of Passchendaele. They then encountered and overcame resistance from pillboxes and shell holes at the northern exit of the village. By 8.45am the Canadian 2nd Division had completed an advance of 800 yards and the entire objective along the eastern crest beyond the village had been gained.

The 1st Canadian Division, on the left flank, attacked along a 380 yard front on the Bellevue – Meetcheele spur to its junction with the main ridge. They also carried out a flanking attack eastwards astride Goudberg spur. They were immediately met by machine gun fire but managed to overrun all opposition. They surrounded the garrison strongpoint at Mosselmarkt and outflanked the shell-hole position behind that was covering the garrison. By 7.45am they had reached a line stretching from the ridge highway a couple of hundred yards north of the northern exit of Passchendaele to the tip of the Goudberg spur.

The Germans launched a series of determined counter-attacks but failed to win back any of the land they had lost.[46]

6 Nov. 'A' and 'D' Companies worked by night on drain D. 'B' Company worked on the trench both ways from the drain. 'C' Company constructed a drain to New Cross Street. 'D' Company commenced work on the trench working both ways from drain C.

Lt.-Col. Storr attended a conference presided over by Major-General Wood at Advanced Brigade H.Q. east of Wulverghem at North Midland Farm at 2.45pm. They discussed arrangements for the completion by the battalion of New Cross Street through to right company H.Q. in the support line by the morning of 15th.

Two men were wounded.

1 Edmonds, *Military Operations, France And Belgium, 1917 Vol. 2,* p. 302
2 Borastan (Editor), *Sir Douglas Haig's Despatches (December 1915 – April 1919),* p. 125
3 Edmonds, *Military Operations, France And Belgium, 1917 Vol. 2,* p. 299
4 Ibid., p. p. 303-315
5 Ibid., p.p. 364-365
6 Everard Wyrall, *The Die-Hards in the Great War, Vol.1,* p. 134
7 *Soldiers Died In The Great War 1914 -1919* p. 102; Commonwealth War Graves Commission casualty details; 1911 Census; London Metropolitan Archives, Holy Trinity, Tottenham, Register of marriages, DRO/066
8 Ibid.
9 Ibid., p. 103
10 Ibid.
11 Ibid
12 Ibid., p. 105
13 Lt.-Col P.D. Ionides Army Service Record, National Archives, WO 374/36434
14 *Soldiers Died In The Great War 1914 -1919* p. 102; Commonwealth War Graves

Commission casualty details
15 Ibid., p. 104
16 Borastan (Editor), *Sir Douglas Haig's Despatches (December 1915 – April 1919)*, p. 128
17 Edmonds, *Military Operations, France And Belgium, 1917, Vol. 2*, p.p. 327-328
18 Ibid., p. 330
19 Ibid., p.p. 335-337
20 Ibid., p. 334
21 Blake (Editor), *The Private Papers of Douglas Haig 1914 -1919*, p. 259
22 McBride Army Service Record
23 Borastan (Editor), *Sir Douglas Haig's Despatches (December 1915 – April 1919)*, p. 129
24 Edmonds, *Military Operations, France And Belgium, 1917, Vol. 2* p.p. 341-343
25 Ibid., p. 364-365
26 Commonwealth War Graves Commission casualty details; British Army WW1 Medal Rolls Index Cards 1914-1920
27 Blake (Editor), *The Private Papers of Douglas Haig 1914 -1919*, p. 260
28 Everard Wyrall, *The Die-Hards In The Great War, Vol. 1*, p. 211
29 Order of Battle of Divisions Part 3B – New Army Divisions (30-41) & 63rd, Compiled by Major A.F. Becke, p. 35
30 *Soldiers Died In The Great War 1914 -1919* p. 104; Commonwealth War Graves Commission casualty details; Private Herbert Ollerhead Army Service Record, National Archives, WO 363
31 98th Machine Gun Company War Dairy, National Archives, WO 95/2427, Image Ref 459
32 Edmonds, *Military Operations in France And Belgium, 1917, Vol. 2*, p. 346
33 Ibid.
34 Ibid., p. 347
35 Ibid., p.p. 349-351
36 Ibid., p.p. 364-365
37 *Soldiers Died In The Great War 1914 -1919* p. 104; Commonwealth War Graves Commission casualty details
38 Ibid., p. 105
39 98th Machine Gun Company War Dairy
40 Edmonds, *Military Operations, France And Belgium, 1917, Vol. 2*, p. 351 & p. 353
41 Borastan (Editor), *Sir Douglas Haig's Despatches (December 1915 – April 1919)*, p. 132
42 Edmonds, *Military Operations, France And Belgium, 1917, Vol. 2*, p.p. 353-355
43 Ibid., p.p. 364-365
44 *Soldiers Died In The Great War 1914 -1919* p. 103; Commonwealth War Graves Commission casualty details
45 British Army Lists
46 Edmonds, *Military Operations, France And Belgium, 1917, Vol. 2*, p.p. 355-357

CHAPTER FOUR

7th November 1917 to 7th December 1917

Consolidating in Flanders
Bethléem Road
Goldfish Château
Savile Road Camp east of Ypres
Duckboard Track

Planning the Allied strategy for 1918 was a very difficult process. Prime Minister Lloyd George had two major criticisms of the way the war had been prosecuted so far.

In a letter to President Wilson on 3 September 1917 Lloyd George stated 'The direction of the War on (the Allies) side has remained in the hands of four separate Governments and four separate General Staffs (namely those of France, Great Britain, Italy and Russia) each of which is possessed of complete knowledge only of its own front and its own national resources, and which draws up a plan of campaign which is designed to produce results mainly on its own section of front. The defects of this system have not been lost sight of. From time to time of late with greatly increased frequency there have been International Conferences to discuss the Allied war plans. But up to the present these Conferences have done little more than attempt to synchronise what are in reality four separate plans of campaign'.[1]

Lloyd George held the view that there was a 'common defect throughout the whole campaigns of the Allies during the past three to four years...the lack of co-ordination amongst the Allies had brought disaster on one or two occasions'.[2]

Lloyd George further advised President Wilson that 'The policy we have pursued hitherto has been to concentrate all our attacks on Germany on the ground that Germany is the mainspring of the hostile alliance, that it is therefore sound policy to try and knock out her army first, even though it is the strongest

with which we are confronted, because if we succeed, all the rest will collapse with it. In consequence, for more than three years, the armies of the main Allies have been engaged each summer in a series of terrific and most costly offensives against the strongest part of the enemy line – offensives which have never yet produced any decisive results in breaking down the enemy military organisation'.[3]

On the Somme in 1916 and continuing in Passchendaele, Allied troops had been engaged in uncoordinated attacks against the Germans strongest points. They failed to break through, became entangled in lengthy battles of attrition, captured very little ground and suffering enormous casualties. Lloyd George was determined to avoid a repetition of these disasters and came up with 'an alternative plan of campaign' for 1918.[4]

His alternative plan was to establish the Allied Supreme War Council on a permanent basis, with its own staff to 'determine the future strategy of the War'.[5] He also proposed that the principles of siege warfare be applied. 'In a siege you do not seek out the strongest part of the enemy line, but the weakest, in the hope that if you break down the defence there, the position as whole will be turned'.[6]

7 Nov. On 5 to 7 November 1917, in the wake of the Italian defeat by the Germans at Caporetto, representatives of the Italian, French and British Governments held a conference at Rapallo. The conference agreed to Lloyd George's proposal to set up a Supreme Inter-Allied War Council. Its remit was to 'watch over the general conduct of the War. It was to prepare recommendations for the decision of the Governments, and keep itself informed of their execution and report thereon to the respective Governments'.

'The first question referred to the new Council was the situation on the Italian Front. It was directed to report immediately on the position'. In consultation with the 'Italian General Headquarters they were to examine into the present state of affairs, and, on a general review of the military situation in all theatres, should advise as to the amount and nature of assistance to be given by the British and French Governments, and as to the manner in which it should be applied'.[7]

7 Nov. 'A' and 'D' Companies carried out night work on drain D. 'B' Company worked on the trench both sides of drain A. 'C' Company worked on the construction of a drain to New Cross Street. 'D' Company worked on the trench both sides of drain C.

8 Nov. 'A' and 'D' Companies were given a night's rest. 'B' Company worked on both sides of drain A. 'C' Company had small working parties employed by day working on the drain between Undulating Support and Undulating Trench from New Cross Street to drain B.

70 infantrymen were provided by 98th Infantry Brigade to bring materials forward from Currie Dump to Bethléem Road. However the tramway was heavily congested and it took more than four hours longer than anticipated to get the materials forward. As a result the 90 men of 'B' Company and 'C' Company, who had been designated to carry these materials forward from Bethléem Road, were brought back to camp because they did not have any work to do.

9 Nov. 'B' and 'C' Company were given a night off. Twenty men of 'A' Company deepened drain D. The rest of 'A' Company and 'D' Company and the battalion drummers carried materials forward from Bethléem Road.

70 infantrymen were again placed at the disposal of the battalion and by 5.15pm they had brought forward ten truck loads of materials from Currie Dump. All the materials carried forward the previous evening, as well as those carried forward during the day, were taken forward to the front line. The total amount of materials carried forward was 582 man loads.

10th November – Second Battle of Passchendaele – Third Battle of Ypres

At 6.45am 1st Canadian Division attacked northwards for another 500 yards along the main ridge east of the highway. On the left the 2nd Canadian Division and the 1st British Division provided the 1st Canadian Division with flank protection. Their attack in a rain storm secured the flank on the main ridge north of the Goudberg re-entrant.

The Germans retaliated with concentrated artillery fire and a series of counter-attacks. The Canadian main line of resistance was consolidated in a precarious salient astride the main ridge, but with advanced outpost groups on the eastern slope of the ridge strategically placed as to give the German artillery no good target.[8] This was the ultimate assault of the Third Battle of Ypres.

Field Marshal Haig's Flanders offensive came to an end. He blamed the 'immense natural difficulties, accentuated manifold by abnormally wet weather, rather than the enemy's resistance, which limited our progress and prevented

the complete capture of the ridge'.[9] Nevertheless, Haig claimed the Third Battle of Ypres as a victory. In his fourth despatch he stated 'Without reckoning, therefore, the possibilities which have been opened up by our territorial gains in Flanders, and without considering the effect which a less vigorous prosecution of the war by us might have had in other theatres, we have every reason to be satisfied with results which have been achieved by the past year's fighting. The addition of strength which the enemy has obtained, or may yet obtain, from events in Russia and Italy has already largely been discounted, and the ultimate destruction of the enemy's field forces has been brought appreciably nearer'.[10]

In fact the Third Battle of Passchendaele was an extremely costly failure for Haig and the British, Colonial and Allied forces. The British front line had only been extended by approximately five miles and did not even come close to capturing the Passchendaele – Staden Ridge which was the first objective of the campaign. Haig's three strategic objectives of liberating the Belgium coast, taking Ostend and Bruges and achieving a decisive break through German lines, had long since ceased to be achievable objectives of the Flanders campaign. In reality they were never achievable in the first place.

The cost in human life was monumental. 200,000 Germans were killed, wounded or taken prisoner. The British and Colonial Armies had 275,000 casualties and the French had 8,500 casualties.[11] The Canadian Corps between 26 October and 11 November lost 12,403 men killed, missing or wounded.[12]

The losses of men seriously weakened armies at the disposal of the British High Command leaving them depleted in numbers, poorly equipped, exhausted and demoralised.

The Germans still held the northern end of the main Passchendaele – Westroosebeke ridge. The five miles of ground taken east of Ypres created salient around Passchendaele which was exposed, difficult to defend and vulnerable to a concerted attack by the enemy. The new British front line in Flanders offered the Germans an extremely easy point of attack for their spring 1918 offensive.

On 24 October 1917 six German divisions and nine Austrian divisions achieved a major break through the Italian front at Caporetto. In the ensuing two weeks the Italian troops were driven back seventy miles, lost more than 600,000 men and more than 3,000 guns together with huge quantities of ammunition.[13]

As soon as the news of Caporetto was brought to Lloyd George by Sir William

Robertson C.I.G.S. the Prime Minister suggested that immediate arrangements should be made to send the necessary assistance. Robertson demurred at first, but acting under pressure, communicated with the French and Italian staff in order to put into operation, without delay, the plans made at the Rome Conference in January 1917 which had been carefully prepared in anticipation of an event such as this. Lloyd George recorded that the 'Rome Conference saved Italy'.[14]

The 23rd and 41st Divisions were sent to Italy.[15]

On 28 October Haig received telegram 44115 from Robertson informing him that he may be called upon to provide four more divisions for the Italian front. Haig replied to Robertson on 31 October in secret letter O.A.D. 688 setting out his views for the War Cabinet on the probable impact of reducing the number of troops on the Western Front.

Haig's first intention was, subject to having the necessary force being left at his disposal, to continue the offensive on the Flanders front. Haig was of the view that despite the advanced season and bad weather he could still take Passchendaele and the high ground round it by the middle of November or sooner. Haig pointed out the tactical importance of capturing the ridge giving him a defensive line for the winter with dry trenches, excellent coverage to the rear and secure flanks. He also pointed out the strategic advantage of holding the ridge as a starting point for the following year's campaign. Failure to take the ridge, he warned, would leave the portion of his lines on the west of the ridge in a low-lying position, water-logged, overlooked and difficult to hold against a determined attack causing wastage (loss of men) from enemy fire and sickness.

Haig cautioned that a decision to send additional troops from the Western Front to Italy would force him to abandon his drive to complete the capture of Passchendaele and ridge and other planned campaigns elsewhere on the Western Front (Cambrai). To strengthen his argument Haig expressed his view that the Germans had considerably reduced their defences on the Western Front and many parts of the front were weak and vulnerable to surprise attacks which would only be met by feeble resistance.

Haig feared that abandoning the Flanders offensive and giving up the initiative would allow the Germans to gather their forces and go on the offensive with options of further attacks in Italy or Salonika or advancing through Switzerland or elsewhere on the Western Front. The only gain Haig could see for sending more British troops to Italy was that this would stop the rout and enable the Italians to hold on.

Sending more troops to Italy would mean that the Allies would not be in a position to go on the offensive in 1918 and would have to wait until sufficient U.S. troops were available for deployment which would probably be not before 1919. Haig therefore saw two options. Option one was to adopt a purely defensive stance on the Western Front and send all the British and French troops that could be spared to reinforce the Italian army. Option two was to assist indirectly by exerting the greatest possible pressure on the Western Front but not sending any additional troops and using the Allied troops already ordered to Italy to restore confidence and enable her to rally her own armies.

Haig felt option two risked losing Italy from the alliance however if option one was chosen he saw the risk of losing the war. Not surprisingly Haig favoured option two.[16]

Following the massive defeat of the Italian Army at Caporetto a conference at Rapallo was held between 5 – 7 November 1917 which was attended by political and military leaders from Italy, France and Great Britain. The conference heard how serious the defeat had been for Italy. Signor Orlando, on behalf of the Italian Government, explained that they needed Allied help to defend the Trentino and Piave fronts and asked for at least 15 divisions. Lloyd George informed the conference that four of the best French divisions were already in Italy or on their way and two of the best British divisions were to be deployed to join the two British divisions already in Italy.[17]

The two divisions already in Italy were the 23rd and 41st which Lloyd George had instructed Haig to send on 26 October. On the 8 November Lloyd George gave another order to send two more divisions to Italy. The 7th and 48th Divisions were thus deployed.[18]

Field Marshal Haig, on receiving orders to send Plumer and British reinforcements to Italy recorded in his diary 'Was ever an Army Commander and his Staff sent off to another theatre of War in the middle of a battle?'[19]

At the follow-up conference held on 8 November 1917 at Peschiera it was decided that the six Allied divisions already in Italy should be moved to the points of greatest danger on the Italian front.[20]

10 Nov. The winter work of consolidating the new British lines in Flanders began. It rained heavily at intervals throughout twenty-four hours. As a result working conditions were extremely difficult.

70 infantrymen were again placed at the disposal of the battalion. They moved ten truck loads of materials forward from the Currie Dump to Bethléem

Road. Part of 'D' Company and the drummers carried revetting materials forward from there to Bethléem Road. The other companies worked on the excavation of New Cross Street.

11 Nov. All companies made a revetted and anchored breastwork along either side of a 70 yard stretch of the proposed new section of New Cross Street. This section of trench was where it crossed a hollow east of drain D. Here the trench was only deep enough to direct water into drain A and not deep enough to provide cover for day work. The work was completed in three shifts during the night.

The 70 infantrymen were again placed at the disposal of the battalion and they moved ten truck loads of materials from Currie Dump to Bethléem Road. A further 80 infantry men were detailed to carry the material from Bethléem Road in three journeys to the work on New Cross C.T. Only 40 infantry men arrived and only half of the materials were moved forward.

The officer commanding 5th Australian Pioneers visited battalion H.Q. between 1 and 2.30pm to make arrangements about the relief of the battalion.

One man was wounded.

12 Nov. Work on revetting New Cross C.T. continued by day and on digging by night. Infantrymen continued to work as carrying parties. The 40 men who failed to arrive the previous night were sent to carry their loads.

A luncheon was held in Paris where French Premier M. Painlevé announced the setting up of the Supreme Inter-Allied War Council. Speaking at the luncheon Lloyd George gave what he called a candid survey of the military position which had led to the creation of the Supreme War Council.[21]

In his speech he pointed out 'The Allies have the advantage of the command of the seas. They have had advantage of numbers, in weight of men, and in materials, in economic resources, and beyond all, in the justice of their cause. This combined superiority ought to have ensured for them victory, or at least ought to have carried them much further along the road to victory than they are now'.[22]

Lloyd George did not blame the armies for this failure.[23] He ascribed the reasons for Allied Forces failing to achieve their purpose to 'almost entirely to lack of unity in their War Direction'.[24] By the time he wrote his war memoirs Lloyd George had reached the view the failure 'had been entirely due to the absence of real unity in the war direction of the Allied countries'.[25]

For these reasons the Allied countries had decided to set up the Supreme War Council.

Lord Derby, Secretary of State for War, was concerned that Sir Douglas Haig would feel Lloyd George's speech reflected on him and his men. Lord Derby wrote to Haig and assured him that he had his entire confidence which he would probably show in an outward and visible way. Haig did not read the speech but saw a summary of it by Reuter and recorded 'I gather that it is more likely to hearten the enemy and discourage the Italians than any other language!'[26]

13 Nov. The battalion worked on revetting by day and digging by night.

Two men were wounded by inhaling mustard gas.

14 Nov. The battalion carried on revetting by day. A quantity of materials was stolen from dumps on the work. 70 men had to be employed carrying up materials to replace it by night. The digging to complete New Cross C.T. to within 60 yards of right company H.Q. was done by night.

Two men were gassed with mustard gas.

Lloyd George explained in a statement to the House of Commons on 14 November 1917 that 'The object of the Allies has been to set up a central body charged with the duty of continuously surveying the field of operations as a whole and, by the light of information derived from all fronts and from all Governments and Staff, of co-ordinating the plans prepared by the different General Staffs, and, if necessary, of making proposals of their own for the better conduct of the war'.[27]

15 Nov. The battalion carried on revetting by day. New Cross C.T. was completed to within 60 yards of right company H.Q. by noon.

Accommodation was found in camp for one company of the 29th Australian Infantry Battalion for the night. The 8th Australian Infantry Brigade sent its band to play in camp from 2.30pm to 3.30pm.

The battalion received Divisional Order 249 at 4pm and orders for the move of the battalion on 16th were issued.

Haig wrote to Sir William Robertson C.I.G.S. 'I note that I am to be prepared to relieve some or all of the Divisions in Italy from other Divisions in France'. Haig told Robertson he was very concerned about the security of the Franco-Belgian front following the decision to send French and British

divisions to help the Italians after their defeat at Caporetto. He feared attacks on the British and French in order to check the number of Allied troops being sent to Italy or to exploit the Allied weakness on the Western Front.[28] Haig failed to take into account the fact that six German divisions had been moved from the Western Front to Austria for the attack on Caporetto.

Bailleul

16 Nov. The battalion marched at 10am to Bailleul arriving at 12.30pm and went in to billets. Lt.-Col. Storr accompanied Major-General Wood to Ypres and visited the camp of the Pioneer Battalion (124th Battalion) of the 4th Canadian Division to make arrangements about the relief of the battalion. The Canadian pioneers were formerly the Governor-General's Bodyguard.

The two officers returned to Bailleul in the evening.

17 Nov. The battalion remained in billets in Bailleul.

A conference of officers was held at 10am to discuss the arrangements necessary for moving the battalion to north-east of Ypres.

Orders were issued at 3pm for the battalion personnel to move by bus and transport by road on the 18th.

Permission was received at 10pm from 33rd Division for the transport to move earlier than the time indicated in Divisional Order 249, but to be close to Locre by 10am. Arrangements were made accordingly.

Fifty men were transferred to the Royal Engineers base depot at Rouen.

Saint Jean

18 Nov. The battalion paraded in the station road at Bailleul at 7.45am ready to embus at 8am as ordered by 33rd Division. The buses arrived at 8.40am, twenty minutes earlier than ordered. The number of buses was fewer than had been ordered.

The Quarter Master did not notify arrangements for the transport of the battalion's blankets until 8.45am so each man had to carry his own blankets.

The transport started at 8.15am and arrived at Ypres simultaneously with the battalion, which debussed near the asylum at about noon and marched the

two miles to Saint Jean north-east of Ypres. The battalion occupied quarters vacated by 124th Canadian Battalion (Pioneers).

The camp and the whole surroundings had been left in a most filthy condition.

The transport marched to Goldfish Château via Ouderdom. The vehicles that were required to unload at Saint Jean marched via Dickebusch and proceed to Goldfish Château after unloading. The transport lines were filthy and unsanitary.

2nd Lieut. Woodgate and fifty other ranks were allocated to 214th Army Troops (A.T.) Company Royal Engineers at Poperinghe.

19 Nov. Reconnaissance of the work to be undertaken by the battalion was carried out by officers from each company. Arrangements were made to construct a camp within the Divisional area on the west side of Savile Road and only 600 yards north-east of the Menin Gate. 'D' Company was given the job of safeguarding the site so they moved on to it and set up their bivouacs.

One man was wounded.

By early August the deployment of tanks at Passchendaele had been rendered impossible by the weather conditions and deepening mud. Lieutenant-Colonel John Frederick Charles Fuller, Chief General Staff Officer Royal Tank Corps, therefore drew up plans for a large scale tank attack to strike 'a theatrical blow' against the Germans before the winter elsewhere on the Western Front. Cambrai was chosen as the site for the attack and General Byng's Third Army was chosen for the offensive.[29]

The intention was to operate as actively as possible for forty-eight hours. This was the period calculated as the minimum necessary for the arrival of fresh German reserves. Failing adequate success within forty-eight hours Haig intended to close down the operation and concentrate on establishing the best winter position on such ground as had been captured.[30]

20th November – Battle of Cambrai

At 6.20am, in a surprise attack, 476 tanks started towards the German front line without the usual artillery bombardment. Haig recorded the 'Infantry were covered by a number of tanks which cut lanes through the wire at intervals of roughly 50 yards or more. The attack was made against the famous Hindenburg

lines of defence, which consist of two main systems, each most stiffly wired, with a reserve system in the rear.

Our troops rapidly passed the first two systems of trenches and occupied the third line about Masnières and Marcoing with the Canal Crossings. Havrincourt, Ribécourt and La Vacquerie were taken early in the day; all were found carefully prepared for defence.

The 51st Division was checked in front of Flesquières, but the 62nd pressed on and took Graincourt and Anneux before nightfall, and extended N. to beyond the Bapaume – Cambrai main road'.[31]

The Times recorded that the Hindenburg Line had been broken on a ten mile front facing Cambrai to a depth of five miles. Bonavis, Lateaux Wood, La Vacquerie, Welsh Ridge, Ribécourt, Couillet Wood, Flesquières, Havrincourt, Marcoing, Neuf Wood, Graincourt and Anneux had been taken. The Third Army had advanced to within five miles of Cambrai.[32]

Prime Minister Lloyd George described the offensive as 'a brilliant success'. When the news of this 'great triumph reached London, the War Office ordered that all the church bells of the metropolis should be set a-ringing'. [33]

20 Nov. One platoon each of 'A', 'B' and 'C' Company and two platoons of 'D' Company prepared the new Savile Road campsite. An immense amount of water was drained off the area. Filth from the site was collected and burnt.

The rest of 'A' Company went out to work on Artillery Road but was prevented by hostile shelling. The rest of 'B' and 'C' Companies worked on the communication trench forward of Hamburg. The remainder of 'D' Company worked on a mule track between Seine and Hamburg half a mile from the front.

21 Nov. The Third Army made good progress north-west of the Canal de l'Escaut and pressed towards the Bourlon – Fontaine Ridge. By the end of the forty-eight hours they held Noyelles, Cantaing, Fontaine and the southern end of Bourlon Wood.

The 29th Division were less successful. They failed to capture the last German trench system south-west of Cambrai and by the evening of 21 November it was clear that no possibility remained of enveloping Cambrai.[34]

21 Nov. 'A' Company worked on Artillery Road and 100 infantrymen carried material for them. 'B', 'C' and 'D' Companies prepared the new camp.

2nd Lieut. Caprara and one other man were wounded.

Sergeant P.W.737 George Mowat born in South Leith, Midlothian and enlisted in Edinburg was killed in action nine days short of his 30th Birthday. He was a general labourer by trade, 5′ 2¾″ tall and weighed 124 lbs. He married Alesandrina Wilson Shanks at the Manse South Leith on 4 December 1908 and at the time they lived at 3 Wilkie Place, Leith. They had a daughter Mary Roberta Henrietta dob 23 May 1911. By the time George Mowat attested on 18 March 1915 he had separated from his wife and was single and he was living at Victoria House, Rosewell, Midlothian. He listed his aunt Miss Linton of 5 Main Street, Newhaven as his next of kin.

Mowat was initially posted to the 18th Middlesex but transferred to the 19th Middlesex on 1 May 1915 and then to the 25th Middlesex on 7 June 1915. On 13 January 1916 he was posted back to the 18th Middlesex and sailed from Folkestone to France. He joined the 18th Middlesex in the field on 7 February. He progressed through the lower ranks and was made Sergeant on 30 September 1916. He took 10 days home leave on 16 August 1917. Following his death his daughter was awarded a pension of 10 shillings a week with effect from 10 June 1918. This was paid to Mary's guardian Mrs Johnston the Secretary of the Families Sub Committee 7 Wellington Place, Leith.

Sergeant Mowat's personal effects of identification disc, letters, photos, 2 letter cases, metal cigarette case, watch and chain, purse, 2 souvenirs and a franc note were sent to his father Mr Henry Mowat 49 Iona Street, Leith. Likewise Mowat's medals were sent to his father. He is buried on Tyne Cot Cemetery.[35]

22 Nov. Field Marshal Haig decided that the Bourlon sector should be attacked and occupied because it would force the enemy to withdraw rapidly from the whole of their salient between the Canal du Nord and the Scarpe. Haig therefore continued operations in that sector beyond the forty-eight hours originally planned, even though he recognised that further progress north of Bourlon would temporarily accentuate the salient created by his advance and increase the length of the line to be held by his troops.[36] In response the Germans counter-attacked and recaptured the village of Fontaine.[37]

22 Nov. The battalion worked on site of new camp and in the forward area.

Two men were wounded, one man slightly wounded.

23 Nov. The British Third Army took the greater part of Bourlon Wood and part of Bourlon village. However, it proved impossible to secure the whole of

Bourlon – Fontaine Ridge. The Germans in turn tried to force the British out of Bourlon Wood and off Bourlon hill but did not gain any advantage.[38]

23 Nov. Three lorries took 88 men of 'B' and 'C' Companies to work at Devil's Crossing. This was where the Ypres to Roulers railway line crossed the Ypres to Broodseinde road two miles back from the front.

24 Nov. The work of 'B' and 'C' Companies on the communication trench was handed over to infantry under Royal Engineer supervision.

'B' and 'C' Companies commenced repairing and completing the triple duckboard 'H' Track between Godley Road and junction of 'H' Track with Royal Army Medical Corps track running north from Frezenberg. The three lorries for transporting men of 'A' and 'D' Companies arrived about two hours late and the men had to march to work.

25 Nov. Repair work on the triple duckboard track was carried out.

26 Nov. Two platoons of 'B' Company continued on the mule track between Zonnebeke Station and Seine. The other two platoons worked in the new camp. Three platoons of 'D' Company were employed on the mule track between Seine and Manx Corner in Moorslede right up to the new front line and one platoon on the new camp. The battalion H.Q. moved to the new camp.

27 Nov. The British Third Army increased their hold on Bourlon Wood and ridge. Haig believed this advance made it possible to hold those features against the strong attack which would undoubtedly be made. Haig made defensive dispositions on the assumption that the Fontaine – Bourlon ridge would be the enemy's chief objective.[39]

Savile Road Camp

27 Nov. Heavy rain in the early hours of the morning delayed work both in the forward area and in the new camp. 'C' Company completed the repair to H track between Godley Road and the junction of H track with RAMC track.

Major-General Pinney, on his way back to his Division, met Lt.-Col. Clive Wigram, Equerry and Assistant Private Secretary to the King, at General Head

Quarters. Wigram told Pinney that Major-General Wood had been unfavourably reported on and he was to replace him.[40]

28 Nov. Two platoons of 'C' Company continued the mule track between Zonnebeke Station and Seine and two platoons continued on the new camp.

Three platoons of 'B' Company and two platoons of 'D' Company continued the mule track between Zonnebeke Station and Seine. One platoon of 'D' Company continued the mule track between Seine and Manx. Three platoons 'A' Company continued on Artillery Road. One platoon each of 'A', 'B' and 'D' Companies worked on the new camp.

Four Lewis guns and teams were put in position under G.S. memorandum No. 5, one at Gravenstafel, two at Seine and one west of Zonnebeke Station.

Major-General Pinney returned and resumed full command of the 33rd Division.

29 Nov. Six lorries were provided to take men up to work on a daily basis until further orders. The lorries made a second journey for materials.

Corporal P.W.651 Horace Norman aged 33 of 'D' Company, born in Nottingham and enlisted in Cockspur Street, Middlesex, was killed in action by shell fire. He was 5 feet 8½ inches tall and weighed 163 lbs. He married Crescentia Theresa Modell at St. Pauls Church Newington on 5 September 1908. They lived at 13 Cavour Street, Penton Place, London SE17 and had four children. He attested on 16 March 1915, was promoted to Acting Lance Corporal on 16 December 1915 and made Corporal on 6 March 1916. He suffered a gunshot wound to the forehead on 18 July 1916 which he recovered from and returned to duty.

Mrs Norman received a 35 shillings a week pension with effect from 17 June 1918 for herself and her four children. The belongings of Horace Norman returned to her included two photos, letters, cards, Attestation Form, Cash Payment Card and a small brass object. Corporal Horace Norman is buried in the Gwalia Cemetery – Ieper, West-Vlaanderen.[41]

30 Nov. Haig reinforced the infantry at Bourlon. He had three fresh divisions in the line between Cantaing and the Canal du Nord. On the extreme right flank south of Twenty-Two Ravine Haig did not reinforce the line because the troops in that sector were holding the original trench system and were therefore in possession of defences which had been organised against attack for several months.

The major German Cambrai counter-attack took place. The Germans were held and beaten off in the Bourlon Sector and on the right flank on the Canal de l'Escaut. On the extreme right of the British position the Germans broke through on the Banteux Ravine and south of Twenty-Two Ravine. They took the villages of Villers-Guislain and Gonnelieu. This in turn forced the British to withdraw from the Bourlon sector to the Flesquières position.[42]

30 Nov. Two platoons of 'C' Company were taken off the mule track and commenced straightening and relaying track 'H' between Oxford Road and Godley Road. Oxford Road linked the Ypres to Wieltje road and the Ypres to Zonnebeke road.

Brigadier-General H.W. Rushton, Chief Engineer VIII Corps, visited battalion H.Q. about 10am. Lt.-Col. Storr attended a conference at Divisional H.Q. at 6pm on the subject of the formation of a works battalion in the Division. One Lewis gun was damaged by shellfire and a fresh gun sent up in its place.

1 December 1917. One platoon from 'A', 'B' and 'D' Companies and two platoons from 'C' Company worked on the new camp at Savile Road less than half a mile north-east of the Menin Gate at Ypres.

'C' Company relieved the drummers who were loading wagons with bricks and materials in Ypres. The drummers made huts in camp. The rest of 'A' Company worked on Artillery Road. The rest of 'C' Company worked on 'H' Track between Godley Road and Oxford Road. The rest of 'D' Company worked on the mule track, partly between Zonnebeke and Seine and partly between Seine and Manx Corner.

2 Dec. Major-General Pinney visited the new camp and expressed himself highly pleased with the progress made.

The battalion received Divisional Order 258 at 9.40pm which gave the co-ordinates for the new Divisional boundaries.

3 Dec. The battalion worked on the new camp, Artillery Road, 'H' Track and the mule track.

4 Dec. The tramway between Kansas Cross and Seine was in a very bad condition. So much so, that mule mats for the track from Seine to Manx Corner

could seldom be moved forward by it. As a result, much time was wasted and energy lost. 'D' Company was taken off the mule-mat work and set to work on laying a double trench board track from east of Bavaria House towards Levi Cottages north of Hill 40.

The battalion received Divisional Order 259 at 10am for the relief of 100th Infantry Brigade by the 98th Infantry Brigade.

5 Dec. The British War Cabinet considered newspaper accounts claiming that:– 1) the recent German counter-attack in Cambrai came as a complete surprise to British troops despite the air being full of British aircraft at the time; 2) the surprise nature of the attack had not been reported to the War Cabinet; 3) how could such a surprise attack have been inflicted on British troops if aerial superiority was as complete as it had been alleged, and if defensive arrangements were properly organised.

The Rt. Hon. the Earl of Derby, Secretary of State for War, informed the War Cabinet that a British Division had been completely overwhelmed and the British line had been breached after the German surprise attack had been affected.

The Rt. Hon. Sir Eric Geddes, the First Lord of the Admiralty informed the War Cabinet that he had been with Sir Douglas Haig on 30 November and Haig had stated that he could not expect to obtain details of what had happened for some days.

The War Cabinet decided to leave it up to the Field Marshal Commanding-in-Chief to enquire into the question of responsibility. They also recorded their view that the official telegrams on the subject had not given sufficient indication of the extent of the reverses suffered.[43]

5 Dec. 'A' Company worked in camp during the morning and had a bath and change of clothes at Ypres in the afternoon. At approximately 3.45pm a German aeroplane flew over the battalion position and was shot down by one of the battalion's Lewis guns at Abraham Heights on the Beecham to Gravenstafel road. The plane crashed at Crest Farm south-west of Passchendaele. This brought rousing cheers from all the lads.

6 Dec. The baths at Ypres suffered a direct hit by enemy shellfire so 'B' Company missed their bath and change of underclothes. Instead, they worked in the camp.

Two men were wounded, one slightly.

2nd Lt. Charles Gordon Sothers aged 32, died of his wounds. He was a Clerk to a Coffee Merchant by trade. He initially joined the London Rifle Brigade and rose through the ranks to be commissioned. He was the husband of May Kathleen Sothers of 15 Paget Road, Stoke Newington, London. His estate was valued at £162 18s. and 11d. He is buried in the Potijze Château Grounds Cemetery – Ieper, West-Vlaanderen.[44]

7 Dec. The German counter-attack at Cambrai was completed. They had regained most of the land they lost on 20 November. British troops hung onto a section of the Hindenburg Line around Havrincourt, Ribécourt and Flesquières. The Germans extended their front by almost a mile between Gonnelieu and Vendhuille.

The British failure to consolidate and then exploit the break through at Cambrai was due to the fact that the offensive took place without having reserves in support. Lloyd George held the view that what 'converted victory into a defeat was a total lack of reserves. When it was essential that there should be fresh troops available to support and exploit the attack, there was not a single platoon in reserve. They were all floundering in the Flemish slough'.[45]

Field Marshal Haig took a different view. He concluded his 5th Despatch stating 'the sudden breaking through by our troops of an immense system of defences has had a most inspiring moral effect on the Armies I command, and must have a correspondingly depressing influence upon the enemy. The great value of the tanks in the offensive has been conclusively proved. In view of this experience, the enemy may well hesitate to deplete any portion of his front, as he did last summer, in order to set free troops to concentrate for decisive action at some other point'.[46]

1 Lloyd George, *War Memoirs Vol. 2*, p.1415
2 Hansard, House of Commons, 19 November 1917, Vol. 99, Columns 894-895
3 Lloyd George, *War Memoirs, Vol. 2,* p.1415
4 Ibid., p.1416
5 Ibid., p.1417
6 Ibid., p.1416
7 Ibid., p.p. 1439-1441
8 Edmonds, *Military Operations, France And Belgium, 1917, Vol. 2*, p. 358.
9 Borastan (Editor), *Sir Douglas Haig's Despatches (December 1915 – April 1919),* p. 133
10 Ibid., p. 135

11 Nigel Steel and Peter Hart, *Passchendaele – The Sacrificial Ground*, Cassell & Co, London, 2000, p. 303
12 Edmonds, *Military Operations, France And Belgium, 1917, Vol. 2*, p. 359
13 Rowland, *Lloyd George*, p. 421
14 Lloyd George, *War Memoirs, Vol. 2,* p. 1394
15 Edmonds, *Military Operations, France And Belgium, 1917, Vol. 2*, p. 352
16 Haig's letters to CIGS, National Archives, WO 158/24
17 Lloyd George, *War Memoirs, Vol. 2*, p.p. 1397 – 1398
18 Edmonds, *Military Operations, France And Belgium, 1917, Vol. 2*, p. 352
19 Sheffield and Bourne (Editors), *Douglas Haig War Diaries and Letters 1914 -1918*, p. 339
20 Lloyd George, *War Memoirs, Vol. 2,* p. 1403
21 Ibid., p. 1442
22 Lloyd George Paris luncheon speech, U.K. Parliamentary Archives, LG/f/234
23 Lloyd George, *War Memoirs, Vol. 2*, p. 1442
24 Lloyd George Paris luncheon speech
25 Lloyd George, *War Memoirs, Vol. 2*, p. 1442
26 Blake (Editor), *The Private Papers of Douglas Haig 1914 -1919,* p. 267
27 Hansard, House of Commons, 14 November 1917, Vol. 99, Col. 390-391
28 Blake (Editor), *The Private Papers of Douglas Haig 1914 -1919,* p. 267
29 Lloyd George, *War Memoirs, Vol. 2,* p.1334
30 Report by Sir Douglas Haig summarizing the operations between November 20 and December 7 1917, 23 December 1917, National Archives, CAB/24/37, Image Reference 0098
31 Blake (Editor), *The Private Papers of Douglas Haig 1914 -1919*, p. 268
32 *The Times Diary & Index of The War 1914 -1918*, p. 126
33 Lloyd George, *War Memoirs, Vol. 2*, p.p. 1335-1337
34 Report by Sir Douglas Haig summarizing the operations between November 20 and December 7 1917, 23 December 1917
35 *Soldiers Died In The Great War 1914 -1919*, p. 104; Commonwealth War Graves Commission casualty details; Sergeant Mowat Army Service Record, National Archives, WO 363
36 Report by Sir Douglas Haig summarizing the operations between November 20 and December 7 1917, 23 December 1917
37 Ibid.
38 Ibid.
39 Ibid.
40 Private Papers of Major-General Pinney, Book 7
41 *Soldiers Died In The Great War 1914 -1919*, p. 104; Commonwealth War Graves Commission casualty details; Corporal Horace Norman Army Service Record, National Archives, WO 363
42 Report by Sir Douglas Haig summarizing the operations between November 20 and December 7 1917, 23 December 1917

43 Minutes of the War Cabinet 292 5 December 1917, National Archives, CAB/23/4, Image reference 0066

44 Commonwealth War Graves Commission casualty details; 1911 Census; England & Wales National Probate Calendar (Index of Wills and Administrations) 1858-1966

45 Lloyd George, *War Memoirs, Vol. 2,* p.1335

46 Boraston (Editor), *Sir Douglas Haig's Despatches (December 1915 – April 1919),* p. 173

CHAPTER FIVE

7th December 1917 to 27th January 1918

Digging in for the winter between Ypres and Passchendaele

7 Dec. Portions of 'C' and 'D' Companies were bathed and worked in camp.

The battalion received Divisional Order 260 at 8.30am for the move of the Division to Steenvoorde and Divisional Order 261 at 10am for the readjustment of the frontage.

One man was slightly wounded.

8 Dec. Portions of 'D' Company and 'H.Q.' Company were bathed.

Alterations to the deployment of front line troops and subsequent reliefs meant infantrymen were not available for work.

Divisional H.Q. instructed the battalion to carry 150 trench boards from Devil's Crossing, where the railway crossed the Ypres to Zonnebeke road, past Tyne Cot, to just north of Hamburg. 'B' Company and a portion of 'C' Company carried out this work. 'A' Company worked on Artillery Road. The rest of 'C' Company worked on 'H' Track. The battalion also worked on the new camp.

One man was slightly wounded.

The Rev. Ridsdale was transferred as chaplain to the Divisional Artillery. The Rev. H.C.C. Lewis took over as the battalion chaplain.

9 Dec. The rest of 'H.Q.' Company bathed.

'D' Company worked on the track east of Bavaria House to Levi Cottages.

2nd Lieuts. B.E.V. Butcher and C.V. Sampford joined the battalion and were posted to 'D' and 'B' Companies respectively.

Four officers and four N.C.O.s of 1/7th Battalion Durham Light Infantry arrived to be shown the work underway and were attached to their respective

companies. The 1/7th Battalion Durham Light Infantry were the Pioneer battalion of the 50th (Northumbrian) Division. 'A' Company moved into the new camp in the afternoon.

10 Dec. 'B' Company and parts of 'C' Company had a bath. The rest of 'C' Company and 'D' Company carried trench boards from Devil's Crossing to just north of Hamburg.

'A' Company worked on Artillery Road.

The battalion received Divisional Order 262 at 6.25pm for the 33rd Division to be placed in the Corps reserve and for infantry brigades to be prepared to move.

11 Dec. 'A' Company had a bath. 'B' Company worked on the mule track from Zonnebeke Station to Seine. 'C' Company worked on 'H' Track. 'D' Company started on a new track.

2nd Lieuts. A.C. Wilson and Herbert Sydney Barber joined the battalion and were posted to 'A' and 'C' Companies respectively. 2nd Lieuts. A.A. Woodland and B.E. Davey joined and were posted to 'D' Company.

12 Dec. 'A' Company worked on Artillery Road.

The officers and N.C.O.s of 1/7th Durham Light Infantry (Pioneers) left to re-join their battalion which had arrived at and was billeted in the adjoining camp.

Lt.-Col. C.M. Browne, the C.R.E. 8th Division, under whose orders the battalion would be working from 14th onwards visited battalion H.Q. about 3pm. Major-General Pinney visited battalion H.Q. at 3.40pm. He interviewed Lt.-Col. Storr who had been badly reported on.[1]

13 Dec. Three platoons of 'A' Company with one platoon of 'D' Company and three platoons of 'B' Company with one platoon of 'D' Company, started draining the formation for a plank road. This started just north of the Brands Gully and the Ypres to Roulers railway.

Three platoons of 'C' Company worked on 'H' Track. One platoon of 'A' Company, one platoon of 'B' Company, one platoon of 'C' Company and two platoons of 'D' Company worked in camp.

14 Dec. 'A' and 'B' Companies and attached platoons drained off the formation south of the Zonnebeke River. Three platoons of 'C' Company with one platoon of 'D' Company started draining the formation north of the Zonnebeke

River. One platoon from each company worked in the camp. 'C' Company moved into the new camp in the afternoon.

15 Dec. 'A' Company worked on clearing the channels of the Zonnebeke River below the proposed road crossing. 'B' and 'C' Companies worked on formation drainage. The rest of 'H.Q.' Company, excluding transport, moved into the new camp.

16 Dec. The battalion worked on the Zonnebeke River channels and formation drainage.

17 Dec. The C.R.E. 8th Division placed Lt.-Col. Storr in charge of the construction of the new plank road from near Devil's Crossing via Windmill Cabaret on the west side of Hill 40 to Seine. One infantry company of the 16th Battalion King's Royal Rifle Corps was also placed under his orders. The infantry pumped out shell holes and carried fascines forward to near the Zonnebeke River.

The battalion made good progress confining the Zonnebeke River to a definite channel. 'B' Company moved into the new camp after work. The whole battalion (less transport) was now accommodated there.

18 Dec. The battalion worked on the new plank road.

19 Dec. The company of infantrymen was not available for work. Two platoons of the 33rd Division's 'B' Works Company, totalling eighty-six other ranks, came under the battalion and carried planks and fascines.

20 Dec. Three companies of the 1/9th Battalion Durham Light Infantry came under the battalion for work. A platoon of the D.L.I. worked with a platoon of the battalion on preparing the formation. The two platoons of 'B' Works Company carried materials. 'C' Company was given a day in camp.

The battalion laid planks connecting a short length of track to South Road. Other plank laying was stopped because the ground was frozen, work being confined to preparation on this formation.

Two men were wounded.

Corporal G/2247 Ernest Frederick Osman, aged 27 of 'C' Company, was killed in action. He was born in Bermondsey, Surrey and enlisted in London.

He was the son of Elizabeth and James John Osman. He was the husband of Catherine Osman (nee Holden). They were married on 26 May 1916 and they lived at 22 Pepler Road, Peckham. He is buried in the Potijze Château Grounds Cemetery.[2]

21 Dec. 'D' Company had a day in camp. 'A', 'B' and 'C' Companies and attached infantrymen laid planks.

Corporal T.F.238055 Charles David Dollery died of his wounds suffered on 20 December. He had shrapnel wounds to his right leg and one to his right arm which had to be amputated. He was aged 33, born in Portsea and enlisted in Portsmouth, Hants. He was 5′ 11½″ tall and weighed 168 lbs. Dollery had enlisted on 28 September 1914 but only went to France on 21 September 1917 to join the 18th Middlesex. He suffered a gunshot wound to his forehead on 6 December. He suffered another head wound on 15 December. He was a bricklayer by trade and the son of Rebecca and Henry Dollery of 47 Reginald Road, Portsmouth. He was the husband of Ellen Teresa Dollery of 149 Eastfield Road, Eastney, Portsmouth. He is buried in the Lijssenthoek Military Cemetery.[3]

22 Dec. 'B' Company had a day in camp. 'A', 'C' and 'D' Companies and attached infantrymen laid planks.

The C.E. VIII Corps visited the work.

One man was wounded.

23 Dec. 'A' Company had a day in camp. 'B', 'C' and 'D' Companies and attached infantrymen laid planks.

2nd Lieut. L. B. Wright left for England to join the Tank Corps.

24 Dec. 'C' Company had a day in camp and had a bath. 'A', 'B' and 'D' Companies and attached infantry laid planks.

25 Dec. Christmas Day and the Corps Commander granted a holiday.

Lt.-Col. Storr held church parades by companies, in the Nissen hut used as a church, at 9.15am, 10.45am, 11.30am and 12.15pm. 'A' Company not only got a day's holiday they got a bath as well.

26 Dec. 'D' Company was given a day in camp and they bathed. 'A', 'B' and 'C' Companies laid planks with the attached infantry. Sixteen other ranks (B1) joined from the base.

Pioneer Battalions and Labour Corps Shoulder Badge

27 Dec. 'B' Company were given a day in camp and they had a bath. 'A', 'C' and 'D' Companies laid planks.

One man suffered a self-inflicted wound.

28 Dec. 'A' Company was given a day in camp. The other companies and attached infantry worked on the formation for the plank road. 78 other ranks (B1) joined from base.

The London Gazette published on Friday 28 December 1917 carried the following notice:

OFFICERS' AND SOLDIERS' BALANCES UNDISPOSED OF.

> In pursuance of "The Regimental Debts Act, 1893." Notice is hereby given that there is available for distribution amongst the Next of Kin or others entitled the sum of money set opposite to the name of each of the deceased Officers and Soldiers named in the lists which are published with this notice in the London Gazette and the "Army List," and are also to be seen at the Regimental Depots throughout the United Kingdom.
>
> Applications from persons supposing themselves entitled as Next of Kin should be addressed by letter to "The Secretary, War Office, Imperial Institute, South Kensington, London, S.W.7" and mark outside "Effects".[4]

Private G/4768 William Madden who died of his wounds 27 October 1916

had a personal estate of £10. 17s. 6d. for distribution amongst his next of kin or others entitled which remained unclaimed.[5]

29 Dec. 'C' Company was given a day in camp. The other companies worked with 'B' Works Company on the formation of the plank road. The infantry companies were not available for work.

30 Dec. 'D' Company was given a day in camp. The other companies worked on the formation of the plank road. A draft of 78 other ranks left to join the 11th Battalion Middlesex Regiment, which was an infantry battalion in the 36th Infantry Brigade of the 12th Division.

31 Dec. 'B' Company was given a day in camp. The other companies and 'B' Works Company worked on the plank road. One platoon of 'A' Company and one platoon of 'B' Works Company started widening a fascine road between Bavaria House and Ibex Avenue running parallel to the Hanebeek River.

Orders were received that the transport lines occupied by the battalion near Goldfish Château must be evacuated by noon on the 2 Jan.

1 January 1918. 'A' Company was given a day in camp.

One platoon 'B' Company and one platoon 'B' Works Company widened the fascine road running south from Bavaria House which was just over two-and-a-half miles north-east of Ypres on the road to Zonnebeke. This area of work was in the old German front line prior to the Flanders offensive.

'C' Company, three platoons of 'B' Company and 'D' Company with two platoons of 'B' Works Company, continued preparing formation for the plank road between Devil's Crossing and Windmill Cabaret.

A draft of 75 other ranks left to join the 1st Battalion Middlesex Regiment which was part of the 98th Infantry Brigade of the 33rd Division. They proceeded by route march to Poperinghe.

The battalion received Divisional Order 266 at 6.15am for the relief of 50th Division by 33rd Division and the move of Divisional H.Q. from Steenvoorde to Brandhoek.

Temporary 2nd Lieut. Henry Cecil Fisher was awarded the Military Cross in the New Years Honours List.[6]

Sergeant 790 J.H. Heath and Sergeant 881 W.T. Williams were awarded the Distinguished Conduct Medal in the New Years Honours List.[7]

Major-General Pinney recorded in his diary that Temporary Captain W.H. Coles (P.F.), Temporary Captain E.H. Bennett, Lieut. S. Mcl. Colvin, Company Sergeant Major 652 G. Blackwell and Company Sergeant Major 7734 H. Cartwright received the New Year Honour of being Mentioned in Despatches.[8]

2 Jan. 'C' Company was given a day in camp. 'A' Company took over the work of 'C' Company on the plank road. The transport moved in the morning from near Goldfish Château to the new lines at the camp in Savile Road. They found the stables incomplete. The battalion received 33rd Division Engineers Order 22 at 6pm. This order arranged the exchange of work with 1/7th Durham Light Infantry (Pioneers of the 50th Division) on 5 Jan.

On 1 January 1918 The Secretary of State for War forwarded to the War Cabinet the Report of the Enquiry into the events of the Battle of Cambrai produced by Field Marshal Sir D. Haig. Lieutenant-General Jan Smuts, a member of the British War Cabinet, went through the papers contained in Haig's Report and submitted a memorandum to the War Cabinet on 3 January. In his memorandum Smuts stated that the 'German attack on the position held by the 12th and 55th Divisions was not met with serious opposition and the Germans rapidly reached Gouzeaucourt'. He went on to state 'what happened was a short and intense enemy bombardment destroyed the wire entanglement, the enemy poured forward without resistance into two ravines which led behind our lines. As soon as British troops found the enemy behind as well as in front of them they either surrendered or retired without resistance and the machine gunners retired with the infantry'.

Smuts dismissed the suggestion that the success for the Germans was due to their attack being a surprise as their 'attack had been expected as early as 28th November'. However he then went on to confirm 'front parts of the British front line were overpowered without any resistance and the British support lines unexpectedly found the enemy on them before they knew what had happened in front of them'.

Smuts exonerated the British High Command in their role in the Cambrai affair. On the role of Brigade and Regimental commanders he refused to express an opinion and passed the book to Field Marshal Haig. Smuts recognised that the '55th Division...had some two months before lost 7,000 officers and men in fighting further north, and that the Division had been filled up with fresh drafts'. He then placed the blame for the defeat at Cambrai firmly on the shoulders of the 55th Division 'junior officers, N.C.O.s and men and especially in regard to the machine

gunners the standard of training had not been such as to qualify them for the sort of situation which arose with the German onslaught on 30th November'.[9]

Despite his findings Smuts did not offer any criticism of Haig or Byng for putting a largely untrained Division in the line, nor did he criticise those responsible for failing to train the Division to the necessary standard for the job it was ordered to do.

Among the papers considered by Lieut.-Gen. Smuts in respect of Haig's enquiry into Cambrai was a memorandum dated 3 January 1918 by General Sir William Robertson Chief of the Imperial General Staff, Major-General Sir Frederick Maurice Director of Military Operations and Major-General Sir Charles Edward Callwell, former Director of Military Operations submitted to the Rt. Hon. the Earl of Derby, Secretary of State for War.

They concluded that in the 'portion of the old front line, held by 55th Division, which was pierced, it suggests itself to us that the concentration of our resources upon offensive operations during the past year had resulted in these defences being less complete than would otherwise have been the case'. They went onto state 'The 55th Division was holding 11,000 yards of front, which is not an excessive length for a Division at normal strength occupying a carefully prepared defensive position. This particular Division had however been heavily engaged in Flanders in August and September and had suffered great losses during these two months; it therefore necessarily contained an inordinate proportion of newly joined drafts. It furthermore was considerably below strength'. They attributed the failure to hold the right of General Byng's battle-line to 'the fact that the units involved were considerably below establishment,...they had not long previously been engaged in arduous offensive operations in Flanders and were very tired, and ...there had been no opportunity for training the new drafts and subordinate commanders adequately'.

They went on to state 'A risk was taken by Sir Douglas Haig in allotting a somewhat extensive front to troops in the condition described above. But some risks must be taken by Commanders in defence, in order to be strong for attack, and we do not consider that, in this case, and viewing the circumstances as they appeared at the time, the risk taken was undue'.[10]

Like Smuts; Robertson, Maurice and Callwell did not criticise Haig or Byng for ordering a tired, largely untrained and under-strength Division to hold a front line position with incomplete defensive systems.

3 Jan. 'D' Company was given a day in camp. The battalion worked on the plank

road and the fascine road. 'C' Company took over work from 'D' Company. A bomb dropped on the road between Bavaria House and Frost House at about 6am. It scored a direct hit on part of 'C' Company marching to work. Twenty-six men were wounded, including two who were slightly wounded.

The following five soldiers were killed in action and are buried in the Potijze Château Grounds Cemetery.

Private G/29748 Albert Burrows aged 30 years, born in Holbrook, Suffolk and enlisted in Ipswich. He was the son of Emma and Walter Burrows of Holbrook, Ipswich. He was the husband of May Burrows (nee Kirby) of Pin Mill Road, Chelmondiston, Ipswich.[11]

Lance Corporal G/355 William Henry Chalcroft aged 29, was born in Kennington, Surrey, enlisted in London and lived at 30 Henry Street, Vauxhall, London. He was the son of Selina and Frederick Chalcroft, was single and a Ledger Clerk by trade. He enlisted on 13 August 1914 and served with the 11th, 5th, Base Depot and 2nd battalions of the Middlesex Regiment before being posted to the 18th Middlesex on 13 March 1917 and travelled to France. He joined the 18th Middlesex in the field on 25 April 1917. He was made Lance Corporal on 13 December 1917.[12]

Private T.F.238089 James Arthur Colbourne aged 24, was born and enlisted in Portsmouth, Hants. He was the son of Sarah and Henry Colbourne of 5 Newcastle Street, Fratton, Portsmouth. He was a trade painter by trade, 6 feet tall and weighed 168 lbs. Colbourne enlisted on 31 May 1915 and was posted to 508th (Wessex) Reserve Field Company Royal Engineers. He was posted to the 18th Middlesex on 22 September 1917 and joined them in the field on 4 October 1917. He was the husband of Margaret Colbourne (nee Ford) of 19 Northam Street, Fratton. They married on 16 September 1915 and had a daughter Margaret Cecilia in December. On 13 May 1918 Mrs Colbourne was sent her husband's effects of a disc, letters, photos, wallet, religious card, locket, cards and a defaced 50 cent note. She was awarded a pension of 20 shillings and five pence per week for herself and her daughter with effect from 22 July 1918. She also received a Separation Allowance of 19 shillings and sixpence and an Allotment of pay of 7 shillings.[13]

Private P.W.732 Arthur Henry Frisby aged 30, born in Westbere, Kent, enlisted in Canterbury and lived in Herne Bay. He was the son of Kate Emma Frisby of Westbere, Canterbury. By the time Arthur was 3 years old he was living with his Aunty Elizabeth Frisby. By the time he was 13 years old he was a pauper living in the Blean Union Workhouse. By the time he was 23 he was working

as a potman (Publican's assistant) in a hotel. He attested on 17 March 1915 and gave his occupation as a navvy. He was posted to the 18th Middlesex and went with the battalion to France on 12 November 1915.[14]

Private T.F.238148 Edmund Borlais Warren aged 26, was born in Plymouth and enlisted in Exeter, Devon. He was the son of Mary Ann and William Warren of 4 Headwell Terrace, St. James, Well Street, Exeter.[15]

Sergeant P.W.727 John Kelly aged 44, who was born, enlisted and lived in Chiswick, Middlesex, died of his wounds at the 10 Casualty Clearing Station. He was a labourer by trade and the husband of Fanny Kelly (nee Burton) of 188 Devonshire Road, Chiswick, London. He is buried in the Lijssenthoek Military Cemetery.[16]

Private P.W.615 Solomon Hearne died of his wounds. He was born on 24 November 1888 in Watford, lived at 40 Shirley Gardens Hanwell, London and enlisted in Hanwell on 15 March 1915. He was a navvy by trade, 5′ 11″ tall and weighed 151 lbs. He married Rosina Smart on 20 December 1913 at St. Mellitus Church Hanwell and they had two children Britannia dob 2 May 1911 and Rosina Gwendolyn dob 4 April 1914. Mrs Hearne received 28 shillings Separation Allowance and was awarded a pension of 25 shillings and 5 pence with effect from 15 July 1918 for herself and her two children. She also received her husband's personal effects of letters, photos, two testaments, cards, cigarette case, tobacco box, waist belt, and metal ring. Private Hearne was the son of Mary and Meshach (Mesheck) Hearne. He is buried in the Ypres Reservoir Cemetery – Ieper, West-Vlaanderen.[17]

The battalion had a bloody start to the New Year.

4 Jan. 'B' Company had a day in camp. The battalion worked on the plank road and fascine road. 'D' Company took up the work previously done by 'B' Company. The work plans were handed over to 1/7th Battalion Durham Light Infantry (Pioneers).

5 Jan. 'A' Company had a day in camp.

One platoon of 'D' Company cleared out 'pillboxes' near Hamburg. 'B' and 'C' Companies laid ribands on the plank road between Zonnebeke Station and Seine. The rest of 'D' Company repaired the plank road between Devil's Crossing and Zonnebeke Station.

Six Lewis guns were mounted as aircraft defences for batteries in relief of Lewis guns of 1/7th Battalion Durham Light Infantry (Pioneers).

2nd Lieuts. A.V. Bromham and C. Cooper joined the battalion and were posted to 'B' Company.

6 Jan. 'C' Company had a day in camp. One platoon of 'D' Company worked clearing out 'pillboxes'. A small party of 'D' Company spiked ribands. The rest of 'D' Company cut drains for formation towards Seine.

The battalion received Divisional Order 267 at 6pm for the 100th Infantry Brigade to relieve the 19th Infantry Brigade in the line, the 98th Infantry Brigade to move up into the support area above Potijze and Ypres and for the 19th Infantry Brigade to move into divisional reserve at Brandhoek.[18]

7 Jan. The British War Cabinet discussed the defensive arrangements on the Western Front. They had before them a letter dated 3 January 1918 from Sir Douglas Haig detailing the defences in place on the Western Front. In his letter Haig referred to paragraph 11 of the 'Memorandum On Defensive Measures' by Lieutenant-General L.E. Kiggell, Chief of the General Staff, issued on 14 September 1917.

In the memo Kiggell pointed out that 'the paucity of reinforcements which (the British Army) were likely to receive during the next few months will make it impossible for our units to be brought up to establishment. In consequence the British Army in France will probably have to adopt a defensive attitude for some time to come and be prepared to meet a strong and sustained hostile offensive, adequately supported by artillery'.

Kiggell's memo contained instructions on the arrangements for the General Scheme of Defence, the aim of which was to ensure the main resistance of any German attack would take place on ground favourable to British troops. The first line of resistance would be the outpost zone 'established and organised for defence in depth and sufficiently garrisoned to guard against surprise. The back bone of the defence in this zone will be machine guns skilfully concealed in combination with wire entanglements'.[19]

Field Marshal Sir Douglas Haig informed the War Cabinet that the 'forward zone is designed to delay an attack in great force so as to give time for bringing up reinforcements to the fighting zone as may be required'.[20]

The next and main line of resistance would be the battle zone where the enemy were to be met and repelled. 'The battle zone will be organised in great depth, varying from 2,000, to at least 3,000 yards and will consist of strong successive systems of defence. Diagonal switch lines, supporting points and

defended localities must be constructed within the battle zone'. 'The more important localities in the battle zone will be permanently garrisoned'.[21]

Haig informed the War Cabinet that the battle zone had 'been designed to include all ground which for various reasons should be held at all costs'.[22]

The third and final line of resistance was the rear zone 'established some 4 – 8 miles behind the battle zone and prepared for defence as labour becomes available'.[23]

Haig informed the War Cabinet that the third or rear zone was 'placed at such a distance in rear of the second as to compel the enemy to move forward his artillery and make fresh preparations before he can attack'. He then went on to make the point with regard to the rear zone defences that 'labour was not available to carry on all these works at once and experience shows that the upkeep of back line trenches as a whole is impracticable'. To meet the situation some tactical localities were to 'be prepared for defence in the rearward zone, trenches will be marked out so that they can be easily dug when wanted, and continuous wire obstacles will be maintained along the whole line'.[24]

In his 14 September 1917 memo Kiggell issued an order of priority for the construction of the defence system:

> '(I) Wire.
> (II) Shell proof accommodation, including machine gun emplacements, observation posts and battle headquarters.
> (III) Communications, including road, tracks and communication trenches.
> (IV) Earthworks'.

Kiggell went on to state 'The constant improvement of road, railway and trench tramway systems for carrying materials, ammunition and supplies is of great importance in the construction of positions. A good tramway system is of particular importance when it is intended to undertake concrete work'.[25]

These priorities were clearly reflected in the work being carried out by the 18th Battalion Middlesex Regiment.

7 Jan. 'D' Company had a day in camp. One platoon 'C' Company cleared out 'pillboxes' whilst the rest of 'C' Company, 'A' and 'B' Companies laid plank tracks towards Seine. Lieut. J.F. Chapman rejoined for duty and was posted to 'B' Company.

8 Jan. 'B' Company had a day in camp. The battalion worked on 'pillboxes' and the plank track.

Four men were wounded.

9 Jan. 'A' Company was given a day in camp. The battalion worked on 'pillboxes' and plank tracks.

Captain Stanley Edward Montague Lawrence joined the battalion and was attached to 'A' Company. He was born on 15 September 1887, was 5 feet 8½ inches tall and a brewer by trade. He lived at Cranleigh, 18 Wolverton Avenue, Kingston Hills, Surrey. He attested on 20 May 1915 and was posted to the Inns of Court Officers Training Corps as a Private. He applied for a commission on 21 June 1915 and joined the 10th Battalion Queen's Royal West Surrey Regiment as 2nd Lieutenant on 16 September 1915. Lawrence had been run over by a coal cart in1897 which left him with a large scar on the inside of his left thigh which caused him pain after exertion and interfered with his marching prowess. A medical board on 4 March 1916 decided that he should relinquish his commission on medical grounds. Lawrence requested that he be retained in the service as he was a qualified Bombing and Signalling Instructor and this was accepted and he joined the 12th Queens (Reserve) Battalion Royal West Surrey Regiment but was designated as not fit for service overseas.[26] On undergoing a further medical board he was declared category Bii fit. He joined the 18th Battalion Middlesex Regiment in Flanders.

10 Jan. 'C' Company had a day in camp.

Two platoons of 'A' Company worked on clearing out five 'pillboxes'; the rest of 'A' Company, 'B' and 'D' Companies worked on the plank track between Zonnebeke Station and Seine. The remaining ex-Royal Engineers were ordered back to the R.E. training camp at Rouen.

11 Jan. 'D' Company had a day in camp. The battalion worked on the 'pillboxes' and plank track.

The battalion received Divisional Order 268 at 4.50pm about brigade reliefs between 12 and 15 January. The 98th Infantry Brigade was to relieve 100th Infantry Brigade in the line, 19th Infantry Brigade to move to the support area and 100th Infantry Brigade to move to the divisional reserve.[27]

12 Jan. 'B' Company had a day in camp. The companies of the battalion had

become quite weak so platoons were amalgamated for work. This released some young officers for a class of instruction.

A class of seven officers started under the Lt.-Col. Storr.

A draft of 77 ex-Royal Engineers left for Rouen.

'A', 'C' and 'D' Companies worked on 'pillboxes' and the plank track.

Six men were wounded, one slightly.

Private T.F.315100 Henry (Harry) James Hutchinson, aged 40, born in St. Luke's, Middlesex, and a porter by trade was killed in action. He was the son of Mary Ann and Thomas Hutchinson. His widowed mother lived at 28 Gopsall Street, Hoxton. He married Caroline Hulford (nee Simms) at St. John the Baptist Hoxton on 7 February 1914. She was a widow and 11 years older than him and they lived at 96 Wenlock Street, Hoxton. He is buried in the Potijze Château Grounds Cemetery.[28]

13 Jan. 'A' Company rested in camp.Two platoons of 'B' Company cleared out 'pillboxes'. The rest of 'B' Company, 'C' and 'D' Companies worked on the plank track.

14 Jan. 'C' Company rested in camp.

'A' and 'C' Companies were to have dug a trench by night leading to an observation post near Passchendaele. However the snowfall in the morning meant that the position would have shown up so the work was cancelled. 'A' Company was sent to repair six direct hits on the plank track near Devil's Crossing.

Two platoons of 'B' Company worked on 'pillboxes' the rest of 'B' Company and 'D' Company pushed planks on the track from Kansas Cross to Seine. Kansas Cross was where the Zonnebeke to Langemarck road crossed the Wieltje to s'Gravenstafel road.

15 Jan. 'D' Company had a day off work. Two platoons of 'B' Company worked on 'pillboxes' while the rest of 'B' Company, 'A' and 'C' Companies worked on the plank track. Thirty infantrymen were obtained for pushing trucks of planks from Kansas Cross to Seine. They only made one journey with five trucks.

The battalion received Divisional Order 269 at 7pm for the 19th Infantry Brigade to relieve the 98th Infantry Brigade, 100th Infantry Brigade to move into the support area and the 98th Infantry Brigade to move into the divisional reserve.[29]

16 Jan. There were heavy gales and rainstorms during the night and into the morning.

'B' Company had a day in camp. Two platoons of 'D' Company worked on 'pillboxes' and two platoons worked on the plank track.

'A' and 'C' Companies worked by night and completed a communication trench to an observation post on the high ground less than half a mile south-west of Passchendaele.

Capt. H.I.E. Ripley from the Worcestershire Regiment joined the battalion on attachment and was posted to 'C' Company.

17 Jan. 'A' and 'C' Companies rested in camp.

'B' and 'D' Companies worked on 'pillboxes' and the plank track.

18 Jan. A draft of 22 other ranks, to complete the 100, left at 2pm to join 11th Battalion Middlesex Regiment.

'C' Company had a day off work.

'A', 'B' and 'D' Companies worked on the plank track.

Private G/27964 Frederick James Field aged 34, born in Poplar, Middlesex on 31 March 1884 died at the 3 Australian Casualty Clearing Station from wounds suffered on 12 January. He married Ethel Crowe on 5 February 1906 at St. Peter's Church Brandon Suffolk. They had three children and at the time of the 1911 Census lived at the Fox and Hounds in Thetford Road Brandon where Frederick was the publican. He was formerly 15970 of the Royal West Surrey Regiment and enlisted on 12 July 1916 at Guilford. He joined the British Expeditionary Force in France on 23 March 1917. On his death his Company Commander wrote to Mrs Field saying 'Your husband was in my company, and I cannot speak too highly of him. He was a splendid man and his death is a great loss to my company'. He was the son of Eliza and Frederick James Field of Brandon, Suffolk. He is buried in the Nine Elms British Cemetery – Poperinghe, West-Vlaanderen.[30]

19 Jan. 'D' Company had a day in camp. 'B' Company worked on the plank track. 'A' and 'C' Companies pushed material on the track from Kansas Cross to Seine.

20 Jan. 'B' Company had a day's rest.

'A' Company pushed material on trucks from Kansas Cross to Seine. 'C' and 'D' Companies worked on the plank track.

On 17 January 1918 Adjutant-General Lieutenant-General Sir George Fowke issued orders for a Court of Enquiry on the action fought south of Cambrai on November 30 1917 to assemble at Hesdin at 10am on 21 January 1918.

Major-General Reginald John Pinney went to Hesdin as a member of that Court of Enquiry.

The President of the Enquiry was Lieutenant-General Sir Alexander Hamilton-Gordon Commander of the IX Corps. The other member of the Enquiry was Lieutenant-General Sir (Frederick) Ivor Maxse Commander of XVIII Corps. Major Frank Boyd Merriman from the General List acted as secretary. Their remit was to enquire into the cause of the German success on 30 November 1917 on the fronts of the III and VII Corps. In particular they were to take and record evidence on the sequence of events in the areas occupied by the 55th, 12th, 20th and 29th Divisions, especially as to where the Germans first broke through the British lines, the cause of this, and the order in which, and direction from which, each portion of ground was successfully captured by the Germans. The Court was to record their opinion as to the sequence of events and the causes of the German success.[31]

Brigadier-General C.G. Stewart C.M.G., D.S.O. took over temporary command of the 33rd Division.[32]

21 Jan. 'A' Company rested.

'B' Company pushed planks on trucks from Kansas Cross to Seine. 'C' and 'D' Companies worked on the plank track.

22 Jan. Lt.-Col. Storr went to England on short leave. Major Coles assumed command of the battalion.

'C' Company rested.

'A', 'B' and 'D' Companies worked on the plank track.

23 Jan. 'D' Company rested. 'A', 'B' and 'C' Companies worked on the plank track.

24 Jan. The battalion received Divisional Order 272 at 8.30am giving details of the brigade and battalion reliefs to take place between 24 and 27 January. The 98th Infantry Brigade was to relieve the 100th Infantry Brigade which in turn was to go into the divisional reserve. The 19th Infantry Brigade was to move into the support area. The battalion received Divisional Order 273 at 7.45pm for the relief of the 33rd Division by 50th Division between 26 and 30 January.[33]

Major-General Pinney called at battalion H.Q. at 10.55am. 'A', 'C' and 'D' Companies worked on the plank track. 'B' Company rested.

25 Jan. 'A' Company rested. 'B', 'C' and 'D' Companies completed the plank track.

26 Jan. 'C' Company rested. 'A', 'B' and 'D' Companies made passing places on the plank track.

27 Jan. Sixty men loaded the battalion transport onto trains. A further sixty men carried wire from Seine to Heine House one mile south-west of Passchendaele. The anti-aircraft Lewis gun posts were relieved by 1/7th Durham Light Infantry (Pioneers).

The transport moved to Tilques Training Area via Oudezeele.

1 Private Papers of Major-General Pinney, Book 7

2 *Soldiers Died In The Great War 1914 -1919*, p. 104; Commonwealth War Graves Commission casualty details; London Metropolitan Archives, Saint Mark, Cobourg Road, Register of marriages, P73 MRK2, Item 013

3 *Soldiers Died In The Great War 1914 -1919*, p. 103; Commonwealth War Graves Commission casualty details; Corporal Dollery Army Service Record, National Archives, WO 363, 1891 Census; 1911 Census

4 Supplement to the London Gazette, Friday 28th December 1917, Published 28th December 1917, Gazette Issue 30449, p. 13582

5 Ibid. p. 13592

6 Supplement to the London Gazette, Friday 28th December 1917, Published 1st January 1918, Gazette Issue 30450, p. 36

7 Ibid., p. 60 & p. 65

8 Private Papers of Major-General Pinney, Book 7

9 Lieutenant-General J. Smuts memorandum to the War Cabinet 3 January 1918, National Archives, CAB/24/37, Image reference 0098

10 Sir William Robertson memorandum to the Secretary of State for War 3 January 1918, National Archives, CAB/24/37. Image reference 0098

11 *Soldiers Died In The Great War 1914 -1919*, p. 102; Commonwealth War Graves Commission casualty details; 1911 Census; England & Wales Marriage Index 1837-1915

12 *Soldiers Died In The Great War 1914 -1919*, p. 102; Commonwealth War Graves Commission casualty details; Lance Corporal Chalcroft Army Service Record, National Archives, WO 363

13 *Soldiers Died In The Great War 1914 -1919*, p. 104; Commonwealth War Graves Commission casualty details; Private Colbourne Army Service Record, National Archives, WO 363; England & Wales Birth Index 1837-1915

14 *Soldiers Died In The Great War 1914 -1919*, p. 103; Commonwealth War Graves Commission casualty details; Private Frisby Army Service Record, National Archives, WO 363; 1871 Census; 1891 Census, 1901 Census; 1911 Census

15 *Soldiers Died In The Great War 1914 -1919*, p. 104; Commonwealth War Graves Commission casualty details; England & Wales Birth Index 1837-1915

16 Ibid., p. 103; Sergeant Kelly Army Service Record, National Archives, WO 363

17 Ibid.; Private Hearne Army Service Record, National Archives, WO 363; London Metropolitan Archives, Hillingdon St. John the Baptist, Register of Baptism, dro/110, Item 009

18 33rd Division War Diary

19 Lieut.-Gen. L.E. Kiggell Memorandum On Defensive Measures 14 September 1917, National Archives, CAB/24/38, Image Reference 0011

20 Sir Douglas Haig's letter to the Chief of the Imperial Staff, 3 January 1918, National Archives, CAB/24/38, Image reference 0011

21 Lieut.-Gen. Kiggell Memorandum On Defensive Measures

22 Sir Douglas Haig's letter 3 January 1918

23 Lieut.-Gen. Kiggell Memorandum On Defensive Measures

24 Sir Douglas Haig's letter 3 January 1918

25 Lieut.-Gen. Kiggell Memorandum On Defensive Measures

26 Captain S.E.M. Lawrence Service Record, National Archives, WO 339/36035

27 33rd Division War Diary.

28 *Soldiers Died In The Great War 1914 -1919*, p. 102; Commonwealth War Graves Commission casualty details; Private Hutchinson Army Service Record, National Archives, WO 363; 1881 Census; 1891 Census; London Metropolitan Archives, Saint John The Baptist, Hoxton, Register of marriages, P91/JNB, Item 070

29 33rd Division War Diary

30 *Soldiers Died In The Great War 1914 -1919*, p. 103; Commonwealth War Graves Commission casualty details; De Ruvigny's Roll of Honour, 1914-1924, Vol. 4, p. 56; 1911 Census

31 Cambrai Court of Enquiry, National Archives, WO 158/53

32 33rd Division War Diary

33 Ibid.

CHAPTER SIX

28th *January 1918 to* 28th *February 1918*

Away from the Front
Training
Back to Passchendaele for God's Battle

Wizernes

28 Jan. On relief by 1/7th Durham Light Infantry (Pioneers), the battalion moved to Wizernes by train. The billet was just south of Gondardennes and east of Wizernes.

29 Jan. The battalion spent the day adjusting the billet accommodation, cleaning the billets, cleaning equipment and arranging training programmes.

30 Jan. Company commanders inspected clothing, equipment and tools.

31 Jan. Training commenced. Lieutenant-General Sir Aylmer Gould Hunter-Weston, the G.O.C. VIII Corps presented Private P.W. 3024 Percy Foster from Congleton with the Military Medal.[1]

Hunter-Weston was the Member of Parliament for North Ayrshire. He was the first serving M.P. to command an army corps in the field. His nickname was Hunter-Bunter because his VIII Corps had the highest level of casualties and failed to take any of its objectives during the first day of the Battle of the Somme.

1 February 1918. Companies trained. Special attention was paid to squad drill, saluting and march discipline. The battalion had no access to a proper training ground so companies had to use vacant ground near their billets.

2 Feb. Training. The armourer inspected the battalion's rifles and had muzzle protectors fitted to the guns.

Allied Plans for Spring 1918

Field Marshal Haig had previously made it clear that he intended to relaunch his Flanders offensive in the spring of 1918.[2] However as preparations were being made for the Allied Supreme War Council meeting at Versailles at the end of January 1918 Sir Douglas changed his mind about the 1918 campaign.

Haig and General Pétain raised their concerns about the effectiveness of the troops and assets they had at their disposal on the Western Front. Both Commanders-in-Chief believed that they would face a major spring offensive by the enemy which they would have difficulty in defending. In turn that would seriously weaken their forces and render them unable to launch a major counter-attack which would lead to the defeat of Germany. They pressed the case for a defensive posture throughout 1918 and wait until 1919 when the arrival of American troops would 'afford us substantial aid in the battle'.[3]

Lloyd George took a contrary view. His appraisal was that 'The effectives of each army standing alone might seem poor next to the German. The united effectives of the two Allied Armies were still richer, and at the climax of the German strength were equal in numbers and more powerful in machinery than the German'.[4]

The Allied Supreme War Council, including the Commanders–in-Chief of the British and French Armies and the Italian Minister of War, met at Versailles between 30 January and 2 February to determine the strategy for the 1918 campaign. The War Council resolved:-

1) The organisation of the whole of the forces of the Allies for defence against the German attack on the basis of a united front. To achieve this aim, power to be given to a Central Authority to form and direct a General Reserve available for use at any part of the front where that Authority deemed it advisable to throw them in for defence or counter-attack. The Council appointed General Foch President of an Inter-Allied body of Generals who constituted the authority in control of the General Reserve. In the West, Foch was ultimately given the sole command of the Allied Armies.

2) To watch the situation in case an unexpectedly favourable development should furnish an opportunity for vigorous offensive action. The defensive was 'not to be of a merely passive character, but to be worked out definitely

> and scientifically, with the intention of gaining the maximum advantage from any opportunities offered in the Western theatre'.[5]

The Supreme War Council agreed to the creation of the General Reserve without a dissenting voice from any quarter, including Commanders-in-Chief and Chiefs of Staff, Pétain, Haig, Robertson and Foch.[6]

The Cambrai Enquiry

The Enquiry concluded taking evidence on 29 January having heard from twenty-five witnesses including the commanders of the 12th, 20th and 55th Divisions. There were a number of notable absentees from the Enquiry including Major-General Vaughan the Chief Staff Officer to General Byng, Lieut.-General Pulteney (III Corps) and Lieut.-General Snow (VII Corps) and the chief General Staff officers of these two commanders.

The Court found that the German attack was launched at about 7.30am from near Les Rues Vertes in the north to about the Birdcage in the south. By 8am the front line troops of 20th Division in the north had been overwhelmed. The northern portion of the 12th Division was also overwhelmed but the southern sector fought well for some hours.

The left of the 55th Division was posted across the Banteux Ravine. They were overrun by a large force of Germans who continued up the ravine overrunning the reserve battalion of the 12th Division about Cheshire Quarry. These Germans then carried on up the valley surprising four machine guns in reserve at Kitchen Crater. These Germans then pressed on and captured Gonnelieu and Villers-Guislain by 8am.

German artillery continued to heavily shell the 55th Division position on the high ground on the right of Banteux Ravine. At the same time a large force of German infantry advanced up the low ground in the Banteux Ravine. That advance was well to the west of the main front of the 55th Division. It was checked and stopped from advancing west on Villers-Guislain till considerably later in the day.

By 9am the Germans had penetrated the British positions in the south to Gouzeaucourt and the railway south and east of Gauche Wood. By 10am the Germans penetrated the British northern sector to the northern slopes of Welsh Ridge, south of Marcoing and the valley of Marcoing.

The 29th Division held their front and successfully counter-attacked the Germans who had passed their southern flank.

The Court of Enquiry found nine reasons for the German success at Cambrai:-

i) Surprise in the outpost lines. The German attack took place after a very short but intense preliminary bombardment which local British commanders took as little more than of normal character. There also appeared to have been a lack of vigilance in the outpost lines of the 12th, 20th and 55th Divisions;

ii) Warnings from above unheeded. On the days previous to the assault the probability of a hostile attack was noted by the higher command and communicated to the troops but these warnings did not produce the desired vigilance on the part of the troops;

iii) British aeroplane reconnaissance on 30 November failed to detect the massing German infantry due to bad visibility caused by ground mist;

iv) Lack of artillery on the 11,000 yard frontage held by the 55th Division. The 55th Division had been reduced to 44 artillery guns for its immediate protection. The paucity of guns available for S.O.S. action in the southern portion of the British front facilitated the assembly of the Germans and their assault on the British front line. The Third Army justification to the Court of Enquiry for this paucity of artillery was that it expected an attack to take place on the Bourlon front not the 55th Divisional front;

v) Boundaries between corps and divisions. The adaptation of schemes of defence to the new conditions following the British advance between the 20 and 29 November was not facilitated by the rearward boundaries allocated to corps and divisions. In the Banteux Ravine two army corps met. The back area of the 12th Division included Gonnelieu and the ground west of Villers-Guislain but the front trenches opposite the ground west of Villers-Guislain were occupied by the 55th Division. The infantry holding the north side of Banteux Ravine could not see the bottom of its front, no one individual commander was responsible for the defence of both sides of the Banteux Ravine and its eastern entrance and troops of two army corps were involved in the defence of its western slopes. Neither Gonnelieu nor Villers-Guislain were defended localities or provided with infantry garrisons;

vi) Hostile low flying aeroplanes. Germans aeroplanes flew below 100 feet and machine gunned the British infantry in both the front trenches and

rearward positions. The British troops did not know how to take out these planes;

vii) Lack of defence in depth. There appeared to be a lack of training and of understanding on the part of subordinate and lower commanders regarding the application of the method of defence in depth. Troops were allocated to the front line system as being the main line of resistance at the expense of garrisons for defensive localities in the rear and troops destined for counter-attacks;

viii) Lack of doctrine for the defensive battle. The Enquiry held the view that it was essential that subordinate commanders and other ranks should rapidly recognise the difference between offensive and defensive actions, and they should adapt their minds quickly to the conditions with which they were confronted. In defensive battles quick decisions on tactical situations by junior infantry commanders are more decisive in results than in offensive battles. The decisions are more difficult to make but a defensive position, on a day it is overwhelmed, demands resourcefulness and impromptu action on the part of subordinate commanders. The absence of such a doctrine indicated a want of supervision on the part of higher commanders. The Court of Enquiry also found that troops detailed for garrisons of rearward positions and for counter-attack were in many cases exhausted by earlier fighting. They were necessarily employed as working parties, and were therefore not in an efficient condition to fulfil the role originally assigned to them by the commanders who had prepared the schemes of defence;

ix) Propogation (Propagation) of rumours. The Adjutant-General officially brought to the attention of the Court of Enquiry that irresponsible, garbled and in many cases false information, concerning the events of November 30 reached the public before any correct reports could be made use of. The Court recognised their terms of reference did not include suggestions for remedial measures to deal with matters on which they had to report. But in light of the communication received from the Adjutant-General and the general interest which had been aroused by these false rumours, the Court decided to comment on and make suggestions on this issue.

The Court of Enquiry submitted a separate paper on Rumours written by Lieut.-General Maxse with their report. Maxse contended that the British public had been misinformed about the Battle of Cambrai by newspapers, Members of Parliament and the 400,000 officers and men who had proceeded

backwards and forwards on leave during the last two months (December 1917 and January 1918). Maxse, however, placed most of the blame on the wounded for being 'the most prolific propagators of baseless stories'.

Maxse opined that it would be better if newspapers had refrained from filling their columns with a torrent of rubbish, refrained from describing British tank tactics on 20 November and related instead the true story of that day's most successful operations. He concluded his paper with reference to the inadequate means of conveying history and rumours to the public at home which had resulted in the British public seeing the Battle of Cambrai as a German success instead of a British victory. His proposed solution was for senior local commanders on the spot to write, as soon as possible after the event, short semi-official stories of the battles. He also proposed that G.H.Q. should appoint a soldier to help the newspaper correspondents to understand the telegrams which come in during the course of an important battle.

The Court of Enquiry Report was sent to the Adjutant-General Lieutenant-General Sir George Fowke on 29 January 1918. In turn he forwarded the report to the Chief of the General Staff on 2 February with a covering letter from himself and a further paper by Lieut.-General Maxse on the causes of the German success.

Fowke advised the Chief of the General Staff that he did not think any question of disciplinary action would arise out of the report because he doubted it would be possible to allocate blame owing to the number and nature of the causes of the German success.

In his letter he mitigated five of the reasons for the German success given by the Court of Enquiry:

i) The unit commanders principally responsible for the lack of vigilance were no longer with the Army and there was no evidence that this failing was general throughout the divisions involved in the fighting;
ii) The lack of artillery on the 55th Divisional front turned on whether or not the Third Army was justified in acting the way they did on the indications they received that the attack would be made further north;
iii) On the issue of the boundaries between corps and divisions the Third Army explained that they were fixed so 'that the VII Corps defensive front should face East and the III Corps South-east, and that naturally gave BANTEUX RAVINE as a boundary'. Fowke did not know how far this explanation should be accepted;

iv) The Third Army now agreed 'Villers-Guislain and Gonnelieu should not have been described as 'strong defensive localities, with machine guns sweeping all the approaches' in their report of 18 December which had since been modified;
v) In response to the lack of doctrine for the defensive battle Fowke referred to the Court's findings that the time was short for 'recognising whether attack or defence would be the predominant factor in the preparations to be made'. He then cites the General Officer Commanding the 55th Division stating that it soon became clear that the enemy was not going back and that one had to think more of defence.

Lieut.-General Maxse, in his further paper on the causes of the German success, contended that the British the 12th, 20th and 55th Divisions were over-run on 30 November 1917, and the 20th and 55th Divisions did not put up sufficient resistance. He further contended that the Germans reached Gauche Wood, Gouzeaucourt, Vacquerie (exclusive), Bonavis Ridge, the northern slope of Welsh Ridge and L.28 central (3/4 of a mile South of Marcoing, Sheet 57c.N.E.4) and places near this line at walking pace, because they arrived there too soon to warrant the supposition that they were delayed by much fighting on the way, except in the centre. Maxse was able to discover few traces of organised counter-attacks or any methodical resistance during the German's advance across one or two miles of undulating country, and there are several indications that the Germans walked into two British divisions and proceeded through them without being held up and delayed by defended localities or machine gun nests behind the British front. The plans of some local commanders apparently did not result in a distribution of strength in sufficient depth for protracted defence.

Maxse recognised the three divisions were weak in numbers and distributed on a wide front but still felt they should have delayed the German advance for a sufficient time to enable reserve troops to counter-attack. Having criticised the three divisions for not standing Maxse dispelled the rumour that there was a panic retreat. He found that the men withdrawing from the front line were the walking wounded who had been caught unarmed by the suddenness of the German bombardment and compelled to retire.

To support his assertion that there was no panic he pointed out that the infantry battalions of the 12th, 20th and 55th Divisions in the forward zone did not retreat or run away. They were surprised to such an extent that only two men got back out of the left battalion of the 55th Division. Less than 100 men

got back from most of the battalions engaged in the three divisions, which had a fighting strength of around 400 to 500 men. He was also of the view that the German attack on 30 November 1917 was not a surprise to the higher command who had foreseen and warned the troops. On the strength of this analysis Maxse concluded the root cause of the failure to stop the Germans, or even delay them in defended localities, was ignorance of the rudiments of successful defence and inexperience in handling sections, platoons and machine guns as fire units in the field.

In summary Maxse cited two causes of what he called the local success of the Germans at Cambrai:-

1) Lack of battle-training in the infantry;
2) Lack of battle-training and discipline in the Machine Gun Corps.[7]

So the Court of Enquiry blamed the troops for lack of vigilance in the outposts, lack of vigilance following warnings from the higher command, the inability to deal with low flying German aeroplanes, lacking in the doctrine of the defensive battle, being over-run and failing to hold the Germans whilst reserves were brought forward.

Local commanders were blamed for not realising that the artillery fire on 30 November was preliminary bombardment to the German attack, lacking in training and understanding how to conduct a defensive battle, lacking in the doctrine of the defensive battle and for spreading misinformation and baseless stories about the true outcome of the battle.

The Court of Enquiry completely failed to criticise the higher commanders in spite of being provided with some significant evidence about the Third Army failures in respect of corps and divisional boundaries, the deployment of artillery elsewhere and the failure to provide defensive garrisons and machine guns to the villages of Gonnelieu and Villers-Guislain. No questions were asked about the decision by Haig to continue the attack after forty-eight hours, the lack of reserves to exploit any breakthrough or consolidate the ground gained. The Enquiry referred to the three divisions used for the battle being under strength, in fact they were only at half strength, yet it did not question why such under strength units were used. Likewise the Enquiry referred to the inability of the British troops to deal with the German aeroplanes but did not ask why British aeroplanes were not on hand to engage in the aerial battle.

The Court of Enquiry found that rumours, misinformation, baseless stories, and false statements about the Battle of Cambrai informed British public opinion which had come to regard Cambrai as a German success and British defeat. The

Enquiry placed the blame for this squarely on the shoulders of the junior officers, other ranks and in particular the wounded who had achieved the early success at Cambrai and then were left to face the German counter-offensive tired, exhausted, depleted, in exposed positions and without support. However the Enquiry chose to totally ignore the actual facts their report confirmed which are that Cambrai was ultimately a German success and a British failure.

In an act of extreme self-denial the Enquiry failed to address the real question of why, at Cambrai, Haig and his generals snatched defeat from the jaws of victory and why they failed to let the War Cabinet know the full extent of the British defeat suffered on 30 November as it occurred and why they tried to place the bulk of the blame for this defeat on the junior officers and the other ranks.

3 Feb. A church parade was held at 9.30am. The battalion received Divisional Order 274 at 10pm for the reorganisation of the 33rd Division on the nine battalion system.[8]

Private T.F.315701 William Henry Stevens aged 41, born in Holborn, Middlesex enlisted in Sidcup, Kent on 22 February 1916. He was posted to 10th Middlesex and then onto 32nd Middlesex both battalions were stationed in England. He was posted to the 18th Middlesex on 19 December 1917 and joined them in the field on 21 December. He suffered shrapnel wounds to his head and leg on 3 January 1918 and admitted to the 3 Canadian Casualty Clearing Station. He was transferred to the 83 General Hospital in Boulogne on 10 January and was taken back to England on H.M.H.S. St. Denis on 24 January. He was admitted to the 2 London General Hospital at Chelsea where his brain injury was superseded by meningitis and he died at 4.50am. He was the son of Sarah and Benjamin Stevens of St. Pancras, London. He married Elizabeth Maud Stevens (nee Booth) on 7 August 1899 in Eltham. They lived at 6 Stanley Road, Sidcup and had three children. He is buried in the Sidcup (St. John) Churchyard – Kent.[9]

4 Feb. Training.

5th Feb. Training. Major Coles attended a conference at 33rd Divisional H.Q. at 5pm.

6 Feb. The battalion was allotted a training ground just over two miles south-west of St. Omer on the road from Longuenesse to Wisques in the Tilques Training area. Tilques was a large training area with firing ranges, bayonet

fighting grounds, bombing grounds, Trench Mortar School, trench mortar grounds, Artillery School, Calibration Range and Central School. Physical Training (P.T.) and Bayonet Fighting (B.F.) instructors were attached to the battalion to assist training.

'Instructions for the training of platoons for offensive action, issued in February 1917 by the General Staff' made it clear that the 'rifle and bayonet, being the most efficient offensive weapons of the soldier, are for assault, for repelling attack or for obtaining superiority of fire. Every N.C.O. and man in the platoon must be proficient in their use'. The instructions stated all ranks must be trained in 'steady drill and ceremonial' which were 'necessary to inculcate discipline, of which cleanliness, smartness and steadiness are bedrock'. All ranks were also required to train in 'bayonet fighting' which 'produces lust for blood'.[10]

Billets were redistributed to provide accommodation for a draft expected from 16th Battalion Middlesex Regiment. The battalion was billeted as follows: 'H.Q.' Company (less transport) in Gondardennes, transport in Poudrerie west of Esquerdes, 'A' Company in Gondardennes, 'B' and 'C' Companies in Wizernes, and 'D' Company in Etréhem (Estrehem Sheet 57 A. & 36 D. W.10.d.).

Lt.-Col. Storr returned from leave and went to visit the pioneer course at the Royal Engineer training camp, Rouen.

7 Feb. There was strong wind and heavy rain.

Private P.W.196 Arthur Lee died of his wounds. He had transferred to the 822nd Area Employment Company, Labour Corps. He is buried in the Chocques Military Cemetery – Pas de Calais.[11]

8 Feb. A draft of eight officers and 227 other ranks from the disbanded 16th Battalion Middlesex Regiment arrived at 5.30pm.

9 Feb. Major-General Pinney inspected the battalion on parade at 9.30am. He said he was satisfied with the appearance, work and transport of the battalion.

10 Feb. Rev. B.G. O'Rorke, D.S.O. the former Senior Chaplain of the 33rd Division, preached at the church service held at 9.30am. The service was followed by a parade. Lt.-Col. Storr resumed command of the battalion.

11 Feb. Training.

12 Feb. Lt.-Col. Storr addressed the draft from the 16th Battalion Middlesex Regiment on parade at 11.45am.

13 Feb. The battalion was due to take part in an exercise with the 19th Infantry Brigade involving low-flying aeroplanes attacking and encountering cloud gas and smoke. After marching half an hour towards the position, very wet weather forced the cancellation. Despite the weather training continued under company arrangements. Lt.-Col. Storr inspected the transport lines and billets.

14 Feb. The previous days cancelled training exercise was rescheduled but at 8.15am it was cancelled again owing to heavy morning mist. The battalion received Divisional Order 275 at 8.45pm for the relief of 50th Division by 33rd Division in the Passchendaele sector.[12] Officers from the 16th Battalion started a course of instruction.

15 Feb. The 'C' range, a firing range for over 30 yards, 1,000 yards north-east of Cormette was placed at the disposal of the battalion and allotted to 'D' Company. The 60 yard firing range constructed by the battalion 2,000 yards east of Wizernes was allotted to 'B' Company. 'A' and 'C' Companies, supervised by the Divisional Gas Officer, constructed an instructional trench system for gas demonstration purposes 700 yards north-west of Tatinghem.

16 Feb. 'A' and 'D' Companies constructed trenches for gas demonstrations. 'B' Company trained. 'C' Company was allotted the 60 yard firing range.

17 Feb. A church parade was held at 9.30am. A conference of company commanders and staff at 11am made arrangements for the move forward.

18 Feb. The battalion was put through gas huts to get firsthand experience of using gas masks. 'D' Company went through the 19th Infantry Brigade hut. The remainder of the battalion went through the hut in Wizernes. One platoon of 'A' Company completed the instructional trench system for gas demonstrations.

19 Feb. The transport, without four field kitchens, two water carts and one mess cart, marched under orders of 100th Infantry Brigade. They passed Wizernes by 10.30am and marched to billets in Renescure.

The battalion marched out to X Corps area north of Tatinghem, leaving Wizernes at 8.30am. 'D' Company joined the column at Tatinghem where the exercise planned for the 13 Feb. took place. It was supposed to be a demonstration with six low flying aeroplanes and with gas and smoke clouds. Only one aeroplane turned up and the very light shifting wind spoilt the gas and smoke demonstration. The battalion reached its billets by 2.45pm.

Pioneer battalions were instructed immediately to reduce establishment from four to three companies to be implemented forthwith.

20 Feb. The transport marched from Renescure to Oudezeele. An advance party of two officers and seven other ranks proceeded by rail from Wizernes to Ypres to take over work and accommodation from the 1/7th Durham Light Infantry (Pioneers). 'D' Company had the use of 'C' Range.

Sunderland Camp

21 Feb. The four field kitchens, two water carts, one mess cart and necessary personnel and animals left Wizernes by rail at 8am. They detrained at Vlamertinghe and marched to Sunderland Camp. Three lorries with blankets left Wizernes at 8am and reached camp at 1pm.

The battalion entrained at Wizernes leaving at 10.15am and detrained at Ypres at 1.10pm and then marched to camp. The transport marched from Oudezeele to Middlesex Camp, which was next to the Sunderland Camp. The battalion arrived back at the Flanders front line at 3pm.

Middlesex Camp – Savile Road

22 Feb. 'A' and 'C' Companies worked on a formation for a tramway near Crest Farm on the ridge south-west of Passchendaele. They left Pickering Junction by light railway at 5.15am to Van Isackere Farm. They returned by light railway from Delva Farm at noon.

Two platoons of 'B' Company repaired and maintained tracks. The other two platoons worked on the tramway with 'A' and 'C' Companies. 'D' Company remained in camp and in line with orders received on 19 Feb was disbanded. The men were distributed among the other three companies.

In the afternoon, after the departure of 1/7th Battalion Durham Light Infantry (Pioneers), the battalion moved into Middlesex Camp. 2nd Lieuts. G.W. Green, W. Howard, and C.M. Hopkinson joined on transfer from 16th Battalion.

At 9pm a German raiding party of 50 men attacked No. 1a and No. 4 advanced posts occupied by the 1/5th Cameronians (Scottish Rifles) at Decline Copse. 14 other ranks were taken prisoner, three men were killed and three men were wounded. The Germans captured three Lewis guns due to the fact that in error an extra Lewis Gun and team had been sent to post No.1a when it should have been sent to post No.10. The 1/5th Cameronians were found to be negligent in not putting out listening posts, not sending out a reconnoitring party to the front and putting out insufficient wire on the flank.[13]

23 Feb. 'A' and 'C' Companies worked on the tramway. One platoon 'B' Company was employed in camp, one platoon on 'pillboxes' and two platoons on maintenance of tracks.

24 Feb. 'A' and 'C' Companies worked on the tramway. One platoon each of 'B' Company worked just south of Tyne Cot Cemetery on the drainage of post S13 in Marne, on 'pillboxes' and maintenance of tracks, and in camp. Capt. Ripley of the Worcestershire Regiment had his attachment to the battalion terminated. Capt. Lawrence was transferred to the base.

25 Feb. 'A' and 'C' Companies worked on the tramway. One platoon each of 'B' Company worked at post S13, on 'pillboxes' and drainage of 33rd Divisional H.Q. Two platoons carried camouflage material for a trench to be dug in Passchendaele. 2nd Lieut. V.S. Copping joined from the 16th Battalion.

Two men were wounded, and one slightly wounded.

Private P.W.1139 Aaron White born and lived in Dukinfield, Cheshire and enlisted in Ashton-under-Lyne, Lancashire, was killed in action. He had served in France with the battalion since 14 November 1915. He was 49 years old and a Railway labourer before he joined up. He was married to Hannah White of 74 Ashton Street, Dukinfield. They had three daughters Clara aged 20, Sarah-Jane 17 and Dora 10. They had two sons Ernest 25 and Thomas 9.[14] He is buried in the Tyne Cot Cemetery.[15]

26 Feb. 'A' and 'C' Companies worked on the tramway. One platoon each of 'B' Company worked at post S13, on 'pillboxes' and track maintenance. Two

platoons of 'B' Company dug and camouflaged a trench across the road to the entrance to a dugout on the south-west outskirts of Passchendaele. This was completed at night, in three reliefs.

Major-General Pinney visited the camp about 3pm.

Private P.W.3240 Jesse Henry Scott, born in Merton, Surrey aged 37 died at the 3 Australian Casualty Clearing Station of shell wounds to his abdomen and right arm suffered on 25 February. He was the son of Caroline and Henry Scott, a navvy by trade, 5´ 3″ tall and weighed 134 lbs. He married Maud Jane Baird on 25 December 1901 at Merton Parish Church. They lived at 103 Nelson Road, South Wimbledon. Scott attested at Kingston, Surrey on 27 May 1915 and stated he had three daughters Jessie May dob 19 May 1902, Hilda Eliza dob 11th February 1908 and Lilian Maud dob 19 March 1912.

He was posted to the 19th Battalion Middlesex Regiment on 28 May 1915, he transferred to the 25th Middlesex on 7 August 1915 and then to the 18th Middlesex on 29 September 1915. He arrived in France with the 18th Middlesex on 12 November 1915. On 11 February 1917 Private Scott was posted to work at the XV Corps laundry. He went on special leave to England between 22 April 1917 and 6 May 1917 following the death of his daughter Lilian. Scott rejoined the 18th Middlesex on 28 August 1917. He was slightly wounded by a gunshot wound to his right arm on 21 November 1917 but returned to duty on 23 November.

Mrs Scott received 26 shillings and sixpence Separation Allowance and was awarded a pension of 20 shillings and five pence for herself and one child with effect from 9 September 1918. She also received her husband's personal effects of 2 discs, 2 letters, 2 photos, photo case, knife, scissors, metal ring, farthing, wrist disc, chain and linen bag. Mrs Scott married William Penfold in the 3rd quarter of 1920. Private Scott is buried in the Nine Elms British Cemetery.[16]

27 Feb. 'A' Company worked the on tramway. One platoon 'B' Company worked on 'pillboxes' and track repair. By night three platoons of 'B' Company and 'C' Company started on a trench through to Passchendaele town centre.

General Sir William R. Birdwood, Commander of the Australian Imperial Force, visited the battalion camp between 12.55 and 1.15pm and said he was pleased with its condition.

Field Marshal Sir Douglas Haig had a very low opinion of Birdwood and the lack of discipline in the Australian Army, which he put down to their refusal to award capital punishment to any Australian soldier. Haig cited the fact that nine per thousand Australian troops were in prison compared to the one per

thousand British troops. The introduction of suspended sentences in the British Army in February 1915 had cut prison numbers and increased the number of troops available for service. Haig saw this absence of crime in the Army as 'quite wonderful'.

28 Feb. 'A' Company worked on the tramway. One platoon of 'B' Company worked on 'pillboxes' and track repair. Two platoons of 'B' Company had a night's rest. One platoon of 'B' Company and 'C' Company, by night, worked on the trench started the previous night through Passchendaele.

Field Marshal Haig anticipated that he would soon have to defend against a large scale German offensive on the Western Front. He wrote to his wife Doris and said 'I feel quite confident, and so do my troops. Personally, I feel in the words of 2nd Chronicles, XX Chap., that it is "God's battle" and I am not dismayed by the numbers of the enemy'.[17]

1 Third Supplement to the London Gazette 31st March 1918, Published 2nd April 1918, Gazette Issue 30606, p. 4018
2 Lloyd George, *War Memoirs, Vol. 2*, p.1615
3 Ibid., p. 1625-1627
4 Ibid., p. 1628
5 Ibid., p. 1642
6 Ibid., p. 1637
7 Cambrai Court of Enquiry
8 33rd Division War Diary
9 *Soldiers Died In The Great War 1914 -1919*, p. 104; Commonwealth War Graves Commission casualty details; Private Stevens Army Service Record, National Archives, WO 363
10 Instructions for the training of platoons for offensive Action 1917, Issued by the General Staff p. 7 & p. 12
11 Commonwealth War Graves Commission casualty details
12 33rd Division War Diary
13 Ibid.
14 1911 census
15 *Soldiers Died In The Great War 1914 -1919*, p. 105; Commonwealth War Graves Commission casualty details; British Army Medal Rolls Index 1914 -1920
16 *Soldiers Died In The Great War 1914 -1919*, p. 104; Commonwealth War Graves Commission casualty details; Private Scott Army Service Record, National Archives, WO 363; 1911 Census; England & Wales, Marriage Index 1916 -2005
17 Blake (Editor), *The Private Papers of Douglas Haig 1914 -1919*, p.p. 290-291

CHAPTER SEVEN

1st March 1918 to 3rd April 1918

Digging-in in Passchendaele
German Spring Offensive
Black Saturday and Black Sunday

Middlesex Camp Savile Road

1 March 1918. 'A' Company, by day, constructed an embankment through Haalen Copse half a mile south-west of Passchendaele on the Passchendaele tramway.

One platoon of 'B' Company worked on 'pillboxes' and track repairs. Both these parties went by light railway train, leaving Manners Junction at 5.15am and returning from Van Isackere Junction at noon. By night the rest of 'B' Company and 'C' Company worked on the trench through Passchendaele. They went by train leaving Manners Junction at 9pm. The return train was due to leave Van Isackere Junction at 3.45am. Two trains failed to turn up and the companies had to march five and half miles back to camp.

2 Mar. 'A' Company worked on the tramway embankment in Haalen Copse. One platoon of 'B' Company worked on 'pillboxes' and track repairs. Two platoons of 'B' Company worked by night on the trench.

The remaining platoon of 'B' Company and 'C' Company had a night's rest.

The large scale attacks of the 1917 campaign on the Western Front ceased by the end of December. This gave the British Army time to prepare and fortify its new front line defences following the German strategic withdrawal to the Hindenburg Line. British Forces held the front line on the Somme, the Scarpe, at Vimy, Messines and Passchendaele.

Field Marshal Haig concentrated the lion's share of his resources in Flanders. The First Army was deployed to the right of Passchendaele with

sixteen divisions, twenty-nine brigades of artillery, fifteen siege battalions and fifty-six companies of Royal Engineers along thirty-three miles of front.

The Second Army was deployed in the Passchendaele sector with fourteen divisions, thirty-four brigades of artillery, twenty-five siege battalions and sixty-eight companies of Royal Engineers along twenty-three miles of front.

The Fifth Army was deployed along the Somme with fourteen divisions, three Cavalry divisions, (which were equivalent to one infantry division) forty-six brigades of artillery, fifteen siege battalions and fifty-six companies of Royal Engineers along forty-two miles of front.

The Third Army was slightly better manned than the Fifth Army but not as well as the First and Second Armies in Flanders. The Third Army was stationed to the right of the Fifth Army in front of Doullens and opposite the Flesquières salient. They had fifty-four companies of Royal Engineers along twenty-eight miles of front.[1]

Haig's concentration of troops in Flanders was strange to say the least, as the wet weather would prevent a German spring offensive in that sector. 'Haig had in his December memorandum intimated to his subordinate Commanders that both (Passchendaele and Flesquières) these salients were indefensible and were to be abandoned in the event of a heavy attack'.[2]

On 2 March Haig presided at a Conference of Army Commanders in Doullens. At the meeting his Intelligence Officer Brigadier-General Edgar William Cox, of G.H.Q. Intelligence, told him that the 'enemy is preparing to attack on the fronts of our Third and Fifth Armies'.[3] He also gave Haig 'the exact area of the attack' and 'the exact date on 20th or 21st March' of the attack.[4] Haig concluded the attack would probably take place.

Haig emphasised to his commanders 'the necessity for being ready as soon as possible to meet a big hostile offensive of prolonged duration'. He said 'I was very pleased at all I had seen on the fronts of the three Armies which I had recently visited. Plans were sound and thorough, and much work had already been done. I was only afraid that the enemy would find our front so strong that he will hesitate to commit his Army to the attack with the almost certainty of losing very heavily'.[5]

3 Mar. Two platoons of 'A' Company worked in Haalen Copse and two platoons had a day's rest.

Three platoons of 'B' Company and two platoons of 'C' Company dug the

trench by night. Two platoons of 'C' Company brought wire and pickets forward from Seine to Haalen Copse by day and then took it to dumps near the places to be wired. One platoon of 'B' Company also had a day's rest.

4 Mar. Two platoons of 'A' Company worked in Haalen Copse and two platoons had a day's rest.

One platoon of 'B' Company worked on 'pillboxes' and track repairs. By day two platoons of 'C' Company carried wire entanglement materials forward to Passchendaele.

By night one platoon of 'B' Company and two platoons of 'C' Company put out 200 yards of wire entanglements on the eastern side of Passchendaele. The train taking them to work broke down and they arrived two hours late.

Two platoons of 'B' Company had a night's rest.

5 Mar. Sir Auckland Geddes, Minister for National Service, informed the War Cabinet that he anticipated practically all the post-war miners who were fit enough to serve in the Army would be withdrawn from the mines by the middle of March. He asked the War Cabinet to issue a decertification order, withdrawing all certificates of exemption from 50,000 pre-war miners aged between 18 years and 8 months to 25 years so that they could be recruited into military service. The War Cabinet agreed.[6]

In an effort to secure the support of The Miners' Federation of Great Britain, Lloyd George invited their leaders to 10 Downing Street. Up till then the Miners' Federation had offered practical resistance to the proposal to take 50,000 young miners out of the pits and into the Army. Lloyd George showed the men a map indicating the depth of German penetration on the British front and the number of German divisions massed opposite the Allies. This graphic visual aid helped the Prime Minister to secure the assent and assistance of the Miners' Federation.

Lloyd George recorded that when the process of recruiting young miners began he received an 'alarming appeal, not from the miners themselves, but from the Coal Controller as to the disastrous effect upon the production of coal'.[7]

5 Mar. 'A' Company worked on the tramway. One platoon of 'B' Company worked on 'pillboxes' and track repairs. Three platoons of 'B' Company and three platoons of 'C' Company worked by night in Passchendaele.

The enemy artillery was more active than usual. They also sent over some 'Blue Cross' gas.[8]

The Blue Cross shell was a 'double purpose' gas missile containing a substance called diphenyl chloroarsine (DA). This gas was a lachrymator causing crying, a sternutator causing sneezing and vomiting and a respiratory irritant. It did not contain a vesicant (blistering agent) like mustard gas.[9] Contact with Blue Cross gas caused uncontrollable nausea or sneezing, forcing troops to remove their gas masks and exposing them to further doses of gas.

The Controlling Board of The Supreme War Council decided on 6 February that Britain should contribute ten divisions to the Inter-Allied General Reserve. This information was communicated to Haig in the Versailles Note. The Cabinet received Haig's reply on 6 March. He informed them 'An enemy offensive appears imminent on both the English and French Fronts. To meet this attack I have disposed of all the troops at present under my command, and if I were to earmark six or seven divisions from these troops the whole of my plans and dispositions would have to be remodelled. This is clearly impossible, and I therefore regret that I am unable to comply with the suggestion'.[10]

6 Mar. 'A' Company worked on the tramway. One platoon of 'B' Company worked on 'pillboxes' and track repairs. During the day one platoon of 'C' Company carried forward materials for wire entanglements. Two platoons of 'B' Company and one platoon of 'C' Company worked by night on the trench through Passchendaele. One platoon of 'B' Company and two platoons of 'C' Company had a night's rest.

7 Mar. 'A' Company worked on the tramway. One platoon of 'B' Company worked on 'pillboxes' and track repairs. One platoon of 'C' Company worked, by day, on the trench through Passchendaele.

Three platoons of 'B' Company and three platoons of 'C' Company put out wire east of Passchendaele but Fritz dropped gas bombs on the area making it too dangerous to work, so these companies worked on the trench instead.

Four men were wounded. Several men suffered slightly from the effects of gas.

8 Mar. 'A' Company worked on the tramway. One platoon of 'B' Company and two sections of 'C' Company worked on track repairs and 'pillboxes'. Two sections of 'C' Company brought forward materials for wire entanglements.

Two platoons of 'B' Company and one platoon of 'C' Company had a night's rest. One Platoon of 'B' Company and two platoons of 'C' Company put out 150 yards of wire by night.

Private T.F.315739 Edward Thomas Bennetts was born in Shoreditch, Middlesex on 7 August 1880 and was the son of Emma Annie and Charles Philip Bennetts of 12 Craven Street, Hoxton New Town, Middlesex. He married Martha Tarr on 12 April 1903 in Charlton Kent. They had one son Edward William dob 10 March 1907 and they lived at 1 Hardens Manorway, Charlton. He was a Timber Inspector by trade, 5´ 6½″ tall and weighed 125 lbs. He attested on 9 June 1915 at Woolwich. He was enlisted into the Army on 17 June 1916 and was posted to 10th Middlesex stationed at Chiswick. He moved to the 63rd Provisional Battalion at Great Yarmouth on 24 June 1916 and then onto the 32nd Middlesex at Gorleston on 1 January 1917.

Bennetts joined the B.E.F with the 1/7th Middlesex on 17 July 1917, transferred to the 16th Middlesex on 7 August 1917 and then onto the 18th Middlesex on 8 February 1918. He suffered a gunshot wound to the head on 7 March and died from his wounds. Mrs Bennetts received her late husband's personal effects of 2 discs, ring, 2 wallets, letters, cards, purse, club book, New Testament, watch and strap, steel mirror, cigarette case, lighters, Cap badge, match box, coin, photos, photo case, handkerchief and pen holder. She received a Separation Allowance of 23 shilling and was awarded a pension of 20 shillings and 5 pence per week with effect from 16 September 1918 for herself and her son. Private Bennetts is buried in the Nine Elms British Cemetery.[11]

Private G/96186 George Brooker, born in Charlwood, lived in Horley, enlisted in Redhill, Surrey, was killed in action. He was formerly 18100 Royal West Surrey Regiment. He is buried in Potijze Château Grounds Cemetery.[12]

Private G/96190 Charles Smith, aged 42, born in Exeter, Devon and enlisted in Finsbury, Middlesex, was killed in action. He was the son of Mary and Charles Smith and the husband of Florence Amy Smith of 110 Corporation Buildings, Farrington Road, London. He was formerly R.28201 of the King's Royal Rifle Corps. He is buried in Potijze Château Grounds Cemetery.[13]

9 Mar. 'A' Company worked on the tramway. One platoon of 'B' Company worked on tracks and 'pillboxes'. One platoon of 'C' Company worked on the Passchendaele trench by day. Three platoons of 'B' Company and three platoons of 'C' Company worked on the trench and put out 125 yards of wire by night.

Two men were wounded, one of them slightly.

10 Mar. 'A' Company worked on the tramway. 'B' Company worked on tracks, 'pillboxes' and night wiring. 'C' Company worked by day on the trench and by night wiring. Between them 'B' and 'C' Companies put out 125 yards of wire.

Lt.-Col. Storr assumed temporary command of the 19th Infantry Brigade. Major Coles assumed command of the battalion.

11 Mar. 'A' Company worked on the tramway. One platoon of 'B' Company worked on the tracks and 'pillboxes' and three platoons worked on the trench. 'C' Company had one platoon wiring and two platoons working on the trench.

Three men were wounded. One man was accidentally wounded, shot during a Lewis gun instruction course in the camp.

12 Mar. A report for Sir Henry Wilson, Chief of the Imperial General Staff (C.I.G.s.), prepared by Brigadier-General P. de B. Radcliffe Director of Military Operations at the War Office confirmed that 'The Forward and Battle Zones (of the Fifth Army's position on The Somme) were only partially wired, and a beginning had been made towards preparing certain localities for defence, but the rest of the main line of defences in the rear zone, was only spit-locked'.[14] This meant the defences had only been marked out on the surface with a pickaxe.

Meanwhile the Chief of the Imperial General Staff informed the War Cabinet that 'there were signs of the enemy concentrating in the area opposite the line from Arras to St. Quentin'. He further informed the War Cabinet 'that he felt no certainty that an attack was coming as it must depend upon whether or not the Germans felt confident of their ability to defeat us in the field'.[15]

12 Mar. The battalion carried on with work from the previous day.

13 Mar. One platoon of 'A' Company worked on the tramway, the rest of the company was given a day's rest. Three platoons of 'B' Company started work on the divisional reserve line and one platoon was rested. One platoon of 'C' Company carried wire and pickets by day and three platoons wired by night.

Lt.-Col. Storr D.S.O. was wounded whilst commanding the 19th Infantry Brigade.

Ten of the officers who became supernumerary to the establishment on re-organisation left to join the Northamptonshire Regiment, eight to the 2nd Battalion and two to the 6th Battalion.

14 Mar. Three platoons of 'A' Company worked on the divisional reserve line and one platoon was rested. One platoon of 'B' Company worked on cleaning and painting the names on 'pillboxes' and three platoons worked on the divisional reserve line. One platoon of 'C' Company worked on the Passchendaele trench and three platoons rested.

A prisoner was taken at 9.30pm south of Tiber. Information gained from him was that the enemy intends to raid British posts at 1am the following day. Counter-preparations were ordered and patrols activated across the whole front.[16]

General Edmonds and Brigadier-General H. Biddulph, Royal Engineers, were sent by the Engineer-in-Chief to report on the Fifth Army defences on the Somme. They 'found that only the front line of the rear zone was marked out by a continuous ribbon of trenches, seven feet wide and a foot deep, with occasional small belts of wire (tactical wire sited for sweeping by machine-guns; protective wire was to follow later). The sites for machine-guns and strong points were marked by notice boards'.[17]

Despite the fact that 'so little had been done to prepare a Rear Zone in the Fifth and Third Army areas'[18] and acknowledging at the end of February 1918 that it was 'probable that the enemy would make his initial effort from the Sensée River southwards'[19], Field Marshal Haig did not redeploy Infantry, Royal Engineers or Pioneer troops from unthreatened Flanders to the threatened Somme.

15 Mar. At 1am under cover of a barrage the enemy raided posts from Tiber to Grun 900 yards south of Passchendaele. They were met with machine gun and rifle fire, which broke up the attack and caused many German casualties.[20]

Three platoons of 'A' Company worked on the divisional reserve line and one platoon on the tramway. Three platoons of 'B' Company worked on the divisional reserve line and one platoon on tracks. One platoon of 'C' Company carried and prepared wire by day and three platoons erected wire by night round Passchendaele.

Three officers left to join 6th Battalion Northants Regiment.

Orders were received to send 2nd Lieut. Percival George Clay to England for six months duty.

16 Mar. One man was wounded by gas whilst at work.

Two large shells fell in the camp at about 2am. One of them destroyed the recreation hut with a direct hit.

The following three soldiers were killed in action and are buried in the Potijze Château Grounds Cemetery.

Sergeant Drummer G/750 John Bathurst Hern was born in Twickenham in the 2nd quarter of 1883. He was the son of John and Mary Ann Hern. He married Lillian Clara Cowling on 6 September 1913 at the Willesden Registry Office and they lived at 20 Wesley Road, Stonebridge Park, Willesden. They had three children before they married but only their daughter Lillian Clara born on 6 December 1911 survived. George aged 2 years died in the 3rd quarter of 1912. John Bathurst Field born on 30 September 1907 died of acute nephritis (inflammation of the kidney) and heart failure on 30 September 1914. Mrs Lillian Hern received an award from the War Office of 2 shillings and 7 pence in respect of her son's death. Their fourth child, Reginald Henry, was born on 23 November 1913.

John Hern attested in Willesden on 1 September 1914 at the age of 31 years and 4 months. He was 5´ 10″ tall and weighed 140 lbs. He was a tram driver by trade and had previously served for 12 years with the Leicestershire Regiment. He was posted to the 6th Battalion Middlesex Regiment on 4 September 1914 and made Acting Corporal on 1 April 1916. He transferred to the 18th Middlesex on 28 November 1916. On 3 January 1917 Hern joined the 33rd Division Band. He rejoined the 18th Middlesex on 7 August 1917. He was made Corporal on 11 August 1917 and Sergeant on 16 August 1917.

Following the death of Sergeant Hern his wife Lillian moved on 30 March 1918 to 4 Wallace Road, Neath, South Wales. She received 27 shillings Separation Allowance and a pension of 27 shillings and 11 pence for herself and two children with effect from 30 September 1918. She also received her late husband's personal effects of a disc, lanyard, ribbons on metal, letters and photos. She married Thomas Meredith in the 1st quarter of 1921 and moved to 1 Gower Street, Port Talbot.[21]

Lance Corporal Drummer L/11242 Joseph Willmore was born in Chelsea in 1887. He attested in London on 30 July 1906. He was a labourer by trade and was posted to the 5th Battalion Middlesex Regiment and served in India. He was 5´ 5″ tall, his girth fully expanded was 34½″ and he weighed 120 lbs. After 6 months service and a course in gymnastics he was 5´ 7″ tall, his fully expanded girth was 35″ and he weighed 135 lbs. He was admitted to hospital on 15 August 1910 suffering from gonorrhoea and discharged on 1 October 1910. On 15 September 1914 he received a service endorsement describing him as 'a quiet sober man. Is very willing and has given no trouble'. He did not have

any record of drunkenness on duty or any ordinary cases of drunkenness. His military character was described as 'V.G.' (very good).

Joseph Willmore married Ellen Martin on 12 June 1915 at the Parish Church, Burham and they had one son Douglas Joseph born on 21 September 1916.

Willmore left Folkestone for Boulogne on 28 November 1916. He arrived in Étaples on 29 November and was posted to the 18th Middlesex on 12 December 1916.[22]

Private Drummer G.41423 Edward Aubery Lane was born in Stanton St. John, Oxfordshire on January 1892 and was the son of Julia and Richard Lane of 46 Lower High Street, Thame. He married Ada Ellen Turnbull on 30 October 1915 at St. Pauls Ealing and they lived at 16 Graham Avenue, Ealing. They had one son Aubrey Richard Matthew dob 18 April 1917. At the time of Edward Lane's death Mrs Lane was living at 18 Salisbury Road, Northfield Avenue, Ealing.

Private Lane attested on 9 December 1915 at Wimbledon. He was a compositor by trade and he was placed in the Army Reserve. He was mobilised on 7 April 1916 and posted to the 3/5th Battalion East Surrey Regiment. He transferred to the 3rd East Surrey on 19 October 1916 and then to the 12th East Surrey on 25 October 1916 and went to France. He transferred to the 18th Battalion Middlesex Regiment on 9 November 1916. He was slightly wounded but remained at duty on 25 May 1917.[23]

17 Mar. One officer left to join 6th Battalion Northants Regiment.

One man was wounded.

Brigadier-General Cox, head of the GHQ Intelligence Branch, reported to Haig 'that the enemy had 187 divisions now on the West Front: of these 80 are believed to be in reserve'.[24] Russia exited from the war against the Central Powers in November 1917 following the success of the Bolshevik revolution. This enabled Germany to relocate men and guns in serious numbers from the eastern front to the Western Front

18 Mar. 'C' Company completed wiring around Passchendaele.

Five men were wounded, one of whom remained at duty.

19 Mar. One platoon of 'A' Company worked on the tramway and three platoons worked on the divisional reserve line. One platoon of 'B' Company worked on

maintaining tracks and three platoons worked on the divisional reserve line. 'C' Company dug the Passchendaele trench by night.

Two men were wounded.

20 Mar. 'A' Company worked on the tramway and 'B' Company maintained the track and the divisional reserve line. 'C' Company started wiring around support posts at Hillside Farm starting 100 yards north-east of the corner of Tyne Cot Cemetery.

Two officers left to join 7th Battalion and one officer to join the 2nd Battalion Northants Regiment.

At about 10.15am two large calibre shells completely destroyed the signal office and equipment, killing the Sergeant signaller and wounding the operator on duty.

Sergeant P.W.1068 Albert Edward Johnson, aged 34, born and lived in Fenton and enlisted in Stoke-on-Trent, Staffordshire, was killed in action. He was the son of Prudence and Samuel Johnson of Fenton, Stoke-on-Trent. He is buried in the Ypres Reservoir Cemetery.[25]

21 Mar. The Germans launched their spring Operation Michael offensive.

Ludendorff, at a conference at Crown Prince Rupprecht's headquarters in Mons on 11 November 1917, set the foundations to deliver a blow on the Western Front. He estimated that he had 35 divisions and 1,000 heavy guns which were sufficient to launch one offensive without any diversions elsewhere. Ludendorff set down three conditions for the attack:

1) to strike at the end of February or the beginning of March; 2) to attack before the Americans could throw strong forces into the scale; 3) the British Army must be beaten.[26]

On 10 March 1918 Paul von Hindenburg, Chief of the General Staff of the Central Powers, received approval from Kaiser Wilhelm II for Operation Michael to take place on 21 March.[27]

Operation Michael was a three pronged attack. The objective of Michael 1 and 2 was to cut off the British in the Cambrai Salient. The Seventeenth Army's first Michael 1 task was to take the line Croisilles – Bapaume – Péronne – mouth of the Omignon. It was then to press onto the Arras – Albert line in a general north-westerly direction.

Under Michael 2 the Second Army was to attack the Arras – Albert line in a westerly direction and press on Albert. The Seventeenth and Second Armies

were then to develop their attack in the direction of Arras. Plans were in place for an immediate exploitation of the Michael attack by rolling up the front, north of Fontaine-lès-Croisilles.

Under Michael 3, on the left flank, part of the German Eighteenth Army was to reach the Somme and take the Crozat Canal south of the Omignon and be ready to extend its right flank as far as Péronne. If they got forward rapidly they were then to launch strong forces via Beauvois – Tertry north-west in the direction of Péronne.[28]

'Shortly before 5 a.m. on the 21st March, a bombardment of great intensity, with gas and high explosive shell from all natures of artillery and trench mortars was opened against practically the whole fronts of the British Fifth and Third Armies from Oise to the Scarpe River, while road centres and railways as far back as St. Pol were engaged by high velocity guns'.[29]

The combination of explosives, phosgene, chlorine and tear gas created a lethal cocktail of poisonous gases which combined with the early morning fog and hung over the British front line trenches like a shroud.

'The hour of the enemy's assault varied in different sections, but by about 9.45a.m. a general attack had been launched on a battle front of fifty-four miles between the Oise and Sensée Rivers'.[30] In all, at least sixty-four German divisions took part in the operations of the first day of the battle.[31]

Facing the attack was the exhausted and depleted British Fifth Army under General Sir Hubert de la Gough. He had fourteen divisions to defend forty-two miles of front. The Third Army, under General the Hon. Julian Hedworth George Byng, had 16 divisions to defend 28 miles of front.[32]

Field Marshal Haig gives slightly different figures showing the Fifth and Third Armies combined had 'twenty-nine infantry divisions and three Cavalry divisions, of which nineteen infantry were in line'.[33] Regardless of this minor difference, the British troops were severely outnumbered and out gunned.

Day one of Operation Michael was a major success for Germany. 'At the end of the first day...the enemy had made very considerable progress but he was still held firmly in the battle zone'.[34] The British III Corps was forced to withdraw behind the Crozat Canal. The 36th Division withdrew to the line of the Somme Canal. The V Corps and 9th Division were forced to withdraw from the Flesquières salient.[35]

21 Mar. 'A' Company worked on the tramway, 'B' Company worked on track

maintenance and the divisional reserve line and 'C' Company carried on wiring around support posts at Hillside Farm.

Lieut. Tristain Noel Marchand Buesst left to do a six months tour of duty in England.

Private P.S.3767 Walter James Peacock aged 22, born in Camberwell, London and enlisted in Farnborough, Hants, died of his wounds. He was the only son of Clara and Walter Hugh Peacock of 430 Lower Addiscombe Road, Addiscombe, Croydon, London. He is buried in the Nine Elms British Cemetery.[36]

22 Mar. 'A' Company worked on the tramway, 'B' Company rested and 'C' Company worked on wiring Hillside Farm.

Three men were wounded.

Sergeant G/50517 Albert Kirk born in Southwark, Surrey, lived in Sheffield, Yorkshire and enlisted in Mill Hill, Middlesex, died of his wounds. He is buried in the Ypres Reservoir Cemetery.[37]

Black Saturday 23 March. Operation Michael saw the Germans swiftly regaining considerable ground on the old Somme battlefield.

Field Marshal Haig recorded 'I then went on to Villers-Bretonneux and saw General Gough, Commanding Fifth Army. [I was surprised to learn that] his troops are now behind the Somme and the River Tortille. Men very tired after two days fighting and long march back. On the first day they had to wear gas masks all day which is very fatiguing [but I cannot make out why the Fifth Army has gone so far back without making some kind of a stand]...'.[38]

The Fifth Army desperately needed support to shore up their line, but behind 'the British right there was no reserve at all'.[39] The British troops concentrated in Flanders by Field Marshal Haig were isolated from this offensive.

For the first time shells from one of the German long-range guns fell in and near Paris. The gun had a 8.26-inch calibre barrel and a range of 75 miles and was located in La Sapinière in the Forest of St. Gobain, to the south-west of Crépy Station between Laon and la Fère.[40]

British Prime Minister David Lloyd George received information from General Headquarters (G.H.Q.) 'that on the Fifth Army Front the enemy had succeeded in penetrating our battle zone and reserve lines, and that a retirement had in consequence been made to the line of the Somme. A more serious

indication of the state of affairs came with the report that our casualties were 40,000 and that not less than 600 guns had been lost. Even then there were reassuring items in the report. On the Third Army Front we were told that the enemy had in the main been held firmly in the battle zone except at Mory, and enormous slaughter had undoubtedly been inflicted on the enemy in places'.[41]

Lloyd George 'had a feeling that the position was much graver than the G.H.Q. messages would imply. It looked as if Gough's tired army was giving way before the fierce onrush of the German hordes. It was evident that our line was broken and that we were relying upon patchwork defences hastily improvised to stop a victorious army'.[42]

Lloyd George told Sir George Riddell, his long standing friend and golf partner who was also the proprietor of the News of the World, that 'the news is very bad. I fear it means disaster'.[43]

Lloyd George postponed the Cabinet meeting and instead went to the War Office to take matters in hand to see 'what could be done to throw all available reinforcements into France with the greatest attainable celerity'. Lloyd George wanted to know how many troops were in Britain, how many could be spared for deployment to France and how many per day could be sent across the channel.[44]

Major-General Sir Robert Hutchison, the Director of Operations in the War Office, advised Lloyd George that there were 170,000 trained men in England who were immediately ready for the draft. This figure includes 50,000 trained youths between the ages of 18½ and 19. Parliament had been given a pledge that men under the age of 19 would not be sent into action unless there was a national emergency.

Lloyd George decided this was a national emergency and gave instructions to rush the 170,000 troops available in Britain to France with the utmost urgency. Arrangements were made to transport 30,000 men a day to France. The 88,000 soldiers on leave in England were immediately recalled to the Western Front. [45]

23 Mar. 'A' Company was given a day of rest. 'B' Company worked on the divisional reserve line and tracks. 'C' Company completed the wiring of support posts at Hillside Farm and worked on the Passchendaele communication trench.

24 Mar. Black Sunday. After four days of intense fighting the 'Fifth Army was no longer an Army. It was broken into fragments – still fighting as it drifted

back...(and) was on average over 16 miles behind the line which it held at dawn on 21st and further retreats were inevitable'.[46]

'The Third Army was also in full retreat. It had been driven miles behind the original line'.[47]

Had Field Marshal Haig acted upon the Supreme War Council decision to set up an Inter Allied General Reserve, troops would have been available to reinforce the Fifth Army and prevent its defeat by the Germans. Likewise if Haig had acted upon the intelligence he had received he would have deployed the bulk of his troops to the Somme.

Lloyd George commented 'Unless President Wilson hurries up, he may be too late. He has wasted too much time; he has been nine months in the war and has done very little which is of real service at the front'.[48]

24 Mar. 'A' and 'B' Companies worked on the divisional reserve line. 'C' Company worked on the Passchendaele communication trench and carried wire.

Major-General Pinney visited the battalion H.Q. at 5.15pm.

Sergeant G/10824 Edward Charles Kent, aged 37, born in Lee, Kent and enlisted in Warley, Essex, died of his wounds. He was the son of Maria and Thomas Kent. He is buried in the Nine Elms British Cemetery.[49]

The following five soldiers were killed in action and their names are on the Pozières Memorial – Somme.

Lance Corporal G/5757 Henry Bull was born and lived in Walworth, Surrey. Formerly of the 12th Battalion Middlesex Regiment he enlisted in Southwark, Surrey.[50]

Lance Corporal G/52118 Henry John Pennifer was born in Stafford and lived Kensal Rise, Middlesex. Formerly of the 12th Battalion Middlesex Regiment he enlisted in London.[51]

Private F/776 Sidney Tomkins was born in Marylebone and lived in Edgware, Middlesex. He was formerly of the 12th Battalion Middlesex Regiment and enlisted in Kingsway, Middlesex.

Lance Corporal G/40672 Charles Ernest Wall, aged 21 was born in St. Paul's Middlesex. He was the son of Martha Ann and William John Wall of 1 College Place, Kinnerton Street, Knightsbridge, London. Formerly of the 12th Battalion Middlesex Regiment he enlisted in Chelsea, Middlesex.[52]

Private G/52107 John Poole, aged 18 was born in Luton, Bedfordshire. He was the son of Mary Ann and John Poole of 100 Albert Road, Luton,

Bedfordshire. Formerly of the 12th Battalion Middlesex Regiment and 3rd Bedfordshire Regiment he enlisted in Luton.[53]

25 Mar. Field Marshal Haig reached the view that the 'progress made by the enemy on our right and along the valley of the Somme makes it evident that it can only be a question of time when the French and English Armies are driven apart'.[54] Haig was preparing to take immediate steps to restore the situation by uncovering Amiens and falling back on the Channel ports.[55]

General Pétain was considering a similar move for the French armies to retreat to the south and 'cover Paris at all costs'.[56]

25 Mar. 'A' and 'B' Companies worked on the divisional reserve line and 'C' Company worked on the communication trench and wiring at Passchendaele.

Five men were wounded by gas.

Second Lieutenant Julius Brinkley Shaw was killed in action whilst on attachment to the 7th Battalion Northamptonshire Regiment. He was born on 21 March 1882 in Clapham, London. In civilian life he was a Professor of Music having attended Sutton Valance School and St. John's College Cambridge. He married Emily Stevenson on 17 April 1913 and lived at 39 Clarendon Road, Holland Park, London, W11.

He attested on 8 April 1915. He was 5 feet 6¼ inches tall and was posted to the 16th Public Schools Battalion Middlesex Regiment. He was promoted to Corporal and then Lance Sergeant on 5 April 1916. A day later he was promoted to Sergeant. He was discharged from the 16th Middlesex on 25 September 1917 on being commissioned as a 2nd Lieutenant with the 5th Battalion Middlesex Regiment.

He was reported missing on 25 March 1918. Enquires through the Netherlands Legation did not produce any results and he was recorded missing, presumed dead on the date. He did not leave a will and his estate was £20. 4s. 7d. At some stage his wife Emily moved to 10 Milward Crescent Hastings.

2nd Lieut. Shaw's name is recorded on the Pozières Memorial, – Somme.[57]

26 Mar. A Conference was held at Doullens between the French and the British to determine their response to Operation Michael. Before the conference convened French Commander-in-Chief Pétain and Field Marshal Haig reached the same pessimistic view about the outcome of the German offensive. Pétain

had planned a French retreat to the south and Haig had planned a British retreat to the north.

French Chief of General Staff, Foch held a completely different view to Haig and Pétain. He counselled that 'common sense indicates that where the enemy wishes to begin making a hole, you do not make it wider. You close it, or you try to close it. We have only got to try and to have the will; the rest will be easy. You stick to your ground, you defend it foot by foot. We did that at Ypres, we did it at Verdun'.[58]

The Doullens Conference placed General Foch in charge of co-ordinating the actions of the Allied Armies on the Western Front and work to this end with the Commanders-in-Chief.[59] He immediately issued orders to General Pétain and General Fayolle for the protection of Amiens.[60]

26 Mar. 'A' and 'B' Companies worked on the divisional reserve line. Three platoons of 'C' Company were rested before taking up day work. One platoon 'C' Company worked on the Passchendaele communication trench.

27 Mar. The German offensive in Picardy continued. The Germans occupied Montdidier without opposition. However from Noyon to Canny the French 5th Corps held the line.[61]

The Germans made determined attacks against the British positions north of the River Somme, losses were heavy on both sides but the Germans gained only slight advantages north of Albert, north of Ablainzevelle, west of Serre and Rossignol Wood.[62] The British retreat on the Somme back towards Amiens started to slow.

27 Mar. Three platoons of 'C' Company took over the work on divisional reserve line from 'B' Company. One platoon of 'C' Company rested. Three platoons of 'B' Company continued wiring round Passchendaele and one platoon maintained tracks. Three platoons of 'A' Company worked on divisional reserve line and one platoon on the tramway.

Three men were wounded by gas.

28 Mar. The Fifth Army on the Somme started to hold the German advance. 'At nightfall we held approximately the Amiens defence line on the whole front south of the Somme from Mezières to Ignaucourt and Hamel'. After a full week of fighting Haig decided to relieve Gough of his command of the Fifth Army

and replace him with General Sir H.S. Rawlinson. Haig placed Gough in charge of 'construction of new defence lines made necessary by the enemy's advance'.[63]

North of the Somme the Germans 'struck at great force along the valley of the Scarpe at Arras'. The objectives of the attack were to take Arras, the heights above the town and Vimy Ridge. They also attacked southwards beyond Bucquoy and further south at Dernancourt. The Third Army repulsed all the German advances. 'With this day's battle, which ended in the complete defeat of the enemy on the whole front of his attack, the first stage of the enemy's offensive weakened'.[64]

28 Mar. 'A' and 'C' Companies worked on the divisional reserve line, tracks and completed the tramway. 'B' Company finished the wiring in Passchendaele.

One officer left to join the 2nd Battalion Northants Regiment.

29 Mar. Prime Minister Lloyd George sent a secret telegram to Lord Reading, the British Ambassador to the United States, to be conveyed to President Wilson, pointing out that the Germans had proved their capacity to break through the Western Front on a wide front and it was certain that they would begin to re-fit immediately for another blow at the earliest possible moment. British losses in the present battle, which had only lasted a week, amounted to 120,000 men. Drafting in all of the remaining reserves of trained and partially trained men would barely make good the losses.

Lloyd George went on to point out that that there would be a dangerous gap in the months of May, June and July when Britain would not be able to make up any further troop losses. The only way of holding the line and preventing the Germans from winning the war on the Western Front was for 120,000 American infantry troops to be sent to Europe each month between April and the end of July.

Lloyd George concluded his telegram by stating 'I believe that the whole future of the war will depend on whether the Allies or the Germans are first in making good the losses of this great war. Unless we can re-fit as fast as they can we shall simply give Germany the chance to deliver the knock-out blow with which its leaders hope to win the war'.[65]

29 Mar. 'A' and 'C' Companies worked on the divisional reserve line and tracks. They also started on support and reserve posts. One platoon of 'B' Company carried wire to Waterfields just over a mile west of Passchendaele. Three platoons of 'B' Company rested in order to commence work by day.

Lieut. Buesst joined the 5th Battalion Middlesex Regiment at Chatham.[66]

30 Mar. 'A' and 'C' Company worked on the Divisional Reserve Line. 'B' Company started wiring Bellevue Switch one mile west of Passchendaele. They also laid a duckboard track connecting the No. 5 track with the Crest Farm track 500 yards south-west of Passchendaele.

2nd Lieut. F.J. Smith and four men were wounded by gas.

Private G/15599 Thomas Edwin Hall, aged 24, born in Islington and enlisted in Holloway, Middlesex, died of his wounds. He was the son of Catherine Ann and Thomas Henry Hall of 12 Queen's Square, Queensland Road, Hornsey Road, London. He is buried in the Nine Elms British Cemetery.[67]

Mar 31. Under Divisional Order 289 the 19th Infantry Brigade and one company of the 33rd Battalion Machine Gun Corps moved by bus to the Grand-Rullecourt area and came under the orders of the Third Army.

'B' Company commenced wiring Abraham Heights Switch 400 yards east of s'Gravenstafel. They completed one belt. 'A' and 'C' Companies worked on the divisional reserve system.

Three men were wounded.

1 April. One platoon of 'B' Company completed the duckboard track connecting F Track and Brick Kiln Road, Zonnebeke. One platoon wired Abraham Heights Switch and the two remaining platoons had a day's rest.

'A' and 'C' Companies worked on the divisional reserve system.

Lt.-Col. H.C. McNeile M.C. Royal Engineers joined and assumed command of the battalion.

One man was wounded at work.

Private Tommy McBride arrived back in France. He was one of the 88,000 troops on leave in Britain and urgently summoned to return to the Western Front by Lloyd George. He was posted to the 19th Middlesex, the pioneer battalion of the 41st Division stationed at Gommecourt.[68]

By this time, almost twelve months after declaring war on Germany the United States had 'less than 320,000 American officers and men in France, of which about 100,000 were necessarily engaged in the Services of Supply'.[69]

2 April. The battalion received Divisional Order 290 at 1.45pm for the relief of the 98th Infantry Brigade by a brigade of the 29th Division.

3 April. 'B' Company completed the wiring of Abraham Heights Switch. 'A' and 'C' Companies worked on the divisional reserve line.

At the end of the day's work, all works in progress, or proposed, were handed over to 6/7th Royal Scots Fusiliers, the pioneer battalion of the 59th (2nd North Midland) Division.

The battalion received Divisional Order 291 at 7.30am for the relief of 33rd Division by 59th Division.

Two men reported wounded from gas.

1 Lloyd George, *War Memoirs, Vol. 2*, p. 1703 and p. 1705
2 Ibid., p. 1705
3 Blake (Editor), *The Private Papers of Douglas Haig 1914 -1919*, p. 291
4 Peter E. Wright, *At the War Council,* G.P. Putnam's Sons, London, 1921, p. 130
5 Blake (Editor), *The Private Papers of Douglas Haig*, p. 291
6 War Cabinet 5 March 1918, National Archives, CAB/23/5/, Image reference 0051
7 Lloyd George, *War Memoirs, Vol. 2,* p. 1774
8 33rd Division War Diary
9 Foulkes, *'Gas' The Story of the Special Brigade*, p.p. 248-249
10 Lloyd George, *War Memoirs, Vol. 2,* p.p. 1712-1714
11 *Soldiers Died In The Great War 1914 -1919*, p. 102; Commonwealth War Graves Commission casualty details; Private Bennetts Army Service Record, National Archives, WO 363; London Metropolitan Archives, Finsbury St. Luke, Register of Baptisms, p. 76, Item 021; 1881 Census
12 Ibid.
13 Ibid., p. 104
14 Edmonds, *Military Operations, France And Belgium 1918, Vol.1*, Macmillan, London, 1935, p. 123
15 War Cabinet 364 minutes 12 March 1918, National Archives, CAB/23/5, Image reference 0056
16 33rd Division War Diary, National Archives, WO 95/2406
17 Edmonds, *Military Operations, France And Belgium 1918, Vol.1*, p.123
18 Ibid.,
19 Boraston (Editor), *Sir Douglas Haig's Despatches (December 1915 – April 1919),* p. 182
20 33rd Division War Diary
21 *Soldiers Died In The Great War 1914 -1919*, p. 103; Commonwealth War Graves Commission casualty details; Drummer Sergeant Hern Army Service Record, National Archives, WO 363; 1911 Census; England & Wales, Marriage Index: 1916 -2005
22 Ibid., p. 105; Lance Corporal Willmore Army Service Record, National Archives, WO 363; 1911 Census

23 Ibid., p. 103; Private Lane British Army WW1 Pension Records 1914 -1920, National Archives, WO 364; 1911 Census; London Metropolitan Archives, Saint Pauls, Northfield, Register of marriage, DRO/102, Item 003

24 Sheffield and Bourne (Editors), *Douglas Haig War Diaries and Letters 1914 -1918*, p. 388

25 *Soldiers Died In The Great War 1914 -1919*, p. 103; Commonwealth War Graves Commission casualty details, p. 103

26 Edmonds, *Military Operations, France And Belgium 1918, Vol.1*, p.p. 138-140

27 Ibid., p. 147

28 Ibid., p.p. 150-151

29 Boraston (Editor), *Sir Douglas Haig's Despatches (December 1915 – April 1919),* p. 186

30 Ibid.

31 Ibid., p. 185

32 Lloyd George, *War Memoirs, Vol. 2,* p. 1735

33 Boraston (Editor), *Sir Douglas Haig's Despatches (December 1915 – April 1919),* p. 185

34 Ibid., p. 190

35 Ibid.

36 *Soldiers Died In The Great War 1914 -1919*, p. 104; Commonwealth War Graves Commission casualty details

37 Ibid., p. 103

38 Sheffield and Bourne (Editors), *Douglas Haig War Diary And Letters 1914 -1918*, p. 391

39 Lloyd George, *War Memoirs, Vol. 2,* p. 1734

40 Edmonds, *Military Operations, France And Belgium 1918, Vol.1*, p. 327

41 Lloyd George, *War Memoirs, Vol. 2,* p. 1726

42 Ibid., pp. 1726-1727

43 Rowland, *Lloyd George*, p. 437

44 Lloyd George, *War Memoirs, Vol. 2,* p. 1727

45 Ibid., pp.1727-1728

46 Ibid., p. 1737

47 Ibid.

48 Rowland, *Lloyd George*, p. 437

49 *Soldiers Died In The Great War 1914 -1919*, p. 103; Commonwealth War Graves Commission casualty details

50 Ibid., p. 76

51 Ibid., p. 80

52 Ibid., p. 82

53 Ibid., p. 80

54 Lloyd George, *War Memoirs, Vol. 2,* p. 1739

55 Ibid., p. 1738

56 Blake(Editor), *The Private Papers of Douglas Haig*, p. 297

57 Commonwealth War Graves Commission casualty details; 2nd Lieut. Shaw Service Record, National Archives, WO 374/61696

[58] Lloyd George, *War Memoirs, Vol. 2,* p. 1740

[59] Ibid., p. 1740

[60] Edmonds, *Military Operations, France And Belgium 1918*, *Vol.1*, p. 538 & p.p. 542-544

[61] Edmonds, *Military Operations, France And Belgium 1918*, *Vol. 2*, MacMillan, London, 1937, p. 12

[62] Ibid., p.p. 28-29

[63] Boraston (Editor), *Sir Douglas Haig's Despatches (December 1915 – April 1919),* p. 210

[64] Ibid., p. 211 & p. 213

[65] Lloyd George's telegram to Lord Reading 29 March 1918, National Archives, CAB/24/46, Image reference 0088

[66] Lieut. Buesst Army Service Record

[67] *Soldiers Died In The Great War 1914 -1919*, p. 103; Commonwealth War Graves Commission casualty details

[68] Wyrall, *The Die Hards in the Great War*: Vol. 2, 1916 -1919, Harrison & Sons Ltd., London, 1926, p. 214

[69] Lloyd George, *War Memoirs*, *Vol. 2*, p. 1811

CHAPTER EIGHT

4th April 1918 to 14th April 1918

Back to Flanders
Operation Georgette
Defence of Méteren and Bailleul

Camps 32 and 33 one mile north-west of Vlamertinge

4 April. The battalion was relieved by the 6/7th Royal Scots Fusiliers and moved by route march to camps 32 and 33 a mile north-west along the Vlamertinge to Vuila Seule Cabaret road.

The battalion received Divisional Order 292 at 6.45pm for the move of the 33rd Division to X Corps Third Army area by train. The 18th Middlesex Battalion was listed to travel on train no. 5 at 10.15pm.[1]

Two men were wounded by gas.

Battle of Avre

At 5.15am the Germans opened a heavy artillery barrage on the British front line, artillery positions and back areas in Villers-Bretonneux. Their infantry attack followed at 6.30am. The sector of the British front line attacked was held by the 14th and 18th Divisions. The 14th Division held their ground throughout the morning. However the 18th Division was forced back along its front. In the afternoon the Germans pressed hard and nearly reached the Démuin – Villers-Bretonneux road.

The British and Australian troops counter-attacked at 5.45pm and swept back the advancing Germans. By 7pm the counter-attack had succeeded and the line east of the village was securely established.[2]

5 April. The battalion remained in camp. The battalion kit was inspected and the men were ordered to clean their equipment.

Major-General Pinney visited the camp at 6.15pm.

On 5 April, after sixteen days of great struggle Operation Michael came to a complete stop and failed in its objective to separate the British and French front. General Erich Ludendorff, Commander of the German Army, conceded that Britain's resistance was beyond German power to break. He did not want to get drawn into a battle of attrition which would not suit either the strategic or tactical situation. He therefore ordered the abandonment of 'Michael'.

This brought to an end the most formidable onslaught so far in the war. The German attack between Barisis and Arras had made major gains but ultimately failed to break through the British lines.[3]

6 April. The battalion marched at 9.15pm to Hopoutre to entrain for Aubigny.

Lattre St. Quentin west of Arras

7 April. The battalion arrived at Aubigny, detrained, and marched to the camp at Lattre St. Quentin. Major-General Pinney visited the battalion at 4.30pm.

8 April. As usual the battalion spent the day cleaning up their billets and settling in.

A conference of company commanders was held and a training programme arranged.

Major-General Pinney gave a lecture at 3.30pm on the situation to all officers and N.C.O.s.

The situation was that in Operation Michael the German attack in France had taken 1,200 square miles of territory and they had captured enormous quantities of weapons and materials. Their new line was only seven miles from Amiens, whose vital railway complex was heavily shelled on a daily basis. The Germans had fifty more miles of front line that would be difficult to defend. In the process they had lost over 250,000 men.[4]

Edmonds in 'Military Operations, France and Belgium' records that gross British losses were 177,639 men killed, missing or wounded. He calculated net losses at 160,000 after accounting for missing soldiers who returned later to their units. He extrapolated 22,000 were probably killed, 96,000 were wounded or gassed and 42,000 were unwounded prisoners.[5]

The Germans come perilously close, but ultimately failed to separate the British and French Armies.

Despite the overwhelming gains made by the Germans they failed to take their objectives of Arras and Amiens and they were held fifty miles north of Paris.

The British front line had been forced back and ran for the eastern outskirts of Arras, south past Colincamps, west of Albert, east of Villers-Bretonneux, and south of Montdidier and east to south of Noyon.[6]

9 April. The battalion spent the day in training and rifle practice.

The battalion received Divisional Order 294 at 1pm which cancelled the move of the 33rd Division from the First Army to the Third Army.[7]

Private G/32331 George Clark, aged 39, from Willesden, Middlesex, was killed in action. He was on attachment to the 2/2nd Battalion of the London Regiment (Royal Fusiliers). He was the son of Ellen A. and James Clark and the husband of Caroline Clark of 83 Tewkesbury Road, South Tottenham, London. His name is on the Pozières Memorial.[8]

Operation Georgette

On 7 and 8 April, the Germans directed an intense bombardment, including mustard gas on Armentières firing an estimated 30,000 to 40,000 shells into the town.[9] This was a precursor to the launch on 9 April of Operation Georgette attacking up both sides of Armentières and simultaneously on to Hazebrouck and Messines in Flanders.[10] The aim of the offensive was to drive the British Army into the North Sea and out of the war.

At 4.15am a heavy bombardment with phosgene gas and heavy shells opened on the back areas of the line between the La Bassée Canal and Frélinghien, but mainly directed at the Givenchy – Laventie sector which was the front of the 55th and Portuguese Divisions. More mustard gas shells were directed at Armentières.[11] This marked the beginning of the Battles of the Lys.[12]

By nightfall the Germans had made a ten-mile wide and five-and-a-half mile gap in the British front line and their line now ran behind the Lawe and the Lys.[13]

10 April. Divisional Order 294 was cancelled at 10.30am and the battalion placed under one hour's notice to move.

A party of officers were sent to reconnoitre the line at Adinfer. This was a wasted exercise as the battalion was posted back to Flanders.

The battalion received Divisional Order 295 at 7pm. The battalion marched to Aubigny and entrained. The battalion had two H.D. horses, six L.D. horses, two riders, four cookers, one mess cart, two water carts and one maltese cart.

Corporal James Knight M.M. had a strain whilst on duty which caused an aggravated hernia. He was subsequently awarded a £40 gratuity for this injury. Knight attested on 24 May 1915 at the age of 38 years and 275 days. He had previously served as a regular soldier with the 3rd Battalion Royal Sussex Regiment. He enlisted on 10 January 1893 for six years. He entered the Militia Reserve on 27 May 1898 and joined the Special Services Section of the Militia on 2 June 1998. He was recalled to permanent service with the regular Forces on 26 June 1900 and served until 9 August 1902 when he was discharged at his own request. Before rejoining the Army in 1915 he was a Labourer at the Waterworks in Sheffield.[14]

The Germans attacked the southern flank of Sir Herbert Plumer's Second Army in the Lys Valley. The Germans took Armentières, Erquinhem, Messines and Ploegsteert. Seven miles south of Méteren they captured Merville and Estaires.

The British line held and made a strategic and methodical retreat. This retreat shortened the British line and provided a base from which to defend Béthune and Hazebrouck.[15]

North of Méteren Veld

11 April. The battalion, having only just moved to northern France was moved straight back to Flanders, detrained at Caëstre and proceeded by route march to Méteren to join the defensive action against Operation Georgette.

At 5.35pm unconfirmed air reports showed the enemy was in La Crèche south-east of Bailleul. One company, together with 222nd Field Company R.E., were sent to picquet the south and south-east exits from Méteren which were under threat from the German advance.

The 18th Battalion Middlesex Regiment were ordered, until further notice, to place picquets on all approaches to Méteren from the Méteren – Noote Boom road, inclusive and thence by the east and north to the Méteren – F in Fontaine Houck road inclusive.

The 222nd Field Company, Royal Engineers, were ordered to place picquets on all approaches to Méteren from Méteren – Noote Boom road exclusive, thence west to the Méteren – Caëstre road.

The elements of the 18th Middlesex, 222nd Field Company R.E. and the 33rd Battalion Machine Gun Corps not on picquet duty were kept together as they arrived and placed on notice to be ready to move at short notice.[16]

> SPECIAL ORDER OF THE DAY BY FIELD-MARSHAL SIR DOUGLAS HAIG K.T., G.C.B., G.C.V.O., K.C.I.E. Commander-in-Chief, British Armies in France.
>
> To ALL RANKS OF THE BRITISH ARMY IN FRANCE AND FLANDERS.
>
> Three weeks ago to-day the enemy began his terrible attacks against us on a fifty-mile front. His objects are to separate us from the French, to take the Channel Ports and to destroy the British Army.
>
> In spite of throwing already 106 Divisions into the battle and enduring the most reckless sacrifices of human life, he has as yet made little progress towards his goals.
>
> We owe this to the determined fighting and self-sacrifice of our troops. Words fail me to express the admiration which I feel for the splendid resistance offered by all ranks of our Army under the most trying circumstances.
>
> Many amongst us now are tired. To those I would say that Victory will belong to the side which holds out the longest. The French Army is moving rapidly and in great force to our support.
>
> There is no other course open to us but to fight it out. Every position must be held to the last man: there must be no retirement. With our backs to the wall and believing in the justice of our cause each one of must fight on to the end. The safety of our homes and the Freedom of mankind alike depend upon the conduct of each one of us at this critical moment.
>
> Signed D. Haig. F.M.
> Commander-in-Chief,
> British Armies in France.[17]
>
> General Headquarters,
> Thursday April 11th 1918.

12 April. The 31st Division fell back to Merris creating a yawning three-mile gap in the British front line between that village and Bailleul. The 33rd Battalion Machine Gun Corps and the 19th Infantry Brigade moved to fill the gap.[18]

Two platoons 18th Middlesex picqueted the road junctions west of La Barrière Calverdans and south on the road from Appetite Farm where it met the Méteren to Armentières road.

At 9.40am reports were received that the enemy had broken through at Merville and cavalry was reported at Neuf Berquin. Together with the 33rd Battalion Machine Gun Corps, the battalion was ordered to be ready to defend Méteren in the event of the 19th Infantry Brigade being ordered elsewhere.[19]

At 1.30pm, together with the 222nd Field Company Royal Engineers, the battalion was ordered to report to the 19th Infantry Brigade Headquarters.[20]

At 2pm orders were received to dig a switch line starting 1,000 yards east of Méteren on the road to La Barrière Calverdans going north for 1,600 yards then going 1,000 yards north-east towards St. Jans Cappel and finishing at the track from Punkah Farm to Heaton Cross Roads 1,000 yards south-west of St. Jans Cappel. This switch line was to be held if necessary. The switch line going north for 1,600 yards from the Méteren Road became known as Scots Trench and Scots Alley. The further 1,000 yards of trench became known as the Rathfriland Support and the Rally Support.

The residue of the 93rd Infantry Brigade appeared about 3.30pm on the main Méteren – Bailleul road. They were ordered to dig in and occupy part of the switch line.

At 5pm the battalion was placed under orders of the 19th Infantry Brigade together with 222nd Field Company R.E., one company 33rd Battalion Machine Gun Corps, New Zealand Entrenching Battalion, IX and XXII Corps Cyclists. They were ordered to hold the Strazeele (Exclusive) to Steam Mill (Moulin a Vapeur) (Inclusive) Line.[21]

At 8pm the battalion was relieved by the 1/5th Cameronians and they withdrew and concentrated east of Halte Porte Farm at 8.30pm.

Five men were wounded.

Private G/87604 Arthur John Leach, aged 32, born in Peterborough, Northants and enlisted in Northampton, was killed in action. He was the husband of Kate Leach of 191 Cromwell Road, Peterborough. His name is on the Ploegsteert Memorial – Comines-Warneton, Hainaut.[22]

Overnight on 12/13 April, the withdrawal of British troops from Passchendaele and the Ypres salient ordered by Field Marshal Haig took place.

As a result the British positions on Passchendaele Ridge were only held by outposts.[23]

13 April. At 2.40am the battalion was placed in the 19th Infantry Brigade reserve at Fontaine Houck.

At 5.30am the battalion had two and half companies in reserve near Battalion Headquarters. The remainder of the battalion occupied the switch line started the previous day.[24]

At 7.30am 'B' Company was sent to reinforce the 1st Queen's Battalion and 'C' Company was sent to reinforce XXII Corps Reinforcement Battalion.

At 8.30am the situation at the junction between the 1st Queen's and XXII Corps Reinforcement Battalion on the left of the front line was obscure because contact between the two units was never established. Reports from the 1st Queen's suggested the enemy had broken through the XXII Corps Reinforcements Battalion just south of Méteren. One company of the 18th Battalion Middlesex Regiment were ordered to counter-attack and restore the line of the XXII Corps Reinforcement Battalion.[25] The report by 1st Queen's proved to be incorrect.[26] The attack by 18th Middlesex did not take place.[27]

At 10.30am the enemy was reported to have broken through a portion of the front held by the XXII Corps Cyclists. The 18th Middlesex were sent as reinforcements to counter-attack and restore the front line position which they did.[28]

The 19th Infantry Brigade was being forced northwards back towards Méteren by the German Operation Georgette.

There was heavy shelling throughout the afternoon on the Méteren – Bailleul road.

At 8pm information from a prisoner confirmed the enemy had been ordered to take Méteren at all costs. Preparations were ordered to defend against further attacks the following day.[29]

At 9pm half of 'A' Company was taken to reinforce the Cameronians by filling gaps in the front line.

Forty men were wounded.

The following five soldiers were killed in action and are buried in the Méteren Military Cemetery – Nord.

Private G/32551 William Beard, born in St. Peters, Worcestershire, lived in Southall and enlisted in Hounslow, Middlesex.[30]

Private G/24962 Frederick Henry Gilmour aged 37, born in Bethnal Green

and enlisted in Mill Hill, Middlesex. He married Maud Elizabeth Tyrell on 15 March 1908 at St. Matthews Church Islington, London. They had two children by the time of the 1911 Census. Walter was born in 1909 and Gladys in 1910. At the time of their marriage they were neighbours living at 46 and 48 Rotherfield Street Islington. Gilmour was a Farrier Cutter by trade and the son of Frederick and Charlotte Gilmour. At the time of his death his wife and family lived at 121 Sydney Road, Hornsey London.[31]

Private G/57941 Alfred Thomas Grace, born in Peckham, Surrey on 17 June 1899 and enlisted in West London. He was only 2 months short of his 19th birthday. He was the son of Ellen and Isaac Grace of 121 Stephendale Road, Fulham, London.[32]

Private G/42954 Bertram Gladstone Stokes, aged 20, a native of Nunhead, London, lived in Tottenham and enlisted in Mill Hill, Middlesex. He was the son of Eliza Ann and Walter Charles Stokes of 9 Waldeck Road, West Green, South Tottenham.[33]

Private G/40011 Frederick James Thomas, aged 25, born in Pembroke Dock, Pembrokeshire, lived in York and enlisted in High Beech, Essex. He was formerly 23376 Royal Fusiliers. He was the son of Annie and James Thomas of 12 Grove Street, Pennar, Pembrokeshire.[34]

The following twelve soldiers were killed in action. Their names are on the Ploegsteert Memorial.

Lance Corporal P.W.857 Joseph Bullock, aged 21 was born in Longton and lived at 178 Sutherland Street. He enlisted in Fenton, Staffs on 24 March 1915 and was a Moulder in the Pottery Industry. On 21 August 1915 Bullock was medically examined under the terms of an 'Application for Discharge of a Recruit as not likely to become an efficient soldier'. He was found to have flat fleet and could not march. However the application was rejected. He went to France on 12 November 1915 with the battalion and was promoted to Lance Corporal on 4 January 1918. He was the son of Hannah Maria and the late George Bullock. His mother was his next of kin and she lived at 25 Marsh Street, Longton. She received a Separation Allowance of 12 shillings and sixpence. She also received the photos and cards which were the personal effects of her son. By 25 June 1919 she had moved to New Street, Cheadle, Staffs.[35]

Lance Corporal G/40372 Reginald Morgan Daly, aged 37, was born in Hemel Hempstead, Herts. He married Susie Worsell on 12 August 1903 in East Grinstead. They had a son Reginald John born on 4 July 1904. They lived at 120 Whitley Road, Eastbourne. Daly enlisted in Eastbourne, Sussex on 9

November 1915. He was an Estate Agent's assistant, 6′ 4″ tall, had varicose veins in both legs, a hammer toe on his left foot and weighed 201 lbs. He was formerly G/12599 of the Royal Sussex Regiment, he transferred to the 16th Battalion Middlesex Regiment on 28 September 1916. He was promoted to Lance Corporal on 1 October 1916 and transferred to the 18th Middlesex on 8 February 1918. He was the son of Virginia and John Daly. His wife Susie received his personal effects of a wallet, photos and a disc. She was awarded a pension of 20 shillings and 5 pence for herself and her son with effect from 11 November 1918.[36] At probate his estate was valued at £3,932. 3s. 7d.

Sergeant P.S.1795 Edmund Thomas Etherton, aged 36, was born in Lewisham, Kent. He married Ethel Coppard from Dane Hill Uckfield on 8 September 1912. They had two children Ellen dob 23 March 1913 and Doris 5 June 1914 and they lived at 39 Hambro Road, Streatham, Surrey. He attested on 26 March 1915 in London and was a male nurse by profession. He was posted to the 16th Middlesex on 30 March 1915, he made the rank of Lance Corporal on 1 October 1916 and Corporal on 25 January 1917. He suffered a gunshot wound to his right forearm on 23 April 1917 which resulted in him being sent back to England and admitted to hospital. He was discharged from hospital on 1 October 1917 and posted to the 6th Middlesex. However he was back in hospital on 4 October 1917 where he had a cyst the size of a wren's egg removed from his right groin under local anaesthetic. He was discharged from hospital on 24 October 1917. On 22 January 1918 he rejoined the 16th Middlesex and he was made a Sergeant on 5 February 1918. He transferred to the 18th Middlesex on 8 February 1918. Mrs Etherton received 27 shillings in Separation Allowance and Attachment of pay. She was awarded a pension of 27 shillings and 11 pence for herself and her two children with effect from 18 November 1918. Following the death of her husband Mrs Etherton moved to North Woodlands Farm, Dane Hill, Uckfield, Surrey and she married William Tyrell in the 3rd quarter of 1919.[37]

Private P.W.798 John Hamilton was born in Littletown, Durham and enlisted in Hornsey, Middlesex. (Soldiers Died in the Great War p. 103 records that Private Hamilton lived in Ferry Hill Village, Staffordshire. However Ferryhill is in Durham). The 1911 Census has a John Hamilton living with his parents John and Elizabeth Hamilton at 5 Siemans Street, Dean Bank, in the Parish of Ferryhill, Durham. He was a coal mine underground labourer aged 15. He had served on the Western Front with the 18th Middlesex since 12 November 1915.[38]

Private G/89285 Hubert Charles Kent, aged 19, born in Bethnal Green,

Middlesex, lived in Deptford, Kent and enlisted in Camberwell, Surrey. He was the son of Walter Kent of 26 Grinstead Road, Deptford Park, Deptford, London.[39]

Private G/60502 Phillip Maguire, born in Fulham, lived in St. Pancras, Middlesex and enlisted in west London.[40]

Private T.F.315937 Sidney Parkhouse was born in Ashreigney, Chulmleigh, Devon in 1886. He lived 128 East Street, South Molton and was a baker by trade. He attested in Devon on 31 August 1916 aged 30. His medical on enlisting shows he was 5´ 0¾″ tall, weighed 118 lbs., and suffered from kyphosis (curvature of the spine). He was called up for service on 12 October 1916 and was posted to the 2/1st Hertfordshire Regiment. On 14 December 1916 he transferred to the 2/9th Middlesex and then to the 32nd Middlesex on 22 January 1917. He was posted to the 18th Middlesex on 19 December 1917 and joined the battalion on 21 December. He was the son of Ellen and Robert Parkhouse of Great Lee, Riddlecombe, Ashreigney, North Devon. His father was his next of kin and he received Sidney's personal effects of a diary, photo wallet, wallet, tin box containing a watch and strap and other photos.[41]

Private G/41278 Ernest Alfred Sharp, aged 22, born in Small Hythe and enlisted in Tenterden, Kent. He was the son of Charles Sharp of Ashenden, Small Hythe, Tenterden, Kent. He was formerly 7011 East Kent Regiment.[42]

Private G/57987 Harold Stewart Skinner was aged 18, born in Edmonton, and lived at 78 Coldback Buildings, Rosebery Avenue, Islington, Middlesex. He enlisted on 28 July 1917 in Whitehall, was 5´ 7½″ tall and weighed 130 lbs. He was posted to the 102nd Training Reserve on 29 July 1917. He transferred to the 250th Infantry Battalion in November 1917 and was promoted to unpaid Lance Corporal on 16 January 1918. He was posted to the 18th Middlesex on 5 April 1918 and embarked for France and reduced in rank back to private. He joined the 18th Middlesex in the field on 9 April 1918. He was wounded and missing 4 days later. He was the son of Annie and John Skinner of 46 Harman Street, Kingsland Road, Shoreditch, London.[43]

Corporal P.S.2166 John Edwin Smith, aged 27, born in Aston, Warwickshire, lived in Herne Hill and enlisted in Lambeth, Surrey. He was the son of Ada and John Smith of 22 Mayall Road, Herne Hill, London.[44]

Private G/21108 Frank Edward Stubbs M.M, aged 21, born in Hackney, lived in Leyton, Essex and enlisted in Mill Hill, Middlesex. He was the son of Annie Elizabeth and Henry Edward Stubbs of 21 Wilson Road, East Ham, London.[45]

Private P.W.3494 Frank Welch, born in Brighton, enlisted in Chichester, Sussex on 19 November 1915, a month short of his 34th birthday. He was a milkman by trade and he married his wife Florence Henrietta on 24 March 1907 in the Parish Church, Brighton. They lived at 38 Bute Street, Brighton and had three children Frank Edwin dob 27 March 1908, Robert George dob 7 January 1911 and Leslie Victor dob 7 May 1913. Private Welch was 5´ 2½″ tall and weighed 132 lbs. He was placed in the Army Reserve. He was mobilised on 3 June 1916 and posted to the 24th Middlesex. He transferred to the 5th Middlesex on 18 September 1916 and then to the 20th Middlesex on 29 November 1916. He was then posted to the 18th Middlesex on 9 December 1916 joining them in the field on 20 December 1916. Mrs Welch received a Separation Allowance of 28 shillings and was awarded a pension of 29 shillings and 7 pence for herself and three children with effect from 11 November 1918. By June 1918 Mrs Welch had moved to 43 Whippingham Road, Brighton.[46]

This was the bloodiest day so far in the history of the 18th Battalion Middlesex Regiment. Seventeen men were killed. This really was back-to-the-wall stuff for the miners' battalion.

The following message was received by the battalion from Lieutenant-General Sir Alexander Hamilton-Gordon, Commander of the IX Corps.

'aaa Ninth Corps Commander wishes to congratulate all ranks on the magnificent fighting qualities which they are displaying under very arduous conditions against heavy odds aaa Reinforcements are coming up to our assistance and the enemy has suffered very heavy losses in his attempts to break through the British Armies aaa The enemy will not succeed aaa The Royal Air Force to-day crashed 47 enemy aeroplanes of which 39 were on this battle front'.[47]

14 April. The 19th Infantry Brigade, including the 18th Battalion Middlesex Regiment, covered Méteren and had a particularly hard day being strongly attacked by the German 81st Reserve Division three times at 8am, 2pm and 7pm.[48]

The situation in the morning remained the same, with enemy attacks on and around Méteren. Reports were received that the Germans were massing near Bailleul.

Three platoons of 'A' Company picqueted the Appetite Farm – Méteren road. Appetite Farm was just over a mile east of Méteren village.

At 11am the Germans had occupied buildings at four points either side of the Strazeelle to Bailleul road south-west of Méteren. They then brought forward

machine guns into these houses and several light trench mortars came into action in the enclosures round them. Enemy infantry then began to gather south of Strazeele to Bailleul road between Brahmin Bridge and Alwyn Farm. They crawled forward in twos and threes and dug in on that line. They carried on a lively fight with British posts further north but made no effort to advance across the open.[49]

Immediately in front of the Germans on the Strazeele to Bailleul road were two platoons of the 18th Middlesex. They were in trenches astride the road running south from Les Ormes to the Strazeele to Bailleul road.

At 12.15pm the two platoons from the 18th Middlesex, having fired off most of their ammunition at small targets, and having come under machine gun fire from their left front, withdrew without warning and for no adequate reason. They suffered several casualties in doing so. Orders were issued for this trench line to be occupied at nightfall by the platoons that had left it. This was done.[50]

The rest of the battalion was relieved overnight from their positions in the front line.

The German 81st Reserve Division attack was eventually held up and it failed to get within 200 yards of the main British line. A counter-attack by the 2nd New Zealand Entrenching Battalion and the 33rd Battalion Machine-Gun Corps stopped the German advance. Méteren and the ridge it stands on were held. During their attack the Germans captured the Steam Mill but abandoned it overnight.[51]

Fourteen men were wounded. One of those men was Private Alfred Enoch Price. He was struck by a machine gun bullet in the lumber region of his back. This gunshot wound (GSW) penetrated his spine leaving his legs paralysed.[52]

Private G/1034 Arthur Brockett aged 36, born in Hornsey and attested in Willesden on 3 April 1915. He was a navvy by trade and married Connie (Constance Amy) Hookham at the Registry Office in Hendon on 3 May 1908. They had two children Hilda May dob 4 November 1908 and Cyril Arthur Frank dob 26 June 1916 and they lived at 47 Villiers Road, Willesden Green. He went to France with the battalion in November 1915. He was wounded on 5 October 1916 suffering a gunshot wound to the lower right jaw. He had two weeks leave in Calais from 4 February to 18 February 1918. His widow moved to live at The Dell, Chorley Wood, Hertfordshire in 1918. She received a Separation Allowance of 24 shillings and sixpence. She was also awarded a pension of 25 shillings and 5 pence with effect from 4 November 1918 for herself and her children. He is buried in the Méteren Military Cemetery.[53]

Private G/57947 Cyril Reginald Hoddinott, aged 18, born in Lawrence

Road, East Ham and enlisted in Stratford, Essex, died of his wounds. He was the son of Edith Alice and Reginald John J. Hoddinott of 431 Green Street, Upton Park, London. He is buried in the Godewaersvelde British Cemetery – Nord.[54]

Private 20817 Alexander Leo Humphrey, aged 32, born in the 2nd quarter of 1886 in St. Pancras and enlisted in Mill Hill, Middlesex, died of his wounds. He was the son of Charlotte and James Humphrey and the husband of Ada May Humphrey (nee Stead) of 234 Shirland Road, Paddington, London. The 1911 Census has Mr and Mrs Humphrey being married for 1 year. However they actually married on 3 January 1916 at St. Peter's Church, Cricklewood. At the time of their marriage they were living at 154 Cricklewood Lane. Private Humphrey was an electrician's mate by trade but had already joined the Army by the time of his marriage. They had one daughter Violet May born in the 2nd quarter of 1910. He is buried in the Haringhe (Bandaghem) Military Cemetery – Poperinghe, West-Vlaanderen.[55]

Private G/57967 Albert John Merhoff, born in Battersea on 3 July 1899, aged 18, died of his wounds. He was the son of Florence Ellen and Henry John Merhoff of 60 Estcourt Road, North End Road, Fulham, London. As a child he went to Battersea Park Road School being admitted on 14 May 1906. The admission entry shows his date of birth to be July 1900. At this time the Merhoff family were living at 41 Warriner Gardens, Battersea. Private Merhoff attested in West London on 30 September 1916, he was a gardener by trade, was 5´ 5″ tall and weighed 120 lbs. He was posted to the 102nd Training Reserve on 1 August 1917. He joined the 250th Infantry Battalion on 24 November 1917. He then moved onto 52nd (Grad.) Battalion Middlesex Regiment. On 5 April he left Folkestone and arrived in Boulogne and joined the 18th Middlesex in the field on 9 April. He suffered serious gunshot wounds to the chest and was admitted to the 2 Canadian Casualty Clearing Station where he died at 12.30pm. He had spent only 6 days at the front. He is buried in the Lijssenthoek Military Cemetery.[56]

2nd Lieut. Frederick Charles Wright, aged 25, was killed by shellfire. He was the son of Florence May (nee Burchell) and George Samuel Wright of 51 Boston Park Road, Brentford, Middlesex. His father was his next of kin and he worked as a superintendant with the Grand Western Railway at Brentford docks.

Frederick Wright attended Rothschild School Brentford and in civilian life was a Clerk with Messer's Heal and Sons. He was 5 feet and 10½ inches tall

and lived at 11 Francis Street, Gordon Square, London. He enlisted on 24 February 1913 and was posted as a rifleman to the 16th Battalion London Regiment. His Regimental number was 1522. He joined The Queen's Westminster Association on 24 July 1913. On 2 September 1914 Frederick Wright signed an agreement to serve outside the United Kingdom in the event of a national emergency.

He suffered a gunshot wound to the leg on 3 January 1915. He was promoted to Lance Corporal with pay on 27 March 1915. On 29 September 1915 he was promoted to Corporal. On 30 September 1915 he suffered an I.C.T. (either a inflamed connective tissue injury or internal cruciate tear) to the leg and was hospitalised in Boulogne. He was shipped back to England on 7 October. Back in service Wright was promoted to Lance Sergeant.

He transferred to the Officer Cadet Battalion at Oxford on 7 August 1916 and was appointed to a commission with the 3rd Special Reserve Battalion Middlesex Regiment on 1 December 1916.

He was then posted to the 18th Middlesex on 7 January 1917 as a 2nd Lieutenant and joined 'A' Company.

Mr George Samuel Wright received a telegram on 3 May 1918 from the Secretary of the War informing him that his son had been killed in action and offering the condolences of the Army Council. His personal effects included a wrist watch, one officers advance book, a leather case containing portraits, one leather pocket case, letters, post cards, one A.B. 439, photos etc. and overseas chevrons.

He was single and died without leaving a will. The gross value of his estate was £173. 1s. 2d.

His family was informed by the War Office that his body was buried 1,000 yards north of Méteren and south of Poperinghe and his grave was marked by a durable cross with an inscription bearing full details. He is buried in the Méteren Military Cemetery.[57]

The following three soldiers have their names on the Ploegsteert Memorial.

Private T.F.315104 Stanley Parrish James was killed in action aged 20. He was born on 26 November 1897, enlisted in Hornsey on 27 May 1915 aged 17 and was posted to the 4/7th Middlesex. He transferred to the 63rd Provisional Battalion on 22 January 1916, moved to the 32nd Middlesex on 1 January 1917 and was posted to the 18th Middlesex on 19 December 1917 and joined them in the field on 28 December. He was the son of Emily and John James of 116 Maryland Road, Wood Green, London.[59]

Private G/20322 Frederick Stanley Moore born in St. Helens, Suffolk, lived in Ipswich and enlisted in Bury St. Edmunds was killed in action.[60]

Private P.S.3457 Thomas Woolven, born in Cowfold in the 4th quarter of 1883 was killed in action. He attested on 10 December 1915 and was placed in the Army Reserve. He was a Farm Stockman by trade, he was 5´ 7½″ tall and weighed 127 lbs. He married Victoria Ida Ellen Johnson on 16 January 1909 at Steyning. They lived at Banfields Cottage, Parkminister, Partridge Green. They had two children Mary Jane dob 27 May 1909 and Maurice James dob 10 April 1912. Private Woolven was mobilised on 3 June 1916 and posted to the 24th Middlesex on 6 June 1916. He arrived in France on 20 October 1916, was posted to the 18th Middlesex on 5 November joining them in the field on 7 November 1916. Victoria Woolven received his personal effects of letters and photos on 28 July 1918. She received a pension of 25 shillings and 5 pence for herself and her two children with effect from 11 November 1918.[61]

1 33rd Division War Diary, National Archives, WO 95/2407
2 Edmonds, *Military Operations, France And Belgium 1918, Vol. 2*, p.121, p. 123, & p.p. 126-127
3 Ibid., p. p. 135-136
4 Barrie Pitt, *Purnell's History of the 20th Century, Vol. 4*, New Caxton Library Service Limited, London, 1972, p. 852; Asprey, *The German High Command At War*, p. 391
5 Edmonds, *Military Operations, France And Belgium 1918, Vol. 2*, p. p. 490-491
6 Ibid., Sketch Map 12 facing p. 111
7 33rd Division War Diary
8 Commonwealth War Graves Commission casualty details
9 Edmonds, *Military Operations, France And Belgium 1918, Vol. 2*, p. 163
10 Ibid., p. 150
11 Ibid., p. 164
12 Ibid., p. xxvii
13 Ibid., p. 184
14 Corporal James Knight British Army WW1 Pensions Records 1914-1920, National Archives, WO 364, Piece 2022
15 Edmonds, *Military Operations, France And Belgium 1918, Vol. 2*, p. 163
16 33rd Division War Diary
17 Edmonds, *Military Operations, France And Belgium 1918, Vol. 2*, p. 512
18 Ibid., p. 270
19 33rd Division War Diary
20 Ibid.
21 Ibid.

22 *Soldiers Died In The Great War 1914 -1919*, p. 103; Commonwealth War Graves Commission casualty details

23 Boraston (Editor), *Sir Douglas Haig's Despatches (December 1915 – April 1919)*, p. 229

24 33rd Division War Diary

25 1st Battalion Queen's Royal West Surrey Regiment Battalion War Diary, National Archives, WO/95/2422 Image Reference 1/478

26 1/5th Cameronians (Scottish Rifles) Battalion War Diary, National Archives, WO 95/2422, Image Reference 1/481

27 1st Queen's Battalion War Diary

28 33rd Division War Diary

29 Ibid.

30 *Soldiers Died In The Great War 1914 -1919*, p. 102; Commonwealth War Graves Commission casualty details

31 Ibid.; p. 103; London Metropolitan Archives, Saint Matthew, Essex Rod, Register of marriages, P83/MTW, Item 014; 1911 Census

32 Ibid.; London Metropolitan Archives, Camberwell Christ Church, Register of Baptism, p.73/ctc, Item 007

33 *Soldiers Died In The Great War 1914 -1919*, p. 104

34 Ibid.

35 Ibid., p. 102; Lance Corporal Bullock Army Service Record, National Archives, WO 363; 1911 Census

36 Ibid., p. 103

37 Ibid.; Sergeant Etherton Army Service Record, National Archives, WO 363; England and Wales Marriage Index 1837-1915; England and Wales Marriage Index 1915-2005

38 Ibid.; 1911 Census; British Army WW1 Medal Rolls Index Cards, 1914 -1920

39 Ibid.

40 Ibid.

41 Ibid., p. 104; Private Parkhouse Army Service Record, National Archives, WO 363; England & Wales Birth Index, 1837-1915; 1891 Census

42 Ibid.

43 Ibid.; Private Skinner Army Service Record, National Archives, WO 363

44 Ibid.

45 Ibid.

46 Ibid., p. 105; Private Welch Army Service Record, National Archives, WO 363

47 1/5th Cameronians (Scottish Rifles) Battalion War Diary

48 Edmonds, *Military Operations, France And Belgium 1918, Vol.* 2, p. 308

49 1st Queen's Battalion War Diary,

50 Ibid.

51 Edmonds, *Military Operations, France And Belgium 1918, Vol. 2*, p. 308

52 Private Price British Army WW1 Pension Records 1914 -1920

53 *Soldiers Died In The Great War 1914 -1919*, p. 102; Commonwealth War Graves

Commission casualty details; Private Brockett Army Service Record, National Archives, WO 363

54 *Soldiers Died In The Great War 1914 -1919*, p. 103; Commonwealth War Graves Commission casualty details; 1911 Census

55 Ibid.; 1911 Census; London Metropolitan Archives, Saint Peter, Cricklewood, Register of marriages, DRO/082, Item 009; England & Wales Birth Index 1837-1915

56 Ibid., p. 104; Private Merhoff Army Service Record, National Archives, WO 363; London Metropolitan Archives, School Admissions and Discharges 1840 -1911

57 Commonwealth War Graves Commission casualty details; 2nd Lieut. Wright Service Record, National Archives, WO 339/68725

58 *Soldiers Died In The Great War 1914 -1919*, p. 103; Commonwealth War Graves Commission casualty details; London Metropolitan Archives, Camberwell St. George, Register of Baptism, p. 73/geo, Item 008; Private James Army Service Record, National Archives, WO 363

59 Ibid.

60 Ibid., p. 105 (The book has his name as Woolman, C.W.C.G. has it as Woolven); Private Woolven Army Service Record, National Archives, WO 363

CHAPTER NINE

11th April 1918 to 20th April 1918

Defence of Méteren
Bailleul
Mont des Cats

On 11 April 1918 the 2nd Battalion Worcestershire Regiment of the 33rd Division took over a section of the front line east of Neuve Église. On 12 April German troops launched an all out attack on the village and broke through on the right flank of the line. The enemy was rejected and the line restored. However early in the morning on 13 April the enemy attacked again and reached Neuve Église village. An immediate counter-attack by the 2nd Worcestershires forced the Germans out of the village annihilating the enemy in the village and destroying their machine guns.

At 6pm the enemy attacked again on the left in great numbers forcing the 2nd Worcestershires back. The Battalion Headquarters was moved into the Mairie in the village and set up as a strong point. During the night the Germans launched wave after wave against the 2nd Worcestershires and Battalion H.Q. lost contact with its left sector.

At dawn on 14April the enemy occupied Neuve Église in strength and the Mairie was completely surrounded by 8am. 2nd Lieut. Johnson volunteered to try and make his way through to Brigade and report the situation. His gallant attempt was unsuccessful and he did not return.

A Lewis gun was posted in an upstairs window and every available sniper was placed in a position of observation. 2nd Lieut. Turley directed rifle grenade fire on the out buildings of the Mairie, the adjacent houses and the roads.

This well directed defence cleared the rear of the Mairie. The Germans withdrew to the high ground on the right and to the vicinity of the church in the village centre. Nevertheless the position of the Battalion H.Q. in the Mairie was under considerable threat and the rear of the building had to be kept clear.

2nd Lieut. Crowe volunteered to take a small party and clear the rear of the Mairie. On reaching the road Crowe's party were met by sniper fire and a hostile party with a machine gun. 2nd Lieut. Crowe drove off the Germans to the high ground. Crowe and his men pressed forward and forced the Germans from the high ground into the village where Crowe followed them and opened fire upon the enemy as they collected in the doorways of the houses.[1]

2nd Lieut. Crowe then left two N.C.O.s and five men to guard the road. With two men he worked round the outer flank of the high ground and he attacked two machine guns which were sweeping the post. Crowe killed both gunners with his rifle and prevented any others from reaching their guns and bringing them into action. He then turned upon a party of the enemy who were lined up in front of him. He killed several of them and the remainder withdrew at once. He captured both guns, one of which was the 2nd Worcestershire's Lewis gun which had been captured by the enemy on the previous day. [2]

A line of defence was established close to the crest of the high ground, a strong point created on the road and communications maintained with Battalion H.Q. at the Mairie.

The enemy withdrew to the centre of the village where they regrouped.

At 1.30pm German troops were observed from the top windows of the Mairie moving forward in fours. The Mairie came under a barrage of trench mortar, machine gun and rifle fire.

The 2nd Worcestershires earlier call for reinforcements had not been answered. The men on the high ground could not hold their ground if attacked in force and the Battalion H.Q. at the Mairie was once again in danger of being completely surrounded.

At 1.45am Major G.J.L. Stoney M.C., 2nd in Command of the 2nd Worcestershires, in order to save the Battalion H.Q. and regain touch with their troops on either flank, gave the order to evacuate the Mairie and fall back to the railway where British troops had already taken up their positions. [3]

2nd Lieut. Crowe made his way to the men in position on the high ground and the post on the road and instructed them to cover the withdrawal. The withdrawal of the entire garrison and also the covering party was achieved without loss. Three men severely wounded prior to the evacuation had their wounds treated and were left in the cellar of the Mairie.

2nd Lieut. John James Crowe aged 41 was awarded the Victoria Cross 'for conspicuous bravery, determination and skilful leadership...Throughout the seven days of operations 2nd Lieut. Crowe showed an utter disregard of danger

and was recklessly brave. His personal example and cheerfulness contributed largely to the determination of the garrison of the post to hold out. It may safely be said that but for his coolness and skill at the last moment, when he personally placed the covering party in close proximity to the enemy, who were again closing round, and were also forming up in fours nearby, the garrison of the post could never have effected its escape. The valour and zeal displayed by 2nd Lieut. Crowe were of the highest order'.[4]

15 April. The 1/5th Cameronians and half of 'A' Company 18th Middlesex holding the line south of Méteren were relieved and moved to Fontaine Houck.[5]

Three platoons of the battalion were posted north of the main Bailleul Road. The remainder of the battalion rested during the day. (The 33rd Division War Diary records that at 8.15am the 18th Battalion Middlesex Regiment had two companies at the Axe Mill Windmill on the Méteren to Fontaine Houck road and one company with the 1st Cameronians).[6]

At 3.10am the Division was informed that reports from prisoners stated the enemy intended to make further attacks on Bailleul that day.[7]

The battalion received 19th Infantry Brigade Order 334 which was cancelled verbally. Divisional Order 296 for the relief of the battalion and placing it in the divisional reserve at Berthen was not received by the battalion.

At 2.50pm information from a prisoner captured by the 1st Cameronians indicated that the enemy was likely to attack the right front and Strazeele was the immediate target.[8]

At 5pm the Germans gained some high ground north of Bailleul.

At 7.50pm Divisional Order 296 amended was issued. The 2nd Battalion Argyll and Sutherland Highlanders were instructed to stand fast and not relieve the troops in the line from south of Méteren Veld to Steam Mill.[9]

Acting under orders issued by the 19th Infantry Brigade the 18th Middlesex manned the Méteren – St. Jans Cappel Switch Line and reinforced the 5th Tank Battalion. The 5th Tank Battalion held the front with Lewis guns. The battalion deployed behind the Tank Battalion in the switch line south of Méteren Veld to the north of Blauvenlandt and south of St. Jans Cappel.[10] These 19th Infantry Brigade orders were the only ones received before the night of the 16th.

Six men were wounded.

Sergeant P.W.1296 William Till M.M., aged 37, born and lived in Longton

The grave of Sergeant William Till M.M. Haringhe (Bandaghem) Military Cemetery

and enlisted in Stoke-on-Trent, Staffs, died of his wounds. He was the son of Sarah and John Till of Longton and the husband of Harriet Maria Till of 228 Uttoxeter Road, Longton, Stoke-on-Trent. He is buried in the Haringhe (Bandaghem) Military Cemetery.[11]

By 9pm the Germans took the smouldering and ruined village of Bailleul. British troops were compelled to fall back to positions between Méteren and Dranoutre. Overnight British troops completed their withdrawal from Passchendaele Ridge taking up positions along the line of the Steenbeek River and the Westhoek and Wytschaete Ridges.[12] Passchendaele Ridge had been won at an enormous cost over many months of desperate fighting in the most appalling conditions. Haig had been forced to give it up in a day.[13]

16 April. Early in the morning the New Zealand Rifles were ordered to withdraw through the Méteren – St. Jans Cappel Switch Line held by the 18th Middlesex and the 5th Tank Battalion. The right flank of front line in the switch line fell back with them.

At 9.40am the Germans gained a footing in Méteren. The 18th Battalion right company made a brave attempt to halt them but failed, suffering very

heavy casualties.[14] The Germans made strong local attacks along the Méteren – Wytschaete Line and broke through establishing positions in both villages.

The 4th Battalion King's (Liverpool) Regiment had been deployed in the Passchendaele sector on the left of the 33rd Division front line from the 6 to 9 March. They were bombarded with gas shells and suffered twenty-two casualties. After five days rest in St. Jean Camp they returned to the front on the 15th. On 20th they were raided by the enemy and two other ranks were killed, four wounded and two missing. On 27 March they relieved the 1st Queen's in support in Hamburg. They were relieved on 3 April by the Royal Guernsey Militia and moved to the rest area at Brandhoek. On the 11 April the train they were travelling in, back to the front, was hit by German artillery fire and 35 men were killed. On 13 April they were deployed to Méteren to support the 19th Infantry Brigade.

On 16th the 4th King's were engaged along the road running south from Méteren. They had the 1/5th Cameronians on their right and troops from the Tank Corps on their left. The Tank Corps troops fell back. Two platoons were sent to fill the gap but were prevented by a German attack. The right stood firm. The left fell back to the line through Méteren and 'C' Company 4th King's practically disappeared. They had a further twenty-six men killed.[15]

Under Operation Georgette by nightfall on 16 April the German's had gained Armentières, Bailleul, Merris, Merville, Messines, Méteren, Neuf Berquin, Neuve Église, Nieppe, Outtersteene, Vieux Berquin and Wytschaete. They were in position to attack the strategic and commanding heights of Mont Kemmel.[16]

Thirty-five men of 18th Middlesex were wounded, 5 of whom remained at duty.

The following eleven soldiers were killed in action and their names are on the Ploegsteert Memorial.

Private T.F.242359 (formerly 7724) Leonard Frederick Ayres, aged 19, was born in Cheltenham, Gloucestershire and lived at Firland Villa, St. Thomas's Terrace, Wells, Somerset. He was a hairdresser by trade and he enlisted in Taunton on 3 March 1916. During a medical at the Military Hospital York on 16 March he was found to have poor physical development and an I.C.T. on his right foot. He was 5′ 4″ tall and weighed 106 lbs. He was called up for service on 22 April and posted to the Somerset Light Infantry the next day. He transferred to the 3/10th Middlesex on 4 May 1916 and onto the 1/8th Middlesex on 30 November and left Folkestone for France on the same day. He was posted

to T.F. Depot on 20 January 1917 and then to the 7th Middlesex on 24 January. He returned home to England on 20 April 1917. He was sent back to France on 5 December 1917 rejoining 1/8th Middlesex. He moved to the 16th Middlesex on 9 December and then joined the 18th Middlesex on 8 February 1918. He was a third class shot. He was the son of Elizabeth Isabella and James Ayres of 36 Marle Hill Parade, Cheltenham.[17]

Private G/52684 John Henry Barry, aged 19, born in Clapton Park lived at 21 Pedro Street, Clapham Park, London. He enlisted in Stratford, Essex on 16 September 1916 aged 17 years and 11 months. During a medical at Stratford on 10 February 1917 he was found to be in good condition. He was a leather case maker by trade, was 5′ 6½″ tall and weighed 120 lbs. On 23 November he was posted to the Base Depot and embarked for France. He was transferred to 3/10th Middlesex on 25 November 1917. He was posted to the 18th Middlesex on 6 March 1918 and joined the battalion in the field on 9 March. He was reported wounded and missing on 16 April 1918. He was the son of Elizabeth Barry of 10 Lockhurst Street, Clapton Park, London.[18]

Lieut. Harry Pendry Boreham, aged 28, was killed by rifle fire. He was the son of Emma and Harry White Boreham of Coverdale, Lowe Park Road, Hastings. His father Harry White Boreham received a telegram on 22 April stating 'Deeply regret 2nd/Lt. H.P. Boreham Middlesex Regiment Killed in Action April sixteenth. The Army Council expresses sympathy' (Boreham was promoted to Lieutenant on 26 March 1918). Probate sent Mr Boreham senior £107. 8s. 6d. settling the estate of his late son. Death duties were remitted.[19]

2nd Lieut. Harry Claude Bradbury was killed by shellfire. Harry Bradbury was born on 22 July 1894. His father lived at 44 Strawberry Hill Road, Twickenham. Harry was a clerk in his father's business before joining up. He attested on 23 September 1914 and was posted to 1/5th Battalion London Regiment where he attained the rank of Lance Corporal. He was nominated for a commission in the 23rd Battalion Middlesex Regiment on 3 July 1916 and accepted for admission to No 7 Officer Cadet Battalion to join at The Curragh. He received his commission 25 October 1916 and was posted to the 23rd Middlesex on 8 November 1916. He transferred to the 18th Middlesex on 18 December 1916. He spent two weeks from the 14 to 28 March 1918 with the London Rifles and then rejoined the 18th Middlesex.

2nd Lieut. Bradbury's personal effects were sent to his father and they included 1 portrait, 1 leather purse, 1 small leather photo case and photos, 1 Advance book, 1 Cheque book, 1 letter and a farthing. He left the whole of his

estate worth £577 and 14 shilling to his step mother and because she was not a blood relative her inheritance was not exempt from death duties.[20]

Private P.W.202 James Cheek was born in Quebec, Durham on 1 June 1884. He married Mary Jane Slater on 16 November 1908 in Lanchester, County Durham. They had four children James dob 25 January 1909, Charles dob 25 September 1910, Margaret Rachel dob 23 December 1913 and Georgina dob 3 November 1917. They lived at 22 Hallgarth Terrace, Ferryhill village, County Durham. James Cheek enlisted in Ferryhill on 27 February 1915. He was miner by trade and was posted to the 18th Middlesex. His medical showed he had dental defects that required treatment. He was 5´ 2½″ tall and weighed 145 lbs.

On 10 September 1915 he overstayed his pass until 8am. He was reported by Sergeant Lynch, admonished by Captain Hill and he forfeited 2 day pay, rations and water. He arrived in France on 14 November 1915 with the battalion. On 22 November he was admitted to the 21st Field Ambulance with pediculosis (body lice) and was discharged 2 days later. On 17 October 1916 he was admitted to the 43 Casualty Clearing Station with piles. On 21 October he was transferred to the 3 Canadian General Hospital at Boulogne. On 23 October he was taken back to England on H.M.H.S. St. Denis. Cheek was posted to 6th Middlesex on 30 December 1916.

On 4 May 1917 he returned to France and rejoined the 18th Middlesex in the field on 2 June 1917. On 19 October 1917 he was admitted to the 19th Field Ambulance with influenza, was discharged on 25 October and returned to duty. He was admitted to the 99th Field Ambulance on 13 November transferred on the same day to the 101st Field Ambulance. On 19 November he was taken back to the 99th Field Ambulance and discharged on 25 November. He rejoined the 18th Middlesex on 13 December 1917. From the 1 March 1918 Cheek had 2 weeks leave.

Mrs Cheek was awarded a pension of £1. 13s. 9d. for herself and 4 children with effect from 25 November 1918.[21]

Sergeant G/8862 William Eastgate was born in and enlisted in Derby.[22]

Private G/50845 John Edward Ellsey, aged 20, was born and enlisted in Brighton, Surrey. His parents were Alice and John Henry Ellsey of 83 Bonchurch Road, Brighton.

Lance Corporal 291488 John Henry Ellsey also served in World War 1. He attested in Whitehall on 18 August 1915 aged 41 years and 6 months. He was well sinker by trade. He was posted to the Royal Engineers Labour Corps and whilst he served with them his Regimental number was 115765. Only a week

later, on 25 August, Mr Ellsey senior embarked for France. He transferred to the Labour Corps 708 Labour Company on 31 July 1917. On 25 January 1919 he proceeded to England for demobilisation and transferred to the Z Army Reserve on 23 February 1919.[23]

Private G/23226 Frederick William Fowle, aged 25, was born and lived in Appledore. He enlisted in Canterbury. He was the son of Sarah and Albert Fowle of Court Lodge Road, Appledore, Kent.[24]

Private G/40239 George Frederick Gladman, aged 21, was born and lived in Hounslow, Middlesex. He enlisted in Ealing, Middlesex. He was the son of Mary Ann and John Charles Gladman of 9 Clarence Terrace, Hanworth Road, Hounslow.[25]

Lance Corporal P.W.228 James Hinson of 'A' Company, aged 30, was born and lived in Wood Green, Middlesex. He enlisted in Mill Hill, Middlesex. He was the son of Esther and Walter Hinson of 12 Grainger Road, Lordship Lane, Wood Green, London, and the husband of Rosina Hinson (nee Herbert) of 56 Acacia Road, Lordship Lane, Wood Green, London.[26]

Sergeant P.W.882 George Lewis M.M., aged 31, was born in Cranford, Middlesex and enlisted in Birmingham on 26 March 1915 aged 28 years and 180 days. He lived at Rowton House, Allcester Street Birmingham, was a navvy by trade, had a mole on his left breast, was 5´ 2½″ tall and weighed 140 lbs. He was posted to 19th Middlesex on 26 March and transferred to 18th Middlesex on 28 March. He travelled to France with the battalion 12 November 1915. He was promoted to Acting Lance Corporal on 1 June 1915, Lance Corporal on 5 June 1915 and Acting Corporal on 26 June 1915. On 9 July 1915 he reverted to the rank of Private for inefficiency and mulcted (fined) 7 day's pay.

He was once again promoted to Lance Corporal on 18 December 1915, made Corporal 21 July 1916, made Lance Sergeant on 28 October 1916 and Sergeant on 12 November 1916. Whilst he held the rank of Corporal he elected 'under A.C.1. 1632 of 1916 to claim the 2d per day authorised for pioneer battalions under the conditions of War Office letter 30/Gen No/3593 (A.G.1.) of 3rd December 1916'.

He was awarded the Military Medal for Gallantry in the Field and Gazetted on 17 December 1917. Following the death of Sergeant Lewis there was an exchange of letters between i/c No 1 Infantry Record Office Hounslow and Mrs Emily Wells of 13 Harvist Road, Holloway, London regarding the disposal of his medals and personal effects. The Record Office wanted to know what her relationship was to Lewis. She informed the Record Office that she was to

be his future wife. She received his personal effects of a medal ribbon and wallet. She also received Sergeant Lewis's medals including the Military Medal.[27]

The following four soldiers were killed in action and are buried in the Méteren Military Cemetery.

Private T.F.315067 John Thomas Cook, aged 39, was born in Leighton Buzzard, Bedfordshire and enlisted in Northampton. He was coal carter by trade and was the son of Mr and Mrs George Cook of Leighton Bromswold, Hunts. He married Edith Mary Lenton on 24 April 1905. They lived at 6 Carlton Street, Kettering and had a daughter Gladys Mary dob 13 July 1911.[28]

Private F/120 Charles William Luker, aged 42, born in Stepney on 2 April 1876, lived in Hackney, enlisted in Kingsway, Middlesex. He was a barman/servant by trade. He was the son of Elizabeth and Henry Luker of 86 Mayola Road, Lower Clapham, London.[29] His brother Lance Corporal 493719 Chris Arthur Luker served with the 13th Kensington Battalion of the London Regiment and was killed in action on 30 October 1917 and his name is recorded on the Tyne Cot memorial. Both their parents were Licensed Victuallers and their mother Elizabeth was born in St. Anne's Bay Jamaica in 1854.[30]

Private P.W.369 Alfred James Peacock, aged 40, enlisted in Deptford, Kent. He was the son of Margaret Jane and George Peacock of Dartford, Kent. He was a labourer by trade, he married Eliza Ann Cutter on 11 October 1903 and they lived at 28 Watergate Street, Deptford. They had three children by 1911 George aged 7, Frank 3 and Violet 1. At some point between 1911 and 1918 Mrs Peacock moved to 49 Armada Street, Deptford, London.[31]

Private T.F.315368 Walter Edwin Searle, aged 33, was born and enlisted in Chelsea, Middlesex. He lived in Battersea and was a Civil Servant, Senior Clerk with the Crown Agents. He was the only son of Sarah and Henry Charles Searle of 23 Anhalt Road, Battersea, London.[32]

Mont des Cats

17 April. The battalion was relieved at 3am by the 2nd Battalion Argyll and Sutherland Highlanders. The battalion route marched to the Convent des Trappistes at Mont des Cats and arrived at 7am. Here they came under the orders of the 98th Infantry Brigade and were placed in the divisional reserve.

Captured German Operation Orders showed that an extensive attack by the 81st Reserve Division, in conjunction with other Divisions of the Sixth German

Army, was to be made all along the 33rd Division front line on the morning of 17 April. The leading waves of the German attack were unable to leave their positions because of the intensity of British artillery and machine gun fire starting at 10.30am. The attack was completely repulsed.[33]

At 11.40pm a congratulatory message was received by the 33rd Division from Army and Corps Commanders thanking troops for their magnificent behaviour in recent fighting.[34]

Sergeant P.W.790 James Henry Heath was awarded the Distinguished Conduct Medal in the 1918 New Years Honours List. The citation for his award, published in the London Gazette, reads 'For conspicuous gallantry and devotion to duty, and consistent good work during a long period. He has maintained a high standard of discipline and efficiency among his men, and has always shown great skill and determination at his work'.[35]

Sergeant Heath was born in 1874 and was a regular soldier only being discharged on 17 January 1914. He was a navvy by trade and married Mary Elizabeth Jane Best on 18 December 1896. They lived at 92 Clarendon Road, Hove. They had six children. Heath re-enlisted on 23 March 1915 and served continually with 18th Middlesex and was finally discharged on 4 April 1919 having served 4 years and 14 days. He received the 1914-15 Star, the British War Medal and the Victory Medal. He decided against having a public presentation of his D.C.M.[36]

Sergeant P.W.881 William T. Williams was also awarded the D.C.M. in the New Years Honours List and his citation reads 'For conspicuous gallantry and devotion to duty and consistent good work during a long period. He has always shown great skill and energy at his work, and on many occasions his personal example and contempt of danger have inspired his men to carry out difficult tasks under trying circumstances'.[37] Sergeant Williams also received the 1914-1915 Star, British War Medal and Victory Medal.[38]

The Germans attacked the commanding feature of Kemmel Hill. The assault was launched after a preliminary bombardment of great intensity, and was accompanied by strong attacks in the Méteren and Merris sectors. The attacks on Kemmel Hill were completely repulsed by troops of the 34th, 49th and 19th Divisions. The attacks on Méteren and Merris sectors were beaten off by the 33rd Division and the 1st Australian Division. [39]

The 4th Battalion King's (Liverpool) Regiment defended the road running south from Méteren. At 6pm the Germans attacked the headquarters of 'D' Company 4th Battalion King's Regiment which was a farm on the British front

line west of Méteren. A conference of five officers was taking place at the time of the attack. The Germans succeeded in surrounding the farm and Captain and Battalion Adjutant G.H.E. Warburton M.C. and Intelligence Officer 2nd Lieut. G.C. Gibb were killed trying to fight their way out. The other three officers were captured. The farm was recaptured by a French counter-attack and the front line restored.

Overnight on the 18 March the remnants of the 4th King's were relieved and marched to camp at Boeschepe. Their casualties in defending the Méteren Road between 15 and 18 April were 20 officers and 469 other ranks killed, missing or wounded.[40]

18 April. The battalion started work on digging and wiring a defensive line to the east of Mont des Cats.

Mont des Cats had to be held at all costs. Loosing this high ground would have forced the British to retreat completely from the Ypres salient and the Yser position. This in turn would have cut the British Army off from the channel ports and its most vital supply lines.

The battalion received Divisional Order 297 at 2.20pm for the withdrawal of all French troops of 133rd Infantry Division from 33rd Division area on the night of 18/19 April. This order was cancelled at 3.20pm.[41]

Private P.W.1124 Alfred Enoch Price arrived back in England having suffered a serious gunshot wound in his spine earlier in April.[42]

19 April. A prisoner captured by 1st Australian Division stated that the enemy intended to attack between Méteren and Strazeele at 5am. A prisoner captured by the French also stated that the enemy were to attack the front held by the 2nd Argyll and Sutherland Highlanders at the same time. The 33rd Division Artillery took counter-preparations and the enemy attacks did not materialise.[43]

The battalion worked furiously on defensive lines in front of Mont des Cats.

A congratulatory telegram from Belgian H.Q. was forwarded to all units.[44]

Divisional Order 298 was received at 6pm for the relief of the 33rd Division by 1st Australian Division. Divisional Order 299 instructed the 33rd Division to transfer to the VIII Corps area by route march from Monts des Cats to the Staple area.[45]

One man was wounded.

Sergeant G/7447 Gilbert Thomas Stevens, aged 37, born in Rockbeare, Devon and enlisted in Tottenham, Middlesex, died of his wounds. He served

with the 2nd Royal West Kent Regiment during the Boer War and served in the Great War for two years and four months. He was the son of Emmie and George Stevens and the husband of Rebecca Caroline Stevens (nee Beauchamp) of 63 Barbot Street, Lower Edmonton, London. He is buried in the Wimereux Communal Cemetery – Pas de Calais.[46]

20 April. The battalion received Divisional Order 299 at 2.15am. As a result the battalion left the Mont des Cats area at 8am and proceeded by route march to the VIII Corps area at Staple.

Private 50600 Maurice Wicker, aged 34, born in Halstead and enlisted in Warley, Essex, died of his wounds. He was a brewer carman by trade and the son of Sarah and Walter Wicker. He married Ada Howlett in the first quarter of 1908 at Bethnal Green. By 1911 they had two daughters Edna aged 3 and Sybil aged 2 and they lived at 66 Tidings Hill, Halstead, Essex. He is buried in the Wimereux Communal Cemetery.[47]

Between 11 and 20 April the 33rd Division had 30 officers and 425 other ranks killed. 77 officers and 1,386 other ranks were wounded. 38 officers and 1,491 other ranks were missing.[48]

Major-General Pinney recorded that 'At the risk of losing a few 18 Pdrs., forward guns should always be used. The sudden opening fire of a field gun at close range has a most demoralising effect on the enemy and the opposite effect on our troops.

These operations once more and, it is hoped, finally decided that the rifle and bayonet are the infantry weapons. Too much time can never be devoted to musketry. The enemy never waits for cold steel'.[49]

1 2nd Battalion Worcestershire Regiment War Diary
2 Sixth Supplement To The London Gazette, Tuesday 25th June, 1918, Published 28th June 1918, Gazette Issue 30770, p.p. 7618-7619
3 2nd Battalion Worcestershire Regiment War Diary
4 Sixth Supplement To The London Gazette, Tuesday 25th June, 1918, Gazette Issue 30770 p.p. 7618-7619
5 1/5th Cameronians (Scottish Rifles) Battalion War Diary
6 33rd Division War Diary
7 Ibid.
8 Ibid.
9 Ibid.

10 Ibid.

11 *Soldiers Died In The Great War 1914 -1919*, p. 104; Commonwealth War Graves Commission casualty details

12 Boraston (Editor), *Sir Douglas Haig's Despatches (December 1915 – April 1919)*, p. 229

13 Edmonds, *Military Operations, France And Belgium 1918, Vol. 2*, Sketch Map 21 opposite p. 285

14 Everard Wyrall, *The Die-Hards in the Great War, Vol. 2*, p. 230

15 4th King's (Liverpool) Regiment Battalion War Diary, National Archives, WO95/2427, Image Reference 456; *Soldiers Died In The Great War 1914 -1919*, Part 13. King's (Liverpool Regiment), J.B. Haywood & Son, Suffolk, 1989

16 Boraston (Editor), *Sir Douglas Haig's Despatches (December 1915 – April 1919)*, p.p. 222-230

17 *Soldiers Died In The Great War 1914 -1919*, p. 102; Commonwealth War Graves Commission casualty details; Private Ayres Army Service Record, National Archives, WO 363; 1911 Census

18 Ibid.; Private Barry Army Service Record, National Archives, WO 363

19 2nd Lieut. Boreham Service Record; Supplement to London Gazette 6th February 1917, Published 7th February 1917, Gazette Issue 29932, p. 1348; Commonwealth War Graves Commission casualty details; British Army Medal Roll Index Card 1914-1920

20 2nd Lieut. Bradbury Service Record, National Archives, WO 339/57983; 2nd Supplement to the London Gazette, 26th January 1917, Published 27th January 1917, Gazette Issue 29922, p. 1034; Commonwealth War Graves Commission casualty details

21 *Soldiers Died In The Great War 1914 -1919*, p. 102; Commonwealth War Graves Commission casualty details; Private Cheek Army Service Record, National Archives, WO 363

22 Ibid., p. 103

23 Ibid.; Lance Corporal John Henry Ellsey Army Service Record, National Archives, WO 363

24 *Soldiers Died In The Great War 1914 -1919*, p. 103; Commonwealth War Graves Commission casualty details

25 Ibid.

26 Ibid.

27 Ibid.; Sergeant Lewis Army Service Record, National Archives, WO 363; Third Supplement to The London Gazette 14th December 1917, Published 17th December 1917, Gazette Issue 30431, p. 13192

28 Ibid.

29 Ibid.; 1911 Census

30 Commonwealth War Graves Commission casualty details; 1901 Census

31 *Soldiers Died In The Great War 1914 -1919*, p. 104; Commonwealth War Graves Commission casualty details; London Metropolitan Archives, Woolwich St. Mary

Magdalene, Register of Baptism, p97/mry/ Item 084; London Metropolitan Archives, St. Nicholas, Deptford, Register of marriages, p78/NIC, Item 032; 1911 Census

32 *Soldiers Died In The Great War 1914 -1919*, p. 104; Commonwealth War Graves Commission casualty details; 1911 Census

33 33rd Division War Diary Narrative on Operations carried out by 33rd Division less artillery April 5 – April 20

34 33rd Division War Diary

35 Third Supplement to the London Gazette 16th April 1918, Published 17th April 1918, Gazette Issue 30636, p.p. 4666-4667

36 Sergeant Heath Army Service Record, National Archives, WO 363

37 Third Supplement to the London Gazette 16th April 1918, p. 4691

38 British Army Medal Rolls Index Card 1914 -1920

39 Boraston (Editor), *Sir Douglas Haig's Despatches (December 1915 – April 1919),* p. 230

40 4th King's (Liverpool) Regiment Battalion War Diary

41 33rd Division War Diary, Divisional Order 297

42 Price Army Service Record

43 33rd Division War Diary

44 Ibid.

45 33rd Division War Diary, Divisional Orders 298-299

46 *Soldiers Died In The Great War 1914 -1919*, p. 104; Commonwealth War Graves Commission casualty details; England & Wales Marriage Index, 1837-1915

47 Ibid., p. 105; England & Wales Marriage Index 1837-1915; 1911 Census

48 33rd Division War Diary

49 33rd Division War Diary, Narrative of Operations carried out by 33rd Division less artillery April 5 – April 20

CHAPTER TEN

21st April 1918 to 2nd June 1918

Front line in Flanders
German Spring offensives
Operation Georgette and Operation Blücher

Staple

21 April 1918. The French Prime Minister Georges Clemenceau inspected representative troops of the 33rd Division at les Trois Rois, south-west of Bavinchove. Lt.-Col. McNeile, two officers and fifty other ranks represented the battalion at the inspection. The remnants of the 4th King's were in attendance.

Captain Paul Gottlieb Julius Gueterbock of the Gloucestershire Regiment temporarily took over the duties of General Staff Officer 2nd Grade 33rd Division from Lieut.-Col. H. C. Sparling D.S.O. of the Queen's Regiment.[1]

The Red Baron, Captain Manfred von Richthofen, first of the great German Aerial Chaser Formations ('Circus') with eighty victims to his name, was killed in action.[2] He was shot down by Canadian airman Roy Brown.

Private 3075 Charles Smart, who was seriously wounded with a fractured spine on 14 April 1918, died of his wounds. He attested on 25 May 1915 and was carman by trade. On enrolment he stated he had been married to Catherine Clarissa Smart (nee Davis) for four years. In fact at the time of his enlistment they were only living together at 80 Hythe Park Road, Staines, Middlesex and Catherine's surname was Nethercliff Ing. She had married Frederick Charles Ing on 14 February 1892 at St Marys Church Staines and they lived at 9 George Street, Staines. They had two children Albert Adolphus Ing dob 25 February 1892 and Catherine Carissa Annie Ing dob 29 May 1895.

By the census on 31 March 1901 Katherine Davis (Catherine Clarissa Nethercliff Ing) was living with John Davis at 33 Alexandra Road, Ealing. They had a daughter Winifred Elizabeth Ethel dob 3 April 1901.

Frederick Charles Ing filed for divorce in 1907 on the grounds of his wife's adultery and co-habiting with a Charles Snelling at Penns Cottage, Adelaide Road, Ashford. The divorce became final on 20 January 1908.

By the census on 2 April 1911 Clarissa Smart (Catherine Clarissa Nethercliff Ing) was living with Charles Smart at Penns Cottage, Adelaide Road, Ashford Middlesex with Catherine's two daughters Annie (Catherine Carissa) and Winifred. On 25 April 1911 Catherine gave birth to Charley Edmund Smart. She actually married Charley Smart on 19 December 1917 in Windsor whilst he was home on leave.

Smart was posted to the 19th Middlesex on attestation, he transferred to the 25th Middlesex on 7 August 1915. On 25 September 1915 he left his guard and remained absent from 4pm until 10pm, and he struck an N.C.O. He was sentenced to 14 days detention by Lt.-Col. Ward. He transferred to 18th Middlesex on 13 January 1916 and joined them in the field in France on 7 February. He then transferred to 285th Area Employment Company, Labour Corps on 20 September 1917 and had the Army number 396866. Whilst serving with the 285th Area Employment Corps he was found guilty of drinking in a Cafe during prohibited hours at 11.20am contrary to General Routine Order (GRO) 1661 and he forfeited 2 days pay.

Mrs Smart received 19 shillings and sixpence Separation Allowance and was awarded a pension of 21 shillings and eight pence for herself and 1 child with effect from 4 November 1918. She also received Charley Smart's personal effects of a bag, 1 pipe lighter, 2 pipes, 1 gold ring, 1 metal ring, 1 camping knife, note book, photos, letters and 1 oil bottle. He is buried in the St. Sever Cemetery Extension, Rouen – Seine-Maritime.[3]

22 April. The battalion had their kit and equipment inspected. Items lost or destroyed in action were replaced.

2nd Lieut. Clifford Cooper aged 21, died of his wounds. He was the son of Sarah Ann and Edward Charles Cooper of 49 Spring Bank, Hull. He was 5 feet 9½ inches tall and a bank clerk in civilian life. At the age of 19 years and 3 months he went to the Central Hull Recruiting Office to enlist on 24 January 1916 and his attestation was witnessed by 2nd Lt. Stanley Thompson. Between then and 5 July 1916 he served with the 26th, 31st and 1st Battalions Royal Fusiliers where he reached the rank of Lance Corporal.

Whilst serving with the 31st Royal Fusiliers Private 23613 Cooper left a will, which he signed on 28 August 1916. In the event of his death he left his Roll

Top Desk and £5 to his father. He gave the remaining balance standing to his account at the London City & Midland Bank Hull to his mother.

He was recommended for a commission by Major-General Sir John Capper, Commanding Officer of the 24th Division. He joined the Officer Cadet Battalion on 6 July 1917. He joined the 18th Middlesex on 5 January 1918 and sometime after that was attached to the 6th Battalion Northamptonshire Regiment. 2nd Lieut. Cooper's Service Record shows two lists of personal effects. The first drawn up on 10 May 1918 lists the following:-

A Pass Book, Book of Views Le Touquet Paris Plague, F.E. Directory, Address Book, New Testament, Book Straight Tips for Subs, Poems of To-day, French Grammar, Field Entrenchment, Knowledge For War, Platoon: Company Drill, 4 books on Musketry, 2 Pelham's Books, 1 copy King's Regulations, 2 Books Lecture Notes and 1 Field Service Pocket Book.

By the 13 May His personal effects were listed as:-

1 A.B.439, a Leather Wallet, Protractor, Cheque Book, Advance Bk., Photos, Tobacco, pipe, pouch, 2 statements of a/c, Metal Cigarette Case, Receipts, Wooden Match Box, Poems, 2 Cap Badges, National Registration Card, 2 Metal Badges, 2 Pencils, COX Cheque Book, Letters, Postcards and two Handkerchiefs.

2nd Lieut. Cooper was killed accidently and there was a Court of Enquiry into his death. However efforts by the War Office to get a copy of the Court proceedings were unsuccessful. On 17 November 1918 Lieutenant Charles Hall, writing on behalf of the Officer commanding the 6th Battalion Northampton Regiment, informed the War Office that he had interviewed Lt. Fergusson and he could not remember a Court of Enquiry being held. However Fergusson was able to confirm that Clifford Cooper was killed accidently whilst examining rifles in the line near Gentelles.

On 28 April Mr Cooper received a telegram informing him that his son had been killed accidently on 24 April and the Army Council expressed their sympathy.

2nd Lieut. Clifford Cooper is buried in the Gentelles Communal Cemetery – Somme.[4]

Camp 2,000 yards north on the Eecke – Steenvorde Road

23 April. Major-General Pinney inspected the battalion on parade at 11.15am.

At 2pm the battalion proceeded by route march to a camp 2,000 yards north

on the Eecke – Steenvoorde road at the junction with the track between Grail Farm and Bliss Cottage.

24 April. The battalion commenced work on the Caestre – Watou Line from Meulewalle north to the Steenvoorde to Poperinghe road just short of the French – Belgian border and 300 yards west of the chapel at Menham Cross.

The Germans deployed thirteen new tanks in their attack on Villers-Bretonneux on the Somme to great effect. During the battle wherever the tanks appeared the British front line was broken. The British responded with six heavy tanks and seven whippet tanks, to good effect, but were unable to stop Villers-Bretonneux falling to the enemy. This was the first battle in which tanks were used by both sides.[5]

2nd Lieut. William Howard was killed in action. He was on attachment to the 2nd Battalion Northamptonshire Regiment. His name is on the Pozières Memorial.[6]

25 April. The battalion worked on the Caestre – Watou Line.

The following officers joined the battalion from England: Capts. H.K. Banks and G.V. Tate, Lieut. B.L. Fish, 2nd Lieuts. B.C. Palmer, R.A.M. Hughman and M.W. White.

The Germans captured Mont Kemmel south of Ypres. Field Marshal Haig commented 'The French 28th Division did not fight well. We all thought Kemmel practically impregnable, yet the place was abandoned by the French troops after two hours' fighting. General De Mitry, Commanding the French Corps in the Second Army, had to employ French Cavalry to collect the French fugitives from Kemmel and prevent a rout. What Allies to fight with!'[7]

26 April. The battalion worked on the Caestre – Watou Line.

Training in musketry and the Lewis gun commenced.

The Lewis gun was a weapon of opportunity. Its chief uses were to kill the enemy above ground and to obtain superiority of fire. Its mobility and the small target it and its team presented rendered it peculiarly suitable for working round an enemy's flank or for guarding one's own flank.[8]

The battalion received Divisional Order 300 at 8.30am placing the 33rd Division in Second Army reserve and for it to concentrate in the vicinity of Sainte-Marie-Cappel.[9]

One man wounded.

27 April. The battalion worked on the Caestre – Watou Line. Training in musketry and the Lewis gun continued.

The reserve line was reconnoitred. It started 2,500 yards east of Eecke at Baeck Houck and went north to the Steenvoorde – Poperinghe road just short of the French – Belgian border 600 yards west of Menham Cross Chapel.

28 April. Work and training.

Private John McFarlane 4th Battalion King's (Liverpool) Regiment, 98th Infantry Brigade, 33rd Division, faced a General Field Court Martial accused on three charges under Section 12 (1.a.) of the Army Act 1881 of 'When on active service deserting His Majesty's Service'.

Circular Memorandum A.G./737/P.S. for a Field General Court Martial required Private McFarlane to be provided with someone to defend him. However McFarlane refused to accept any assistance from a prisoner's friend. He was not represented and nobody was instructed to act on his behalf at the Court Martial.

In any event the Court Martial Officer Captain A.B. Whitfield confirmed it would have been very difficult to obtain the services of an accused's friend for McFarlane because the Division moved on the day of the trial and he did not consider it advisable to adjourn the case. Whitefield advised McFarlane that in the absence of an accused's friend it was his duty as Court Martial Officer to do everything in his power to help him.

Whitfield warned McFarlane more than once of the seriousness of his position and tried to elicit from him any facts that might help. McFarlane refused to make a defence and Whitfield had to extort the few facts that were stated in mitigation.

The court heard the three charges of desertion:-

1) That on 15/3/18 McFarlane missed roll call at 6.10pm and did not proceed to the trenches with his platoon. He missed the whole tour of duty. He was apprehended by Military Police at noon on 16/3/18 at Cassel;
2) On 31/3/18 in the field McFarlane absented himself from the support line trenches at Hamburg in the Passchendaele sector. He was apprehended by Military Police in St. Omer at 6pm on 1/4/18;
3) On 11/4/18 he absented himself from the line of march at 9.30pm when the battalion was proceeding to the front line in the Bailleul area. He surrendered himself to the Military Police in the Rue de L'Arsenal in St. Omer on 12/4/18.

Private McFarlane pleaded not guilty to all three charges. In mitigation it was stated McFarlane was in the Territorials and was time expired a fortnight before war broke out. He re-enlisted voluntarily for one year and after that he was retained. He absented himself because he had not been given a month's leave after his time had expired, although he had applied for it on 5 August 1915 and 5 August 1916.

He was found not guilty on the first and third charge of desertion but guilty of the lesser charge of being absent without leave. On the second charge he was found guilty of desertion and sentenced to death.

Brigadier-General J.D. Heriot-Maitland, the Commanding Officer of the 98th Infantry Brigade, found McFarlane's record as a soldier, judging by his conduct sheet, was a very poor one and his desertion seemed to be deliberate and likely to be repeated. He recommended that the sentence be carried out.

Lieut.-Col. S.E. Norris D.S.O., the Commanding Officer of 4th Battalion King's (Liverpool) Regiment was required to report on Private McFarlane following his Court Martial. Lieut.-Col. Norris advised that McFarlane had only been with the battalion since January 1918 and he had no possibility of judging him as he deserted at once every time he came into the shelled area. Lieut.-Col. Norris considered that the crime was deliberately committed and he recommended the extreme penalty be inflicted on account of the bad effect this man's conduct had on the large number of young soldiers in the ranks.[10]

29 April. The battalion completed the work on the Caestre – Watou Line. The Steen Akker Switch Line was reconnoitred. The line ran west to east from a point 1,500 yards north of Godewaersvelde to Steen Akker 1,000 yards south-west of the Belgian border.

The battalion received Divisional Order 301 at 3.45pm for the move of the 33rd Division to Blaringhem – Wardrecques – Racquinghem. These orders were subsequently cancelled and troops were ordered to return to their former billets due to the enemy attack in the neighbourhood of Scherpenberg.[11]

One man was wounded but remained at duty.

Operation Georgette saw the German's advance their front line forward to Voormezeele, Locre, Bailleul, Méteren, Vieux Berquin, Pacaut Wood, Festubert and Givenchy.

Encouraged by the capture of Mont Kemmel the Germans made a determined effort to break through the British and Allied front line positions

from west of Dranoutre to Voormezeele. A German bombardment of exceptional intensity was launched at 3.10am and followed at 5am with a series of strong attacks. Very heavy fighting rapidly developed on the whole front. On more than one occasion the British drove the Germans back with the bayonet. The French held onto their line including Mont Scherpenburg and Mont Rouge. The British troops held the line only giving a little ground about Voormezeele.

In concert with this attack the Belgian positions astride the Ypres – Staden railway were again attacked. The Germans initially gained ground but vigorous counter strokes by Belgian troops promptly restored the line. In both operations the Germans failed in their attempt to break the British and Allied lines.[12]

The German attack was met by very strong defences organised in depth which was supported by artillery also organised in great depth and by machine gun fire. These defences proved particularly hard for the Germans to overcome and presented far greater difficulties than the Germans had previously experienced. By 6pm it was reported that the offensive power of the German troops was exhausted. On advice from Lossberg, Lundendorff suspended Operation Georgette. Lossberg took stock of the situation and considered it would take ten to twelve fresh divisions to capture Poperinghe, Mont Rouge and Mont Noir and as these could not be made available the German Fourth Army had for the moment to pass onto the defensive and Operation Georgette was called-off.[13]

The German advance to the North Sea under Operation Georgette was halted by the British, French and Belgians.

In the forty days from 21 March to 30 April it is estimated that the British lost 9,704 officers and 230,089 men killed, missing or wounded. The French losses in total were 92,004. The reported German casualties for the same period were 12,300 officers plus 336,000 other ranks.[14]

30 April. The whole battalion completed the work on the Steen Akker Switch. So no training was undertaken.

General Sir Herbert Plumer, the Commanding Officer of the Second Army, sent a wire to the 33rd Division stating 'I wish to take this opportunity to express to Genl. PINNEY and to the officers and men of the 33rd Division my thanks for the splendid fight made by troops of their Division at NEUVE EGLISE on the 14th April, and also for the gallant action performed by them South of MÉTEREN in the earliest days of the LYS Battle, when the enemy was still pressing his

advance strongly in that direction aaa The determined resistance offered by the 33rd Division at that stage of the fight was of the upmost value aaa Ends aaa'.[15]

1 May. 'C' Company completed the remaining work on the Steen Akker Switch.

It was reconnoitred. The Abeele Line ran west to east from a point 250 yards west of St. Éloi Inn to 100 yards south of Sligo Cottages on the Abeele to Poperinghe road. In total the line was almost four miles long.

The battalion received Divisional Order 302 at 3.45pm for the move of the 33rd Division to Blaringhem.

2 May. The battalion was employed digging the Abeele switch line and completed it.

3 May. The battalion engaged in training.

The battalion received Divisional Order 303 at 2.30am instructing the 33rd Division to move the Abeele area on the French – Belgian border.[16]

Camp two miles west of Poperinghe

4 May. The battalion moved by route march to bivouac two miles west of Poperinghe less than 300 yards south-east of Melton Fork.

The Ouderdom Line from Ottawa Camp to Red Horse Shoe Camp was reconnoitred.

Divisional Order 304 was issued instructing the 98th Infantry Brigade to relieve the 56th Infantry Brigade overnight. The order also instructed the G.O.C. 33rd Division to take over command of the front line from a point 320 yards east of Kruisstraathoek running south-west to a point 900 yards west of Vierstraat, next to Godezonne Farm on Cheapside.[17] The front line then ran further south-west between Scherpenberg in Allied hands and Mont Kemmel in German hands.

5 May. The battalion worked on the Ouderdom Line 5,000 yards south-east of Poperinghe.

Private G/32983 Royden Charles Bird aged 20 and born in East Runton, Norfolk, lived in Grosvenor Square, Middlesex and enlisted in London, was killed in action. He was the son of Amanda and Arthur Bird of 2 Garden Cottage, East

Runton. His oldest brother Private 240766 Arthur Bird served with the 'C' Company of the 1/5th Battalion Norfolk Regiment died on 25 April 1917 whilst serving in North Africa. Arthur is buried in the Alexandria (Hadra) War Memorial Cemetery. Royden Bird is buried in the Lijssenthoek Military Cemetery.[18]

6 May. The battalion worked on the Ouderdom Line and started patrols and road repairs forward of the Divisional Green Trench (D.G.T.) line.

Two men were wounded but stayed at duty.

7 May. Work continued on the Ouderdom Line, patrols and road repairs in Divisional area.

The front of the 98th Infantry Brigade and 30th Composite Brigade was reconnoitred with a view to carrying out work there.

The battalion received Divisional Order 305 at 8am for the relief of 149th Brigade R.F.A. by 121st Brigade R.F.A.

At 5.30am Orders were issued to 33rd Battalion Machine Gun Corps and to the Commander Royal Artillery to co-operate with an operation to be carried out by 32nd and 129th French Divisions to strengthen their line from Butterfly Farm to Cheapside, just east of the Milky Way light railway junction, a mile north of Kemmel.[19]

2nd Lieut. Barber and eight men were wounded.

On 7 May General Sir Alexander John Godley, the Commander of XXII Corps, produced a report on German tanks following their use in the attack on Villers-Bretonneux. He recorded that German tanks have a black cross on a white background. Their vulnerable points are the four flaps on the cab on top of the tank, the machine gun points, two on each side of the tank, and the gun shield at the front of the tank. French A.P. bullets penetrate the cab. Ordinary bullets pass through apertures if the flaps are open and through the space between the gun shield and front of the tank. The 'splash' of ordinary bullets is effective against the cab and against machine gun emplacements. The armour plating of the tank is of poor quality and there is no protection against the 'splash' of ordinary bullets. The tank cannot cross a large trench of eight feet or more, or large shell holes. A direct hit by artillery puts them out of action. The Germans are using Tanks of their own making and captured British and French Tanks. The latter had probably been provided with a dome-shaped armoured shield giving it the appearance of a Turtle or inverted basin. The Germans give their tanks names such as Cyclops or put the skull and cross

bones sign on them. They generally have three tanks per regiment which they use against strong points or machine gun nests. The tanks follow the infantry and come into action if the infantry cannot make progress. The tank personnel do not appear to have been well trained as they repeatedly failed to take advantage of good targets.[20]

8 May. Work on roads continued. Work on the Ouderdom Line was handed over to 11th Battalion South Lancashire Regiment 30th Division Pioneers. The work planned on the brigade fronts was cancelled as both brigades were in action in the battle to recapture Ridge Wood.

Two men were wounded and four men were wounded by gas.

During the successful British counter-attack on Ridge Wood the enemy put up various kinds of lights: double reds, double greens, golden rain, double oranges and strings of three white lights. It was impossible to work out the meanings of these signals.[21]

Waratah Camp Poperinghe

9 May. The battalion worked on roads. Work on the Vlamertinge Line was commenced at night. The battalion moved by route march to Waratah Camp 2,200 yards south-east of Poperinghe on the road to Reningelst.

At 7.30pm the battalion received orders, together with the 30th Composite Brigade and the 33rd Battalion Machine Gun Corps, to withdraw from the line as early as possible to move by bus to Lederzeele area on 10/11 May.[22]

One man was wounded by gas.

10 May. The battalion received Divisional Order 307 at 6.30am for the relief of the 33rd Division by 14th French Division.

Work on the roads continued.

The other work being carried out by the battalion was discontinued due to the pending relief by the French.

11 May. Work on the roads was completed. Work on the Vlamertinge Line was handed over to the 7/1st French Engineers.

Divisional Orders 308 and 309 were received at 9am and 8.30pm respectively for the transfer of the 33rd Division to II Corps.

Camp two miles west of Poperinghe

12 May. The battalion moved by route march to their former camp west of Poperinghe.

The Ouderdom – Vlamertinge line was reconnoitred.

Divisional Order 310 received at 8pm transferred the Divisional Artillery from XXII Corps to II Corps.[23]

13 May. Work began on the Vlamertinge Switch Support Line.

14 May. Work continued on the Vlamertinge Switch Support Line.

2nd Lieut. H.L. Wilson and 2nd Lieut. S.F. Hedgecoe joined the battalion and were posted to 'A' and 'B' Companies respectively.

Major-General Pinney went on leave to Boulogne. Brigadier-General C. G. Stewart C.M.G., D.S.O. of the Royal Artillery and Commander of the 33rd Divisional Artillery assumed temporary command of the 33rd Division.[24]

Private T.F.292546 Daniel Lake aged 27, who enlisted in west London, died of his wounds. He was the son of Jane and Alfred George Lake of 19 St. James Street, Hammersmith, London. He is buried in the Gwalia Cemetery.[25]

15 May. 'C' Company started work on the East Poperinghe Line. It ran south to north from three miles from Condiment Cross west of Reningelst to Ride Camp east of Poperinghe. The remainder of the battalion work on the Vlamertinge Switch Support Line.

Major F.G. Trobridge D.S.O. arrived and took over the duties of General Staff Officer 2nd Grade of 33rd Division.[26]

Three men were wounded.

2nd Lieut. Herbert Sydney Barber aged 38, died of his wounds. He was the husband of Alice Mary Barber of 5 Hereford Road, Southsea, Portsmouth. He is buried in the Arneke British Cemetery – Nord.[27]

Private G/57966 John Mayho, born in Southwark, lived in Bermondsey and enlisted in Whitehall, died of his wounds. He is buried in the Manor Park Cemetery – Essex.[28]

Private G/43533 Sidney Southey of 'B' Company aged 24, born in Hornsey, lived in Wood Green and enlisted in Tottenham, was killed in action. He was the son of Sarah Ann and Henry Ernest Southey of 114 Hoppers Road,

Winchmore Hill, London. He was a tailors warehouseman by trade. He is buried in the Esquelbecq Military Cemetery – Nord.[29]

16 May. Work continued on the Vlamertinge Switch Support Line and on the East Poperinghe Line.

The battalion received Divisional Order 311 at 3.40pm for the relief of 98th Infantry Brigade by the 19th Infantry Brigade.[30]

The 18th Battalion Middlesex Regiment did not celebrate Albuhera Day. The 1st Middlesex was given a days' holiday and held a sports meeting and had a football match against the 98th Brigade. The officers held a celebratory lunch.[31]

17 May. Work continued on the Vlamertinge Switch Support Line and on the East Poperinghe Line.

18 May. The battalion worked on Vlamertinge and East Poperinghe lines.

Private G/1301 Albert Green aged 35, born in Chesterton, lived in Shelton, Staffordshire and enlisted in Hornsey, died of his wounds. He is buried in the Stoke-on-Trent (Hanley) Cemetery – Staffordshire.[32]

19 May. Work continued on the Vlamertinge and East Poperinghe lines.

Major-General Pinney returned to his command of the 33rd Division.[33]

One man was wounded by gas.

20 May. 'A' Company worked on the Vlamertinge Support Line. The rest of the battalion was inspected by the Second Army Commander General Sir Herbert Charles Onslow Plumer.

Private G/25885 Walter John Cressey enlisted in the Army on 16 November 1915 and posted to the 2nd Battalion Middlesex Regiment. At some stage he transferred to the 18th Middlesex and posted to the 4th platoon of 'A' Company. On 20 May 1918 he was discharged from the Army under Paragraph 392 (XVI) of the King's Regulations being no longer physically fit for War Service. He was awarded the Silver War Badge and certificate number 392070.[34] He was also awarded the British War Medal and the Victory Medal.[35]

Cressey had been gassed, left blind and lost four fingers. Whilst being treated at Queen Alexandra's Military Hospital in London he made a number

of beaded necklaces and a headband as part of occupational therapy. These are now deposited at the Imperial War Museum.[36]

Cressey was born on 27 July 1891 in Westminster and his parents were Eliza and Stephen Cressey. He was christened in Westminster on 11 October 1891. Stephen Cressey was a Police Constable and at the time of the 1891 Census he and his family were living at 245 Sandringham Buildings, St. Anne, Soho. London. By the 1901 Census Stephen Cressey was still a Police Constable and he and his family had moved to 72 Sandringham Buildings. On 25 March 1895 Walter was admitted to St. Martin-in-the-Fields Infant School at the age of 3. On 1 March 1899 Walter transferred to St. Martin-in-the Fields Boys School.[37]

By the 1911 Census Stephen Cressey had retired from the Police Force and was working as a Bank Porter. Walter Cressey was by then working as a messenger for a journalist. The Cressey family had moved to 14 Ellerslie Road, Shepherds Bush West, Hammersmith, London.[38]

Stephen Cressey died on 15 January 1916 and his estate, valued at £192. 4s. 10d. passed to his wife Eliza.[39]

By 1919 Eliza Cressey had moved to 109 New Oxford Street London, W.C.1 and her son Walter John was living with her.[40]

Walter John Cressey continued to live with his mother at 109 New Oxford Street until he married Kate Steer in the second quarter of 1932 at Pancras. Kate died in 1947 at the age of 48. By 1951 Walter was resident at 107-111 New Oxford Road. Also resident at that address was Arthur Henry Haynes, Evelyn Haynes and Ethel Johanna Perry. By 1952 Ethel Perry had moved out and a Beatrice Jones had moved in.[41]

Eliza Cressey died in March 1948 in Brentwood aged 82.[42] Walter John Cressey died aged 80 in Canterbury in the second quarter of 1972.[43]

21 May. Work continued on the Vlamertinge Support Line.

On 30 April 1918 Major-General Pinney, Commanding Officer 33rd Division, concurred with the execution of the death sentence on Private McFarlane. On 5 May 1918 General Plumer recommended that the sentence be carried out. On 16 May 1918 Field Marshal Haig confirmed the guilty verdict and confirmed the sentence.

22 May. John McFarlane, aged 27, was shot at dawn at 4.11am.[44] He was bound, gagged, blind folded and a marker was pinned next to his left breast

pocket. He was fastened to a stump and twelve members of his battalion shot him.

The 4th Battalion King's (Liverpool) Regiment were billeted at the Dirty Bucket Camp at the time.[45] The camp was less than a mile north of Brandhoek.

His parents, William and Margaret McFarlane, who lived at 14 Gerard Street, Byrom Street, Liverpool were told he had died on the Western Front. He is buried in the Nine Elms British Cemetery where he is remembered with honour.[46] His headstone is enscribed 'until the day breaks'.

In the afternoon the 98th Brigade had a full parade commanded by Brigadier-General Maitland and inspected by General Plumer. The 1st Middlesex band played during the general salute.[47]

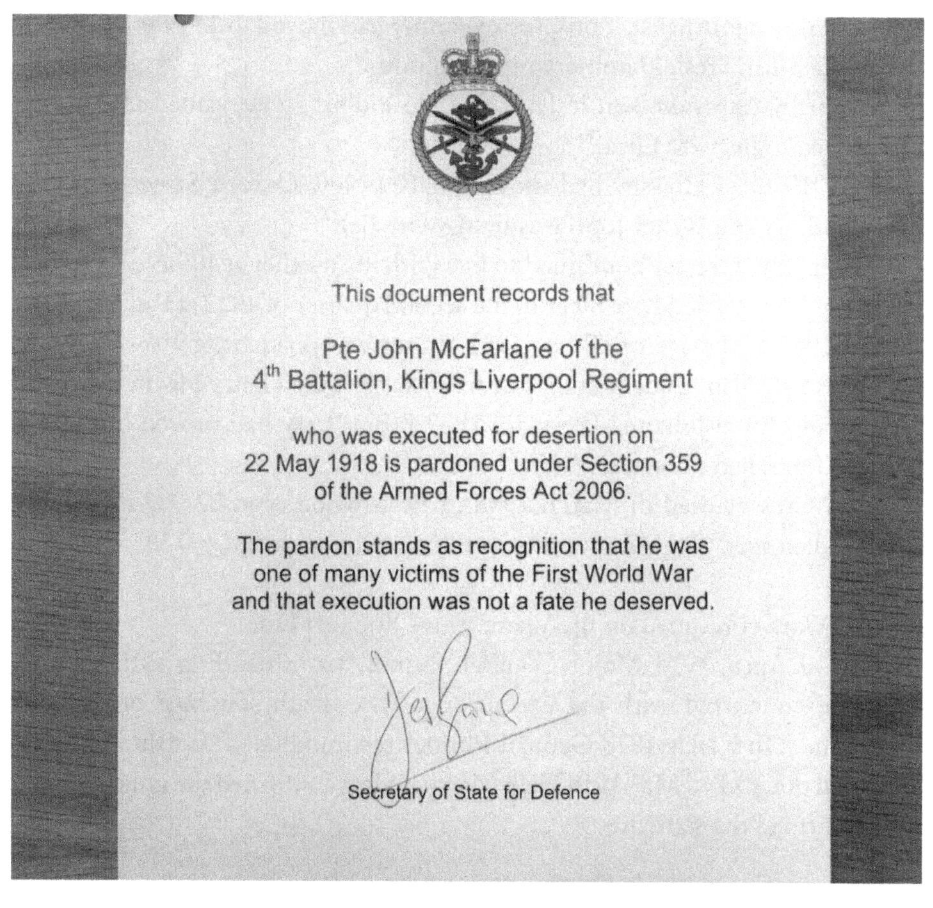

This document records that

Pte John McFarlane of the
4th Battalion, Kings Liverpool Regiment

who was executed for desertion on
22 May 1918 is pardoned under Section 359
of the Armed Forces Act 2006.

The pardon stands as recognition that he was
one of many victims of the First World War
and that execution was not a fate he deserved.

Secretary of State for Defence

Private John McFarlane's pardon [49]

On 8 November 2006 the Armed Forces Act 2006 received Royal Assent. Under Section 359 of the Act Private John McFarlane was pardoned by The Rt. Hon. Des Browne M.P. Secretary of State for Defence.[48]

22 May. Work continued on the Support Line.

The battalion received Divisional Order 312 at 10pm for the relief of the 19th Infantry Brigade by 100th Infantry Brigade.[50]

Two men were wounded, one slightly.

The following three soldiers were killed in action and are buried in the Klein-Vierstraat British Cemetery – Heuvelland, West-Vlaanderen.

Private G/57350 Frank Edwin Cooper, dob 3 November 1898, aged 19, was born in Greenwich, Kent. He attested in Greenwich on 18 September 1916 aged 17 years and 10 months. At this time he was living at 15 Azof Street Greenwich and was a sheet iron worker by trade. He joined the Army on 21 March 1917 and posted to the 2/3rd County of London Yeomanry and given the Regimental number 3020. He was made Lance Corporal on 31 January 1918. On the same day he was admitted to the Field Ambulance at Wroxham with pharyngitis (throat infection) and returned to duty on 7 February. On 13 April he reverted to the rank of Private and was compulsorily transferred to the 18th Middlesex. He was the son of Harriet Jane and Arthur Cooper of 2 Bryant's Cottages, Straight Road, Romford, Essex.[51]

Private G/57958 Samuel Charles Loxdale was born in St. Luke's, London, in the 3rd quarter of 1899. He lived at 49 Grange Road, St. James Street, Walthamstow. His application to join the Army was accepted on 26 July 1917 and he enlisted in Stratford, Essex. On his attestation he listed soldering as his profession. He was posted to 102nd Training Reserve Battalion the following day and given the Regimental number 128133. He transferred to the 250th Infantry Battalion on 24 November 1917. He then joined the 52nd (Grad.) Battalion and was given the Regimental Number 51537. On 5 April 1918 he left Folkestone for Boulogne and was posted to 18th Middlesex joining them in the field on 9 April. He was the son of Elizabeth and Henry Loxdale.[52]

Sergeant G/87296 Joseph Alfred Pring aged 36, was born in Fulham and enlisted in Camberwell. He was the husband of Alice Charlotte Friend Pring (nee Banks) of 61 Mallinson Road, Battersea, London. They got married on 28 June 1913 at St. Mary's Battersea.[53]

23 to 27 May. The battalion worked on the Vlamertinge Support Line.

Ludendorff and the German Supreme Command still held the view that the only way to win the war was to defeat the British and drive them away from the Channel Ports before the U.S troops started to arrive in France in great numbers. With Britain defeated in the field the Germans surmised that France would be compelled to consider terms. In an attempt to drive a wedge between the British and French troops on the Western Front, Ludendorff decided the next attack should be against the French on the Chemin des Dames sector. He hoped this diversionary attack would break through the French lines and pose a serious threat to Paris. In turn this would compel Foch to withdraw his reserves from the north and open up the way for a renewed German offensive against the British.[54]

27 May. The German plan was to attack across the formidable Chemin des Dames on a twenty-two-mile front running south-west from Anizy to Berry-au-Bac which was a 'quiet sector' believed to be weakly held by seven French and four British divisions. The primary objective was the line Soissons – Reims. The German forces, under Crown Prince Wilhelm's army group, comprised of von Hutier's Eighteenth Army, von Boehn's Seventh and von Mudra's First and in total amounted to forty-one divisions.

The German bombardment opened at 2am (1am British time) and was another Bruchmüller spectacular that featured the combined violence of nearly 4,000 guns. Preceded by thousands of gas shells, the barrage exploded seven to eight miles deep throughout the battle zone, while mortar fire concentrated on barbed-wire defences and the densely packed trenches of the immediate front. At 4.40am (3.40am British time) the guns shifted to a rolling barrage, the *Sturmtruppen* moved out. Operation Blücher-Yorck was underway.

Defending the Chemin des Dames was in fact six divisions of General Denis Auguste Duchêne's Sixth Army.[55] They were supplemented by four British divisions of the IX Corps under Lieutenant-General Sir A. Hamilton-Gordon. The 21st, 8th and 50th Divisions were in the line on a front of about fifteen miles between Bermicourt and Bouconville north-west of Reims.[56] These divisions, together with the 25th Division in reserve had been shockingly mutilated in the northern battle (First Battle of the Somme 1918/Operation Michael and the Battle of Lys/Operation Georgette) and had been sent by Foch to the quietest sector of the front line in order to refit and train their recruits.[57] All these divisions had only recently been filled up with young drafts and were in no

condition to take part in major operations until they had rested for several weeks.[58]

In the British sector the IX Corps had the 50th Division on the left, the 8th Division in the centre and the 21st Division on the right in the Berry-au-Bac area. The Germans attacked with storm troops and tanks. The 21st Division fought well. However, the 22nd French Division on the left of the 50th Division retreated without warning. This left a gap between the French and the British which the Germans used to get behind and attack both the 50th Division and 8th Division. The 25th Division in reserve was ordered into the line but was overrun by troops coming back. All four British Divisions suffered heavy casualties.

Prime Minister Lloyd George blamed General Duchêne for the disaster. Duchêne had kept the bulk of his forces massed in forward positions and these were all but annihilated in the opening German bombardment. Duchêne delayed the orders to destroy the bridges over the Aisne. The centre of the French front caved in, the Germans swept over the Chemin des Dames, down to Aisne, crossed the intact bridges and then crossed over the Vesle. In one day the German centre advanced to a depth of 12 miles.[59]

28 May. The battalion trained.

The battalion received Divisional Order 313 at 8.50pm for the relief of the 6th Division by the 33rd Division in the right sector of the Corps front overnight on 3/4 June. The 100th Infantry Brigade relieved the 98th Infantry Brigade in Dirty Bucket Camp.[60]

The Germans launched fresh attacks in great force. The Allies were pressed back to the west of Soissons and south of Fère-en-Tardenois. The IX British Corps was forced to withdraw across the Vesle and then pressed further back in a south-easterly direction between the Vesle and the Ardre.[61]

The Americans had been in the war for almost fourteen months and the doughboys had only seen limited action in the trenches. The first offensive operation of the war was planned for 28 May. The attack was not tactically or operationally important in itself but was massively important as it would demonstration whether or not the Americans had the necessary fighting capability to succeed on the Western Front.

The American 1st Division had taken over the Cantigny sector four miles north-east of Montdidier on 27 April. On 28 May 4,000 U.S. troops of the 28th Regiment attacked the German salient surrounding Cantigny town. This attack was on a 1,700 yard front. They swept through Cantigny and took the high

ground beyond the town. The Germans bombarded the American 1st Division position for five days but the U.S. troops refused to be driven from the town. This sent a clear message to the Allies and Germans that U.S. troops were a force to be reckoned with.[62]

29 May. The battalion worked on the Vlamertinge Support Line.

Private G/40569 Harry (Henry) Burrows aged 30 lived at 16 Glenfield Road, West Ealing. He was married to Mrs A.M. Burrows. He attested on 24 March 1915 in Southall and was posted to the 3/8th Middlesex. He went to France to join the British Expeditionary Force on 31 August 1916 and was posted to the 18th Middlesex. He suffered a gunshot wound to his left thigh on 12 May 1918. On 22 May he was gassed and he died from his wounds in the No. 1 Australian General Hospital in Rouen 7 days later. His wife was sent his personal effects of a disc, photos, pipe, religious medallion, metal ring, diary, wallet, holdall containing 2 razors, a comb, soap, brush, pencil and holder. She received 28 shillings weekly in Separation Allowance and Allotment of pay. She was awarded a pension of 25 shillings and 5 pence for herself and 2 children with effect from 2 December 1918. Private Burrows is buried in the St. Sever Cemetery Extension.[63]

Orders were issued by 98th Infantry Brigade to the 1st Middlesex and the 2nd Argyll and Southerland Highlanders to counter-attack across open country and retake 1,000 yards of the front and support lines of the Vlamertinge Line east of Hospital Farm between Vlamertinge and Elverdinghe. The attack was preceded by a creeping barrage which started at 7.40pm. At 8pm the barrage lifted on to the Vlamertinge Support Trench. Three minutes later it lifted at a rate of one hundred yards every three minutes and then it was held on the final objective.

4.5″ howitzers fired on the Vlamertinge front line until 8pm. At 7.30pm the 1st Middlesex attacked on the left and the 2nd Argyll and Sutherland Highlanders attacked on the right. They were supported by a company of 33rd Battalion Machine Gun Corps and two Stokes Mortars and necessary personnel. The attack was successful.[64]

The following members of the 1st Middlesex Battalion received gallantry honours:-

Lieutenant, Acting/Captain, Thomas William Heather M.C. was awarded the Bar to the Military Cross. His citation reads ‘For conspicuous gallantry and devotion to duty. He carried out a personal reconnaissance of the front line

under heavy machine-gun fire, and obtained information of great value in clearing up the situation. At all times he did good work'. He was gazetted for the Military Cross on 4 June 1917.[65]

Captain Longford Loftus Welman was awarded the Military Cross. His citation reads 'For conspicuous gallantry and devotion to duty. He led a counter-attack successfully, occupying a village and holding up the enemy advance. He showed fine courage and skilfully handled his men'.[66] Welman had been promoted to the rank of Acting Major with effect from 16 May 1918 whilst serving at the 1st Battalion Middlesex Regiment Head Quarters.[67]

Private, acting Lance Corporal, 14218 A. Wilkinson was awarded the Distinguished Conduct Medal. His citation reads 'For conspicuous gallantry and devotion to duty while in charge of a Lewis-Gun team in the front wave of an attack. His team suffered heavy casualties, and he took charge of another team as well. Choosing good targets and directing the fire skilfully. When his company was compelled by heavy fire to withdraw, he hung on to the last and accounted for many of the enemy. He showed fine courage and determination'.[68]

30 May. Work continued on the Vlamertinge Support Line.

Under Operation Blücher-Yorck, General von Boehn and the German 7th Army reached the north bank of the River Marne fifty-miles from Paris. In four days the Germans advanced over 30 miles, took 400 guns and nearly 40,000 prisoners.[69]

31 May. Work continued on the Support Line.

Two men were wounded.

1 June. Work continued on the Elverdinghe – Vlamertinge – Ouderdom Support Line and on the East Poperinghe Support Line.

Lt.-Col. M.O. Clarke D.S.O. took over the duties of General Staff Officer 1st Grade from Lt.-Col. E.C. Gepp D.S.O. who had been appointed General Staff Officer 1st Grade of the Third Army. [70]

Prime Minister Lloyd George recorded that under Operation Blücher-Yorck the Germans inflicted a 'heavy defeat on the French on the Chemin des Dames and the Aisne and the poor fight put up by their divisions, which enabled the enemy at one blow to advance within forty miles of Paris, created for a time a sense not only of despondency but of something tantamount to dismay.'[71]

2 June. Work continued on the Elverdinghe – Vlamertinge – Ouderdom Support Line and on the East Poperinghe Support Line.

1 33rd Division War Diary
2 *The Times Diary & Index of The War 1914 -18*, p. 143
3 Commonwealth War Graves Commission casualty details; Private Smart Army Service Record, National Archives, WO 363; England & Wales, Civil Divorce Records, 1858 – 1911, Divorce Court File 7511; 1901 Census; 1911 Census; General Records Office certificates BXCG 150505, BXCG 137653, MXG 241490
4 Ibid.; 2nd Lt. Clifford Cooper Service Record, National Archives, WO 339/115635
5 Edmonds, *Military Operations, France And Belgium 1918, Vol. 2*, p.p. 388-389 & p.p. 392-393
6 Commonwealth War Graves Commission casualty details
7 Blake (Editor), *The Private Papers of Douglas Haig*, p. 305
8 Instructions for the training of platoons for offensive action 1917, p. 7
9 33rd Division War Diary, Divisional Order 300
10 Field General Court Martial, Private John McFarlane, National Archives, WO 71/644
11 33rd Division War Diary
12 Boraston (Editor), *Sir Douglas Haig's Despatches (December 1915 – April 1919),* p.p. 233-234
13 Edmonds, *Military Operations, France And Belgium 1918, Vol. 2*, p. 454
14 Ibid., p. 490
15 33rd Division War Diary
16 Ibid.
17 Ibid., Divisional Order 304; 1st Battalion Middlesex Regiment War Diary
18 *Soldiers Died In The Great War 1914 -1919*, p. 102; Commonwealth War Graves Commission casualty details; 1911 Census
19 33rd Division War Diary
20 Ibid.
21 Ibid.
22 Ibid.
23 Ibid.
24 Ibid.
25 *Soldiers Died In The Great War 1914 -1919*, p. 103; Commonwealth War Graves Commission casualty details
26 33rd Division War Diary
27 Commonwealth War Graves Commission casualty details
28 *Soldiers Died In The Great War 1914 -1919*, p. 104; Commonwealth War Graves Commission casualty details
29 Ibid.; 1911 Census

30 33rd Division War Diary

31 1st Battalion Middlesex Regiment War Diary, National Archives, WO 95/2426, Image Ref 1/447

32 *Soldiers Died In The Great War 1914 -1919*, p. 103; Commonwealth War Graves Commission casualty details

33 33rd Division War Diary

34 U.K. Silver War Badge Records 1914 -1920

35 British Army WW1 Medal Rolls Index Cards 1914 -1920

36 Imperial War Museum, EPH 1390, EPH 1391, EPH 1392 and EPH 1393

37 England & Wales Death Index 1916 – 2006; England & Wales Christening Records 1530 -1906; London, England, School Admissions and Discharges 1840 -1911; 1891 Census; 1901 Census

38 1911 Census

39 England & Wales, National Probate Calendar (Index of Wills and Administrations) 1858 -1966

40 London, England, Electoral Registers 1832 -1965

41 Ibid.; England & Wales, Marriage Index 1916 – 2005, 2nd Quarter 1932, Pancras 1b 39

42 England & Wales Death Index 1916 – 2006

43 Ibid.

44 Field General Court Martial, Private John McFarlane

45 4th King's (Liverpool) Regiment Battalion War Diary

46 Commonwealth War Graves Commission casualty details

47 4th King's (Liverpool) Regiment Battalion War Diary

48 Field General Court Martial, Private John McFarlane

49 Ibid.

50 33rd Division War Diary

51 *Soldiers Died In The Great War 1914 -1919*, p. 103; Commonwealth War Graves Commission casualty details; Private Cooper Army Service Record, National Archives, WO 363; 1911 Census

52 Ibid.; Private Loxdale Army Service Record, National Archives, WO 363; England & Wales Birth Index 1837-1915; 1911 Census

53 *Soldiers Died In The Great War 1914 -1919*, p. 104; Commonwealth War Graves Commission casualty details; London Metropolitan Archives Saint Mary, Battersea, Register of banns of marriage, 1909 Jul-1913 Dec, P70/MRY2/108

54 Lloyd George, *War Memoirs, Vol. 2*, p.p. 1836 -1837

55 Asprey, *The German High Command At War*, p.p. 412-414

56 Boraston (Editor), *Sir Douglas Haig's Despatches (December 1915 – April 1919)*, p.p. 252-253

57 Winston S. Churchill, *The World in Crisis 1911 – 1918, Vol. IV*, p. 1287

58 Borastan (Editor), *Sir Douglas Haig's Despatches (December 1915-April 1919)*, p. 252

59 Lloyd George, *War Memoirs, Vol. 2*, p. 1841

60 33rd Division War Diary

61 Boraston (Editor), *Sir Douglas Haig's Despatches (December 1915 – April 1919),* p. 253

62 Edmonds, *Military Operations, France And Belgium 1918 Vol. 3*, HMSO, London, 1939, p. 115; James J Cooke, *Pershing And His Generals Command and Staff in the AEF*, Praeger Publishers, Westport, 1997, p.p. 86-87

63 *Soldiers Died In The Great War 1914 -1919*, p. 102; Commonwealth War Graves Commission casualty details; Private Burrows Army Service Record, National Archives, WO 363

64 4th King's (Liverpool) Regiment Battalion War Diary

65 Third Supplement to the London Gazette Friday 13th September 1918, Gazette Issue 30901, p. 10892

66 Ibid., p. 11032

67 Third Supplement to the London Gazette Friday 9th August 1918, Published 12th August 1918, Gazette Issue 30839, p. 9438

68 Third Supplement to the London Gazette, Friday 30th August 1918, Published 3rd September 1918, Gazette Issue 30879, p. 10361

69 Lloyd George, *War Memoirs, Vol. 2*, p. 1841

70 33rd Division War Diary

71 Lloyd George, *War Memoirs, Vol. 2*, p. 1842

CHAPTER ELEVEN

3rd June 1918 to 14th July 1918

Front Line in Flanders
Gas Attack on Verbranden Molen

Following the US declaration of war against Germany on 6 April 1917 two major issues arose:

1) When would US troops actually be deployed in active combat on the Western Front;

2) Under what command structure would they operate?

Time passed by and the conflict moved into 1918. Germany came perilously close to breaking through the Allied lines in March, April and May. However, almost fourteen months after the declaration US troops had only just been sent into combat on the Western Front.

The Allied armies needed massive reinforcements to replace the huge casualties suffered in the German Spring offensive. Allied commanders anticipated even more serious casualty figures for the summer and US troops ready for combat at the front were desperately needed.

To get their fighting units up to numerical strength the Allied leaders wanted to incorporate US troops in Allied formations, temporarily attaching them to Allied divisions. This position was unanimously adopted by the Military Representatives, including General Bliss on behalf of the US, at Versailles on 27 March.[1]

The sticking point was the position taken by General John Joseph 'Black Jack' Pershing, Officer commanding the American Expeditionary Force in Europe. He 'wanted, at the earliest possible moment, to form an independent American Army, with its own bases and transport communications, its own part of the front, all under his separate command'.[2]

Between March and the end of June much time and effort was devoted by the Allied Leaders, particularly Lloyd George, to speed up the number of U.S.

Infantry troops and machine gun parties being sent to the Western Front; and for theses troops to be incorporated into existing Allied combat units.

At the Supreme War Council meeting held on 1 and 2 of June Pershing agreed to bring over U.S. troops who had completed three months training. He also agreed to transport at least 250,000 men in both June and July giving absolute priority to combatant troops. 170,000 combat troops, amounting to six divisions, without artillery, ammunition trains or supply trains to be sent in June. Likewise in July, as an absolute priority, 140,000 combat troops, amounting to four divisions without artillery etc were to be transported.[3]

This marked a very important turning point in the War. Allied commanders could now plan the further prosecution of the war on the basis they would have sufficient combat troops directly at their disposal to replace their losses. They would be able to build numerical superiority over the Germans who were exhausting their front line troops without sufficient reserves to replace them.

The agreement to deploy American troops could not have come sooner. Pershing, on 31 May, had already committed his 2nd and 3rd Divisions in the all-out effort to stop the Germans. The 3rd Division had been deployed to Château Thierry and the 2nd Division was brought up the Paris – Metz highway as the French Government prepared to leave Paris. The 9th U.S. Infantry was placed between the Paris – Metz highway and the Marne facing Vaux. A Regiment of the Marine Brigade was also deployed north of Le Thiolet on the Paris – Metz highway. It was agreed that the Marine Brigade would fight as a unit north of the highway and the 3rd Infantry Brigade to the south of it.

The U.S. 23rd Infantry was deployed to close a breach in the French line to the front and left of the Marines. Thus U.S. troops held a twelve mile line from the 9th Infantry south of the highway, through the Marines to the 23rd Infantry. The Germans held the line from Vaux, to Bouresches to Belleau and occupied Belleau Wood. And the Americans faced them across rolling farmland from Triangle Farm to Lucy to Hill 142. The U.S. troops were ordered to 'Hold the line at all hazards'.[4]

3 June. Work continued on the Support Lines.

The battalion received Divisional Order 316 at 7.30am for the relief of 19th Infantry Brigade by 98th Infantry Brigade.[5]

Coming out of Belleau Wood the Germans attempted to advance on the

U.S. front line. They were met by marines who had dug in shallow trenches and cut them down with deadly rifle fire. The Germans were forced to retreat back through the woods. The Marines held the line. That particular German offensive was finished and Paris was out of their reach for the time being.[6]

4 June. Work continued on Support Lines.

U.S. Major-General Bundy took command of the line held by American troops from the Paris – Metz road north to Triangle Farm, to Lucy onto Hill 142. For the next two days the Germans continued to make local assaults against the line but were thrown back by Marine expert fire.[7]

5 June. Work continued on Support Lines.

6 June. The battalion got a day's rest.

At 3.45am the 1st Battalion 5th Marines attacked Hill 142. As they advanced they were met with machine gun fire from Belleau Wood, which the French had told the Americans was clear of Germans. Heavy fighting and hand to hand combat ensued and the U.S. troops suffered serious casualties. Still they took the hill by the afternoon. The 1st Battalion 5th Marines lost 9 officers and most of 325 men in the process.[8]

At 5pm the 3rd Battalion 5th Marines attacked Belleau Wood and secured a foothold. During this battle the Marines suffered heavy casualties losing 31 officers and 1,056 men.[9]

During Operation Blücher-Yorck the Germans 'gained the north bank of the Marne from Dormans to Château Thierry and advanced astride the Aisne to the outskirts of the Villers Cotterets Forest and across the high ground north east of Attichy. On the eastern flank of the salient created by the enemy's advances, the British forces, at that date under the command of the French Fifth Army, withdrew gradually to the line Aubilly – Chambrecy – Boujacourt where they were able to consolidate.

The day culminated in two determined German attempts upon the important position known as the Montagne de Bligny which commanded the valley of the Ardre, all the attacks were gallantly repulsed and the enemy's advance definitely stayed'.[10]

Operation Blücher-Yorck had been met, held and repulsed with a vital contribution by U.S. troops.

Brandhoek

7 June. The battalion, less transport and quartermaster's stores, moved to a camp on the southern outskirts of Brandhoek and relieved the 11th Battalion Leicestershire Regiment (Pioneers) 6th Division.

8 June. Two platoons of 'A' Company worked on posts in the Intermediate Line. Two platoons of 'A' Company dismantled huts in the Road Camp south of Vlamertinge. 'B' Company dug a communication trench to the Intermediate Line west of Vijverbeek to 200 yards north of Vijerhoek. This took the C.T. right up to the bank of the Vijverhoek to Dickebusch Canal.

'C' Company worked on a communication trench south-east from Café Belge to Kruisstraathoek.

Two officers and twenty-eight men were employed as sector commandants and guides for the Dickebusch – Goldfish Château – Brielen Line and Goed Moet Mill Switch and the Elverdinghe – Vlamertinge – Ouderdom Line.

The London Gazette carried confirmation that Temporary 2nd Lt. C.H. Wight M.C. and Temporary 2nd Lt. G. Cotton were promoted to Temporary Lieutenant on 22 May 1918.[11]

9 June. 'A' Company worked on posts in the Intermediate Line and on dismantling huts in the Road Camp. 'B' Company worked on a communication trench to the Intermediate Line. 'C' Company worked on a communication trench. Two officers and twenty-eight men were employed as sector commandants and guides.

Three men were wounded, one slightly.

Private G/57347 Alfred James Quickfall aged 19 and enlisted in Stratford, Essex, was killed in action. He was the son of Sarah and Frederick Quickfall of 58 Fern Street, Devons Road, Bow, London. He is buried in the Lijssenthoek Military Cemetery.[12]

The Germans attacked the French between Noyon and Montdidier.[13]

10 June. 'A' Company worked on the Intermediate Line and on dismantling huts. 'B' and 'C' Companies worked on the C.T. trenches. Two officers and twenty-eight men worked as sector commandants and guides. In addition one platoon each of 'B' and 'C' Companies patrolled the roads near Moat Farm, Kruisstraat and Withuis (White House) on the south and west approaches to Ypres.

The battalion received Divisional Order 317 at 7.30am for the relief of 100th Infantry Brigade by 98th Infantry Brigade.[14]

The 100th Brigade Trench Mortar Battery remained in the line and came under the orders of 98th Infantry Brigade. The 98th Infantry Brigade Trench Mortar Battery was placed at the disposal of the 46th French Division for operations to be carried out against Ridge Wood.[15]

11 June. 'A' Company worked on the Intermediate Line and on dismantling huts. 'B' and 'C' Companies worked on the C.T. trenches and a platoon each patrolled roads. Two officers and twenty-eight men worked as sector commandants and guides.

The attack between Noyon and Montdidier advanced the German front line a further fifteen kilometres and had taken them to the heights before Compiegne. But the methods of defence exacted a heavy toll and the wise elasticity in the use of ground enabled the French to economise losses.[16] The Germans were held 50 miles from Paris.

12 June. 'A' Company worked on the Intermediate Line and on dismantling huts. 'B' and 'C' Companies worked on the C.T. trenches and a platoon each patrolled roads.

The sector commandants were returned to regimental duty.

One man was injured accidentally.

13 June. The battalion worked on the Intermediate Line, dismantling huts, C.T. trenches and road patrols.

14 June. Night work was cancelled. The battalion worked on dismantling Road Camp and patrolling roads.

General Headquarters considered a heavy attack was imminent. Major-General Pinney attended a Corps Commanders conference at Lovie Château and gave instructions as to the actions to be taken. In attendance were the Lt.-Col. M.O. Clarke G.S.O.1, Major F.G. Trobridge D.S.O. G.S.O.2, Major J. Walker M.C. G.S.O.3, Deputy Assistant Adjutant-General (D.A.A.G.) Major H.C.C. Batten D.S.O., Brigade Major W.A.T. Barstow D.S.O. Royal Artillery, Lt.-Col. G.F. Evans Commander Royal Engineers and Major G.W Williams D.S.O. M.C. Officer commanding Divisional Signals Company, Royal Engineers.[17]

The battalion received Divisional Order 319 at 10pm for the relief of 19th Infantry Brigade by 100th Infantry Brigade.[18]

Three men were wounded.

15 June. The battalion dug a cable trench, buried cable from Query Camp to Oxley Farm and carried out road patrols.

2nd Lieut. L. H. White left to join R.A.F.

16 June. Three platoons of 'A' Company worked on Vlamertinge – Ouderdom Line and one platoon worked at 33rd Divisional H.Q.

Two platoons of 'B' Company worked on the Vlamertinge Line and one platoon dismantled the Givenchy Camp south-west of Vlamertinge.

Three platoons of 'C' Company constructed shelters on the Vlamertinge Line. Platoons from all three companies patrolled the roads.

17 June. The battalion patrolled the roads.

'A' Company worked on the Vlamertinge – Ouderdom Line and at Divisional H.Q.

'B' and 'C' Companies worked together on the Intermediate Line and right flank defences at night.

Private Alfred Enoch Price was officially declared totally disabled from the gunshot wound to his spine suffered in April.[19]

18 June. Battalion platoons patrolled roads. 'A' Company worked on the Vlamertinge – Ouderdom Line and at 33rd Divisional H.Q. 'B' and 'C' Companies worked together at night on the Intermediate Line and right flank defences.

19 June. Three platoons of 'C' Company had a day's rest. The battalion bathed. The men had a good wash and scrub up and were issued with clean underclothing.

At 12.15am on 20 June four officers and 138 men of the 2nd Battalion Worcestershire Regiment and one officer and five men of the Royal Garrison Artillery raided Manor Farm south of Zillebeke Lake. This was a fortified position behind the German front line. They took five prisoners and killed or wounded forty to fifty Germans. The raid, under 2nd Lieut. Boswell was a complete success. The R.G.A. officer and two other ranks 2nd Worcestershire

Regiment were only slightly wounded.[20] Three other ranks were killed and four other ranks were wounded.[21]

20 June. The battalion patrolled roads, worked on the Vlamertinge – Ouderdom Line, Divisional H.Q., on the Intermediate Line and right flank defences.

The battalion received Divisional Order 321 at 9am for a gas attack. A demonstration in connection with this order was carried out at 3pm at Winnipeg one-and-a-half miles east out of Poperinghe on the light railway line adjacent to the main railway line to Ypres. Fortunately no one was accidentally gassed.

21 June. The battalion patrolled roads, worked on the Vlamertinge – Ouderdom Line, Divisional H.Q., on the Intermediate Line and right flank defences.

At 10am a message 'Shovels' was sent out in respect of Divisional Order 321. At 1.30pm a message cancelling 'Shovels' and substituting 'Picks' was sent out. At 5.30pm a message 'Rum' was sent out. These were coded messages relating to the planned gas attack.[22]

22/23 June. Capt. Shaw M.C. and a party of 245 men and seven officers made of two platoons of 'A' Company, three platoons of 'B' Company and two platoons of 'C' Company, left camp at Brandhoek at 8.45pm by motor lorry to carry out the gas attack detailed in Divisional Order 321. The battalion and 'P' Special Company Royal Engineers were assisted by Light Railways and No. 5 Foreways Company, Royal Engineers.

The aim of the gas attack was to destroy Germans and disorganise enemy troops anywhere in the area east of the Ypres – Wytschaete – Messines and south of Zillebeke and Gheluvelt. The 1,853 gas cylinders were packed on three-ton trucks and carried on seven trains each carrying seven trucks and drawn by 40 horse power 'Simplex' tractors. The trains left the Brandhoek yard at 9.30pm at five-minute intervals.

The battalion debussed at the Asylum in Ypres. They marched to their position adjacent to Woodcote House and the light railway Three Kings Junction astride the Lille Road arriving at 10.15pm. They were ready to push the trains to their discharge point 600 yards behind the front line between Sandbag Track north-east of Bedford House and just north of the Klietgatbeek east of Trois Rois. The frontage for the discharge was 350 to 400 yards.

The first two trains arrived at Castle Siding at 11pm and 11.05pm. The

sidings were at the junction where the Shrapnel Corner to Withuis Cabaret road crossed the Canal de L'Yser south of Ypres.

The two trains had to be pushed in silence the final 450 yards from Castle Siding because the tractors were noisy. Their axels had not been checked or properly greased. The battalion got these into position at 11.35pm and 11.40pm.

The five remaining trains were pushed in silence from Trois Rois Spur into position just behind the front line. Further difficulties were encountered with one tractor derailing three times due to a faulty axel between Frankton and Brisbane and a second tractor failing. They were both replaced, one by the spare and the other by the C.R.T. (Canadian Railway Transport) Patrol. Nevertheless the last train arrived at Trois Rois at 11.45pm and was in position just after midnight.

The Brigade in the left sub-sector was ordered to have all troops withdrawn from front line posts by 11.30pm and to reoccupy the posts the following day.

Difficulty was experienced in operating the gas bottles. All the bottles had been fitted with a special electronic device for detonating the nozzles simultaneously. However the bottles were rusted up and had not been greased. The gas was successfully discharged at 12.55am. The noise made by the discharging gas was masked by aeroplane noise above. The wind speed at the time of discharge was seven to nine miles per hour in a north-westerly direction.

220 cylinders did not work because the electrical leads had been cut by splinters of shells and more especially by cartridge spigots after detonation. Captain Shaw and his men stood 50 yards back windward of the trains and watched as the large grey plume drifted and spread its lethal load over the German front line. They did not need their gas masks.

The gas cloud spread over a distance of 3,000 yards to the high ground above Verbranden Molen. It was very dense and it did not drift back over Allied lines. The countryside was bleached and the cloud looked like a sheet being unfolded across the ground.

Once the gas discharge was over, the men had to turn off the cylinders to stop residual gas from escaping. It was impossible to do this by hand so they used spanners.

On the return journey a particular problem was encountered at Bedford Junction. The shortness of the trucks and the size and curve of the track meant that it was not possible to keep all the men windward of the trains.

During the return journey the men had to wear their gas masks because the

trucks were saturated in gas; the undischarged cylinders leaked and they had to push the trucks against the wind. If they had ropes they would have been able to pull the trucks instead of pushing them.

Another problem occurred when fourteen trucks were placed on one train. The coupling pins broke twice. If this had happened on a gradient the train would have rolled back and collided with the following train.

Two men were slightly gassed during the operation.

Six men of 'A' Company were wounded by a shell as they were entering the camp on their return from the gas attack.[23]

The Special Brigade was a secret unit established by Sir John French in 'June 1915 to carry out gas operations against the Germans in retaliation for their introduction of this horror of modern war'.[24]

The rest of the battalion patrolled roads.

Capt. W.H. Adams was admitted to hospital.

23 June. Major-General Pinney visited the battalion.

24 June. Two platoons of 'A' Company worked on the Green Line. One platoon of 'B' Company and two platoons of 'C' Company worked together at night on the Intermediate Line and right flank defences. The battalion also provided road patrols for the area.

A day's rest was given to all ranks taking part in the operation on the previous night.

The battalion received Divisional Order 322 at 12.20pm for the relief of 100th Infantry Brigade by 98th Infantry Brigade in the left sub sector.[25]

A few high velocity shells landed near the camp during the night. Three men were wounded.

25 June. 'A' Company worked on the Green Line. 'B' and 'C' worked together at night on the Intermediate Line and right flank defences. The battalion also provided road patrols for the area.

Private P.W.3127 James Henry Whiting aged 43, born and enlisted in Canning Town, Essex, died of his wounds. He was the husband of Mrs Whiting of 47 Mary Street, Canning Town, London. He is buried in the Lijssenthoek Military Cemetery.[26]

26 June. The battalion worked during the day on the Green Line and at night

on the Intermediate Line and right flank defences. The battalion also provided road patrols.

One man was wounded.

27 June. The battalion worked on the Green Line, the Intermediate Line and right flank defences and road patrols.

28 June. Work continued on the Green Line and Intermediate Line trenches, right flank defences and road patrols.

An artillery demonstration was carried out by the 33rd Divisional Artillery and 11th Army Brigade R.F.A. at 3.10am. The enemy reply to the barrage was not heavy and was fired in response to red and green lights.[27]

Under cover of the bombardment at 3.10am, the 4th King's (Liverpool) Regiment rushed an enemy post on the south bank of the Etang de Zillebeke but found it unoccupied.[28]

Corporal P.W.2948 Arthur Barley died of his wounds. He attested on 25 May 1915 in Woolwich, Kent. He was a dock labourer by trade and he married Jane Godfrey on 31 July 1910 at St. Paulinus Parish Church Crayford. They had three children Stephen Arthur dob 15 May 1910, George dob 16 August 1911, and Lilian dob 21 June 1915. They lived at 1 Westbourne Grove, Bexley Heath. He was posted to the 18th Middlesex on 25 May 1915, transferred to the 25th Middlesex on 8 August 1915 and then moved back to the 18th Middlesex on 29 September 1915. He suffered a gunshot wound to his arm on 7 December 1915. He was made unpaid Acting Lance Corporal on 7 May 1916, paid Acting Lance Corporal 16 May 1916, Acting Corporal 21 August 1916, and Corporal on 21 August 1916. On 10 January 1917 he was tried and found guilty by a Field General Court Martial of 'when on Active Service absenting himself without leave'. Unfortunately his Army Service Record does not record what punishment he received. His wife received a Separation Allowance of 28 shillings and she was awarded a pension of 30 shillings and 10 pence a week for herself and three children with effect from 6 January 1919. Corporal Barley died in the 2 Canadian Casualty Clearing Station. He is buried in the Esquelbecq Military Cemetery.[29]

29 June. Work continued on the Green Line and Intermediate Line trenches, defences and patrols.

The camp was shelled by high velocity bombs and hit by shrapnel, but the battalion sustained no casualties.

30 June. Two platoons of 'A' Company took over the work of the two platoons of 'B' Company on Intermediate Line and right flank defences.

'B' Company took over work on two posts from the 212th Company Royal Engineers. 'C' Company worked at night on Intermediate Line and right flank defences.

Lt.-Col. McNeile attended a conference at Divisional H.Q at 2.30pm.

Brandhoek

1 July. Two platoons of 'A' Company worked on posts in the Intermediate Line and two platoons worked during the day on shelters in the Green Line.

Three platoons of 'B' Company worked on posts and wire in the Intermediate Line during the night. One platoon of 'B' Company worked in three eight hour shifts on general road repairs throughout the area south-west of Ypres at Den Groenen Jager Cabaret to Kruisstraat to north-east of Café Belge.

Three platoons of 'C' Company worked on right flank defences between Vijverhoek and Kruisstraathoek. One platoon of 'C' Company worked in three eight hour shifts on general road repairs south of Vlamertinge, from Section Bend north of Givenchy Farm to 1,000 yards north of Assam Farm and from Vlamertinge Station to north of Assam Farm.

(The 18th Battalion War Diary shows a new map reference for the camp at Brandhoek but does not show the battalion actually moving camp).

One man was wounded.

2 July. Two Alsatians from 10th Company 330th Infantry Regiment deserted south of Zillebeke Lake and came over to the 33rd Division lines. They both complained bitterly about their treatment. One prisoner said he had not had any home leave for twenty-five months. He went on to say that Alsatians who had property at home are afraid to desert, as all their possessions would be confiscated. Both prisoners said there are some fifteen other Alsatians in the 10th Company equally ready to desert. Neither of the prisoners was prepared to return to their side to bring over these fifteen soldiers.[30]

'A' Company worked on posts in the Intermediate Line and on shelters in the Green Line. 'B' Company worked on posts and wire in the Intermediate Line and on general road repairs. 'C' Company worked on right flank defences

and on general road repairs. However, 'C' Company were unable to work after 12.15am because of the enemy barrage.

Lt.-Col. M.O. Clarke, G.S.O.1, who took up his post on 1 June, called with reference to the gas attack carried out by the battalion on 22/23 June.

Lt.-Col. McNeile proceeded on special leave to England and command of the battalion passed to Capt. Alfred Stanley Hands M.C.

Captain Hands received his Military Cross 'For conspicuous gallantry and devotion to duty. Under heavy machine-gun fire at short range he organised a counter-attack, and sent back a clear report of the situation. Throughout he set a fine example to his men'.[31]

Prior to joining the Army Hands was a commercial clerk with Abram Lyle and Sons Ltd., and former pupil of Chigwell School. Alfred Hands, dob 13/8/1891, joined the Army on 30 March 1909 and signed up for four years. He was 5´7″ tall and in good health. He was posted to 'D' Company 3/5th Battalion City of London Rifles. On 30 January 1913 Lance Corporal 8921 Hands signed up for a further four years. He was promoted to Corporal on 24 April 1914 and embarked for France on 4 November 1914. He suffered a shell shock injury and was hospitalised at Wimereux in France and sent back to England on Hospital Ship St. Andrew on 6 May 1915. Whilst still at home in England, Corporal Hands applied on 14 June for a commission with the 18th Battalion Middlesex Regiment. His application was supported by Captain Norman C. King the Adjutant of 3/5th Battalion City of London Rifles.[32]

On 2 July 1915 Hands was promoted to Temporary 2nd Lieutenant and posted to the 18th Battalion Middlesex Regiment.[33] On 12 November 1915 Hands was promoted to the rank of Temporary Lieutenant.[34] On 26 December 1916 he was promoted to the rank of Temporary Captain.[35] On 24 March 1918 Hands was again promoted, this time to the rank of Acting Major.[36] He lost his rank as acting Major on 5 May 1918. He had been admitted to hospital with influenza on 23 April and returned to England on 8 May for three weeks sick leave. He returned fit to France 1 June 1918.[37]

It is somewhat ironic that a battalion commanded for so long by Lt.-Col. Storr who had little time for men promoted from the ranks should be commanded by such an officer.

German high velocity shells peppered Brandhoek and the main road.

Two men were slightly wounded in camp. Ten men were wounded at work including four who remained at duty.

3 July. 'A' Company worked on posts and on shelters. 'B' Company worked on posts and wire in the Intermediate Line and on general road repairs. 'C' Company worked on right flank defences and on general road repairs.

Private T.F.292539 Frederick John Way aged 39 attested in Portsmouth on 11 December 1915. He was single, a waiter by trade, lived at 140 Francis Avenue, Southsea and was placed in the Army Reserve. He was mobilised on 15 May 1916 and posted to the 10th Middlesex, he transferred to the 2/8th Middlesex on 25 May 1917 and then onto the 18th Middlesex on 27 May 1918. He suffered a shell wound to the back which pierced his lung. He died of wounds in the 2 Canadian Casualty Clearing Station. He was the son of John E. and Laura J. Way of Ashton Villa, 25 Swiss Road, Weston-Super-Mare, Somerset. His mother received his personal effects of letters, photos, diary, dictionary and note book. Private Way is buried in the Esquelbecq Military Cemetery.[38]

4 July. 'A' Company worked on posts and on shelters. 'B' Company worked on posts and wire and on general road repairs. 'C' Company worked on right flank defences and on general road repairs.

A strain of what was called 'Spanish Flu' or 'La Grippe', reached the Western Front in mid June. It pole-axed troops on all sides.

A sick bay was constructed in camp for slight cases of influenza. Serious cases were immediately put in isolation.

Private P.W.112 William Symcox died of shrapnel wounds to his back and left leg in the 2 Canadian Casualty Clearing Station. He attested on 22 February 1915 at Longton Staffordshire. He was a miner by trade, aged 30. He listed his mother Johannah Symcox as his next of kin and they lived at 57 Victoria Street Sandford Hill, Longton. His father was the late William Symcox. Private Symcox was posted to the 18th Middlesex and travelled to France with them on 11 November 1915. On 30 January 1918 he married Louisa Spare at the Registry Office in Stoke-on-Trent and she lived at 72 Lonsdale Street, Stoke. Louisa Symcox received her husband's personal effects of photos, 3 religious medallions, crucifix, badge, knife, comb, purse, handkerchief, 1 German 5 mark note and 3 German coins. She also received a Separation Allowance of 12 shillings and sixpence and was awarded a pension of 13 shillings and 9 pence per week for herself with effect from 13 January 1919. Private Symcox is buried in the Esquelbecq Military Cemetery.[39]

5 July. 'C' Company completed two saps in a communication trench less than half a mile north-west on the road out of Kruisstraathoek.

2nd Lieut. Drage rejoined the battalion from the Foreways Company.

6 July. The 33rd Division took over the section of front line held by the 6th Division which ran from 350 yards east of Kruisstraatheok to the southern corner of Middlesex Wood 300 yards west of Elzenwalle.[40]

'A' Company was working on a dugout at Pigment Farm when it was blown up by a direct hit.

The following three soldiers were killed in action and are buried in the Hagle Dump Cemetery – Ieper, West-Vlaanderen.

Private G/87575 William Staveley Forth aged 38, was born and lived in Dover, Kent. He enlisted in Canterbury. He was the son of Elizabeth and George Frederick Samuel Forth of 5 Church Hill, Temple Ewell, Dover.[41]

Private P.W.1442 Alfred James Johnson attested on 13 April 1915 in Fenton, Staffordshire. He was 34 years and 1 month old and a Collier by trade. He married Emily Colclough on 26 December 1904 and they had four children Sidney dob 23 January 1909, Alfred James dob 28 April 1910, William dob 9 July 1912 and Ethel dob 29 November 1914. They lived at 35 Duke Street, Fenton. Private Johnson was posted to the 18th Middlesex and went with the battalion to France on 12 November 1915. He suffered a gunshot wound to his left leg on 28 October 1916 and returned to England on 20 October. He spent time in the Military Hospital at Chatham. He was posted to the 6th Middlesex on 15 March 1917 and returned to France to rejoin the 18th Middlesex on 20 April 1917. On 17 October 1918 the War Office sent his personal effects to his wife Emily comprising a disc and strap, broken pipe, 2 knives, pencils, letter and a 5 cent coin. She received 31 shillings Separation Allowance and was awarded a pension of 33 shillings and 9 pence per week for herself and four children with effect from 27 January 1919.[42]

Corporal G/41526 George Ralph lived in Portslade and enlisted in Hove, Sussex. He was formerly 4817 of the East Kent Regiment.[43]

7 July. A soldier from the 33rd Division who succeeded in escaping from the Germans reported that he saw during his captivity men in khaki, in service jackets without top coats, wearing the regulation steel helmet and carrying English and French gas-masks. They spoke to a German Officer and then, without saluting him, set off in the direction of the frontline. The same man

saw six men, dressed as French soldiers, wearing French jackets and steel helmets, who were talking with an officer in German. Those dressed in khaki, were clean-shaven, whilst those who were dressed as French soldiers had moustaches.

Division drew everyone's attention to this possible method of spying by the enemy.[44]

Work continued on the Intermediate Line and Green Line.

One N.C.O. and eleven other ranks of 'C' Company were sent back to the transport lines to start work on two wells either side of the chapel just over two miles west of Poperinghe on the road to Rhodes Corner.

Six men were wounded, one of whom remained at duty.

8 July. During the evening there was a ferocious thunder and lightning storm and torrential rain.

Private P.W.1124 Alfred Enoch Price was discharged from the army.[45]

9 July. 'A' and 'B' Companies commenced a second belt of wire in front of the Intermediate Line. The battalion started digging another well west of Poperinghe 300 yards south of Rhodes Corner between Davidson Camp and Perron Camp.

The Fifth Supplement to the London Gazette of Tuesday 9 July 1918 confirmed that King George V had given permission for Regimental Quartermaster Sergeant P.W.124 Joseph Mawbey from Doncaster to wear the Croix de Guerre awarded by His Majesty The King of the Belgians.[46]

Mawbey was born in St. Fagans, Drope, South Wales in September 1887. By 1911 his family had moved to 7 Cross Street in the model village of Maltby and he was a Pit Sinker by trade. He married Emily Makin at Maltby Parish Church on 27 August 1912. They had a daughter Emily Winifred born on 17 March 1913. Mawbey enlisted for the duration of the war on 22 February 1915 and by then he lived at 9 Edward Street Rossington near Doncaster. He was 5' 5¾" tall and weighed 148 lbs. He had two toes missing on his right foot but this slight defect was not sufficient to cause his rejection from the Army.

Mawbey was posted to the 18th Middlesex on 25 February 1915, made Acting Lance Corporal on 4 May 1915, Acting Corporal 16 July 1915, Acting Sergeant 7 August 1915 and Regimental Sergeant Major on 6 November 1915. In 1918 he became a candidate for a commission and went on probation to 255th Tunnelling Company on 10 July. On 2 October 1918 he went back to England pending his

commission. He was made Regimental Quarter Master Sergeant and transferred to the 5th Battalion Middlesex Regiment. He was transferred to the Army Reserve on 14 February 1919 and finally discharged from the army on 31 March 1920. He had 4 years and 357 days service counted towards his pension. On 28 March 1922 he received the Diploma to his Belgian Croix de Guerre.[47]

10 July. The battalion had another bath. This was the second bath they had in less than seven weeks.

The battalion wired in front of the Intermediate Line and continued the three wells started the previous day.

Eight men were wounded.

Private G/41434 George Ernest Luck aged 41, lived at 2 Rose Cottage, Clay Hill, Goudhurst, Kent was killed in action. He was 5´ 6″ tall and a labourer by trade. He attested on 23 November 1914 at Cranbrook, Kent giving his age as 33 years and 7 months. However it is clear he lied about his age because his birth was registered in the 2nd quarter of 1877 at Cranbrook, Kent. He joined the 2nd Battalions The Buffs on 25 November 1914 at Ashford, Kent and was given the Regimental number 2095. He transferred to the 2/5th Buffs on 11 December 1914. He was discharged from the Army at Chattenden Farm Camp on 24 March 1916 with 'his services being no longer required'. Sometime later he joined the East Kent Regiment and had the Regimental number 3884 and subsequently transferred to the 18th Middlesex.

He was the son of Alice and Thomas Luck of Spring Cottage, Risebridge, Goudhurst, Kent. He is buried in the Hagle Dump Cemetery.[48]

11 July. 'B' Company worked one platoon by day on the Intermediate Line. A small working party of 'C' Company worked in the Maida Vale Trench. The rest of the battalion worked on wiring and digging wells.

12 July. 'C' Company commenced two fire bays at the west end of the Maida Vale Trench. (The 18th Battalion Middlesex Regiment War Diary records that this work was done to enable fire on the Germans in the Café Belge area [H.29.b.]. However this area was 1,250 yards behind the British front line.)

Private G/41459 George Penfold who was born in Hartley and enlisted in Cranbrook, Kent, died of his wounds. He was formerly 2174 East Kent Regiment. He is buried in the Croix-Rouge Military Cemetery, Quaedypre – Nord.[49]

13 July. 'A' Company plus one platoon and fifty infantrymen commenced a new track from Halifax Camp on the Vlamertinge to Ouderdom road to the Vijverbeek Canal. One platoon of 'B' Company worked by day on the Intermediate Line. 'C' Company worked on two fire bays at the west end of Maida Vale trench. The rest of the battalion worked on wiring and digging wells.

Major-General Pinney visited the battalion.

Lieut. Deric William Parkes M.C. reported for duty. Temporary Lieut. D.W. Parkes was awarded the Military Cross for 'conspicuous gallantry and devotion to duty. He led a successful raid against the enemy's trenches, and inflicted many casualties. He set a splendid example to his men'. This citation appeared in the Fifth Supplement to the London Gazette 9 March 1917.[50]

14 July. British troops in Flanders advanced east of the Etang de Dickebusch on a 2,000 yard front near Ridge Wood.[51]

Two companies of the 1st Middlesex Battalion were attached to the 18th Infantry Brigade for the 6th Division attack on the right Division front. The objective of the attack was to retake the GHQI Line in Elzenwalle. 'A' and 'C' Companies of the 1st Middlesex and men of the 2nd Battalion Durham Light Infantry carried out the attack.

The attack was preceded by an artillery bombardment starting at 5.55am. At 6am one party attacked across the broad gauge railway line and one party down the German trench.

The attack was completely successful and the gains made were consolidated. Three men were killed and nine wounded. During the attack 41 prisoners and four machine guns were captured and an attempted counter-attack was stopped by Lewis gun fire.[52]

Following the attack three platoons of 'B' Company commenced work on a communication trench from Château Segard through the north-east corner of Kruisstraathoek to 500 yards north-west of Voormezeele.

'C' Company took over 'B' Company's work on the Intermediate Line.

Major Hinman returned from leave and took over command of the battalion.

One man was wounded.

Lance Corporal P.S.2726 George Oscar Porter aged 28 died of his wounds in the 3 Australian Casualty Clearing Station. He attested on 1 September 1915 in London aged 25 years and was posted to the 24th Middlesex joining them at Woldingham on 4 September. He was caterer by trade, single and lived with his mother Mary Ann Witham and stepfather Frederick Witham at 78 Hill Street,

Peckham. His father William Charles Porter died in the last quarter of 1897 aged 35. Lance Corporal Porter was transferred to the 16th Middlesex on 14 April 1916 joining them in the field in France. He received a gunshot wound to the back on 2 July 1916 and returned to England on 18 July. He transferred to the 25th Middlesex on 22 September 1916 and then rejoined the 16th Middlesex once again in the field in France on 20 May 1917. He was hit by shrapnel on 11 August 1917 suffering a mild wound to the face. He was made Acting Lance Corporal on 20 November 1917. He transferred to the 18th Middlesex on 8 February 1918.

Lance Corporal Porter listed his mother was as his next of kin and she received a Separation Allowance of 14 shillings and sixpence. She was sent his personal effects on 5 November 1918 comprising photos, note book, cards, religious medallion, 2 letters, cigarette case, purse and a pair of scissors. He is buried in the Esquelbecq Military Cemetery – Nord.[53]

1 Lloyd George, *War Memoirs, Vol. 2*, p. 1813
2 Ibid., p. 1803
3 Ibid., p. 1827
4 J Robert Moskin, *The U.S. Marine Corps Story,* McGraw-Hill Book Company, New York, 1982, p.p.107-108
5 33rd Division War Diary
6 Moskin, *The US Marine Corps Story*, p.p. 108-109
7 Ibid., p. 109
8 Ibid., p.p. 110-111
9 Ibid., p. 99 & p. 102
10 Boraston (Editor), *Sir Douglas Haig's Despatches (December 1915 – April 1919),* p.p. 253-254
11 Supplement to the London Gazette, Friday 7th June 1918, Published 8th June 1918, Gazette Issue 30736, p. 6868
12 *Soldiers Died In The Great War 1914 -1919*, p. 104; Commonwealth War Graves Commission casualty details
13 Boraston (Editor), *Sir Douglas Haig's Despatches (December 1915 – April 1919),* p. 254
14 33rd Division War Diary
15 Ibid.
16 Churchill, *The World Crisis 1911 – 1918, Vol. IV*, p. 1293
17 33rd Division War Diary; 33rd Division Royal Artillery War Diary, National Archives, WO/95/2410/1
18 Ibid.
19 Price Army Service Record
20 33rd Division War Diary

21 2nd Battalion Worcestershire Regiment War Diary
22 33rd Division War Diary
23 Ibid.; Report on Gas Cloud Attack carried out by 33rd Division and "P" Coy. R.E. – assisted by Light Railways & No5 Foreways Coy. R.E., June 22/23
24 Foulkes, *'Gas' The Story of the Special Brigade,* p. vii
25 33rd Division War Diary
26 *Soldiers Died In The Great War 1914 -1919*, p. 105; Commonwealth War Graves Commission casualty details
27 33rd Division War Diary
28 Ibid.
29 *Soldiers Died In The Great War 1914 -1919*, p. 102; Commonwealth War Graves Commission casualty details; Corporal Barley Army Service Record, National Archives, WO 363
30 33rd Division War Diary
31 Third Supplement to the London Gazette 13th September 1918, Published16th September 1918, Gazette Issue 30901, p. 10960
32 Captain Alfred Stanley Hands Army Service Record, National Archives, WO 339/37316
33 Third Supplement to the London Gazette 27th July 1918, Published 29th July 1918, Gazette Issue 29245, p. 7440
34 The London Gazette 12th January 1917, Gazette Issue 29900, p. 504
35 Supplement to the London Gazette 2nd February 1917, Published 3rd February 1917, Gazette Issue 29929, p. 1243
36 Fifth Supplement to the London Gazette 30th April 1918, Published 2nd May 1918, Gazette Issue 30665, p. 5336
37 Third Supplement to the London Gazette 25th June 1918, Published 27th June 1918, Gazette Issue 30767, p. 7582; Hands Army Service Record
38 *Soldiers Died In The Great War 1914 -1919*, p. 104; Commonwealth War Graves Commission casualty details; Private Way Army Service Record, National Archives WO 363; 1881 Census
39 *Soldiers Died In The Great War 1914 -1919*, p. 104; Commonwealth War Graves Commission casualty details; Private Symcox Army Service Record, National Archives, WO 363; 1881 Census
40 33rd Division War Diary
41 *Soldiers Died In The Great War 1914 -1919*, p. 103; Commonwealth War Graves Commission casualty details; 1911 Census
42 Ibid.; Private Johnson Army Service Record, National Archives, WO 363
43 Ibid., p. 104
44 33rd Division War Diary
45 Price Army Service Record
46 Fifth Supplement to the London Gazette, Tuesday 9th July 1918, Published 12th July 1918, Gazette Issue 30792, p. 8180

47 R.Q.M.S. Joseph Mawbey Army Service Record, National Archives, WO 363

48 *Soldiers Died In The Great War 1914 -1919*, p. 103; Commonwealth War Graves Commission casualty details; Private Luck British Army Pension Records 1914 – 1920, National Archives, WO 364; England & Wales Birth Index 1837-1915; British Army WW1 Medal Rolls Index Cards 1914 -1920; 1891 Census; 1911 Census

49 Ibid., p. 104

50 Fifth Supplement to the London Gazette 9th March 1917, Gazette Issue 29981, p. 2479

51 *The Times Diary & Index of The War 1914 -1918*, p. 152

52 1st Battalion Middlesex Regiment War Diary

53 *Soldiers Died In The Great War 1914 -1919*, p. 104; Commonwealth War Graves Commission casualty details; Lance Corporal Porter Army Service Record, National Archives, WO 363; England & Wales Death Index 1837-1915; 1911 Census

CHAPTER TWELVE

15th July 1918 to 29th August 1918

Front Line in Flanders
U.S. Troops attached to the Battalion
Training

15th July – Second Battle of Marne

The Germans launched their expected attack in the Reims sector. The ultimate objective of the attack was to threaten Paris.

The German attack was a pincer movement with two separate simultaneous attacks, with a silent gap of 12 miles between them on each side of Reims, with the objective of biting off the city and the difficult hilly region around it. The Seventh German Army attacked across the Marne to the west of Reims, and the First and Third German Armies to the east. The total width of the offensive, including the gap, was nearly 43 miles. Its general convergence was upon Châlons.

Ludendorff's aim was to draw Allied reserves southwards to defend Paris and this in turn would open the way for Crown Prince Rupprecht, with thirty-one divisions, to attack the British in Flanders, resume the Battle of Lys and drive at the Channel ports.

Generalissimo Foch, acting on intelligence received about the nature and purpose of the German attack, decided to allow the Reims battle to develop and then at the height of the attack to strike at the right flank of the advancing Germans with a heavy counter-stroke. Under the veil of secrecy Foch marshalled an army of more than twenty divisions and 350 small French tanks in the forests around Villers-Cotterets.[1]

In the eastern sector between Prunay and Massiges the Germans were held by General Gouraud's Fourth French Army which included the U.S. 42nd Division. In the west sector of the attack between Coulommes and Fossoy the

Germans advanced by two to three miles and crossed the River Marne at Fossoy.[2]

15 July. 'A' Company worked on the new track. 'B' Company worked on the communication trench. One platoon of 'C' Company worked for the No. 4 Foreways Company on making connections between Pocklington and Stanley. The rest of 'C' Company worked on the Intermediate Line.

16 July. 'A' Company worked on the new track and 'B' Company worked on the C.T. trench. One platoon of 'C' Company made connections between Pocklington and Stanley. The rest of 'C' Company worked on the Intermediate Line.

2nd Lieut. E.J. Robinson reported for duty.

Major-General Pinney went to England on leave and Brigadier-General C.R.G. Mayne D.S.O. assumed temporary command of the 33rd Division.

The officer strength of the 18th Battalion Middlesex Regiment was Lt.-Col. H.C. McNeile in command, Major W.H. Coles 2nd in command, Major C.P. Hinman, Captains R.R. Mills, H.K. Banks, A.S. Hands M.C., A. Shaw M.C., E.H. Bennett, A.W. Hills Adjutant, W.H. Adams, D.W. Parkes M.C. acting Captain, A.M. Baer, H.C. Fisher M.C., Lieutenants C. Taaffe, C.H. Tollemache (attached to the 2nd Battalion Northamptonshire Regiment), J.F. Chapman, N.W.P. Walsh, S. McL.Colvin, R.G. Bineham (Captain with 6th Battalion Northamptonshire Regiment 8 June 1918), G. Prior, P.G. Clay, S.F. Hedgecoe, R.C. Ballard, C.H. Wight M.C., G. Cotton, 2nd Lieutenants A. Payton, T. Tye, F.J. Smith, A. Burgoyne, C.R. Pughe, J.A. Woodgate, H.C.B. Jones, G.M. Lowcock (attached to the 2nd Battalion Northamptonshire Regiment), E.G. Caprara, F.S. Mason (attached to the 2nd Battalion Northamptonshire Regiment), G.W. Squier, C.M. Hopkinson (attached to the 2nd Battalion Northamptonshire Regiment), E.P. Parrish, G.W. Green, E.J. Robinson, A.A. Woodland, B.E. Davey (attached to the 2nd Battalion Northamptonshire Regiment), C.V. Sampford (attached to the 2nd Battalion Northamptonshire Regiment), A.C. Wilson, H.B. Wilson, B.E.V. Butcher, F. Clarke, V. Sang, A.V. Bromham, J.T. Tubbert, R.A.M. Hughman and Lieutenant H. Ladensack Quarter-Master.[3]

17 July. In response to the German attack east and south-west of Reims Pétain, under orders from Foch, employed the elastic front tactic where he lightly held the forward zone which forced attackers to advance beyond the support of their

trench mortars before they met the main body of the defence. This muffled the full force of the German attack.[4] The Germans were held by the French, American and Italian forces on their fronts.[5]

17 July. Two officers and 53 other ranks of the 119th Regiment, and two officers and 53 other ranks of the 120th Regiment United States Reserve (U.S.R.) Pioneer Platoons were attached for instruction to 'A' and 'B' Companies.

Lieut. Hedgecoe was wounded. Four men were wounded, two of whom were slightly wounded and stayed at duty.

18 July. Marshal Foch launched his long prepared great counter-offensive on the front between Château Thierry and Soissons. He supported this successful stroke by vigorous attacks on other parts of the German salient.[6]

Foch's attack was carried out by Mangin's Tenth Army from their concealed positions in the forest of Villers-Cotterets on the western flank of the German salient. He had twenty-two divisions including two British and two American.[7]

Mangin attacked with 330 small Renault tanks without a preliminary artillery bombardment. The tanks ground their way through the German lines. Behind them the French infantry rolled forward in immense superiority. Upon a wide front the Germans were overwhelmed.[8]

By the end of the day the French Tenth Army had penetrated to an extreme depth of ten kilometres, captured 16,000 prisoners and approximately 100 guns.[9]

The Foch counter-stroke was successful, it halted the German advance, the threat to Paris was lifted and it marked a major turning point of the war.

18 July. 'A' Company had two platoons working on Vauban Alley. The rest of 'A' Company completed the track which they were working on. 'B' Company's night party was rested. 'C' Company finished working on the Maida Vale Trench with the exception of a small maintenance party who worked by day.

19 July. Two platoons of 'A' Company worked on the Intermediate Line and two platoons on the Green Line. 'A' Company also provided one section of the maintenance party for the track from the Halifax Camp to Vijverbeek.

'B' Company took over work on the Vauban Communication Trench. 'C' Company's night working party was rested. The battalion provided road patrols.

The battalion received Divisional Order 329 at 12.30pm for the relief of the 98th Infantry Brigade by 19th Infantry Brigade.[10]

The British fight back in Flanders continued and the 9th Division recaptured Méteren. Elsewhere along the Western front gains were made. The French and American troops advanced towards the Soissons – Château Thierry road and Allied troops south of the River Marne took Montvoisin.[11]

Pursued by the French and Americans, overnight on 18/19 July, the Germans in the Marne bridgehead moved the greater part of their guns, transport and stores back across the river. They completed their retreat at 4am 20 July.[12] In this retreat they abandoned the salient created by Operation Blücher.

20 July. Work continued on the Green Line, Intermediate Line, track maintenance and road patrols.

French and British troops attacked the eastern side of the salient south-west of Reims. The British 51st and 62nd Divisions of the XXII Corps attacked on a front of 8,000 yards astride the Ardre River up the open valley bottom flanked on both sides with steep wooded slopes. Both the valley and slopes were studded with villages and hamlets which provided excellent cover to the enemy.[13]

21 July. The whole battalion bathed and was given a clean change of underclothing. This is the second change of underclothes and the third bath the men had had in just over a month.

The French retook Château Thierry.[14]

Middlesex Regiment postcard

22 July. Day work continued on the Green Line, Intermediate Line, track maintenance and road patrols. Due to the expected enemy attack night work was cancelled. Instead the men worked on the Yellow Line trench.

23 July. 'A' Company and 'B' Company changed over work. 'A' Company took on the work on the Vauban Communication Trench and Intermediate Line. 'B' Company was set to work on the Green Line.

The British attack astride the Ardre River met with vigorous and determined opposition but Marfaux was taken as the Germans continued to be forced back.[15]

The British 15th and 34th Divisions attacked the west side of the salient in the neighbourhood of Berzy-le-Sec and Parcy-Tigny south-west of Soissons.[16]

24 July. The light rail train did not arrive and 'A' Company was unable to go to work on the Vauban Communication Trench. They worked instead on the Yellow Line.

Lt.-Col. E.A. Osborne D.S.O. of the Royal Engineers took over the duties of the G.S.O.1 from Lt.-Col. Clarke who moved to become G.S.O.1 of the 20th Division.[17]

Marshal Foch, Commander in Chief of the Allied Armies, presented a memorandum to Allied commanders at the Council of War. He started by 'pointing out that his counter-stroke had not only stopped the fifth German offensive but had turned it into defeat. This defeat must be exploited, not only in Champagne, but on a much wider scale'.[18] Foch decided 'The time has come to abandon the general defensive attitude hitherto necessitated by numerical inferiority and to go over to the offensive'.[19]

Foch devised a two stage approach to the Allied offensive. The first stage was to secure three major railway lines along the Allied front:-

1) The Paris – Avricourt line in the Marne district;
2) The Paris – Amiens line;
3) The Paris – Avricourt line in the Commercy district by reducing the St. Mihiel salient.

Also as part of the first stage Foch wanted attacks to take place in Flanders to free the mining districts of Bèthune from enemy threat and to clear the enemy out of the northern ports.[20]

The second stage of Foch's plans was to launch 'an important offensive at the end of the summer or in the autumn of such a kind as to add to our advantages and to leave no respite to the enemy'.[21]

Lloyd George records that the 'scheme was not acceptable to the French and British Commanders-in-Chief...Haig and Pétain plead the fatigue of their armies: Pershing the inexperience of his. Not one of the three Commanders-in-Chief frames a formal refusal, however, being convinced that events will be responsible for bringing the plans of the General-in-Chief of the Allied Armies back within the bounds of their own conceptions'.[22]

25 July. At the request of Lloyd George Sir Henry Wilson, Chief of the Imperial General Staff (CIGS), produced a memorandum entitled 'British Military Policy 1918-1919'. In producing the memorandum Wilson personally consulted Haig and was fully aware of the views of Pétain.[23]

The report was written following the start of the 2nd Battle of Marne by Crown Prince Rupprecht which commenced on 15 July and was the fifth major German attack on the Western Front in 1918. After weeks of hard fighting Wilson observed that the attack had 'been definitely neutralised...and the threat to Paris has been greatly lessened'.

Wilson confirmed that it was known that preparations had been in hand for an attack on the British Front in Flanders, as well as between Montdidier and Noyon but he was of the view that 'On the whole it appears doubtful whether the Germans can do more than make one further attack on the grand scale' in the rest of 1918.

The best position envisaged by Wilson for the remainder of 1918 was that the 'German offensive may be fought to a standstill before any strategical decision has been obtained, leaving the Allied Armies in effective touch with each other, holding a line from the North Sea to Switzerland, coving the Channel Ports and Paris'.

On the assumption that the stalemate would be accomplished Wilson saw 'the immediate pre-occupation of the Allies must be to secure such a margin of safety for our line in France as will remove all anxiety as to our position. This will enable us to devote our efforts uninterruptedly during the ensuing period to preparation for the decisive phase'. He went on to advise that the Allied Armies 'should fix the culminating period for our supreme military effort on the Western Front not later than 1st July, 1919'.[24]

Gone was the talk of fully exploiting a break through enemy lines and achieving the much sought after decisive victory. Wilson's advice to postpone the Allied offensive until July 1919 was made after the fifth German offensive in Champagne had been severely defeated. The German Army was in retreat,

the Allied Armies had achieved numerical superiority of numbers following the huge influx of U.S. troops, and the initiative of war was firmly in their hands.

25 July. 'A' Company worked the Vauban Communication Trench and the Intermediate Line.

'B' Company worked on the Intermediate Line, Green Line and patrolled roads.

'C' Company worked on the Intermediate Line, road patrols and the demolition of horse standings.

In line with Divisional Order 331 the 98th Infantry Brigade in the right sub sector relieved the 100th Infantry Brigade.[25]

One man was wounded.

26 July. 'B' Company commenced work on four bridges and paths for artillery placements in Dawson south of Belgian Château.

27 July. 'A' Company worked the C.T trench and the Intermediate Line. 'B' Company worked on four bridges and paths for artillery placements 'C' Company worked on the Intermediate Line, patrols and the demolition of horse standings.

One man was wounded.

28 July. British troops retook Montagne de Bligny.[26]

28 July. The battalion worked on C.T. trench, Intermediate Lines, four bridges, patrols and the demolition of horse standings.

Lieut. Hamilton, United States Reserve (U.S.R.) was attached to 'B' Company for instruction.

29 July. A gas attack practice in connection with Divisional Order 332 was held at 2pm. Major-General Pinney was present at the practice.

Owing to the battalion standing by for this operation, slight alterations were made to the work. One platoon of 'A' Company took over road patrols from 'C' Company and the two U.S.R. platoons attached took over the work on the Green Line trench.

In line with Divisional Order 332 a message 'Spanners' was sent out at 10.30am.[27]

Four men were wounded.

30 July. The night party of 'A' Company was given a night's rest. The wind made it unsuitable to carry out the gas attack detailed in Divisional order 332. A message 'Spanners' was sent out at 10.30am.[28]

The XXII Corps in ten days continuous fighting of the most difficult and trying nature took 1,200 prisoners from seven different divisions and advanced four miles.[29]

31 July. The wind was still unfavourable for the operation detailed in Divisional Order 332. A message 'Spanners' was sent out at 10.30am. Work continued as before.[30]

Lt.-Col. McNeile returned from leave and resumed command of the battalion.

1 August 1918. The battalion worked on Vauban Alley, Intermediate Line, Green Line, Halifax – Dawson track running south from Belgian Château and road patrols.

2 Aug. Work continued with Vauban Alley, Intermediate Line, Green Line, Halifax – Dawson track and road patrols.

The battalion received Divisional Order 335 at 9pm for the relief of 98th Infantry Brigade by 19th Infantry Brigade.

One man was wounded.

Corporal P.W.453 Ernest Chidley aged 39 was killed in action hit by a shell. He was born in Macclesfield, Cheshire and at the age of 2 was recorded as a 'nurse child' with Elizabeth Copestick of 75 George Street, Newcastle-under-Lyme during the 1881 Census. By the 1891 Census he was still living with Elizabeth Copestick and had been adopted by her. He married Elizabeth (Lizzie) Farmer in 2nd quarter of 1901. By 1911, under the name of Ernest and Lizzie Copestick, they were living at 16 Wesley Street, Tunstall, Staffordshire and they had 3 children Ernest aged 11, Doris aged 8 and Hilda aged 3. At the time of the 1911 Census Ernest Copestick (Chidley) was employed as a Pawn Brokers Assistant.

Ernest Chidley first joined the Army on 21 September 1914 attesting at Tunstall. He stated his trade as Miners Loader. He was posted to 9th Battalion South Regiment and given the Regimental number 13273. However, he had a deformity of the left foot with hammer toes. He was discharged from the Army on 11 November 1914 under Para. 392 111c of the King's Regulations as not being likely to become an efficient soldier.

Chidley attested again at Tunstall on 5 March 1915. He listed his trade as a Collier. He had a medical on the 6 March which recorded an operation for hammer toes had left him some difficulty in getting up on his toes. Despite this he was passed fit to serve and posted to the 18th Middlesex. He travelled to France with the battalion on 11 November 1915. He was made a Lance Corporal on 27 January 1916 and Corporal on 5 August 1916. On 25 March 1918, contrary to General Route Order G.R.O. 1032 he halted vehicles outside an estaminet. He was reported by Corporal Eagle M.M.P. and reprimanded by Major W.H. Cole on 28 March 1918. On 19 July 1918 he was again reprimanded this time for making a false statement to his superior officer.

He was the son of Martha and Albert Chidley of Newcastle-under-Lyme. At sometime after March 1915 his wife moved to 5A, Victoria Street, Tunstall, Staffordshire. She received 23 shillings Separation Allowance and was awarded a pension of 26 shillings and 8 pence a week for herself and two children with effect from 24 February 1919. On 29 November 1918 she was sent her late husband's personal effects of photos, photo case, religious tracts, notes, wallet, letter, an unused registered envelope, note book, rosary, KRR Badge and two discs. He is buried in the Hagle Dump Cemetery.[31]

3 Aug. 'A' Company and attached Americans working on Vauban Alley were given a night's rest.

Two men were wounded.

4 Aug. Work continued on Vauban Alley, Intermediate Line, Green Line, Halifax – Dawson track and road patrols.

5 Aug. Work continued on the Alley, Intermediate and Green Line, Halifax – Dawson track and road patrols.

Field Marshal Haig recorded that 'The enemy had only maintained himself in the Lys salient under the constant fire of our guns at the expense of heavy casualties, not only to his infantry in line, but to his artillery and troops in back areas. With the abandonment of his projected offensive against the Channel Ports all reason had gone for remaining in so costly a salient, while the threat, carefully maintained by us, of a British attack, provided an additional reason for withdrawing.

Accordingly, from 26th July the enemy had been actively employed in removing the ammunition and stores accumulated for his offensive, and as early

as 5th August he had begun to effect local withdrawals on the southern flank of the salient'.[32]

6 Aug. Thomas McBride's baby daughter Martha celebrated her sixth birthday.

Private P.W.1120 William Thomas Bancroft born in Longport in 1880 died of his wounds aged 37. He enlisted in Stoke-on-Trent, Staffordshire and was a coal miner hewer by trade. He married Sarah Price in 1901 and they lived at 17 John Street, Longbridge Heyes, Wolstanton, Staffordshire. He travelled to France with the battalion on 11 November 1915. He is buried in the Croix-Rouge Military Cemetery.[33]

His Majesty the King presented Captain Crowe of the 2nd Worcestershire Battalion with his Victoria Cross at the Second Army Headquarters.[34]

A representative party from the 100th Infantry Brigade Minimum Reserve, under Captain E. O. Underhill, marched to Divisional Headquarters at La Lovie Château where His Majesty the King drove past the assembled troops.[35] The Château was two miles north of Poperinghe on the road to Krombeke.

7 Aug. Attempts made to carry out Divisional Order 332 to gas the enemy failed owing to bad weather.

8 Aug. The battalion received Divisional Order 336 at 12.10pm for the relief of the 100th Infantry Brigade by the 98th Infantry Brigade in the right sub sector.[36]

The Second Battle of Amiens opened. Generalissimo Marshal Foch placed Field Marshal Haig in overall command of the British, Canadian, Australian and French troops involved in the attack.

Rawlinson's Fourth Army attacked the eleven mile front from Morlancourt north of the River Somme, through Villers-Bretonneux, to just south of Dormart-sur-la-Luce on the Amiens to Roye road. On the right he had the Canadian Corps with the 1st, 2nd and 3rd Divisions in line with the 4th Division in close support. In the centre he had the Australian Corps with 2nd and 3rd Divisions in the line and the 4th and 5th Divisions in support. On the left, north of the Somme, he had the British III Corps with the 18th and 58th Divisions in the line and the 12th Division in support.

General Debeney's French First Army, forty-five minutes after the start of the British attack, attacked on the front of over four miles from Moreuil to the British right just south of the Amiens to Roye road.

The first objective of the attack was to retake the Amiens outer defences to the east between Le Quesnel and Méricourt sur Somme and thus free the Paris – Amiens railway. Once this was achieved the Fourth Army was to press immediately towards Roye and capture the important railway junction at Chaulnes. This in turn would cut the communications of the German forces in the Lassigny and Montdidier area.

At 4.20am Rawlinson's meticulously prepared artillery bombardment smashed the whole front of the attack to devastating effect. At the same time the Fourth Army and the massed British Tank Corps poured forward and rapidly gained Démuin, Marcelcave and Cérisy. By the end of the day the Fourth Army had advanced to a depth of over six miles, taking the Amiens outer defence line, including Caix, Harbonnières and Morcourt. Before daylight Le Quesnel was also taken.

North of the Somme the III Corps was held up at Chipilly.

The first day of the Second Battle of Amiens was a complete success. The Paris – Amiens railway was freed and opened a clear field for measures of exploitation. Over 13,000 prisoners were taken, between 300 and 400 guns and vast quantities of ammunition and stores of all kinds were captured.

At nightfall, east of the line of the British advance, the enemy blew up dumps in all directions whilst transport and limbers streamed eastwards towards the Somme.

The French captured Pierrepont, Plessier, Fresnoy, 3,350 prisoners and many guns.[37]

As the sun set on the 8 August on the battlefield, the greatest defeat which the German Army had suffered since the beginning of the war, was an accomplished fact. The German position divisions between the Avre and the Somme, which had been struck by the Allied attack, were all but annihilated.[38]

9 Aug. Work continued on Vauban Alley, Intermediate Line, Green Line, Halifax – Dawson track and road patrols.

The British Fourth Army met considerable opposition on the line Beaufort – Vrély – Rosières – Framerville south of the Somme. At the end of the day they had taken Méharicourt and they held Bouchoir, Rouvroy, Morcourt and were on the western outskirts of Lihons and Proyart. North of the Somme, the III Corps including the 12th Division and a regiment of the 33rd American Division, gained a line east of Chipilly, Morlancourt and Dernancourt.[39]

10 Aug. Work continued on Vauban Alley, Intermediate Line, Green Line, Halifax – Dawson track and road patrols.

The French First Army under General Debeney attacked and recaptured Montdidier.[40]

11 Aug. The 119th and 120th United States Reserve Pioneer Platoons left the battalion to rejoin their units.

12 Aug. Work continued on Vauban Alley, Intermediate Line, Green Line, Halifax – Dawson track and road patrols.

By the evening the Fourth Army attack north of the Somme had reached the western edges of Bray-sur-Somme. South of the Somme they reached the old German defences of 1916 on a general line west of Damery, east of Lihons, east of Proyart. By nightfall further to the south the advance reached the general line of the old Roye – Chaulnes defences.

Field Marshal Haig observed 'the derelict battle area which now lay before our troops, was seared by old trench lines, pitted with shell holes, and crossed in all directions with tangled belts of wire, the whole covered by wild vegetation of two years, presented unrivalled opportunities for stubborn machine gun defence'.[41]

13 Aug. The Fourth Army attack south of the Somme was met by a heavily reinforced enemy ready to give battle for their positions. Haig, for once, did not press the attack, instead he broke it off. He planned to transfer his attack to the sector north of the Somme with the intention of the Third Army operating in the direction of Bapaume, so as to turn the line of the old Somme defences from the north.

In the five days of the Second Battle of Amiens the town of Amiens and the railway centring upon it had been disengaged. Nearly 22,000 prisoners and over 400 guns were taken and the front line pushed forward to a depth of twelve miles. This gave the Allies their second decisive victory in less than four weeks.[42]

13 Aug. The battalion received Divisional Order 337 at 12.45pm for the relief of the 19th Infantry Brigade by the 100th Infantry Brigade in the left sub sector.[43]

14 Aug. Work continued on trenches, Green Line defences and road patrols.

Marshal Foch urged Haig to press his attack against Chaulnes – Roye front. Haig refused because they could only be taken after heavy casualties in men and tanks.[44]

15 Aug. The battalion worked on trenches, Green Line defences and road patrols.

Lt.-Col. Henry Storr D.S.O., aged 43, the former Commanding Officer of the battalion, died in Queen Alexandra's Military Hospital, Westminster, London. He had suffered from influenza for nine days and had broncho pneumonia of both lungs and heart failure. His death certificated wrongly states that at the time of his death he was the Commanding Officer of the 19th Battalion Middlesex Regiment.[45] He was the son of Marian and Henry Storr of 29 Matfield Court, Matfield Green, Brenchley, Tonbridge, Kent. He is buried in the Matfield (St. Luke) Churchyard to the east of the Church, Brenchley.[46]

16 Aug. The battalion finally got a day's rest. The men had done a great deal to strengthen the fortifications to the front line around the south, the south-west and south-east of Ypres.

Work was handed over to officers of 2nd Battalion 105th American Regiment of Engineers.

The battalion received instructions that the gas attack, in line with Divisional Order 332, would not be carried out on the night of 17/18 August.[47]

Strathcona Camp Proven

17 Aug. 2/105th American Engineers relieved the battalion.

The battalion received Divisional Order 340 at noon for the move of the 19th Infantry Brigade transport.

The battalion was taken by light railway to the Strathcona Camp near Proven.

18 Aug. The battalion got another day's rest.

In Flanders British patrols, whose activities had been constant, made considerable advances opposite Merville.[48]

Ouest Mont

19 Aug. The battalion was transported by train to Watten and marched from there to Ouest Mont six miles north-west of St. Omer.

British troops took Merville. The whole front line in Flanders moved forward from the Lawe River to the Plate Becque.[49]

To straighten, shorten and strengthen their front line, the Germans were forced to retreat further on the Lys. Between 14 and 17 August they had withdrawn from their position about Serre. Overnight on 13/14 August British troops had pushed forward and established posts south and east of Vieux Berquin. By 19 August Outtersteene village and ridge and some 900 prisoners had been captured by the 9th, 29th and 31st Divisions of the Second Army.[50]

Holque

20 Aug. The battalion marched to Holque three miles north-east of Ouest Mont.

General Mangin's French Tenth Army attacked northwards along a twelve mile front near Soissons to its left boundary on the Oise and penetrated the German front to an average depth of over 3,000 yards. The extension of the great offensive to the right and left had begun.[51]

21st August 1918 – The Battle for Bapaume.

The Battle for Bapaume was an extension of the Second Battle of Amiens. Field Marshal Haig planned to make his main attack against the Germans between the River Scarpe and the River Somme. Haig reasoned that the Germans did not seem prepared for an attack in this direction, the left flank of salient held by the enemy was already threatened from the south, the ground north of the Ancre River was not greatly damaged by shellfire and was therefore suitable for tanks, and a successful attack between Albert and Arras in a south easterly direction would turn the line of the Somme defences south of Péronne. This in turn would be a step forward towards the strategic objective of St. Quentin – Cambrai.

As a precursor to the main attack scheduled for 23 August, the British Third Army, supported by tanks, attacked along a nine mile front north of Albert from Miraumont to Moyenneville. The German foremost defences were rapidly carried. The attacking troops reached the general line of the Arras – Albert railway line on practically the whole front, taking Achiet-le-Petit, Logeast Wood, Courcelles, Moyenneville and the northern bank of the Ancre was cleared about Beaucourt. Over 2,000 prisoners were taken.[52]

Field Marshal Haig had lunch with Winston Churchill, Minister for

Munitions. Haig told Churchill 'we ought to do our upmost to get a decision this autumn'. In reply Churchill told Haig the General Staff in London remained of the view that 'the decisive period of the war cannot arrive until next July'.[53]

21 Aug. The battalion was given another day's rest.

22 Aug. Training began with platoon commanders training their own platoons.

The British Fourth Army, supported by a small number of tanks, attacked the Germans between Albert and the Somme. They forced a passage of the River Ancre and captured Albert. The British front line was advanced well beyond the Bray – Albert road. Over 2,400 prisoners were taken.[54]

Haig issued a notice to Army Commanders changing the conditions under which operations were to be carried out. The new instruction read 'It is no longer necessary to advance step by step in regular lines as in 1916 -17 battles. All Units must go straight for their objectives, while Reserves should be pushed in where we are gaining ground'.[55]

Battle of Bapaume

The main attack of the Battle of Bapaume was launched. The British Third Army, together with the divisions of the Fourth Army north of the Somme, attacked along the whole of the thirty-three mile front from the junction with the French north of Lihons to Mercatel. The attacks were supported by about one hundred tanks.

Herleville, Chuignolles, Chuignes and 2,000 prisoners were captured by the Australian Corps.

The III and V Corps recommenced their attack about Albert and captured the high ground east of the town known as Tara and Usna Hills. Two companies of the Welsh Regiment waded the Ancre in the neighbourhood of Hamel and maintained themselves on the east of the river all day.

Gomiecourt, Bihucourt, Ervillers, Boyelles and Boiry Becquerelle were taken together with over 5,000 prisoners and a number of guns. British troops straddled the Arras – Bapaume road and were closing in on the town from the north and north-west. The German position on the Thiepval Ridge salient became perilous.[56]

23 Aug. 'A' Company moved to Inglinghem to construct a rifle range. The rest of the battalion was engaged in training.

24 Aug. The attack resumed on the whole front from the Somme to Neuville-Vitasse. Bray-sur-Somme was taken and the line was carried forward across the high ground between Bray and La Boisselle.

The Third Army carried the Thiepval Ridge. Thiepval village, the high ground above Ovillers, Pozières, Courcelette, Martinpuich, Miraumont, Pys, Irles, Grévillers and Biefvillers were taken and Loupart Wood cleared. Avesnes-lès-Bapaume was reached. Strong opposition was encountered on the high ground between Sapignies and Mory. St. Léger and Hénin-sur-Cojeul were taken and a footing gained in St. Martin-sur-Cojeul.[57]

The battalion trained. Officers of the battalion were given a demonstration by staff of the Inspector General (I.G.) of Training at Serques.

25 Aug. The battalion had another day's rest.

Favreuil was cleared, Sapignies and Behagnies were captured and the Germans were driven from Mory.[58]

26 Aug. 'A' Company returned from Inglinghem. Training was cancelled.

The battalion received Divisional Order 342 at 2.35pm for the 33rd Division, less artillery, to be transferred to the Third Army.[59]

In the French sector south of the Somme the Germans evacuated Roye.[60]

27 Aug. 'C' Company marched to St. Omer to work as a loading party for the 98th Brigade Group.

'A' and 'B' Companies were given a day's rest.

The battalion received Divisional Order 343 at 5.45am for the move by train the following day to Doullens.[61]

Flers was attacked and bitter fighting once more took place in front of Trônes Wood, in Delville Wood and Longueval Wood.[62]

28 Aug. The battalion marched to St. Omer and entrained for Doullens.

Hardecourt and the spur south of it were taken.[63]

29 Aug. The battalion arrived at Doullens and marched to Sombrin.

The Germans evacuated Bapaume and the New Zealand Division promptly occupied the town. The 18th Division entered Combles. North of Bapaume the 56th and 57th Divisions penetrated Riencourt-lés-Cagnicourt. The British line was established in the western and northern outskirts of Bullecourt and Hendecourt.[64]

Taking Bapaume and affecting a decisive break through had been the primary objective of Haig in the 1916 Battle of the Somme.

1 Churchill, *The World Crisis 1911 – 1918, Vol. IV*, p.p. 1324-1325
2 *The Times Diary & Index of The War 1914 -1918*, p. 152
3 British Army Lists
4 Lloyd George, *War Memoirs, Vol. 2*, p.1848
5 Boraston (Editor), *Sir Douglas Haig's Despatches (December 1915 – April 1919),* p. 255
6 Ibid.
7 Lloyd George, *War Memoirs, Vol. 2*, p.1848
8 Churchill, *The World Crisis 1911 – 1918, Vol. IV*, p. 1331
9 Lloyd George, *War Memoirs, Vol. 2*, p.1848
10 33rd Division War Diary
11 *The Times Diary & Index of The War 1914 -1918*, p. 153
12 Edmonds, *Military Operations, France And Belgium, Vol. 3*, HMSO, London, 1939, p.p. 243-244
13 Boraston, (Editor), *Sir Douglas Haig's Despatches (December 1915 – April 1919),* p. 255
14 *The Times Diary & Index of The War 1914 -1918*, p. 153
15 Boraston (Editor), *Sir Douglas Haig's Despatches (December 1915 – April 1919),* p. 255
16 Ibid.
17 33rd Division War Diary, National Archives, WO 95/2407/3
18 Lloyd George, *War Memoirs, Vol. 2*, p.1853
19 Ibid., p. 1855
20 Ibid.
21 Ibid., p. 1856
22 Ibid.,
23 Ibid., p. 1862
24 Sir Henry Wilson, Chief of the Imperial General Staff, *Memorandum British Military Policy 1918 - 1919*, 25 July 1918, National Archives, CAB/25/85 Part 1, Image reference1, p.p. 2-9
25 33rd Division War Diary
26 Boraston (Editor), Sir *Douglas Haig's Despatches (December 1915 – April 1919),* p. 255
27 33rd Division War Diary
28 Ibid.
29 Boraston (Editor), Sir *Douglas Haig's Despatches (December 1915 – April 1919),* p. 255
30 33rd Division War Diary
31 *Soldiers Died In The Great War 1914 -19*, p. 102; Commonwealth War Graves Commission casualty details; Corporal Chidley Army Service Records, National Archives, WO 363; England & Wales Marriage Index 1837-1915; 1881 Census; 1891 Census, 1911 Census
32 Boraston (Editor), Sir *Douglas Haig's Despatches (December 1915 – April 1919),* p. 272
33 *Soldiers Died In The Great War 1914 -19*, p. 102; Commonwealth War Graves

Commission casualty details; England & Wales Birth Index 1837-1915; England & Wales Marriage Index 1837-1915; 1911 Census

34 2nd Battalion Worcestershire Regiment War Diary

35 Ibid.

36 33rd Division War Diary

37 Boraston (Editor), Sir *Douglas Haig's Despatches (December 1915 – April 1919),* p.p. 258-262

38 Edmonds, *Military Operations, France And Belgium 1918, Vol. 4,* HMSO, London, 1947, p.p. 88-89

39 Boraston (Editor), Sir *Douglas Haig's Despatches (December 1915 – April 1919),* p. 262

40 Ibid.

41 Ibid.

42 Ibid., p. 263

43 33rd Division War Diary

44 Blake (Editor), *The Private Papers of Douglas Haig 1914 -1919*, p. 323

45 General Register Office, Death Certificate, COL34964

46 Commonwealth War Graves Commission casualty details

47 33rd Division War Diary

48 Boraston (Editor), Sir *Douglas Haig's Despatches (December 1915 – April 1919),* p. 272

49 Ibid.

50 Ibid., p. 264

51 Edmonds, *Military Operations, France And Belgium, Vol. 4*, p.173

52 Boraston (Editor), Sir *Douglas Haig's Despatches (December 1915 – April 1919),* p.p. 264-266

53 Blake (Editor), *The Private Papers of Douglas Haig 1914 -1919*, p. 324

54 Boraston (Editor), Sir *Douglas Haig's Despatches (December 1915 – April 1919),* p. 266

55 Blake (Editor), *The Private Papers of Douglas Haig 1914 -1919*, p. 324

56 Boraston (Editor), Sir *Douglas Haig's Despatches (December 1915 – April 1919),* p.p. 266-268

57 Ibid., p.p. 268-269

58 Ibid., p. 269

59 33rd Division War Diary

60 Boraston (Editor), Sir *Douglas Haig's Despatches (December 1915 – April 1919),* p. 270

61 33rd Division War Diary

62 Boraston (Editor), Sir *Douglas Haig's Despatches (December 1915 – April 1919),* p. 269

63 Ibid.

64 Ibid.

CHAPTER THIRTEEN

30th August 1918 to 24th September 1918

Training
Back to the Somme
Back to the Hindenburg Line – Villers-Guislain

Sombrin

30 Aug. Platoons trained for two hours.

The Third and Forth Armies front line north of the Somme now ran from Clery-sur-Somme past the western edge of Marrières Wood to Combles, Lesboeufs, Bancourt, Frémicourt and Vraucourt, and thence to the western outskirts of Ecoust, Bullecourt and Hendecourt.[1]

The Germans in a strategic combination of forced retreat and tactical withdrawal once again returned to the formidably fortified Hindenburg Line where they dug-in furiously in anticipation of an all-out allied assault.

31 Aug. Training.

Alfred Enoch Price received a letter from the War Office dated 5 July 'The accompanying war badge and certificate No. 423069 are forwarded hereby to A.E. Price in respect of War service as PW/1124 Middlesex Regiment. The badge will be worn on the right breast or on the right lapel of the jacket, but not in naval or military uniform. Duplicates of the badge and certificate cannot be issued under any circumstances. Receipt of the same are acknowledged hereon'. Alfred Enoch Price signed that he had received the badge and certificate.[2] The certificate read PW/1124 Private Alfred Enoch Price Middlesex Regiment Served with honour and was disabled in the Great War. Honourably discharged on 8 July, 1918. The certificate was signed by King George V.

Overnight on the 30 and 31 August the 2nd Australian Division stormed Mont. St. Quentin, which was a strategic feature commanding the crossing of

the River Somme at Péronne. Flooding and machine gun fire prevented the 5th Australians Infantry Brigade from crossing the river opposite Mont St. Quentin so they crossed two miles further west at Feuillières. By 10.15pm the Brigadc had captured the German trenches east of Cléry.

The Australians used the captured trenches as an assembly point for their attack on Mont. St. Quentin which was launched at 5am. They captured the Mont and then repulsed repeated counter-attacks delivered throughout the day and night with great resolution by strong hostile forces which resulted in extremely severe fighting. Nearly 1,000 prisoners were taken and there were heavy German casualties.

Field Marshal Haig stated that taking Mont St. Quentin 'ranks as a most gallant achievement'.[3]

On 31 August the Fourth Army, supporting the attack at Mont St. Quentin, attacked towards Bouchavesnes, Rancourt and Frégicourt. They took the villages on 1 September.

The Third Army also launched an attack on 31 August. By the evening of 1 September they had captured Sailly-Saillisel, Morval, Beaulencourt, Riencourt-les-Bapaume and established positions on the ridge east of Bancourt, Frémicourt, Vaulx Vraucourt and Longatte.

XVII Corps troops completed the capture of Bullecourt and Hendecourt on 31 August. Overnight they captured Riencourt-lez-Cagnicourt and 380 prisoners.[4]

The 1/7th Battalion Middlesex Regiment took the factory north-east of Bullecourt.[5]

Battle Of Scarpe

The Battle of Scarpe commenced on 26 August and ran simultaneously with the Battle of Bapaume. By 25 August the advance of the British First Army under General Horne had formed a salient of the German position opposite Arras. Field Marshal Haig judged that the time had come to extend the flank of the attack to the north.

The aim of the planned attack was to drive eastwards from Arras, turn the enemy's position on the Somme and cut his system of railway communications which ran southwards across the area. The left flank of the attack was covered by the River Scarpe and the River Sensée.

26 August. The Canadian Corps on the right of the First Army attacked the German positions on a five and half mile front astride the River Scarpe. They were closely supported by the left of the Third Army. By noon they had taken Wancourt and Guemappe and had stormed the hill and village of Monchy-le-Preux. They then pressed east of the three villages making substantial progress and repulsing a strong counter-attack.

North of the Scarpe the 51st Division pushed forward their line towards Roeux and captured Greenland Hill in the evening.

On 27 August the First Army took Chérisy, Vis-en-Artois, the Bois du Sart, Roeux and Gavrelle.

By the end of August the high ground east of Chérisy and Haucourt was gained, Eterpigny was captured and the area between the Sensée and Scarpe rivers west of the Trinquis Brook was cleared. North of the Somme Plouvain was captured.

These actions brought British and Colonial troops to within assaulting distance of the powerful trench system running from the Hindenburg Line at Quéant to the Lens defences about Drocourt, the breaking of which would turn the whole of the enemy's organised positions on a wide front.[6]

Lys Salient

Overnight on 29/30 August, as a result of the dual pressures of constant aggression by troops on the spot and by the urgency of events elsewhere, the enemy commenced an extensive retirement on the whole of the Lys front.

By the morning of 30 August British troops found Bailleul unoccupied by the enemy. Advanced British detachments reached the general line Lacouture, Lestrem, Noote Boom and east of Bailleul.[7]

1 September 1918. Platoons trained.

The 2nd Australian Division captured Péronne.[8]

2 Sept. Major-General Pinney inspected the battalion. He presented some medal ribbons.

The German trench system at the junction of the Hindenburg Line and the Drocourt – Quéant Line was attacked at 5am on a four-and-half-mile front by the 1st and 4th Canadian Divisions. The attack was supported by forty tanks, a

force of mobile machine gun units, Canadian Cavalry and armoured cars. By noon the whole of the elaborate system of wire, trenches and strong points constituting the Drocourt – Quéant Line had been taken.

At the same time, on the right, the XVII corps attacked the triangle of fortifications marking the junction of the Hindenburg Line and the Drocourt – Quéant Line north-west of the village of Quéant. They met stern fighting north and south of Quéant but by early afternoon they had cleared the triangle. The 63rd Division passed through to exploit the breakthrough.

During the afternoon British troops met considerable resistance from German machine gun nests in the woods and villages on the reverse side of Dury Ridge. By nightfall that resistance had been overcome and British troops reached the railway line east of Quéant.

The whole of the German front south of the junction was pushed back by three miles along the Cambrai – Arras road to the outskirts of Buissy. The Allies took Villers-lès-Cagnicourt, Cagnicourt and Dury. 8,000 prisoners and many guns were captured.[9]

3 Sept. Platoons trained.

The Germans fell back rapidly on the whole front of the Third Army and the right of the First Army. By the end of the day the Germans had taken up positions along the general line of the Canal du Nord from Péronne to Ytres and thence east of Hermies, Inchy-en-Artois and Ecourt St. Quentin to the Sensée east of Lecluse.

During the Battle of Scarpe ten British divisions attacked and overthrew thirteen German divisions and forced their general retreat. 16,000 prisoners and 200 guns were taken.[10]

4 Sept. Platoons trained.

Divisional Headquarters moved to Château Lucheux in the village of Lucheux north-east of Doullens.[11]

5/6 Sept. Platoons trained.

7 Sept. Platoons trained. The battalion received Divisional order 345 at 8.15pm for the move of the battalion, together with the 33rd Battalion Machine Gun Corps to Warlincourt.[12]

Private P.W.347 Joseph Edward Corrigan aged 36, was killed in action. He

married Fanny Jupe in 1913 at Farnham, Suffolk and they lived at 4 St. Mary's Place, East Street, Farnham. Fanny was a widow with a daughter Edith Nellie dob 24 November 1901 from her previous marriage to the late Albert Edward Jupe. Together with Corrigan she had a son Harry Edward dob 23 June 1913. Corrigan attested at Farnham on 3 March 1915 and after a medical at Aldershot was posted to the 18th Middlesex on 5 March 1915. He was labourer by trade, 5′ 4½″ tall and weighed 128 lbs. He travelled to France with the battalion on 11 November 1915. He suffered a shell wound to his ribs on 20 March 1916 and was admitted to the 34 Casualty Clearing Station. He was mildly gassed on 27 July 1917. He suffered a more serious mustard gas wound on 1 October 1917, he returned to England and was admitted to the Red Cross Hospital in Hale on 2 October. He was discharged on 3 November 1917 and transferred to the Base Depot. He then transferred to the 19th Middlesex on 30 March 1918 and returned to France. He was gassed again on 8 May 1918. On 13 August 1918 he transferred to the 112th Company of the Labour Corps and given the Regimental number 615499.

Joseph Corrigan was the son of Jane and Michael Corrigan of 4 River Row, Wrecclesham, Farnham. Fanny Corrigan had moved by July 1918 to 3 Holmes Cottages, Upper Hale, Farnham. She received 19 shillings and sixpence Separation Allowance and was awarded a pension of 20 shillings and 5 pence per week for herself and 1 child with effect from 31 March 1919. On 13 February 1919 she received her late husband's personal effects of letters, photos, wallet and note book. Private Corrigan is buried in the Faubourg D'Amiens Cemetery, Arras – Pas de Calais.[13]

Warlincourt

8 Sept. The battalion marched to Warlincourt.

The German retreat gathered pace as they withdrew to the general line from Vermand, Epéhy, Havrincourt and thence along the east bank of the Canal du Nord.

The French took Ham and Chauny on 6 September and by 8 September they had pushed the line back to the Crozat Canal.[14]

9 Sept. Platoon training.

10 Sept. Platoon training.

Field Marshal Haig had a meeting at the War Office with Lord Milner, Secretary of State for War. Haig had requested the meeting to explain how greatly the situation in the field had changed to the advantage of the Allies. Haig considered it of the first importance that the Cabinet should realise how that change affected the plans and methods of the future prosecution of the war. Haig told Milner that 'if we act with energy now, a decision can be obtained in the very near future'. To exploit success and achieve that decisive victory Haig told Milner he needed the troops currently in England, including the reserves and those troops kept for civil defence, to be sent to France immediately. Haig recorded that Milner fully agreed and said he would do his best to help.[15]

11 Sept. Platoons trained.

12 Sept. Platoons trained.

Before a major assault could be launched against the Hindenburg Line the formidable German defences in front of it at Havrincourt and Epéhy had to be cleared. The British Third Army attacked the German positions in the Havrincourt area of the Hindenburg Line on a five mile front. The New Zealand 37th Division took Trescault and the New Zealand 62nd Division took Havrincourt.[16]

The American First Army, assisted by a number of French divisions, drove the enemy out of the St. Mihiel salient and inflicted heavy losses on them in terms of prisoners and guns.[17]

13 Sept. Platoon training.

Private P.W.2723 Frederick Reynolds aged 45, from Richmond died. He attested on 13 May 1915 at Kew Bridge London. He was a carman by trade and was posted to the 18th Middlesex on 17 May 1915. He married Bessie (Elizabeth) Ann Balls at the Trinity Church, Richmond on 3 February 1901. They had a daughter Louisa May dob 12 March 1909 and they lived at 10 Hyde Road, Richmond.

Frederick Reynolds travelled to France with the battalion on 11 November 1915. On 11 February 1918 he was admitted to the 99th Field Ambulance suffering from tonsillitis. He rejoined the 18th Middlesex on 19 February. He reported sick again on 4 April to the Medical Officer suffering from bronchitis, chest pains, sore throat, shortness of breath and a very bad cough.

He was admitted to the 64 Casualty Clearing Station where he complained of a very bad cough, shortness of breath and pain in the small of his back.

He later transferred to 55 General Hospital at Boulogne and was then sent back to England on 11 April 1918. He was admitted to the Edinburgh War Hospital, Bangour where a month after being admitted to hospital in France he had developed twitching of the right side of his face, stertorous breathing, had severe headaches, a very bad cough and was unable to speak or understand what was said to him. His blood pressure was 180 m.m. Doctors removed 30 ounces of blood from his veins and his blood pressure dropped to 150 m.m. His general condition was described as poor. He was medically examined on 4 June 1918 and diagnosed as suffering from arterio sclerosis and bronchitis and was recommended for discharge from the Army as he was permanently unfit for service of any kind under para. 392 (XVI) of the King's Regulations. The degree of his disability was assessed at 50% and whilst this disability was not attributable to service during the war it had been aggravated by his service. He was duly discharged from the Army on 1 July 1918. He was awarded the Silver War Badge.

Frederick Reynolds was the son of Elizabeth and George Reynolds. By the end of the war his wife Elizabeth had moved to 72 Porchester Road, Woolston, Southampton, Hants. He is buried in the Richmond Cemetery, Surrey.[18]

Ginchy

14 Sept. The battalion moved to Ginchy, right back into the heart of the old Somme battlefield, following a lengthy spell of duty at the front in Flanders. The men travelled by bus. The battalion transport went by road.

The battalion received Divisional Order 346 6.30pm for the move of the division overnight.[19]

15 Sept. The battalion was given a day's rest. The transport arrived at Ginchy at 11.30pm.

33rd Divisional H.Q. moved to le Mesnil-en-Arrouaise near the ruined village of Sailly-Saillisel also at the heart of the old Somme battlefield.

16 Sept. More training.

The battalion received Divisional Order 347 at 8.15am placing the 98th Infantry Brigade Trench Mortar Battery at the disposal of the 38th Division and

their move by lorry to 38th Division area and for the 19th Infantry Brigade to be relieved in the line. Major-General Pinney assumed command of the Right Sector V Corps front line.[20]

Private P.W.1124 Alfred Enoch Price died of his wounds. He was one of at least eleven Tommies who lived in and around Ashton-under-Lyne who left England with 18th Middlesex to fight in this Great War.

Whilst he was at the Colchester Military Hospital Price he was diagnosed as having a 100% disability and discharged from the Army on 8 July 1918 under Paragraph 392 (XVI) of the King's Regulations as being 'no longer physically fit for War Service'. He was awarded a War Pension of 27 Shillings and sixpence per week and an allowance of 24 shillings and 2 pence for his five children from 9 July 1918 to 7 January 1919.

He was not fit to return to his family home so was transferred to the House for Disabled Soldiers in Park Lane, Broughton, Salford. Uraemia (azotaemia chronic renal failure) set in on 14 September and he died forty-eight hours later. Alfred Price was forty years old and a coal hewer by trade. He was the husband of Mary Maria Price (nee Shemwell) of 53 Charles Street, Ashton-under-Lyne. They were married on 22 May 1899 at the Parish Church, Hednesford, Staffordshire. They had 6 surviving children. Alfred Price is buried in the Ashton-under-Lyne and Dukinfield Joint Cemetery – Cheshire.[21]

17 Sept. Training.

The 19th Infantry Brigade was relieved in the line. At 6.10am Major-General Pinney gave up command of the line.[22]

As part of the attack to clear the fortifications in front of the Hindenburg Line the IX Corps and Australian Corps captured Holnon village and wood and Maissemy and then moved on Le Verguier and Templeux-le-Guérard.

18 Sept. The Third and Fourth Armies, in torrential rain, attacked the Germans along a seventeen-mile front from Holnon to Gouzeaucourt. The ground over which the attack took place had continuous and well organised defensive belts formed by the old British and German lines. The advancing British troops met strong resistance on the extreme right and in the left centre at Epéhy. Before nightfall the last centres of resistance in Epéhy had been reduced. The front line was advanced a further three miles into previously held German territory.

The French First Army cooperated by attacking south of Holnon.[23]

At 5.20am 17th, 21st and 38th Divisions of the V Corps attacked the German

positions on the south and western outskirts of Villers-Guislain. They took Fives Trench, Beet Trench and part of Guislain Trench. Despite being held up by machine gun fire from Limerick Trench and Lark Spur the advance continued and Meunier Trench was occupied and Gauche Wood entered. They advanced along Leith Walk and pressed the front line up from Leith Walk to Meath Post and from Parrs Trench to Limerick Lane. 18 German officers, 443 other ranks and 877 guns were captured.[24]

At 11.55am the 98th Infantry Brigade was ordered to be held at 30 minutes notice to move. The 19th Infantry Brigade Light Trench Mortar Battery and 98th Light Trench Mortar Battery rejoined their brigades during the morning. Two companies of 33rd Battalion Machine Gun Corps attached to the 21st Division reverted to the command of their own company and were concentrated in between Équancourt and Fins by 1pm.

The two companies of the 33rd Battalion Machine Gun Corps attached to the 17th Division reverted to the command of their own company and were also concentrated between Équancourt and Fins by 8.50pm.[25]

Manancourt

18 Sept. The battalion marched to Manancourt on the banks of the Canal du Nord.

19 Sept. The battalion, less headquarters, moved to bivouacs in Équancourt Wood to the east of Canal du Nord. The battalion was edging once again closer to the front line.

The battalion received Divisional Order 349 at 12.30pm for the relief of the 33rd Division.

At 7.20pm a warning order was received from V Corps that the 33rd Division may have to capture just part of the Red Line on the Divisional front the following night.[26] Here the Red Line ran for just over three quarters of a mile south along Gloster Road from the crossroads with Leith Walk to the crest of Lark Spur between Kildare Avenue and Dados Lane.[27]

20 Sept. At 3.30am Major-General Pinney once again assumed command of the right sector, V Corps front.

Three supply tanks were placed at the disposal of 33rd Division.[28]

Divisional patrols were reported to have reached as far as the Meunier Trench 1,000 yards south of Villers-Guislain between Villers Hill and the Targelle Ravine. The 33rd Division ordered the V Corps to attack, in conjunction with the 58th Division, the front south of Villers-Guislain to Kildare Avenue on the Lark Spur the following day. Zero hour was 5.20am.[29]

Équancourt

The 18th Middlesex Battalion headquarters moved up to Équancourt Wood.

'B' and 'C' Companies moved into forward positions in trenches west of the Sugar Factory in Heudicourt. 'B' Company wired strong points along the 800 yard section from the southern end of Fives Trench east of Chapel Crossing to the beet factory south-west of Villers-Guislain.

One man was wounded.

21 Sept. 'C' Company worked on forward roads. 'B' Company did not work due to military operations.

Material for the construction of the new 33rd Divisional H.Q. was salvaged by 'A' Company from huts.

At 5.20am, in accordance with Divisional order 350, the 33rd Division attacked the outer defences of the Hindenburg Line south of Villers-Guislain. The 98th Infantry Brigade, with one battalion only of the 2nd Argyll and Sutherland Highlanders, attacked the section of Meunier Trench from south of Villers-Guislain to Leith Walk. Their further objectives were to take the Meunier Support Trench and Gloster Road as far south as Leith Walk. The 4th King's (Liverpool) Regiment were held ready to exploit any success and the 1st Middlesex Regiment were held in reserve.

The 19th Infantry Brigade with three battalions, the 1st Queen's on the right and 1st Cameronians on the left and the 5/6th Cameronians in reserve, attacked the front south from Leith Walk to Kildare Avenue. Their objectives were to take the strong points Meath Post and Limerick Trench and the section of Gloster Road from Kildare Avenue up to Leith Walk on the Targelle Ravine.[30]

The 175th Infantry Brigade of the 58th Division attacked Dados Loop on the right flank on the 19th Infantry Brigade front.[31]

The 2nd Argyll and Sutherland Highlanders reached the southern end of the Meunier Trench and Meunier Support but by 10.50am they were forced to

withdraw. The 1st Queen's were held up at Limerick Post.[32] The attack by the 1st Cameronians was met with intense machine gun fire from Meath Post and they were held up by uncut wire. They suffered heavy casualties and the remnants of the battalion collected and organised in Meath Lane.[33] Four platoons of 175th Infantry Brigade were held up in the western end of Kildare Avenue by fire from Limerick Post.

Divisional Order 351 was issued at 2pm ordering the 19th Infantry Brigade to attack at 7.45pm and penetrate the trench system either side of Meath Post and exploit any success by attacking north and south over the open ground. The 98th Infantry Brigade was ordered to attack down both sides of Gloster Road and Meunier Trench in the open. The 175th Infantry Brigade was held ready to attack Kildare Post in the event of Limerick Post being captured.[34]

Elements of the 1st Queen's were in Kildare Avenue with troops from 175th Infantry Brigade 400 yards west of Limerick Post on Lark Spur. The remainder of the 19th Infantry Brigade held the sunken road on the Quail Ravine astride Meath Lane 220 yards west of Meath Post. They also held Meath Lane west of the sunken road and the Targelle Trench across the Quail Ravine.

The 2nd Argyll and Sutherland Highlanders held the Meunier Trench and Meunier Support Trench along the section on Villers Hill. They also held the Beet Trench to the Divisional boundary.

The attack commenced at 'zero' as planned. The protective barrage was reduced to half of its intensity at 8.55pm and ceased at 9.10pm.

By 1am 22 September the 2nd Argyll and Sutherland Highlanders had made progress down Meunier Trench and Meunier Support Trench and had deployed a bombing party up Storar Avenue. However they failed to reach the crossroads with Leith Walk and the numerous attacks on Gloster Road, across open land, failed with the enemy holding the line in strength.

The 5/6th Cameronians captured Meath Post and established a 600 yard line north along Gloster Road from the Targelle Valley to the Targelle Ravine just 80 yards short of Leith Walk. The 1st Queen's failed to capture Limerick Post.

22 Sept. Between 5.20am and 5.40am counter preparation fire was carried out by the Divisional Artillery on Leith Walk, across the Targelle Valley to the road running north-west from Gloster Road to Tyhurst Quarry. Machine gun fire was directed on Tyhurst and Pigeon quarries.

Pockets of enemy troops were still around Leith Walk in the vicinity of the crossroads with Gloster Road.

The 98th Infantry Brigade held Meunier Trench as far as its junction with Storar Avenue and Meunier Support Trench 300 yards north of Leith Walk crossroads. The 19th Infantry Brigade held Limerick Lane from Pigeon Ravine north past Meath Post towards Meath Trench south of Leith Walk.

At 3.30pm the 19th Infantry Brigade unsuccessfully attacked Limerick Post.

A further attack was planned for 9.30pm. The 19th Infantry Brigade was to attack Limerick Post and the trench system and hollow road 400 yards east of it. The 98th Infantry Brigade was to attack Derby Post 800 yards south-east of Villers-Guislain and Gloster Road north of Leith Road. The 175th Infantry Brigade was to attack Kildare Post and Dados Loop.[35]

At 9.30pm 2nd Worcestershire Regiment, attached to the 19th Infantry Brigade, was due to attack Limerick Post but the 19th Infantry guides assigned to take them to their positions got lost in the dark. The 33rd Divisional Artillery barrage came down at 9.15pm and passed before the 2nd Worcestershires were in place. The Germans immediately responded sending down a barrage along Thrush Valley and the sunken road running south along the eastern slope of Thrush Valley to Epéhy. This caused the Worcestershires considerable casualties. They temporarily established themselves in the sunken road by Poplar Trench.[36] Their attack on Limerick Post failed.

The 98th Infantry Brigade was ordered to take Gloster Road and Derby Post and join up with 19th Infantry Brigade at the Gloster Road/Leith Walk crossroads. The primary attack on the objectives was carried out by two platoons of 'A' Company 2nd Argyll and Sutherland Highlander with a platoon from 'C' Company detailed to bomb down Gloster Road on the right and join up with 'D' Company holding a block in the old front line at Storar Avenue.

The three platoons, under the command of Lieut. McLean M.C. formed up in No Man's Land parallel to their objectives and attacked at 9.48pm. They were met by very heavy rifle and machine gun fire but Lieut. McLean and twenty men made it into Gloster Road. They found only one German who was about to fire a machine gun and he was stopped. They then came under rifle and machine gun fire from their right rear from a trench they had crossed and not noticed it was held. Lieut. McLean gathered his remaining men and rushed this trench with determination and ferocity. The garrison surrendered at once and 60 prisoners were taken.

Lieut. McLean returned to Gloster Road and pushed down it to the right affecting a junction with 'D' Company at Storar Avenue. He then took six men and turned northwards up Gloster Road and seized Derby Post where the

enemy had fled in panic. He then sent for reinforcements and two more platoons of 'C' Company pushed up and consolidated Derby Post and Gloster Road.[37] In this operation the 98th Infantry Brigade took 115 prisoners.[38]

The line established the previous day between Meath Post and Gloster Road was withdrawn to the Limerick Trench.[39]

The battalion worked on trenches west of the Sugar Factory, wiring strong points on forward roads and salvaging materials.

The following officers joined the battalion. 2nd Lieut. D.H. French was posted to 'B' Company. 2nd Lieuts. L.S. Powys-Maurice and H.A.A. Howell were posted to 'C' Company and 2nd Lieuts. E.J. Young and G.B. Little were posted to 'A' Company.

Five men were wounded, one only slightly and he remained at duty.

The following five soldiers were killed in action and are buried in the Fins New British Cemetery, Sorel-Le-Grand – Somme.

Lance Corporal P.W.1215 Thomas Atherton aged 39, born and enlisted in Ashton-under-Lyne, was killed in action. He was the husband of Jane Atherton of 111 Wellington Street, Ashton-under-Lyne.[40]

Private T.F.293102 Daniel Nash, aged 30 years and 4 months, attested on 28 September 1916 in Bristol. He was a boot maker by trade and married Sarah Agnes Suter at St. Matthews Moorfields, Bristol on 27 July 1911. They had four children William Gilbert, dob 2 December 1911, Elsie dob 9 March 1915, Percy Lewis dob 22 March 1914 and Violet dob 1 May 1917. They lived at Stanley Terrace, Soundwell, Staple Hill, Bristol.

Following his attestation he had a medical which diagnosed him with slightly flat feet, he was 5′ 2″ tall and weighed 104 lbs. He was posted to the 5th Essex on 2 October 1916, transferred to the 2/10th Middlesex Training Battalion on 14 December 1916, he then joined the 2/8th Middlesex on 19 June 1917. On 20 September 1917 he transferred to the 281st Infantry Battalion. He made his way to France being posted to 1/7th Middlesex on 13 April 1918 and then onto the 20th Middlesex on 14 April 1918 joining them in the field on 17 April. He was posted to 18th Middlesex on 15 July 1918. Mrs Nash received a Separation Allowance of 35 shillings and sixpence and was awarded a pension of 33 shillings and 3 pence per week for herself and her 4 children with effect from 14 April 1919. She also received her late husband's personal effect of letters, photos and letters case. After the war Mrs Nash and her family moved to 5 Jubilee Terrace, Kings Wood, Bristol.[41]

Corporal G/13470 Edmund James Price aged 28, was born in Bristol, Gloucestershire. He lived at 134 Bonvilstone Road Pontypridd, Wales and attested in the town on 5 July 1915. He was single, a shop assistant by trade, 5´ 7¼″ tall, had scar below his right eye and weighed 137 lbs. He arrived at the Middlesex Regiment barracks in Mill Hill London on 8 July 1915 and was posted to the 6th Middlesex on 10 July. He made the rank of Corporal on 9 December 1916. He joined the British Expeditionary Force in France on 12 January 1917 and joined the 20th Middlesex in the field on 14 January. On 6 March 1918 he was wounded receiving gunshot wounds to his left arm and right hip and was admitted to the 13 General Hospital Boulogne. On 12 March 1918 he was transported back to England on H.M.H.S. Princess Elizabeth and admitted to the Wharncliffe War Hospital Sheffield on 13 March. He was discharged on 23 August having spent 164 days in hospital. He was then readmitted on 2 September and discharged on 18 October 1917. He was posted to the 6th Middlesex on 19 October. He passed 1st Class at the Gas Course at the Anti-Gas School at Crowborough on 17 February 1918.

Corporal Price returned to France on 11 May 1918, was posted to the 18th Middlesex on 12 May and joined them in the field on 17 May. He was the son of Sarah Ann and James Price of 9 Nesta Road, Canton, Cardiff.[42]

Private G/41473 George Miles Revell aged 30, was born in Bridge, Kent and enlisted in Ashford, Kent. He was the son of Mary Ann and George Revell of 5 Neal Cottages, Dover Road, Upper Walmer, Deal, Kent.[43]

Corporal T.F.200377 Alfred Henry Woods was born on 25 September 1897 and lived in Edmonton. He attested on 17 June 1914 at Tottenham. He gave his age as 17 but in fact he was only 16 at the time. He was posted to the 7th (Reserve) Battalion Middlesex Regiment on 18 June. He was made a paid Lance Corporal on 2 January 1915 and moved with his battalion to Gibraltar on 1 February. He moved to Egypt with the 7th Middlesex on 24 August. He was promoted to Corporal on 1 November and then unpaid Lance Sergeant on 28 February 1916.

On the 8 May 1916 the 7th Middlesex left Alexandria and sailed for France. They arrived at Marseille on 15 May and then moved to Rouen No. 5 Infantry Base Depot (I.B.D.). Woods was transferred to the 1/7th Middlesex on 23 June 1916. On 7 October he was blown up and suffered shell shock wounds and was taken to the 48 Casualty Clearing Station. On 9 October he was moved, to 22 General Hospital Dannes Camiers, then to the 26 General Hospital at Étaples

on 31 October and then to the 25 General Hospital at Boulogne on 1 November. He was then taken back to England on 29 December 1916.

On 30 December Woods was transferred to the 22nd Middlesex and on 10 April 1917 he returned to the 7th Middlesex. At midnight on 17 June, on active duty as the Battalion Orderly Sergeant, he absented himself until 8am the following morning. He was severely reprimanded by Lt.-Col. Drew, the Officer commanding the 7th Middlesex, and he forfeited 1 days pay, water and rations. Despite his lapse in discipline Woods was promoted to paid Lance Sergeant on 1 July. He made paid Acting Sergeant on 9 February 1918. On 16 July 1918 he moved to the Pioneer Depot. On 25 August he posted to the 18th Middlesex, he reverted back to the rank of Corporal and embarked from Folkestone for France.

Woods was a cabinet maker by trade working at Lebus Ltd., Tottenham. He was 5′ 8″ tall and the son of Emma and Samuel Rush Woods. They lived at 5 Sandal Road, Raynham Avenue, Upper Edmonton. His mother was sent his personal effects of leather letter case and note book, photos, letters, various papers, cigarette case, and 2 testaments. Corporal Woods served in three separate theatres of World War One.[44]

23 Sept. At 2am the 58th Division reported that they had secured Dados Loop and Kildare Post but their left flank was exposed due to the failure of the 19th Infantry Brigade to capture Limerick Post. Major-General Pinney issued immediate orders for the 100th Infantry Brigade to capture Limerick Post.[45]

Overnight the 2nd Worcestershires were reassembled. At 7am they advanced on Limerick Post and occupied it without opposition. They consolidated the position and immediately posts were pushed out in the direction of Gloster Road.[46]

At 8.30am the enemy heavily shelled Meunier Trench and Meunier Support and counter attacked from Leith Walk northwards and retook Gloster Road.[47] Lieut. McLean and the garrison defending Derby Post were killed when the Germans retook the strong point from the rear.[48] The position in Meunier Trench and Meunier Support was restored later in the day but Gloster Road remained in enemy hands. In the evening the Germans shelled Chapel Hill which is the high point between Heudecourt and Villers-Guislain with mustard gas.[49]

During the day the 2nd Worcestershires in Limerick Post came under intense machine gun fire and sniping from the direction of the crossroads of Gloster Road and the road to Tyhurst Quarry adjacent to Kildare Avenue. The 2nd

Worcestershires made more than one attempt to capture the crossroads but failed. An attempt by the enemy to advance from Gloster Road was frustrated by 33rd Division artillery fire.[50]

23 Sept. The battalion worked on forward positions in trenches west of the Sugar Factory, on forward roads and on salvaging materials. 'B' Company finished wiring of support posts.

Sergeant G.S.9480 Ernest Edward Heley was awarded the Distinguished Conduct Medal. His citation reads 'He has done consistent good work the whole time he has been with the battalion. While his platoon was wiring near Villers-Guislain on the night of 22/23 September 1918, the enemy put down a very heavy barrage in their midst. He has many times acted as platoon commander, and has proved especially trustworthy under all conditions.'[51]

Heley was born in 1881 in Penge, Surrey and was a Machine Ruler by trade in the print industry. He married Ann Ellen Hutchinson on 20 June 1903 at St. Philips, Dalton and they had two children Robert Ernest dob 22 March 1904 and Leonard James dob 25 November 1905. He enlisted on 24 March 1915 and was posted to the 5th Battalion Middlesex Regiment on 26 March. He was made Acting Lance Corporal 1 June 1915. On 12 August he was absent from tattoo until 5.30am 13 August. He was admonished by Captain W.C. Dodds and forfeited a day's pay. He was made a full Corporal on 13 October 1915. On 28 November 1916 he was posted to France and joined the 20th Battalion Middlesex Regiment. On 9 December he transferred to the 18th Battalion Middlesex Regiment. He was made a Lance Sergeant on 1 October 1917 and a Sergeant on 23 November 1917. He was finally discharged on demobilisation on 31 March 1920.[52] He died in December 1945.

Eight men were wounded including one slightly.

Private G/53074 Walter Lawrence Webster, born in Greenwich, lived in Deptford and enlisted in Camberwell, Kent, was killed in action. He is buried in the Thilloy Road Cemetery, Beaulencourt – Pas de Calais.[53]

24 Sept. By retaking Gloster Road, Derby Post and holding on to the Meunier Trench and Leith Walk crossroads the Germans established a position between the 19th and 98th Infantry Brigades. Major-General Pinney saw danger in this situation and ordered the 100th Infantry Brigade to attack conjointly the enemy positions in the trench south of Leith Walk, in Meunier Trench and in Gloster Road astride Leith Walk.

At 3am, on the left, the 16th Battalion King's Royal Rifle Corps of 100th Infantry Brigade attacked Gloster Road astride Leith Walk and Limerick Trench from the south 170 yards north of Meath Post to Leith Walk. On the right, the 2nd Worcestershires were to consolidate Gloster Road up the southern slope of the Targelle Valley. The 1st Middlesex of the 98th Infantry Brigade attacked down Meunier Trench and Meunier Support. All these attacks made initial progress but were unable to maintain the positions gained and by noon the British troops were back at their starting points. [54]

At about 11.30am the enemy moved out of the Gloster Road – Kildare Avenue crossroads and attacked and retook the Dados Loop. The 2nd Worcestershires formed a defensive flank along Kildare Avenue.[55]

At 11.42am the 12th Division issued an S.O.S. from Little Priel Farm. Their right brigade front was heavily shelled and the enemy penetrated into Dados Lane on the 12th Division front.

In the four days of fighting from 21 September – 24 September the 33rd Division took six officers and 172 other ranks prisoner.[56]

'A' Company relieved 'B' Company in forward camp at Railton after working on roads, the 100th Infantry Brigade H.Q. and the 33rd Divisional H.Q at Équancourt five-and-half miles back from the front.

'B' Company had a day's rest. 'C' Company worked on erecting air line poles for signals.

Private G/34633 Arthur Richard Brown aged 24, was killed in action. He was born in Tottenham and was the son of Eliza and Richard Brown of 10A Brunswick Road, South Tottenham. He enlisted in Mill Hill, Middlesex on 7 November 1916, he was a milk carrier by trade, 5′ 6½″ tall and weighed 130 lbs. He married Agnes Barbour at the Parish Church, Tottenham on 5 February 1914. They lived at 22 St. George Road, South Tottenham and had one child.

Private Brown was posted to the 13th Middlesex and transferred to 16th Middlesex joining them in the field in France on 13 February 1917. On 19 April 1917 he was wounded in action and admitted to the 87th Field Ambulance. He was moved to 6 Stationary Hospital at Fervent on 22 April. He was discharged on 27 May 1917 and rejoined the 16th Middlesex. He had two weeks leave in England from 30 November 1917 to 14 December. He was posted to the 18th Middlesex and joined them in the field on 8 February 1918.

Mrs Brown was awarded a pension of 20 shillings and 5 pence per week for herself and 1 child with effect from 14 April 1919. Sometime afterwards she

moved to 4 King's Street, Church Road, Tottenham, London. He is buried in the Fins New British Cemetery.[57]

Private P.W.6722 Frederick Clarke aged 40, born in Lowestoft, Suffolk and enlisted in Bury St. Edmunds, was killed in action. He was the son of Lottie and Charles Clarke of Lowestoft and was a gas works labourer by trade. He married Matilda Maud Garner in Mutford, Suffolk in the 4th quarter of 1903, they lived at 2 Primitive Methodist Cottages, St. Peter's Street, Lowestoft and they had two sons. Frederick James Clarke was born in 1904 and William Charles Clarke in 1906. Private Clarke is buried in the Fins New British Cemetery.[58]

1 Boraston (Editor), Sir *Douglas Haig's Despatches (December 1915 – April 1919),* p. 269
2 Price Army Service Record
3 Boraston (Editor), Sir *Douglas Haig's Despatches (December 1915 – April 1919),* p. 270
4 Ibid., p. 271
5 Wyrall, *The Die-Hards in the Great War, Vol. 2*, p. 247
6 Boraston (Editor), Sir *Douglas Haig's Despatches (December 1915 – April 1919),* p. p. 273-274
7 Ibid., p. 273
8 Ibid., p. 270
9 Ibid., p.p. 274-275
10 Ibid., p. 275
11 33rd Division War Diary
12 Ibid.
13 Commonwealth War Graves Commission casualty details; England & Wales Birth Index 1837-1915; 1891 Census; Private Corrigan Army Service Record, National Archives, WO 363
14 Boraston (Editor), Sir *Douglas Haig's Despatches (December 1915 – April 1919),* p. 275
15 Blake (Editor), The *Private Papers of Douglas Haig 1914 -1919*, p.p. 326-327
16 Boraston (Editor), Sir *Douglas Haig's Despatches (December 1915 – April 1919),* p. 276
17 Ibid., p. 277
18 Commonwealth War Graves Commission casualty details; Private Reynolds British Army Pension Records 1914-1920, National Archives, WO 364
19 33rd Division War Diary
20 Ibid.
21 Price Army Service Record; General Register Office, Death Certificate, COL258777; Commonwealth War Graves Commission casualty details; 1911 Census; British Army WW1 Pension Records 1914-1920
22 33rd Division War Diary
23 Boraston (Editor), Sir *Douglas Haig's Despatches (December 1915 – April 1919),* p.p. 276-277

24 V Corps War Diary, National Archives, WO 95/751
25 33rd Division War Diary
26 Ibid.
27 V Corps War Diary
28 33rd Division War Diary
29 Ibid.
30 Ibid.
31 1st Battalion Cameronians (Scottish Rifles) War Diary, National Archives, WO 95/2422, Image reference 1/480
32 33rd Division War Diary
33 1st Battalion Cameronians (Scottish Rifles) War Diary
34 33rd Division War Diary
35 Ibid.
36 2nd Battalion Worcestershire Regiment War Diary
37 2nd Battalion Argyll and Sutherland Highlanders War Diary
38 33rd Division War Diary
39 Ibid.
40 *Soldiers Died In The Great War 1914 -19*, p. 102; Commonwealth War Graves Commission casualty details
41 Ibid., p. 104; Private Nash Army Service Record National Archives WO 363
42 Ibid.; Corporal Price Army Service Record National Archives, WO 363
43 Ibid.
44 Ibid., p. 105; Corporal Woods Army Service Record, National Archives, WO 363; London, England, Birth and Baptisms 1813 -1908; England & Wales Birth Index 1837 -1915
45 33rd Division War Diary
46 2nd Battalion Worcestershire Regiment War Diary
47 33rd Division War Diary
48 2nd Battalion Argyll and Sutherland Highlanders War Diary
49 33rd Division War Diary
50 2nd Battalion Worcestershire Regiment War Diary
51 Third Supplement to the London Gazette 9th March 1920, Published 11th March 1920, Gazette Issue 31819, p. 3050
52 Sergeant Heley Army Service Record, National Archives, WO 363
53 *Soldiers Died In The Great War 1914 -19*, p. 104; Commonwealth War Graves Commission casualty details
54 33rd Division War Diary
55 2nd Battalion Worcestershire Regiment War Diary
56 33rd Division War Diary
57 *Soldiers Died In The Great War 1914 -19*, p. 102; Commonwealth War Graves Commission casualty details; Private Brown Army Service Record, National Archives, WO 363; 1911 Census; London Metropolitan Archives, All Hallows,

Tottenham, Register of marriages, DRO/015/A/01, Item 039

58 *Soldiers Died In The Great War 1914 -19*, p. 102; Commonwealth War Graves Commission casualty details; England & Wales Marriage Index 1837 -1915; 1911 Census; All England & Wales Birth Index 1937 – 1915

CHAPTER FOURTEEN

25th September 1918 to 5th October 1918

Joining the Advance
Work on forward roads
Breach of the Hindenburg Line
Bridging the St. Quentin Canal

25 Sept. 'N' Special Company fired 100 chlorine drums into Villers-Guislain at 12.35am and 100 drums at 1.25am. The enemy retaliated with heavy artillery fire on the area between Fives Trench and Beet Trench west of Villers-Guislain and south of Chapel Street.[1]

Renewed attempts to retake the Dados Loop failed.[2]

One platoon of 'B' Company worked on 33rd Divisional H.Q. and approaches. The rest of 'B' Company together with 'C' Company worked on the preparation of the Étricourt – Heudicourt horse transport track. 'A' Company worked on forward roads.

Lieut. E.C.V. Warde joined the battalion and was posted to 'B' Company. 2nd Lieut. H.C. Yoxall joined and was posted to 'C' Company.

Orders were issued for an attack on 28 September to capture the Brown Line which curved round the eastern side of Villers-Guislain. The same orders contained instructions for an attack on the Green Line to take place on 29 September.

The 19th Infantry Brigade was ordered to relieve the right battalion of the 98th Infantry Brigade and capture the Brown Line from Meunier Trench to Derby Post east of Villers-Guislain. The rest of the 98th Infantry Brigade, supported by three tanks, was to capture the Brown Line from Derby Post to 21st Divisional junction at Glass Street on the northern outskirts of Villers-Guislain.

The 19th and 100th Infantry Brigades were to be ready to attack the Green Line, when the advance on the left by the Fourth Army and the 38th Division

threatened the rear of the enemy holding that line.[3] The Green Line ran south to north parallel to the St. Quentin Canal from 170 yards north of the Catelet Road to 200 yards north of High Street 2,200 yards east of Villers-Guislain.

26 Sept. The battalion worked on 33rd Divisional H.Q., and approaches, and on the preparation of the Étricourt – Heudicourt horse transport track.

2nd Lieut. Howell and four men were wounded.

The following eight soldiers were killed in action and are buried in the Fins New British Cemetery.

Sergeant G/6802 William George Brooks aged 21, born in Islington and enlisted in Marylebone, Middlesex. He was formerly 21304 9th Reserves Cavalry. He was the son of Minnie Jane Brooks (nee Ingram) and George Brooks of 48 Nascot Street, Watford, Herts.[4]

Private G/52693 Henry William Brown born and lived in Walworth and enlisted in Southwark, Surrey, died of his wounds.[5]

2nd Lieut. Arthur William Drage M.M. aged 26, from Hackney, London. He was the son of Mary Ann Louisa and William John Drage of 20 Rushmore Road, Clapton, London.[6]

Private T.F.241513 Ernest James Harris lived at 88 Pellatt Grove, Wood Green, London. He was unofficially married to Marie Harris and they had a son Ernest James Harris born on 1 September 1909. He attested on 20 November 1915 aged 29 years and 2 days and was a salesman by trade. His next of kin was his mother Alice Wallace of 37 Argyle Street, Kings Cross. He was mobilised on 3 March 1916 and posted to the 4/8th Middlesex the following day. On 12 July 1916 he was transferred to the 1/8th Middlesex and travelled to France to join the British Expeditionary Force. He suffered a gunshot wound to his right hand on 15 September 1916 and was treated in the 36 Casualty Clearing Station. He returned to duty on 31 January 1917. On 15 July 1917 he was admitted to the 3 Canadian Stationary Hospital at Boulogne, transferred to the 11 Stationary Hospital at Rouen on 19 July and was taken back to England on 27 July. He was attached to the 23rd Territorial Force Depot on 22 October and returned to France on 7 December and joined the 16th Middlesex in the field on 10 December. He was transferred to the 18th Middlesex on 8 February 1918.

Private Harris was killed in action. Marie Harris, his commonlaw wife, received a Separation Allowance of 25 shillings and sixpence.[7]

Private T.F.202224 Bertram (Bertie) James Keal aged 24 was born in

Croydon in 1893. He attested in Croydon on 16 February 1916, he listed his mother Agnes Sarah Keal as his next of kin, his father Alfred had died in 1912. He lived at 2 Surrey Cottage, Johnson Road Croydon with his grandmother Emma Higgs. He was carman by trade, single, 5′ 6″ tall and weighed 127 lbs. He was placed in the Army Reserve on 17 February and mobilised on 7 March 1916. He was admitted to Dunsdale Hospital, Westerham on 8 May 1916 with tonsillitis. He was discharged on 11 May. He was posted to the 1/7th Middlesex on 31 August 1916, he sailed from Folkestone to Boulogne on 2 September 1916 and joined them in France on 20 September 1916.

Private Keal was admitted to the 7 Casualty Clearing Station on 10 December 1916 suffering from scabies. He was discharged and rejoined his unit on 27 December. He suffered a gunshot wound to the neck on 18 August 1917 and as a result was admitted to the 3 Canadian Casualty Clearing Station on 18 August and on the same day transferred to the 18 General Hospital at Camiers. He was discharged from hospital on 28 August and joined the 41st Base Depot at Étaples. He was posted to 16th Middlesex on 6 September 1917. He had ten days leave in England from 5 October to 15 October.

Keal was posted to the 18th Middlesex on 8 February 1918. He was gassed on 3 April 1918 and admitted to 54 General Hospital at Boulogne, he transferred to the 25 General Hospital on 11 April and onto the 1 General Hospital at Boulogne on 22 April. He was discharged from hospital on 15 May and again went to the Base Depot at Étaples. He rejoined the 18th Middlesex on 25 May 1918.

His grandmother received a Separation Allowance of 10 shillings and 8 pence. His mother, who lived at 73 Queen's Road, West Croydon, was sent his personal effects of a note case, metal mirror in case, photo case, photos, French phrase book, 1 fountain pen, match box case, metal case, letters and cards.[8]

Private G/21227 James Henry Mahoney aged 20, born in Ashford Common and enlisted in Mill Hill, Middlesex. He was the son of Bridget and Michael Mahoney of 2 Alexandra Road, Ashford, Middlesex.[9]

Corporal P.S.2247 Thomas Joseph Parkyns was born in Hoxton in 1889. He married Henrietta Steed on 25 December 1908 at St. Georges, Hanover Square, Westminster. They had a daughter Henrietta Ellen dob 16 May 1911 and they lived 33 Medway Street, Westminster. He was the son of Rosa and Joseph John Parkyns.

He attested at Cockspur Street, London on 25 May 1915 and listed his trade as a barman. He had previously worked as a kitchen porter. He was posted to

the 16th Middlesex and joined them at Woldingham on 27 May. On 17 November 1915 he travelled to France with his battalion. He suffered a gunshot wound to left shoulder on 30 January 1916 and was admitted to the 19th Field Ambulance on 31 January. He was transferred to the 12 General Hospital at Rouen 2 February and was sent back to England on H.M.H.S. St. Denis on 18 February. He was posted to the 24th Middlesex on 19 February.

Private Parkyns returned to France to rejoin the British Expeditionary Force arriving at Boulogne on 15 July 1916. He was posted to the 1st Middlesex and joined them in the field on 26 July 1916. On 26 August he suffered a shell wound to his right shoulder and spent 2 days in the 19th Field Ambulance returning to duty on 28 August. On 15 January 1917 he was admitted to the 99th Field Ambulance suffering from bronchitis. He was moved on 16 January to the 2 Stationary Hospital in Abbeville. On 20 January he was moved to the 2 Canadian General Hospital at Le Treport and then taken back to England on 24 January on H.S. Formosa.

On 16 April 1917 Parkyns was posted to the 2/9th Middlesex. He was made Lance Corporal on 1 May 1917 but reverted back to Private on 18 September 1917. On 19 September he was posted to 3/10th Middlesex and returned to France joining his new battalion in the field on 26 September. He was made an unpaid Lance Corporal on 27 December 1917 and then a paid Lance Corporal on 1 January 1918. On 22 January 1918 he was made Corporal.

Corporal Parkyns transferred to the 18th Middlesex on 23 March and joined the battalion in the field on 25 March only to be posted back to England on 27 March for duty with the 22nd Corps School. He rejoined the 18th Middlesex on 7 June 1918. During his Army service Parkyns qualified as a Grenadier and Lewis Gunner.

Henrietta Parkyns was awarded a pension of 21 shillings and 8 pence per week for herself and her daughter with effect from 14 April 1919. She also received her late husband's personal effects of 5 Army forms, letters, photos, cards, tobacco pouch, pencil case, canvas letters case, key locket, rosary and wallet.[10]

Private T.F.315903 Albert Charles Warry aged 21 lived in Acton Green. He was the son of Emma and Samuel James Warry of 2 Carlton Road, Bedford Park, Chiswick, London. He attested on 28 September 1914 at Stamford Brook Lodge, Ravenscourt Park, London. He had a medical on 24 September, he was 5′ 7″ tall and his vision was good with glasses. He was a Grocer's Assistant by trade. He was posted to 1/10th Middlesex and embarked for the Mediterranean

Expeditionary Force on His Majesty's Troopship S.S. Huntsgreen on 18 July 1915. On 14 August 1915 at Sulva Bay he was admitted to 35th Field Ambulance with debilitating eyes. The Senior Medical Officer from M.S. Ascania at Mudros diagnosed him as being invalided. He was sent back to England and arrived home on 21 September 1915.

He was posted to the 4/10th Middlesex on 8 January 1916 and attached to the Command Depot at Shoreham on 12 January. He joined the 7th Middlesex on 13 January 1917 and moved to the 32nd Middlesex on 23 January. He was made an unpaid Lance Corporal 26 February 1917. He attended the 4th Course at 225th Infantry Brigade School at Yarmouth on the 1 to 30 April but failed because he suffered shell shock. He then attended the 225th Infantry Brigade Hotchkiss Gun School on 13 July and passed as 'good'. On 19 July 1917 he lost his Lance Corporal stripe for neglect of duty.

He was posted to the 18th Middlesex on 19 December 1917 and joined them in the field in Flanders on 21 December.

His father Samuel James Warry was his next of kin and received his late son's personal effects of 1 pipe, 1 cigarette case, 1 purse, photos, 1 packet case, letters, cards, 1 pair of spectacles in a case, 1 cigarette holder in silver case, 1 silver match box, 1 leather guard, 1 memorial card, 1 photo wallet, 1 note book and 1 coin.

Rifleman 318271 Samuel James Warry 1/5th (City of London) Battalion (London Rifles Brigade), the brother of Albert Charles, was killed in action on 10 March 1918. He is buried in Roclincourt Military Cemetery.[11]

Private L/14696 William Mappley was born in Hampstead. He attested at Mill Hill, Middlesex on 4 November 1913 giving his age as 18 years and 3 days. However his birth is registered in the 1st quarter of 1897 and the 1901 Census taken on 31 March 1901 gives his age as 4 years. The oldest William Mappley could have been on 4 November 1913 was 17 years if he was born in the final quarter of 1896 and his parents registered his birth early in 1897. The youngest he could have been when attesting was 16 years and 7 months if he was born before 31 March in the 1st quarter of 1897.

He was a checker by trade, 5′ 4¼″ tall and weighed 118 lbs. Before joining the Army William worked as vanguard for Carter Paterson & Company Limited of 128 Goswell Road. He was posted to 5th Battalion Middlesex Regiment Special Reserve on 4 November 1913. On 25 June 1914 he was charged and found guilty of disobedience of Fort standing orders and confined to barracks for 3 days. He transferred to the 4th Middlesex on 30 August 1914 and travelled

with them to France well before his 18th birthday. He was wounded on 15 October 1914 and was taken back to England on 18 October. He was posted to the 6th Middlesex on 29 December 1914 and made unpaid Lance Corporal on 27 February 1915. He was made a paid Lance Corporal on 9 April 1915. On 30 April he was charged and found guilty of irregular conduct when in charge of an escort because he did not return until the next day. Lt.-Col. G.E. Barker, Officer commanding 6th Middlesex, deprived Mappley of his Lance Stripe as a punishment.

On 25 May 1915 Mappley transferred to the 3rd Middlesex and embarked with them from Southampton. The battalion arrived at Rouen the following day. He was again made an unpaid Lance Corporal on 13 August 1915. On 29 September 1915 he suffered a slight gunshot wound to the head and was admitted to the 3 Canadian General Hospital at Camiers. He returned to duty on the 20 October 1915 joining the 28th I.B.D. at Rouen. On the 25 October 1915 he embarked from Marseilles and disembarked at Alexandria on 31 October 1915 joining the British Mediterranean Expeditionary Force in Salonika. He was admitted to the 1 New Zealand General Hospital on 9 December with rheumatism. Whilst in hospital he was made a paid Lance Corporal on 14 December 1915. He returned to duty on 16 December. He lost his Lance stripe again on 15 June 1916.

On 19 July Mappley was admitted to the 28 General Hospital, Salonika. On 28 July he was taken on S.S. Letitia to Malta where he was admitted on 1 August to St. Patrick's Hospital suffering from malaria. On 17 August he was moved to the Melleha Convalescent Camp and on 26 August he was moved to All Saints Convalescent Camp. On 7 September he sailed on S.S. Nile and arrived back in Salonika rejoining the 3rd Middlesex on 18 September. He fell ill again on 1 October 1916 and was admitted to the 84th Field Ambulance and then moved to the 27 Casualty Clearing Station. On 3 October he was admitted to the 5 Canadian General Hospital suffering from malaria. On 3 November he was taken by His Majesty's Hospital Ship Llandovery Castle back to Malta and admitted to the Spinola Hospital on 8 November. On 9 January 1917 he was moved to the Ghain Tuffieha Convalescent Camp. His condition took a turn for the worst and he was admitted to Manoel Hospital suffering from another bout of malaria accompanied with an outbreak of scabies. He was taken back to England on 11 July 1917.

He was admitted to Huddersfield War Hospital on 21 July still suffering from Malaria. He was moved to 4 Northern General Hospital Lincoln on 2 August and discharged on 7 September. On 17 September he was transferred

to the 5th Middlesex. He had another attack of malaria 30 September and was admitted to Fulham Military Hospital on 1 October. He was discharged on 15 October having not had a malaria attack since his admission.

Mappley, whilst on route back from hospital to the 5th Middlesex, went absent from tattoo on 15 October until 1.30pm on 19 October. He was initially deprived of 10 days pay and confined to barracks for 14 days, but this was reduced to a forfeit of 5 days pay, water and rations.

Mappley remained in England until 3 November when he was posted back to France joining the 16th Middlesex in the field on 11 November. Captain P. Beresford of 'A' Company 16th Middlesex recorded on 5 February 1918 that Mappley was of very good character, his special qualification was marksmanship and he was employed as sniper and sentry at Battalion Headquarters.

He transferred to the 18th Battalion on 8 February 1918. On 26 September he suffered shrapnel wounds to both his legs losing his left leg below the knee. He was taken to the 19th Field Ambulance and then to 43 Casualty Clearing station where he died from his wounds.

Private Mappley was the son of Charlotte and John Mappley and they lived at 105 Mayo Road, Willesden. Their previous address was 34 Netherwood Street Kilburn. On 15 February 1919, Mrs Mappley received her late son's personal effects of 2 discs, letters, photos, pipe, cigarette case, watch (broken), purse, badge and wallet. He is buried in the Thilloy Road Cemetery.[12]

Private T.F.316055 Ernest Powell born in Leighton Buzzard, Bedfordshire and enlisted in Northampton, died of his wounds. He is buried in the Thilloy Road Cemetery.[13]

The British front line once again came up to the Hindenburg Line and Hindenburg Support Line of defences. In total the Hindenburg Line ran from near Vailly on the Aisne north past St. Quentin by Quéant and then north-westwards to the Scarpe in front of Arras. The Wotan Line, which crossed it at Quéant, cut off a smaller part of the front mostly north of the Hindenburg Position, from Sailly-Saillisel northwards to Quéant and in front of Armentières; the portion north of Quéant was known to the British as the Drocourt – Quéant Line.[14]

The success of the next phase of the Allied advance depended on the British breaking the Hindenburg Line in the centre where the German defences were the most formidable and highly organised. Field Marshal Haig was well aware of the importance of the task facing him. The probable results of a costly failure, or, indeed, of anything short of a decided success, in any attempt upon the main defences of

the Hindenburg Line would be large and would go far to reviving the declining morale, not only of the German Army, but of the German people. Nevertheless Haig was convinced that the British attack was the essential part of the general scheme and the moment was favourable. He ordered the attack to proceed.[15]

The British First and Third Armies faced the strongly held German positions covering the approaches to Cambrai between the Canal du Nord and Scheldt Canal and the section of the Hindenburg Line north of Gouzeaucourt.[16] To the south of Gouzeaucourt the Fourth Army front ran from Vendhuille to Holnon just in front of St. Quentin.[17]

Overnight on 26/27 September a very heavy British bombardment took place along the whole of the front of all three armies between Holnon and Sauchy Lestrée. The bombardment was to be followed up by an attack only delivered by the First and Third Armies. This was an attempt to deceive the Germans about the specific point of attack that was to follow and enable the First and Third armies to get nearer to their objectives and simplify the task of the Fourth Army artillery.[18]

27 Sept. Work continued on the horse transport track, the Divisional H.Q. and approaches.

2nd Lieut. H.B. Scammell joined the battalion and was posted to 'C' Company.

Two men were wounded.

Private G/52437 Walter Frederick Andrews born in Doncaster and enlisted in Pontefract, Yorkshire, was killed in action. He is buried in the Fins New British Cemetery.[19]

Divisional Order 354 confirmed the attack on the right of the IV Corps had not been successful. The attack planned for the evening on the Brown Line was postponed until 3.30am on 29th. If that attack was successful then the 33rd Division was to attack the Green Line just in front of the St. Quentin Canal early on the morning of the 29th in conjunction with the Fourth Army. The battalion of the 19th Infantry Brigade in the neighbourhood of Équancourt was held in readiness to move to Genin Well Copse north-east of Railton early on 28 September.[20]

The Battle of Canal du Nord

At 5.20am the British First Army and Third Army with the IV, VI, XVII and Canadian Corps attacked along the thirteen mile front running from Sauchy –

Lestrée north-west of Cambrai to Gouzeaucourt south-west of Cambrai. The Fourth Army front did not attack.

By nightfall, British troops had made significant advances and moved the front line forward to Beaucamp – Ribécourt – Fontaine–Notre-Dame – east of Haynecourt – Epinoy – Oisy-le-Verger and had taken over 10,000 prisoners and 200 guns.[21]

28 Sept. Work continued on the horse transport track, the Divisional H.Q. and its approaches.

By nightfall Palluel, Sailly, Fontaine-Notre-Dame, Noyelles-sur-l'Escaut, Marcoing and Gouzeaucourt were all in British hands. At Marcoing British troops established themselves on the east bank of the Scheldt Canal and on the northern flank entered Aubencheul-au-Bac.[22]

Battle of St. Quentin Canal

29 Sept. In conjunction with the big attack of the Fourth Army on the right and the remainder of the Third Army and part of the First Army on the left, the 33rd Division was to capture Villers-Guislain and push on to the Canal de l'Escaut. The 98th Infantry Brigade with the 4th King's, 2nd Argyll and Sutherland Highlanders and 1st Middlesex were to take Villers-Guislain and the Brown Line from Villers Hill past Derby Post, past Woking Post and around the north-eastern outskirts of Villers-Guislain to Glass Street.[23]

The 100th Infantry Brigade was to take the Green Line with the 2nd Worcestershires on the right and the 1/9th Highland Light Infantry on the left. The Green Line ran north from Stone Lane along Stone and Pigeon trenches to Leith Walk.

At 3.35am, in accordance with Divisional Order 355, the 98th Infantry Brigade attacked and for a time the 4th King's held Villers-Guislain but was forced out again by noon. The 1st Middlesex captured a section of the Brown Line near Derby Post but not the post itself. They also held Gloster Trench and Meunier Trench 330 yards north Leith Walk. The 2nd Argyll and Sutherland Highlanders captured the Brown Line on Petit Saut Ravine and astride the road through Woking Post. The 4th King's were in a trench west of the cemetery on the northern outskirts of Villers-Guislain.[24] The Germans held Villers-Guislain and Villers Trench with the 105th Regiment which was a fresh unit and up to strength.[25]

At 5.50am the 100th Brigade attacked the Green Line. The 1/9th Highland Light Infantry advanced on the left but were met with very heavy machine gun fire from the Sherwood Lane – Leith Walk crossroads and from Seventeen Spur and they were halted on Gloster Road. Some men managed to push forward as far as Pigeon Quarry where they dug in. Some of these managed to return to the British Line under cover of darkness, the remainder were surrounded and captured.[26]

The 2nd Worcestershires attacked on the right and their first objective was to take Sprint Road from Dados Lane north to just before Tyhurst Quarry.

'D' and 'C' Companies led the advance from Limerick Trench with 'A' and 'B' Companies in support. The leading platoons were scattered and those behind were in diamond formation. As the artillery barrage came over the troops went forward. The barrage moved so quickly that the men had to run to keep up with it. Their attack was brought to a standstill before it reached Gloster Road by enemy machine gun and sniper fire from posts at the crossroads of Gloster Road and Kildare Avenue. The right of 'D' Company was held at the tunnel in Kildare Avenue. The left of 'D' Company swung forward towards the crossroads, but as each party got forward they were instantly exterminated.

'C' Company moved down the Targelle Valley and across the small spur which separates it from the Targelle Ravine. They too were cut down by machine gun fire from the crossroads. Those who escaped were met by sniper fire from posts dug in on Gloster Road. Lieut. Wright M.C. was found there shot through the head still grasping a bomb. The whole of his platoon were killed. Likewise, Lieut. Lambert and his platoon were also completely wiped out.

Not a single man of the 2nd Worcestershires was able to get across Gloster Road. By 7am the fighting died down. Those who had escaped being wounded or killed were finding their way back to Limerick Trench. During the day attempts made to bring in the wounded were immediately stopped by fire from machine guns and snipers.[27]

By noon the 100th Infantry Brigade troops that had reached Gloster Road were compelled to fall back to Meath Post by heavy enfilade machine gun fire.

At 2.45pm the 98th and 100th Infantry Brigades were ordered to consolidate their positions, reorganise and be prepared to push forward to the Canal should a retirement by the enemy be detected. During this operation the 98th and 100th Infantry Brigades suffered very heavy casualties with the strength of each brigade being reduced to about 700 rifles and 50 Lewis guns.[28]

At 5.50am, to the south of Villers-Guislain, the British Fourth Army attacked under an intense artillery barrage against the twelve mile front from

Holnon to Vendhuille. On the right of the Fourth Army the French First Army attacked the St.Quentin sector.

The 46th Division captured Bellenglise, stormed the western arm of the Scheldt Canal and gained German positions on the eastern bank of the canal.

The 1st Division, with the 6th Division covering its flanks, crossed the ridge north-west of Thorigny and reached the west end of the le Tronquoy Tunnel. Here they came in touch with the 32nd Division who had passed through the 46th Division and taken Lehaucourt and Magny la Fosse.

North of Bellenglise the 30th American Division, having broken through the deep defences of the Hindenburg Line, stormed Bellicourt and seized Nauroy. The 27th American Division pressed on as far as Bony. Heavily supported by their own reserves and the Australian 3rd and 5th Divisions, the Americans overcame strong resistance at Bellicourt, Nauroy, Gillemont Farm and a number of other points in the intricate defences of the Hindenburg Line.

The 12th and 18th Divisions cleared the slopes of Vendhuille. The Third Army captured Masnières and secured the crossings of the Scheldt Canal between Masnières and the outskirts of Cambrai. The Canadians took St. Olle and Sancourt.[29]

'H.Q.' Company, 'B' Company and the battalion transport moved up to Railton. The 18th Middlesex Battalion H.Q. remained at Équancourt Wood.

Private G/34020 Thomas Alfred Raven born in King's Cross and enlisted in West Ham, Middlesex, died of his wounds aged 34. He was formerly 2024 Essex Regiment. He was married to Minnie Isabel Raven. In 1911 they lived at 11 Chestnut Avenue, Forest Gate, London and they had two sons Frederick Alfred aged 2 and Leonard Arthur aged 1. He worked as Municipal clerk with West Ham Council. He was the son of Kate and Thomas Alfred Raven of 28 Cobbold Road, Forest Gate, London. He is buried in the Terlincthun British Cemetery, Wimille – Pas de Calais.[30]

30 Sept. The Germans evacuated their positions opposite the 33rd Division west of the St. Quentin Canal. The 98th and 100th Infantry Brigades moved forward during the morning and occupied the Green Line with patrols pushed forward to the St. Quentin Canal. By 4pm the 33rd Division held the whole of the Green Line on their front without opposition, from just north of the Catelet Road to just north of High Street. The divisions on both flanks of the 33rd Division also advanced to the Green Line without opposition. The Germans held the east bank of the canal with snipers and machine guns. The enemy destroyed most

of the crossings over the canal. Brigades in the line were ordered to hold any crossings that could be established but not to become heavily engaged with the enemy to force crossings.

11th and 212th Field Companies R.E. escorted by 'E' Squadron 5th Cyclists Regiment moved to Pigeon Ravine and reconnoitred bridges over the canal and collected materials ready to construct bridges when the situation allowed.[31]

'B' and 'C' Companies worked on the forward roads.

The heavy attacks on all fronts on the 29 and 30 September produced a gap in the Hindenburg Line which was enlarged by the capture of Thorigny and Le Tronquoy and that led to the capture of the Le Tronquoy Tunnel. Villers-Guislain and Gonnelieu were abandoned by the enemy as they withdrew behind the Scheldt Canal.[32] (The Canal de l'Escaut, Scheldt Canal and St. Quentin Canal were the same water course which ran from north of Cambrai to south of St. Quentin.)

Railton

1 October 1918. Battalion H.Q. moved up to Railton.

The battalion worked on forward roads.

'B' Company moved to Tétard Wood a 1,000 yards east of the centre of Épehy. 'C' Company moved to a camp just over a mile south-west of the centre of Villers-Guislain, north-east of Vaucellette Farm.

The 1st Battalion Middlesex Regiment held the east side of the St. Quentin Canal and one platoon held posts on both sides of the destroyed bridge over the canal at Honnecourt. The village itself, on the west side of the canal was clear of the enemy but snipers in ruined houses on the west bank of the canal continually fired on the forward troops. Captain Belsham reported that the lock gates at Franqueville were undamaged and the footbridge, although partially destroyed, was passable for infantry in single file.[33]

The IX Corps and Australian Corps, supported by the First French Army that had occupied St. Quentin, took Levergies, Joncourt, Estrées and Bony. In the Cambrai sector the New Zealand and 3rd Division took Crèvecoeur and Rumilly. North of Cambrai the Canadian Corps cleared the high ground west of Ramillies and entered Blécourt.[34]

The British Army adopted the 24 hour clock system which Field Marshal Haig saw as a great convenience.[35]

2 Oct. The battalion worked on forward roads.

Lt.-Col. McNeile broke his ankle.

Divisional Order 358 was issued at 21.15 hours for the relief of the 98th Infantry Brigade by the 19th Infantry Brigade in the left sub sector of 33rd Division front.

The 1st Middlesex were ordered to cross the St. Quentin Canal at the lock gates at Franqueville but found the footbridge to be completely destroyed and they were prevented from approaching the western bank of the canal by heavy machine gun fire.[36]

3 Oct. 'A' Company moved to Fir support in the Thrush Valley east of Peizières.

The battalion worked on forward roads.

One man was wounded.

The Fourth Army attacked between Sequehart and Le Catelet capturing both villages, Ramicourt, Gouy and the Beaurevoir – Fonsomme Line.[37]

4 Oct. Work continued on forward roads.

Lt.-Col. McNeile was admitted to hospital and command of the battalion passed to Major Hinman.

The Germans still held the east bank of the St. Quentin Canal on the 33rd Divisional front (Honnecourt to Ossus) with machine guns and prevented British troops from crossing.[38]

The newly appointed Imperial Chancellor of Germany, Prince Max of Baden, under direct instructions from the German Supreme Army Command, dispatched a Note to United States President Wilson asking him to take in hand the restoration of peace and requesting the immediate conclusion of an armistice on land and sea and in the air.[39]

5 Oct. 'A' Company worked on the approaches to the heavy bridge on the St. Quentin Canal. 'B' and 'C' Companies worked on making roads passable for transport from the old front line to the St. Quentin Canal.

33rd Division dawn patrols crossed the St. Quentin Canal without opposition at Ossus and with little opposition at Honnecourt. Most of the enemy had withdrawn. A line of posts was established on the road Honnecourt – Kingston Quarry – De La l'Eau, under cover of which the two leading battalions of 19th Infantry Brigade, the 1st and 5/6th Cameronians (Scottish Rifles), crossed the canal.

Patrols were rushed forward to the Hindenburg Line followed by the remainder of the 1st and the 5/6th Cameronians (Scottish Rifles). A few of the enemy were discovered holding the trenches about la Terrière. By 15.00 hours these were soon driven out and the Hindenburg Line occupied between Richmond Quarry and Rancourt Farm with a point at Bonabus Farm.

Patrols of the 5th Cyclist Regiment reconnoitred as far as Mortho Wood and the Divisional observers entered Aubencheul-aux-Bois at 15.00 hours. A few hostile machine-guns were encountered in both places, otherwise no opposition was met.

The 1st Queen's, the remaining battalion 19th Infantry Brigade, was assembled in the Hindenburg Line west of la Terrière.

Work on the construction of bridges over the canal was commenced by 11.00 hours. Three infantry bridges had been completed near Ossus by 14.15 hours, one for transport and field guns near Ossus by 18.00 hours. A heavy bridge at Franqueville to carry 12 ton axle loads, was ready for use at 22.00 hours.

The 98th Infantry Brigade moved to the vicinity of Pigeon Quarry in the afternoon and was in position there by 17.00 hours.

During the day the 38th Division advanced across the front of the 33rd Division and occupied a line between Aubencheul and Mortho Wood. The 33rd Division then passed into Corps Reserve. One prisoner was captured.[40]

Montbrehain and Beaurevoir were captured and the Germans evacuated the high ground about la Terrière in the bend of the St. Quentin Canal between La Catelet and Crèvecoeur.

The First, Third and Fourth Armies had stormed the line of the Canal du Nord and broken through the Hindenburg Line driving a wide gap through it and the rear trench systems behind it. The whole of the main Hindenburg defences were in British hands. The German's last and strongest prepared position had been shattered. 36,000 prisoners and 380 guns were captured. At last Haig had achieved a decisive victory.

In Flanders a similar success had been achieved by Belgian and British troops. By the beginning of October Belgian troops had taken Zonnebeke, Poelcapelle, Schaap Baillie, cleared Houthulst Forest and passed the general line of Moorslede – Staden – Dixmude.

The British had captured Wytschaete, Messines, Terhand, Dadizeele, forced the German rearguard out of Ploegsteert Wood and cleared the left bank of the Lys from Comines.

On 2 October the Germans began to fall back from south of Lens to Armentières. On the evening of 4 October, north of Lens, the German retreat halted and the strength of their resistance indicated they intended to stand and fight on the general line of Vendin le Vieil – Wavrin – Erquinghem – Houplines. South of Lens the German retreat slowed and they held the general line Fresnoy – Sallaumines – Vendin le Vieil.[41]

1 33rd Division War Diary
2 2nd Battalion Worcestershire Regiment War Diary
3 33rd Division War Diary, Operations carried out by 33rd Division between 26 September and 3 October 1918
4 *Soldiers Died In The Great War 1914 -19*, p. 102; Commonwealth War Graves Commission casualty details; England & Wales Marriage Index 1837-1915; 1901 Census
5 Ibid.
6 Ibid., p. 103; Private Harris Army Service Record, National Archives, WO 363
7 Commonwealth War Graves Commission casualty details
8 *Soldiers Died In The Great War 1914 -19*, p. 103; Commonwealth War Graves Commission casualty details; Private Keal Army Service Record, National Archives, WO 363; England & Wales Birth Index 1837-1915
9 Ibid.; 1911 Census
10 *Soldiers Died In The Great War 1914 -19*, p. 104; Commonwealth War Graves Commission casualty details; Corporal Parkyns Army Service Record, National Archives, WO 363; 1901 Census; 1911 Census; England & Wales Marriage Index 1837-1915
11 Ibid.; Private Warry Army Service Record, National Archives, WO 363
12 Ibid., p. 103; Private Mappley Army Service Record, National Archives, WO 363; England & Wales Birth Index 1837-1915; 1901 Census
13 Ibid., p. 104
14 Edmonds, *Military Operations, France And Belgium 1918 Vol. 4*, Macmillan, London, 1947, p. 258 f.n.1
15 Boraston (Editor), Sir *Douglas Haig's Despatches (December 1915 – April 1919)*, p. 278
16 Ibid., p. 280
17 Ibid., p. 282
18 Ibid., p. 280
19 *Soldiers Died In The Great War 1914 -19*, p. 102; Commonwealth War Graves Commission casualty details
20 33rd Division War Diary
21 Boraston (Editor), Sir *Douglas Haig's Despatches (December 1915 – April 1919)*, p.p. 280-282

22 Ibid., p. 282

23 2nd Argyll and Sutherland Highlanders Battalion War Diary

24 33rd Division War Diary

25 2nd Argyll and Sutherland Highlanders Battalion War Diary

26 33rd Division War Diary

27 2nd Battalion Worcestershire Regiment War Diary

28 33rd Division War Diary

29 Boraston (Editor), Sir *Douglas Haig's Despatches (December 1915 – April 1919),* p.p. 282-283

30 *Soldiers Died In The Great War 1914 -19*, p. 104; Commonwealth War Graves Commission casualty details; 1911 Census

31 33rd Division War Diary, Operations carried out by 33rd Division between 26 September and 3 October 1918

32 Boraston (Editor), Sir *Douglas Haig's Despatches (December 1915 – April 1919),* p. 284

33 1st Battalion Middlesex Regiment War Diary

34 Boraston (Editor), Sir *Douglas Haig's Despatches (December 1915 – April 1919),* p. 284

35 Blake (Editor), *The Private Papers of Douglas Haig 1914 -1919*, p. 329

36 1st Battalion Middlesex Regiment War Diary

37 Boraston (Editor), Sir *Douglas Haig's Despatches (December 1915 – April 1919),* p. 284

38 33rd Division War Diary

39 David Lloyd George, *War Memoirs, Vol. 2*, p. 1953

40 33rd Division War Diary

41 Boraston (Editor), Sir *Douglas Haig's Despatches (December 1915 – April 1919),* p.p. 284-287

CHAPTER FIFTEEN

6th October 1918 to 25th October 1918

Final advance through Nord
Second Battle of Le Cateau
Bridging the River Selle
Towards Mormal Forest

Franque Wood

6 Oct. The battalion H.Q. moved forward to Rag Trench west of les Tranchées. 'A' Company moved to Bosquet Farm. 'B' Company moved to Franque Wood. 'C' Company moved to Honnecourt Wood. Two platoons of 'A' Company worked on approaches to a bridge over the St. Quentin Canal at the lock in Franqueville. The other two 'A' Company platoons worked on road repairs from Cannon Gate to that bridge.

'B' Company repaired the road from Pigeon Quarry through Honnecourt and across the St Quentin Canal to just south of Noble Ville. 'C' Company repaired roads from north of Honnecourt Wood to Rancourt Farm in the Hindenburg Line.

7 Oct. The battalion H.Q. moved to the north-west edge of Franque Wood. This was within a 1,000 yards of the Hindenburg Line.

'A' Company worked on roads from Franqueville to the south-east of la Terrière and from the centre of la Terrière to the east of the village. They also worked on the approaches to the heavy bridge over the St. Quentin Canal.

'B' Company worked on the road from the crossroads east of Franqueville through la Terrière to Rancourt Farm. This work was inside the defensive fortifications of the Hindenburg Line. One officer and 57 other ranks of infantrymen worked with 'B' Company

'C' Company repaired the road along the west bank of the St. Quentin Canal, from the bridge north of Honnecourt, running south to the lock at Franqueville and the road from the lock to the start of Cannon Gate road south of Les Tranchées. 320 infantrymen worked with the battalion.

8 Oct. Two platoons of 'A' Company repaired the road from the western outskirts of la Terrière, through the village to the northern tip of Basket Wood. The other two platoons made recesses in the bank for huts for 33rd Division H.Q.

'B' Company, with 83 infantrymen, repaired roads from the crossroads south-west of Franque Wood to la Terrière.

'C' Company, together with 80 infantrymen, worked again on the west bank canal road north and south of Honnecourt.

Second Battle of Le Cateau

At 04.30 hours the Third Army attacked and at 05.10 hours the Fourth Army attacked. The combined front for these two attacks was seventeen miles from Sequehart north of St. Quentin to south of Cambrai. British infantry and tanks penetrated the German positions to a depth of between three and four miles.

The French attacked on the British right south to St. Quentin. Further south French and American troops attacked east of Meuse and in Champagne.

Brancourt and Prémont were taken by the American 30th Division. The 66th Division took Serain. The 38th Division cleared Villers-Outréaux. Malincourt was captured in the late afternoon. The New Zealand Division passed through Lesdain and took Esnes. The 2nd, 3rd and 63rd Divisions captured Forenville, Seranvillers and Niergnies. The 57th Division made progress in the southern outskirts of Cambrai.[1]

The 33rd Division moved forward in the afternoon with the 19th Infantry Brigade on the Le Catelet – Nauroy Line, the 98th Infantry Brigade in the Hindenburg Line and the 100th Infantry Brigade in the vicinity of Pigeon Quarry. At 18.50 hours orders from the V Corps were issued for the 33rd Division to continue the pursuit of the Germans at dawn the following day, passing through the outposts of the 38th Division at 05.20 hours. The objective for the 33rd Division was to take Clary and press on towards Bertry. The 66th Division on the right and the 17th Division on the left were to advance at the same time as the 33rd Division.[2]

President Wilson replied to the German Chancellor asking him if the German Government accepted the terms laid down by him in his address to the Congress of the United States on 8 January last and in subsequent addresses. The requested discussions would only be to agree upon the practical details of their application. With specific reference to the requested armistice, President Wilson pointed out that he would not propose a cessation of arms to the Allies as long as German troops remained on invaded territory. He stated 'The good faith of any discussion would manifestly depend upon the consent of the Central Powers immediately to withdraw their forces everywhere from invaded territory'.[3]

9 Oct. Work continued on repairing roads from la Terrière to the northern tip of Basket Wood, from Franqueville to la Terrière and the canal road north and south of Honnecourt. Recesses were made in the bank for huts for Divisional H.Q.

In addition 'B' Company sent one platoon to work on the main road north of Rancourt Farm.

The battalion moved forward by companies and assembled at Angelus Orchard next to Mortho Wood north-west of Villers-Outréaux.

Lieut. C. Taaffe returned to the battalion and reported for duty.

The battalion received Divisional Order 360 at 5.30 hours, 361 at 11.15 hours and 362 at 21.30 hours for the move of the 33rd Division.

The 33rd Divisional front ran south from Mill Wood (Bois du Moulin) to the road 1,500 yards west of Élincourt. At 04.30 hours the 19th Infantry Brigade assembled about Malincourt and advanced through the outposts of the 38th Division. They met little opposition at first which was soon overcome. The Germans had retreated and left a few machine guns as a rearguard. Gard Wood was reported clear of Germans at 06.15 hours. Clary was taken at about 09.00 hours but a further advance was checked for some time by German fire from the high ground just east of the village. A battalion of the 19th Infantry Brigade was sent to work round by the south of the village in conjunction with troops of the 3rd Cavalry Division and press on towards Bertry.

At 09.00 hours orders were issued for the 98th Infantry Brigade to march at 11.00 hours on Clary and the 100th Infantry Brigade to march to Dehéries. At about 10.35 hours V Corps reported that the XIII Corps were pushing on towards Le Cateau. At 11.15 hours orders were issued for the 19th Infantry Brigade to press itself on the high ground beyond the road between Montay and Neuvilly.

The 98th Infantry Brigade was ordered to march on Troisvilles, but in view of the check at Clary was subsequently halted just west of Clary. The 19th Infantry Brigade reported that Bertry was taken at 15.40 hours. At 20.20 hours the 19th Infantry Brigade reported that they held Troisvilles and had established an outpost line east of the village.[4]

The Infantry Brigades of the 33rd Division captured seven objectives during the day; the first was the Selvigny to Élincourt road, second the Caullery to Élincourt road, third and fourth east of Clary Village, fifth Montigny to Ever Spring 1,300 yards south of Bertry, sixth looped east of Bertry and the seventh outposts east of Troisvilles. These outposts stretched from the north-west of Troisvilles clockwise to the south-east of the village. The 33rd Division advanced their front line by over six-and-a-half miles in one day. [5]

In the 24 hours up to 17.00 hours one officer, 117 men and a battery of 77mm guns with horses were captured by 33rd Division.[6]

Overnight Canadian troops captured Ramillies and crossed the St. Quentin Canal at Pont d'Aire. Canadian patrols entered Cambrai from the north and joined up with patrols of the 57th Division working through the south of the town.

At 5.20 hours the Fourth and Third Armies resumed their attack on the whole front, assisted by the Cavalry. By nightfall troops were within two miles of Le Cateau, Bohain had been captured and Caudry was under attack from the south. Cambrai was captured and troops advanced three miles to the east of the town.

Dragoon Guards and Canadian Cavalry were instrumental in the capture of Honnechy, Reumont and Troisvilles.[7]

The 5/6th Cameronians (Scottish Rifles) advanced north-east of Clary. They found the Germans had withdrawn from the village and they did not meet any resistance until they reached the east side of Clary. With the help of the cavalry they overcame that resistance. They took 5 officers and 50 other ranks prisoner. They also captured three field guns and five horses. They did not count the number of machine guns captured.[8]

Iris Farm

10 Oct. The battalion moved to Iris Farm leaving at 05.00 hours. Companies fell out to work on the line of the march.

'A' Company worked on the roads through Malincourt village. 'B' Company worked on the roads through Élincourt village. 'C' Company repaired the roads through Clary village mainly filling in shell holes and mine craters. This was essential work to ensure that the advancing 33rd Division maintained good lines of communication for supplies and reinforcements and did not get overstretched.

2nd Lieuts. H. Cripps and A. Knight reported for duty.

The 4th Battalion Middlesex Regiment marched through Caudry and received a most enthusiastic welcome from many thousands of civilians who had been liberated from the Germans. The battalion formed up at Petit Caudry.[9]

The 33rd Divisional Commander received a letter from V Corps pointing out that the advance of the division had not been sufficiently energetic and several opportunities had been lost.[10]

The 98th Infantry Brigade were ordered to pass through the position held by the 19th Infantry Brigade and continue the pursuit of the Germans and take the high ground north-east of the La Selle River. At 04.00 hours the 2nd Argyll and Sutherland Highlanders moved off from near Clary, marched through Bertry and formed up in artillery formation astride the Bertry – Troisvilles road and led the advance by the 98th Infantry Division across open country. The 4th King's were in support and the 1st Middlesex were in reserve.

The advance made good progress until it reached the Le Cateau – Cambrai road where it was met by an enemy barrage. The 2nd Argyll and Sutherland Highlanders pushed forward and by 07.30 hours established outposts along a 2,000 yard front between Neuvilly and Montay and just 600 yards short of the Neuvilly – Montay road. They paused there because the 17th Division on the left and the 66th Division on the right were not in sight.

At 08.00 hours troops from the 66th Division arrived on the right of the 2nd Argyll and Sutherland Highlanders and the advance was resumed. They were met immediately along the whole line by an intense barrage of Lewis gun and rifle fire and from field guns firing over open sites. The 2nd Argyll and Sutherland Highlanders suffered heavy casualties and they were prevented from crossing the River Selle. The intense enemy shelling continued for the rest of the morning and into the early afternoon.

At around 15.00 hours orders were issued for the resumption of the attack at 17.00 hours with the objective of forcing a crossing of the River Selle and reaching the high ground north-east of it

The 2nd Argyll and Sutherland Highlanders attacked again under an arranged barrage and with the 4th King's in close support. 'C' Company crossed

the river 1,400 yards south-east of Neuvilly and 'B' Company 2,000 yards south-east of the village.

'B' Company advanced beyond the River Selle and made good progress but were held up by machine gun fire 550 yards west of the river and established a post there. They also established a post 300 yards further back on the road, north of Montay on the road to Neuvilly. 'C' Company were forced to withdraw back across the River Selle when they discovered that the 17th Division had gone back and the enemy were working round their left flank from Neuvilly.[11]

In this section of the Western Front the front line ran from Riquerval Wood along the west bank of the River Selle to Viesly then on past St. Hilaire and Avesnes to the St. Quentin Canal at Thun St. Martin.[12]

There was a suspicion among Allied leaders that Germany was not serious about ending the war but was playing for time and the 'peace would only be a truce, under cover of which the redoubtable military leaders of Germany would gather up her strength for a renewed conflict and we should be compelled to prepare for the next struggle'.[13]

General Sir Herbert Lawrence, Chief of the General Staff, met Field Marshal Haig to discuss the proposed armistice with Germany. Lawrence told Haig he was fearful that Britain would find herself in a difficult position if Germany were to counter-attack. Haig 'assured him that the enemy had no means, nor has the German High Command the willpower, to launch an attack strong enough to affect our front line troops. We have got the enemy down, in fact, he is a beaten Army, and my plan is to go on hitting him as hard as we possibly can, till he begs for mercy'.[14]

11 Oct. Overnight all companies working in shifts filled craters on the Selvigny to Clary road. The battalion completed a double lorry way by 07.00 hours.

'B' Company continued improving the Selvigny to Clary road.

'A' Company went forward to make approaches to pontoon bridges being put across the River Selle between Montay and Neuvilly.

Sixty men, comprising the remainder of 'B' Company 2nd Argyll and Sutherland Highlanders and elements of 'A' and 'C' Companies of the 2nd Argylls and a few stragglers of the 4th King's under the command of Lieut. T. Prentice held the forward post north-east of the River Selle. Some men of the 4th King's pushed forward before dawn and occupied the post on the Montay to Neuvilly road behind Lieut. Prentice.

During the day the advanced post was exposed to extremely severe sniping and machine gun fire from the high railway embankment which was strongly held by the Germans and looked straight down on the British position.

At 18.30 hours the Germans counter-attacked the forward post and Lieut. Prentice and his men were forced back to the Montay to Neuvilly road where they held their ground.[15]

Mayor Bonneville of Clary wrote to Major-General Pinney on the liberation of the town. He said 'Thanks to their rapid and vigorous pursuit the brave Scotch troops have succeeded in preventing the enemy from finishing the work of destruction he had commenced in our commune. There has been no accident, no loss of life to deplore, our Church has been preserved to the last minute...We offer our heartfelt gratitude to all the brave soldiers who have so generously poured out their blood in the sacred cause of right, justice and the independence of all people'.[16]

Private T.F.204113 Alfred George Williams was born on 20 December 1897 in Willesden worked in the book department of the British Museum. He attested at Pound Lane Willesden Green on 25 June 1915 and was posted to 3/9th Middlesex. On the 4 August 1915 he undertook a medical at Pound Lane where his age was recorded as 19 years. However, he was only 17 years and 9 months old at the time. On 19 October 1915 he was admitted the Purfleet Military Hospital suffering from influenza and discharged on 25 October.

On 5 February 1916 he was transferred to 63rd Provisional Battalion and moved to the 7th (Reserve) Battalion Middlesex Regiment on 24 November 1916. He was posted to 1/7th Middlesex on 8 March 1917 and travelled to France to join the British Expeditionary Force. He was then 19 years and 3 month old.

On 26 March 1917 he transferred to the 16th Middlesex and joined 'A' Company. On 14 April 1917 he suffered a gunshot wound to his abdomen and was admitted to the 87th Field Ambulance and then transferred to the 6 Stationary Hospital at Frevent on 18 April and then onto the 11 Stationary Hospital at Rouen. On his discharge from hospital Williams joined the 41st Infantry Base Depot at Étaples on 17 June 1917 and rejoined the 16th Middlesex in the field on 30 June.

On 17 July 1917 Private Williams was diagnosed with congenital phimosis (tight foreskin) and was admitted to 88th Field Ambulance and then sent to 63 Casualty Clearing Station for a circumcision operation. He was back in the 63 Casualty Clearing Station on 28 July suffering from Pyrexia of Unknown Origin (P.U.O. – hyperthermia or fever). He was sent back to England on 5 August 1917. He was granted 10 days home furlough from 5 to 15 October.

On 7 December 1917 he once again embarked for France. He rejoined the 16th Middlesex on 12 December in the field. On 15 December he was admitted to 89th Field Ambulance, transferred to 6 Stationary Hospital and was then moved to the 12 Stationary Hospital on 22 December 1917. He was discharged on 19 January 1918 and rejoined the 16th Middlesex in the field.

On 8 February Williams was posted to the 18th Middlesex but his sickness continued. He suffered a bout of influenza and bouts of P.U.O. and was admitted to the 19 Casualty Clearing Station, 3 Canadian Casualty Clearing Station, 54 General Hospital, 6 Convalescent Depot, 15 Convalescent Depot and the 99th Field Ambulance. He rejoined the 18th Middlesex on 30 July. He was seriously wounded on 26 September suffering gunshot wounds to his left arm, left leg, chest and left buttock. He was admitted to the 3 Canadian General Hospital at Dannes Camiers where he died of wounds 40 days before his 21 birthday.

He was the son of Charlotte Susan and Alfred George Williams of 13 Eresby Road, High Road, Kilburn, London. His mother Charlotte received a Separation Allowance of 8 shillings and 9 pence. He is buried in the Étaples Military Cemetery – Pas de Calais.[17]

12 Oct. Divisional Order 363 at 12.45 hours issued the previous evening ordered the bridging of the River Selle. The 11th and 212th Field Companies of the Royal Engineers constructed eleven foot bridges before dawn along a mile stretch of the river starting 1,000 yards north of Montay. Two of the bridges were able to carry pack transport.[18]

'A' Company arrived back in camp at noon having completed the approach roads to the eleven pontoon bridges across the River Selle. They had rested at Bertry for several hours.

'B' Company repaired the Selvigny to Clary road. 'C' Company repaired the Clary – Bertry – Troisvilles road.

The battalion received Divisional Order 364 at 8.00 hours.

Major-General Pinney called to tell the battalion that Lt.-General Sir Cameron Deane Shute, General Officer commanding V Corps, was very pleased with the work done by the battalion on the roads.

The 100th Infantry Brigade of the 33rd Division relieved the 98th Infantry Brigade. During the operations between 9 and 12 October the 2nd Argyll and Sutherland Highlanders had 9 officers and 192 other ranks killed, missing or wounded.[19]

The 100th Infantry Brigade were ordered to capture and consolidate the line from Road Junction 2,000 yards north-east along the track from Montay to Forest

1,300 yards west of Forest, and onto the cross roads 800 yards south of Amerval.[20]

At dawn the 100th Infantry Brigade attacked with the 16th King's Royal Rifles on the left resting on Neuvilly, the 2nd Worcestershires in the centre and 1/9th Highland Light Infantry on the right resting on Montay.[21] The objectives were the Le Cateau – Solesmes railway line and the high ground east of the River Selle south-west of Forest.[22] Without the support of a barrage, the three battalions were ordered to rush the railway line, which was strongly held and wired, and then push onto the high ground.[23] They were met by machine gun and artillery fire. The 1/9th Highland Light Infantry eventually reached the slopes of the spur 1,000 yards north-east of Montay but was forced back by enfilade machine gun fire. The 16th King's Royal Rifles reached its objective but the Division on its left flank failed to clear Neuvilly. The exposed left flank of the 16th K.R.R. was attacked from the north-west and they were forced to fall back across the River Selle. By the afternoon the line was held along the River Selle.[24]

The German Government replied to President Wilson accepting the propositions laid down by him and agreeing to evacuate the occupied territories as a condition of the armistice.[25]

13 Oct. 'B' Company filled in craters and cleared mud off the Selvigny – Clary road. 'C' Company repaired roads in Clary.

Six men were sent to Clary to put the bathhouse in order. It was overcast and raining.

During the Battle for Le Cateau 12,000 German prisoners and 250 guns were taken. Full possession of the important lateral double railway from St. Quentin through Busigny to Cambrai was achieved. The British Army secured the River Selle at all points south of Haspres and established bridgeheads at a number of places.

The Germans, in the face of the French advance along both sides of the Argonne, retreated and Laon was taken by the French.

In northern France the German withdrawal continued south of Lens. The 8th Division captured Biache St. Vaast and Oppy. By the evening of 13 October British troops reached the western suburbs of Douai and were close up to the west banks of the Sensée Deviation and the Haute Deule Canals on the whole front from Arleux (south of Douai) to Vendin le Vieil.[26]

14 Oct. Overnight the 33rd Division was relieved by the 38th Division and went into the Divisional reserve.[27]

'A' Company repaired roads in and around Clary. 'B' Company worked on the Hurtevent Farms – Clary road. Hurtevent Farms were 2,100 yards east of Clary. 'C' Company worked on the Élincourt – Selvigny road and the Élincourt – Walincourt road.

Lieut. E.C.V. Warde was detailed as Divisional Road Reconnaissance Officer. 2nd Lieut. Yoxall was detailed as the Divisional Water Point Officer.

Private P.S.2563 Walter Alfred Webb was born on 18 November 1892 in Walthamstow. He attested on 14 July 1915 at Wood Green, was single, a clerk by profession, 5′ 5¼″ tall and weighed 112 lbs. He joined the Middlesex Regiment on 20 July 1915 at Woldingham. He was posted to 24th Middlesex on 28 July 1915. He was posted to the 16th Middlesex on 23 January 1917 and travelled to France to join the British Expeditionary Force.

He was granted leave to England from 4 to 14 June 1917. He was awarded Proficiency Pay Class I from 14 July 1917. On 2 October 1917 he was struck off the strength of 16th Middlesex and as batman to Major O'Reilly attended a course in England. He rejoined the 16th Middlesex on 1 January 1918 with Major O'Reilly. He transferred to 18th Middlesex on 8 February 1918.

On 14 April 1918 Major O'Reilly was attached to the 29th Divisional Headquarters and based with the 2nd Battalion Hampshire Regiment. Private Webb moved with him. He was killed in action with the 2nd Hampshires in the Final Advance in Flanders – Battle of Courtrai.

Private Webb was the son of Maria Elizabeth and William Walter Webb of 122 Fairbridge Road, Upper Holloway, London. His mother received a Separation Allowance of 6 shillings and 2 pence. He is buried in the Ledeghem Military Cemetery – Ledegem, West-Vlaanderen.[28]

In Flanders at 05.35 hours British, Belgian and French forces, under the command of His Majesty the King of the Belgians, attacked on the whole front between the Lys River at Comines and Dixmude. The British sector extended for a distance of over nine miles from Comines to the hamlet of St. Pieter on the Menin – Roulers road. British troops advanced the line to the southern edge of the rising ground overlooking Wervicq, Menin and Wevelghem. Moorseele was captured and troops got to within a short distance of Gulleghem and Steenbeek. On the left Belgian troops reached Iseghem and took Cortemarck. French troops surrounded Roulers.[29]

President Wilson replied to Germany condemning the illegal and inhuman practices of German submarines sinking passenger ships and the wanton destruction of cities and villages by the retreating German forces in Flanders

and France. He saw this as a direct violation of the rules and practices of civilised warfare. He told Germany that the Allies would not agree to a cessation of arms while acts of inhumanity, spoliation and desolation were being continued.[30]

15 Oct. 'A' Company repaired the roads in and around Clary. 'B' Company repaired roads in Malincourt. 'C' Company repaired roads in and around Walincourt. The Lewis gunners of 'A' Company were excused work so that they could train.

16 Oct. All companies worked on general road repairs in the 33rd Divisional area. 'B' Company Lewis gunners were excused work and trained under the battalion Lewis gun sergeant.

17 Oct. The battalion had another bath.

The battalion worked on roads in the 33rd Divisional area.

'C' Company Lewis gunners trained under the battalion Lewis gun serjeant.

Battle of the Selle River.

The war turned full circle. With communications and logistics in place Field Marshal Haig was ready to move forward again on the Le Cateau front. At 05.20 hours the Fourth Army attacked on a ten mile front from Le Cateau southwards. The French First Army attacked simultaneously west of the Sambre et Oise Canal.[31] British troops attacked the same positions the British Expeditionary Force desperately defended in August 1914.

18 Oct 'A' Company had a day's rest. 'B' and 'C' Companies worked on the roads in the Divisional area.

The battalion received Divisional Order 365 at 20.40 hours for the move of the 33rd Division.

Evacuation of Lille

The British advances north of the Lys put troops far to the east of the German defences on the northern side of Lille. The advances on the Le Cateau front

turned the Lille defences from the south. The position of the German forces between the Sensée and the Lys became very exposed. On 15 October British troops crossed the Haute Deule Canal on a wide front north of Pont-á-Vendin. This attack precipitated a German retreat which was closely pursued by the VIII and XI Corps.

By 17 October the 8th Division entered Douai and the 57th and 59th Divisions entered the outskirts of Lille. On 18 October at 05.50 hours British troops encircled Lille which was clear of the enemy. The British line was carried far to the east of Douai, Lille, Roubaix and Tourcoing.[32]

19 Oct. 'A' and 'C' Companies worked on roads in the 33rd Divisional area. 'B' Company had a day's rest.

2nd Lieut. Palmer was admitted to hospital due to sickness.

The Germans had been driven back across the Sambre et Oise Canal at almost all of the points south of Catillon where the line then followed the Richemont Valley east and north of Le Cateau.[33]

Bertry

20 Oct. The battalion moved at 9.30 hours to billets in Bertry.

The British Army attacked along the River Selle north of Le Cateau and took the high ground east of the river and patrols were pushed out as far as the River Harpies. North of Haspres progress was made on both sides of the St. Quentin Canal reaching the slopes overlooking the left bank of the Écaillon River and occupying Denain.[34]

Flanders

By 16 October British troops held the north bank of the Lys from Frélinghien to opposite Harlebeke and had crossed the river at a number of points. The Germans retreated from Thourout which had been surrounded by Allied troops the previous day. Ostend fell on 17 October. By 20 October the Belgian and French troops had pushed the northern flank of the front line right up to the Dutch border.[35]

Germany responded to President Wilson accepting that military advisers would arrange the terms of the armistice but demanded that the present relative

strength on the fronts must be made the basis of arrangements that will safeguard and guarantee it. They also undertook to order U-boat commanders to stop sinking passenger ships.[36]

21 Oct. Companies worked by shifts on the road running south-west from Montay to Reumont.

'C' Company sent two platoons to north-east of Montay to blow up and crowbar away the demolished railway bridge on the Montay to Forest road.

22 Oct. 'A' Company cleared the debris of the demolished railway bridge north-east of Montay. They also sent a platoon forward to make a track for horsed transport over the River Selle just over 1,000 yards north of Montay. However, they were unable to work because of a German barrage. Another platoon of 'A' Company completed this work later.

'B' Company repaired roads in the 33rd Divisional Area.

Lieut. Maurice Oxenbould reported for duty.

One man was wounded.

The British troops that secured Lille pressed on and gained the general line of the Scheldt Canal on the whole front from Valenciennes to the neighbourhood of Avelghem.[37]

L' Évêque Wood Camp

23 Oct. At 5.10 hours the battalion received orders to move forward. An officer was sent to Divisional H.Q. to obtain instructions from Lt.-Col. Evans on the work to be carried out by the battalion.

As a result 'C' Company were sent forward to repair the main Montay – Forest – Croix road 1,200 yards north-east of Montay just beyond the practice trenches. They were instructed to go as far forward as the situation permitted.

'B' Company was sent forward later in the day and worked in advance of 'C' Company through Forest and Croix. 'A' Company remained in reserve at Montay.

After work the battalion H.Q. moved to L'Évêque Wood camp which was 1,000 yards west of Malgarni. 'B' Company was billeted in Forest.

The capture of the Selle positions opened the way for a larger attack aimed at moving the general line forward to the Sambre Canal along the edge of the Mormal Forest to the neighbourhood of Valenciennes.[38]

The original front for the attack was fifteen miles long and stretched from east of Mazinghien to Maison Bleue, north-east of Haussy. The assault was opened by the Fourth Army at 01.20 hours. The Third Army, including the 33rd Division, were also involved in the attack.[39]

The 33rd Division starting point was the front line on the high ground east of the River Selle overlooking the village of Forest. The line ran south to north from 800 yards north-east on the Montay – Bavay road to 900 yards west of Croisette on a front of 2,500 yards. The 19th Infantry Brigade was to attack on the left, the 98th Infantry Brigade on the right and the 100th Infantry Brigade was in close support. Three tanks were also to be deployed in the attack.[40]

The 19th and 98th Infantry Brigades advanced north-eastwards taking land on both sides of the Montay – Bavay road and the village of Forest. As the 19th Infantry Brigade pushed on to Vendegies Wood, the 98th Infantry Brigade were able to take the second line objective north-west of Calevaux (Caluyaux) and the third line objective north-east of Vert Baudet.[41] By 17.00 hours the two brigades made touch on the line of the road running north-west and south-east of Paul Jacques Farm just short of their fourth objective. Both brigades were held up by machine gun fire from the enemy line running north-west and south-east through Paul Jacques Farm.

At 19.30 hours the farm was surrounded and captured. The two brigades pressed on but were held up by a continuous belt of wire protecting numerous machine gun posts 600 yards south-west of Englefontaine, 100 yards short of their fifth objective. The 18th Division reached Bousies Wood Farm.[42]

Up to 17.00 hours on 23 October 12 officers, 315 other ranks, two batteries of field guns, two single field guns, two trench mortars, about sixty machine guns and two anti-tank rifles were reported as captured by the 33rd Division.[43]

President Wilson replied to Germany stating 'The only Armistice he would feel justified in submitting for consideration would be one which should leave the United States and the Powers associated with her in a position to enforce any arrangements that may be entered into, and to make a renewal of hostilities on the part of Germany impossible'. He went to advise that he was sending the correspondence to the Associated Governments, for their military advisers to work out Armistice terms as will fully protect the interests of the peoples involved and ensure to the Associated Governments the unrestricted power to safeguard and enforce the details of the peace.[44]

24 Oct. Again the battalion were very busy repairing roads and trying to keep open the communications with the vanguard of the attack.

'A' Company moved forwards to billets in Croix and worked on the Montay – Bavay main road from Vert Baudet to southern edge of Vendegies Wood north-east of Herpies Mill.

'B' Company worked on the main road from the church north-east of Croix to Vert Baudet. Later in the day 'C' Company worked forward from Herpies Mill to Paul Jacques Farm.

The advanced battalion H.Q. moved to the outskirts of Forest on the road leading north to Ovillers. The battalion transport remained at L'Évêque Wood.

One man was wounded.

The 19th and 98th Infantry Brigades were ordered to capture the line Englefontaine to Le Coupe Gorge and dig in. The 100th Brigade was then to pass through the village and advance the front to a line running south-east from Futoy, across the Montay to Bavay road and 1,300 yards into the western edge of the Forêt de Mormal.

At 04.00 hours the 19th Infantry Brigade on the left and the 98th Infantry Brigade on the right attacked and encountered heavy fighting and lots of wire. The wire was five rows deep along a line running north-west from Paul Jacques Farm between Vendegies-au-Bois and Wagnonville. The Germans had constructed a line of posts behind the wire. A captured German map showed this position was known as Hermann Stellung II. They overcame that opposition and advanced on Wagnonville.

At 07.40 hours leading troops of the right brigade had advanced along the Montay to Bavay road to a point 800 yards west of Wagnonville. On the way they met considerable opposition. During their advance they encountered a large party of Germans between Poix-du-Nord and Englefontaine and engaged them with concentrated fire from six machine guns inflicting heavy casualties.

The 98th Infantry Brigade made no further progress and by evening they were held just short of the brewery on the road south-west of Englefontaine. They did not take the village.

The 19th Infantry Brigade faced a German counter-attack at 12.30 hours. Two machine guns on the high ground north of Les Tuileries dispersed the German attack inflicting heavy casualties. Some Germans surrendered.

By nightfall the 19th Infantry Brigade established themselves between Wagnonville and Les Tuileries.

The 100th Infantry failed to take Englefontaine and were held on the western outskirts of the village.

In the 24 hours up to 17.00 hours the 33rd Division took 5 German officers and 187 German other ranks prisoner.[45]

In the advance up the Montay to Bavay road the many woods and villages proved difficult to clear. Severe fighting took place in Bois L'Évêque and the villages of Pommereuil, Bousies Forest and Vendegies-sur-Écaillon which was captured late on the day. British troops reached the western outskirts of Forêt de Mormal and were also within a mile of le Quesnoy and north-west of Ruesnes and Maing.[46]

By nightfall the 1st Battalion Middlesex Regiment, which had played a pivotal part in the advance through Nord but sustained heavy casualties, had to be reorganised in the field into one company under Captain Tate and about 90 men.

Over the preceding two day hostilities the 1st Middlesex lost Captain F.B. Broad M.C., Lieut. A.A.T. Morris M.C., Lieut. A.C.T. Kroenig-Ryan all killed. Lieut. F.J. Smith D.C.M. and 2nd Lieut. R.E. Holland were wounded and 2nd Lieut. C.E. Cade was missing.[47]

Lieut. Oxenbould volunteered to transfer from 18th Middlesex to serve with the Die Hards 1st Battalion. He was posted to 'C' Company.

25 Oct. At 05.00 hours the hostile shelling, which had been kept up all night, became very heavy on Poix du Nord and west and south-west of Englefontaine. At 07.30 hours about 75 German troops counter-attacked the British post north of Englefontaine at Le Coupe Gorge on the road to le Quesnoy. The 33rd Division machine guns covering this part of line did good work and the attack was driven off and three machine guns were captured. Spare members of one gun section were posted in houses and knocked out a German light machine gun trying to come into action with their rifle fire.

At 10.30 hours there was a Divisional conference to draw up plans for an attack on Englefontaine. At 12.30 hours the Germans once again attacked British posts in Le Coupe Gorge. Again these attacks were repulsed.

In the 24 hours up to 17.00 hours 33rd Division German prisoners amounted to one officer and 116 other ranks.

Divisional Order 369 was issued at 19.00 hours for the attack the following day on Englefontaine village.[48]

The 18th Middlesex Battalion repaired various roads in the 33rd Divisional area.

Lieut. O.G. Johnson reported for duty.

Lieut. Fish, 2nd Lieut. Poynton and ten men were wounded.

Private G/57940 William G. Glensman who was born and lived in Hackney, Middlesex and enlisted in Stratford, Essex, died of his wounds. He is buried in the Étaples Military Cemetery.[49]

The following four soldiers were killed in action and are buried in the Forest Communal Cemetery – Nord.

Private T.F.315297 Victor John Garratt was born on 14 May 1888. He was a head furniture porter by trade, single, 5´ 8¼″ tall and weighed 133 lbs. He lived at 88 Thrush Street, Walworth. He attested on 23 June 1916 at Camberwell. At his medical he classified as 'B' (one). He was posted to 63rd Provisional Battalion on 24 June and transferred to the 32nd Middlesex on 1 January 1917. He had an inguinal hernia and was fitted with a truss on 13 November. He was posted to the 18th Middlesex on 19 December 1917 and travelled to France. He joined the 18th Middlesex in the field on 21 December. He suffered wounds to his back and left arm on 11 July and returned to duty on 18 July.

He was the son of Matilda Frances and Joseph Garratt. Mrs Garratt received a Separation Allowance of 16 shillings and her son's personal effects of photos and a note book.[50]

Private G/57982 Thomas Plummer, aged 19, was born Holloway, lived in Islington and enlisted in Whitehall, Middlesex. He was the son of Hannah and John Plummer, 50 Rhodes Street, Lower Holloway, London.[51]

Private G/44914 Frederick Smith was born in Hammersmith and enlisted in Chelsea, Middlesex.[52]

Lance Corporal G/9967 George Henry Turpin was born in Islington, lived in Clerkenwell and enlisted in Southwark, Surrey. He was first posted to the British Expeditionary Force in France on 27 September 1915 six weeks before the 18th Middlesex travelled to France. He was the son of Elizabeth and Edwin Turpin. By the time of the 1911 Census his mother had died and he lived with his father at 6 Queens Head Street, Islington.[53]

1 Boraston (Editor), Sir *Douglas Haig's Despatches (December 1915 – April 1919)*, p.p. 287-288

2 33rd Division War Diary

3 Lloyd George, *War Memoirs, Vol. 2*, p.1957

4 33rd Division War Diary
5 Trench Map included in 33rd Division War Diary
6 33rd Division War Diary
7 Boraston (Editor), Sir *Douglas Haig's Despatches (December 1915 – April 1919),* p. 288
8 5/6th Battalion Cameronians (Scottish Rifles) War Diary, National Archives, WO 95/2422, Image ref 1/481
9 Wyrall, *The Die-Hards in the Great War, Vol. 2*, p. 257
10 33rd Division War Diary
11 2nd Argyll and Sutherland Highlanders Battalion War Diary
12 Boraston (Editor), Sir *Douglas Haig's Despatches (December 1915 – April 1919),* p.p. 288-289
13 Lloyd George, *War Memoirs, Vol. 2*, p.1943
14 Blake (Editor), *The Private Papers of Douglas Haig 1914 -1919*, p. 331
15 2nd Argyll and Sutherland Highlanders Battalion War Diary
16 5/6th Battalion Cameronians (Scottish Rifles) War Diary
17 *Soldiers Died In The Great War 1914 -19*, p. 105; Commonwealth War Graves Commission casualty details; Private Williams Army Service Record, National Archives, WO 363; London Metropolitan Archives, London, England, Births and Baptisms 1813 -1906
18 33rd Division War Diary, Divisional Order 363
19 2nd Argyll and Sutherland Highlanders Battalion War Diary
20 33rd Division War Diary
21 2nd Battalion Worcestershire Regiment War Diary
22 16th Battalion King's Royal Rifles War Diary
23 33rd Division War Diary, Report on Operations 11-16 October 1918
24 Ibid.
25 Lloyd George, *War Memoirs, Vol. 2*, p.1961
26 Boraston (Editor), Sir *Douglas Haig's Despatches (December 1915 – April 1919),* p. 289
27 33rd Division War Diary
28 *Soldiers Died In The Great War 1914 -19*, p. 104; Commonwealth War Graves Commission casualty details; Private Webb Army Service Record, National Archives, WO 363; London Metropolitan Archives, London, England, Births and Baptisms 1813 -1906
29 Boraston (Editor), Sir *Douglas Haig's Despatches (December 1915 – April 1919),* p. 290
30 Lloyd George, *War Memoirs, Vol. 2*, p.1962
31 Boraston (Editor), Sir *Douglas Haig's Despatches (December 1915 – April 1919),* p. 291
32 Ibid., p.p. 290-291
33 Ibid., p. 292
34 Ibid.
35 Ibid., p. 290
36 Lloyd George, *War Memoirs, Vol. 2*, p.1966
37 Boraston (Editor), Sir *Douglas Haig's Despatches (December 1915 – April 1919),* p. 291

38 Ibid., p. 292

39 Ibid.

40 33rd Division War Diary, Divisional Operations 22 October – 26 October 1918

41 2nd Battalion Argyll and Sutherland Highlanders Regiment War Diary

42 Ibid.

43 33rd Division War Diary, Report on Operations October 22 – October 30 1918

44 Lloyd George, *War Memoirs, Vol. 2*, p.p. 1966 -1967

45 33rd Division War Diary

46 Boraston (Editor), Sir *Douglas Haig's Despatches (December 1915 – April 1919)*, p. 293

47 1st Battalion Middlesex Regiment War Diary

48 33rd Division War Diary

49 *Soldiers Died In The Great War 1914 -19*, p. 103; Commonwealth War Graves Commission casualty details

50 Ibid. Private Garratt Army Service Record, National Archives, WO 363; 1891 Census

51 Ibid., p. 104; London Metropolitan Archives, London, England, Electoral Registers, 1832 -1965

52 Ibid.

53 Ibid.; British Army Medal Rolls Index, 1914 -1920; 1911 Census

CHAPTER SIXTEEN

26th October 1918 to 2nd January 1919

Taking Englefontaine
Bridging the River Sambre
Armistice
Malincourt Dump Explosion
Demobbed and Home

26 Oct. 'A' and 'C' Companies repaired the road between Croix and Englefontaine.

Half of 'B' Company assisted the 183rd Company Royal Engineers filling in and timbering tunnels under the road between Croix and Englefontaine.

The rest of the battalion worked on roads in Poix–du-Nord.

The battalion received Divisional Order 370 at 14.20 hours for the relief of the 33rd Division by the 38th Division.[1]

Private T.F.315514 George Thomas Chapman who was born and enlisted in Marylebone, Middlesex, died of his wounds. He is buried in the Awoingt British Cemetery –Nord.[2]

At 01.00 hours the 98th Infantry Brigade 4th Battalion King's (Liverpool) Regiment made an enveloping attack on Englefontaine from the south. At the same time the 19th Infantry Brigade 1st Queen's Royal West Surrey Regiment made a similar attack from the north. The 1st Middlesex were established by the brewery south of Englefontaine. The attack was successful and Englefontaine was captured. However the situation on the right was not secure so the 1st Middlesex had to occupy posts south-east of Englefontaine and link up with the 18th Division.[3]

The 100th Infantry Brigade was given the task of mopping up through Englefontaine. This operation was carried out by the 1/9th Highland Light Infantry.[4] They forced their way through Englefontaine and captured many

prisoners. In the 24 hours up to 17.00 hours 5 officers and 425 other ranks were captured.

The attack on Englefontaine caught the German 58th Division being relieved by the 14th Division. Prisoner statements and captured orders showed that the Germans had intended to hold Englefontaine at all costs and a counter-attack was likely to be made to recover the lost ground. Orders were issued for the 100th Infantry Brigade holding the new front line to be reinforced. One company of the 19th Infantry Brigade, one company of the 98th Infantry Brigade and the 98th Light Trench Mortar Battery were sent forward to support the 100th Infantry Brigade in the case of a hostile attack.

The right flank of the 100th Infantry Brigade was exposed because the 18th Division had failed to take Mont Carmel south-east of Englefontaine leaving a gap in their line. This enabled the Germans to launch a counter-attack against the 100th Infantry Brigade on the south-east outskirts of Englefontaine. The counter-attack was repulsed.

The remainder of the day was spent in consolidating the captured positions. The 33rd Division was relieved in the afternoon by the 38th Division.

In the operations between 22 and 26 October the 33rd Division had 15 officers killed, 51 wounded and 5 were missing. Other ranks had 210 killed, 1,109 wounded and 94 missing.[5]

27 Oct. The battalion repaired the road between Croix and Englefontaine, filled in or timbered tunnels under the road and repaired roads in Poix–du-Nord.

The German Government replied to President Wilson stating we now await 'proposals for an Armistice, which shall be a first step towards a just peace'.[6]

28 Oct. The battalion continued to fill in or timber tunnels under the main road.

2nd Lieut. Herbert Lawson Wilson, who had only returned from home leave on 26 October, became ill and the Medical Officer sent him down the line to the hospital.[7]

Private 76024 James William Fenn, aged 35, died of tuberculosis of the lungs. He attested in Lowestoft and enlisted on 1 October 1916. He was an auctioneer's assistant by trade, 5′ 8¼″ tall and weighed 142 lbs. His medical examination on enlistment classified him as B II (two) and he was called up for service on 24 October 1916 and posted to Royal Fusiliers Labour Corp. He

underwent a further medical on 27 November and was assessed as being C II (two) category. On 12 December 1916 he transferred to 29th Middlesex and moved to the 18th Middlesex on 28 February 1917.

On 9 May 1917 he transferred to the Eastern Command Labour Centre, Labour Corps. On 29 October he overstayed his pass from tattoo until 5.20pm on 2 November. He was confined to barracks for 7 days and forfeited 5 days pay, water and rations. On 30 November 1917 he was placed in the Class W Reserve and returned to work in civilian life. His health had seriously deteriorated whilst he served in the Army. He found part-time work with Messrs Read, Stanford and Owles, a local firm of auctioneers. He was employed to work every other week but his health was such that his father, George Albert Fenn, and his wife, Gertrude Ellen Fenn, did the work for him most of the time.

On 13 August 1918 Private Fenn reported to the 325th Field Ambulance at Beccles and immediately transferred to the Norfolk War Hospital, Thorpe, Norfolk. He died there at 1pm on 28 October 1918.

He married Gertrude Fenn (nee Warren) on 18 August 1909 at the Parish Church Beccles. They had four children William Ernest dob 28 October 1909, James Bernard dob 12 July 1911, Lucy May dob 7 July 1913 and Ivy Gertrude dob 5 July 1915.They lived a 25 Ingate Street, Beccles. Mrs Fenn received her late husband's personal effects on 22 February 1921 which comprised of tobacco, cigarettes, correspondence, hair brush, comb, 1 religious book, shaving brush, tooth brush, 1 pair of braces, 1 safety razor, 1 pair scissors, pipe, pencil, 1 civilian suit, cardigan, shirt, 1 pair of pants, 1 pair of socks, 1 pair of boots, 1 civilian cap, collar and tie. She received a Separation Allowance of 31 shillings and was awarded a pension of 33 shillings and 9 pence per week for herself and 4 children with effect from 5 may 1919.

Private Fenn is buried in the Beccles Cemetery – Suffolk.[8]

29 Oct. 'C' Company worked on the approaches to the tank bridge over the River Selle.

Major-General Pinney inspected the battalion and 222nd Field Company Royal Engineers.

Lieut. G. Cotton became sick and complained of fever. He was put in an ambulance and taken to the 45 Casualty Clearing Station, a huge collection of tents where sick and wounded men were first sent before being taken either to hospital or the cemetery. Initially Lieut. Cotton was deposited on the ground

in a large tent among a considerable number of men, some groaning, others past that stage. During the night Lieut. Cotton's servant arrived at the clearing station to check on his officer. The servant had Cotton moved to the officers' tent where he was put in a bed next to 2nd Lieut. Herbert Lawson Wilson.[9]

30 Oct. Work continued on filling in or timbering tunnels under the road and on the approaches to the tank bridge over the River Selle.

Lieut. Benjamin Leslie Fish, aged 25, died of his wounds. He was the son of Frances Ellen and Barrow Fish of Risedale, Priory Road, Hornsey, London. He was a member of the 12th Battalion on attachment to the 18th Battalion. He is buried in the Awoingt British Cemetery.[10]

Turkey abandoned the Central Powers and withdrew from the War. The Armistice with Turkey was signed onboard H.M.S. Agamemnon at Mudros. As part of the Armistice the Allies were given possession of the forts in the Dardanelles and the Bosporus which in turn gave Allied shipping passage through the Bosporus to the Black Sea. In addition all Allied prisoners were immediately repatriated.[11]

31 Oct. Work continued on filling in or timbering tunnels under the road and on the approaches to the tank bridge.

Lieut. Cotton was taken to the No. 8 General Hospital at Rouen.[12]

Private G/89642 George Morgan was born on 22 January 1899 in Llandovery and lived at 2 Hall Street, Ammanford, Carmarthenshire. He attested on 12 April 1916 at Ammanford, was a collier's assistant by trade, single, 5′ 2″ tall and weighed 112 lbs. He was posted to the Royal Engineers as a Tunnelling Mate and joined the Royal Engineering Tunnelling Depot at Clipston, Northant on 24 April.

He went to France on 12 May 1916 and joined the British Expeditionary Force. On 26 May he transferred to the 17th Company of the Royal Engineers and then moved onto the General Base Depot on 1 July. On 19 July he was absent from roll call at 9pm until 9.10pm. He was awarded 2 days Field Punishment No. 2 and placed under open arrest. He returned to England on 9 August 1916.

Private Morgan was posted to 'M' Company Royal Engineers on 22 January 1917, he transferred to the 3rd Provisional Company R.E. on 28 June 1917. He transferred to the 5th Middlesex on 22 January 1918. He then transferred to the 18th Middlesex on 12 May 1918. He reported sick with influenza on 5 October, was admitted to the 3 Canadian Casualty Clearing Station on 6 October and

transferred to the 26 General Hospital Étaples on 10 October where he died of pneumonia on 31 October.

He was the son of Emily and Evan James Morgan of 1 North Bank, Llandilo, Carmarthenshire. Mrs Morgan was sent her late son's personal effects on 2 April 1919 comprising of 4 badges, 3 titles, crucifix, cigarette case, tobacco pouch, coin, bible, cards, razor, wallet, 1 parcel, coat muffler, birth certificate, photos and letters.

Private Morgan is buried in the Étaples Military Cemetery.[13]

During the latter stages of the Battle of the River Selle, Englefontaine was taken. The Allies moved the front line well to the north and east of the le Quesnoy – Valenciennes railway, from the outskirts of the fortified town of le Quesnoy, past Sepmeries and Artres to Famars.

20,000 Germans were taken prisoner. 475 guns were captured and tons of ammunition was left behind. The Germans were unable to replace these losses and their ability to carry on fighting was draining away.[14]

Forest

1 November 1918. The battalion repaired roads near Forest, Croix and Montay. Lt.-Col. A.A. Crookshank assumed command of the battalion.

Field Marshal Haig feared that if the Germans were allowed to make an orderly retreat to shorten their lines they may have been able to prolong the war over the winter. He determined to stop that happening and aimed to make a direct attack upon a centre vital to the German war effort to force an immediate conclusion of the war. He therefore decided to take Valenciennes and then to attack on a thirty mile front from the Sambre, north of Oisy, to Valenciennes.

At 05.15 hours the British Third Army, supported by the First Army Canadian Corps, attacked the six mile section of German front south of Valenciennes.[15]

2 Nov. Work continued on the roads around Forest, Croix and Montay.

2nd Lieut. Burgoyne reported for duty and was posted to 'A' Company.

2nd Lieut. Wilson, aged 25, died of pneumonia. He was the husband of Menzies Lawson Kirkwood Wilson of 15 Montpelier, Edinburgh. He is buried in the Awoingt British Cemetery.[16]

3 Nov. Work on the roads around Forest, Croix and Montay continued.

Divisional Order 371 was received at 10.00 hours for the battalion to move to Englefontaine.[17]

Battle of the Sambe

The British and Canadian troops crossed the Rhonelle River. British troops captured Maresches and Preseau. Canadian troops captured Valenciennes and made progress beyond the town. The Germans withdrew on the le Quesnoy – Valenciennes front.[18]

Englefontaine

4 Nov. The battalion moved to Englefontaine in conjunction with operations by 38th Welsh Division. 'A' and 'C' Companies filled in craters on Route D'Hecq through the Forêt de Mormal.

The First, Third and Fourth British Armies lined up along the thirty mile section of front from Valenciennes in the north to just north of Oisy on the Canal du Sambre in the south. At daybreak, following an immense artillery barrage, the assembled armies attacked. They advanced to a depth of five miles reaching the general line Fesmy – Landrecies – centre of Forêt de Mormal – Wargnies-le-Grand – five miles east of Valenciennes – Onnaing – Scheldt Canal opposite Thiers. During the day 19,000 prisoners and 450 guns were captured.[19]

The Allied Supreme War Council meeting at Versailles agreed the terms of the armistice to be offered to Germany. The Allied Governments informed President Wilson they were prepared to make peace with Germany on the terms laid down by him in his 8 January 1918 address to the Congress of the United States with two provisos. The first related to the freedom of the seas, where the Allied Governments demanded complete freedom on this subject at the Peace Conference. The second was that Germany would pay compensation for all damage done to the civilian population of the Allies and their property.[20]

5 Nov. 'B' Company cleared roads for the advanced guard of 33rd Division. 'A' and 'C' Companies filled in craters on Route D'Hecq and the crater near Croisil Inn on the Route de Landrecies in the Forêt de Mormal.

At 03.55 hours the 100th Infantry Brigade moved on La Tête Noire and Sarbaras (Le Sart Bara). The 98th and 19th Infantry Brigades followed in close support. At 04.19 hours the 98th Infantry Brigade moved to just east of Locquinol. At 08.00 hours the advanced battalions of the 98th Infantry Brigade moved through the position held by the 100th Infantry Brigade and secured a crossing of the Sambre River. By 10.30 hours the 98th Infantry Brigade were reported on the eastern edge of the Forêt de Mormal. At 11.45 hours the rest of 98th Infantry Brigade moved through the position of the 100th Infantry Brigade to a general line west of the Ribaumet to Sassegnies road. The 21st Division took over the portion of Berlaimont captured by the 100th Infantry Brigade.

At 14.00 hours the Germans held the eastern bank of the river and 33rd Division held the western bank. Orders were issued for the bridging of the river with an organised attack, assisted by the Royal Engineers and the use of local enterprise and materials. The first objective was to reach the railway line triangle and factory just east of the river. The second objective was to take Petit Maubeuge.

At 22.30 hours the 98th and 100th Infantry Brigades posted patrols over the river. At 23.25 hours orders were issued that in the event of the 98th Infantry Brigade and 100th Infantry Brigade securing bridges over the river the 19th Infantry Brigade were to be prepared to cross the river and advance eastwards. They were to act as the advanced guard of the 33rd Division with the ultimate objective of securing the Avesnes to Maubeuge road. This order was dependent upon the 98th and 100th Infantry Brigades securing bridges over the river.

At 23.56 hours three companies of the 1st Middlesex Battalion, the leading battalion of the 98th Infantry Brigade, crossed the river and established bridgeheads along the railway line.[21]

6 Nov. At 03.15 hours the footbridge over the River Sambre just south of Mecrimont Farm was completed. At 08.00 hours the rest of the 1st Middlesex Battalion crossed the river and were followed by support. By 08.35 hours two battalions of the Right Brigade had crossed over the river and were advancing on Leval. Six companies of the 100th Infantry Brigade crossed the river. 38 prisoners were captured. At 09.00 hours the Right Brigade was reported entering Leval. At 09.45 hours Petit Maubeuge was captured. At 11.50 hours the transport bridge on the eastern outskirts of Berlaimont was completed but the approaches were in a bad condition.

At 13.20 hours the C.R.E. issued orders for all bridges to be duplicated and

new footbridges to be constructed. 13.50 hours 19th Infantry Brigade advanced along the La Toque to Pot de Vin road. At 14.00 hours Royal Engineers improved the approaches to the Sassegnies Bridge.

At 21.07 hours orders were received from V Corps in respect of the advance to the Beaufort to Floursies Line. At 23.00 hours the 33rd Division issued orders for the attack the following day.[22]

Croisil Inn

The 18th Middlesex marched to the Croisil Inn and worked on the crater in the road just north-east of Croisil.

'A' Company moved to Berlaimont and worked on the approaches to the pontoon bridge on the River Sambre.

P.W. 251 Private Frederick Smith received the very sad news that his wife Sara Jane had died in the West Ham Union Infirmary. He was sent home on 14 days compassionate leave. His wife was 38 years old and had 6 surviving children, 3 daughters and three sons. Her youngest son John Frederick was only born on 1 October 1918. Private Smith attested on 28 February 1915 and was a road constructer/labourer by trade. He had a tattoo on his left forearm 'I.L.S.J. & C.', on his right forearm he had tattoos of a palm tree and a snake. He married Sarah Jane on 9 November 1902 at the Parish Church West Ham and they lived at 53 Blythe Road, Stratford.

Private Smith was posted to the 18th Middlesex on the 28 February 1915 and travelled with the battalion to France on 12 November 1915. He served with the battalion throughout its stay in France and transferred to the Army Reserve on 8 February 1919. After the war he moved to 65 Blythe Road and was diagnosed with a 20% disability due to rheumatism and bronchitis. He was awarded a pension of 5 shillings and sixpence per week for 52 weeks from 9 February 1919.[23]

Private P.W. 88 John Adams was born in Kilpatrick and lived at the Sailors Home, Leith. He attested in Leith on 19 February 1915 and was posted to the 18th Middlesex on 21 February. He was 36 years and 30 days old, a general labourer, single, 5´ 10″ tall and weighed 149 lbs. He had small scar in the middle of his back and mole on his right shoulder. He listed his Uncle Alexander Harvey as his next of kin. His parents were dead and he did not have any brothers or sisters.

He embarked at Southampton on 12 November 1915 and sailed for France with

the 18th Middlesex. On 21 October 1916 he was sentenced to 21 days Field Punishment No. 1. He was granted leave to the United Kingdom from 2 to 12 June 1917 and he had two weeks leave in Calais between the 1 and 15 February 1918.

On 31 October 1918 he was admitted to the 101st Field Ambulance and moved on the same day to 59 Casualty Clearing Station. He was then moved to the 1 Australian General Hospital at Rouen where he died from bronco-pneumonia on 6 November. His aunty Margaret Michie of 14 Maclean Street, Patrick, Glasgow received his personal effects of knife, watch and strap in case, disc, pencil, purse, tobacco pouch, letters, photos and cards.

Private Adams is buried in the St. Sever Cemetery Extension, Rouen.[24]

7 Nov. 06.30 hours the 3rd Hussars joined the 33rd Division for the attack on the Beaufort to Floursies Line.

At 07.13 hours the 19th Infantry Brigade attacked and met little opposition. The Cyclists attached to the 19th Infantry Brigade captured Pot de Vin. At 09.07 hours one battery of field guns crossed the river and went in support of the 19th Infantry Brigade to the area near Pot de Vin. At 08.30 hours the 19th Infantry Brigade reached the outskirts of Écuélin.

At 11.30 hours the 98th Infantry Brigade were ordered to advance on the Avesnes to Maubeuge road. The 100th Infantry Brigade was ordered to follow and, when the road was taken, to pass through the 98th Infantry Brigade position and capture the high ground south of Romeries. The 98th Infantry Brigade was then to move up and capture Floursies.

At 15.30 hours the N.C.O. in command of Divisional Observers reported he was in Écuélin and the village had been captured. Limont-Fontaine was still in enemy hands.[25]

The Guards took Bavay.[26]

Berlaimont

The 18th Middlesex marched to Berlaimont.

'C' Company stayed behind to work on the crater in Croisil. 'A' and 'B' Companies worked on the approaches to the pontoon bridge on the River Sambre.

2nd Lieut. Ernest Joseph Young, aged 25, died of influenza. He was the son of Jane and Edward Young of Willesden Green, London. He is buried in the Rocquigny-Equancourt Road British Cemetery, Manancourt – Somme.[27]

Croisil Inn

8 Nov. The battalion moved from Berlaimont to Croisil Inn to be closer to their work on the approaches to the bridge over River Sambre and on the crater.

Avesnes, Hautmont and Condé were captured. The outskirts of Maubeuge were reached and the Scheldt crossed on a considerable front south of Antoing. The Germans abandoned the bridgehead at Tournai.[28]

The German delegation lead by the Centre Party leader Matthias Erzberger, a member of Prince Max's Government, arrived at the railway carriage in the Forest of Compiegne. Here they met Marshal Foch representing the armies of the Allies and Admiral Sir R. Wemyss representing the navies.

Foch presented the German delegation with the terms of the armistice agreed by the Supreme War Council and gave them seventy-two hours to sign them. The terms were severely punitive and amounted to a surrender that would leave Germany defenceless and subject to whatever peace terms the Allied Governments wished to impose on her. The German delegation was granted permission to get instructions from their Government.[29]

9 Nov. Work continued on the approaches to the Sambre Bridge and on the crater.

The Germans were finally routed and a general retreat opposite the whole British front had begun. The Guards Division entered Maubeuge. The Canadians attacked Mons. Peruwelz, Antoing and Tournai were captured.[30]

Kaiser Wilhelm II of Germany abdicated and fled to Holland. A new Socialist Government took over the running of the newly created German Republic.[31]

Berlaimont

10 Nov. Work continued on the approaches to the Sambre Bridge and on the crater.

The battalion moved to Berlaimont.

Major-General Pinney went on leave to England.

11 Nov. Overnight negotiations with the German delegation on the terms of surrender took place on Foch's train in the Forest of Compiegne. At the

conclusion of those talks French Prime Minister Clemenceau sent a message to British Prime Minister Lloyd George informing him the Germans signed the armistice at five o'clock.[32]

The battalion received news of the signing of the armistice with Germany at 09.00 hours.

At 09.30 hours the General Army Headquarters issued the following order:

'Hostilities will cease at 11am on November 11th. Troops will stand fast on the line reached at that hour, which will be reported by wire to G.H.Q. Defensive precautions will be maintained. There will be no intercourse of any description with the enemy until receipt of instructions from G.H.Q. Further instructions will follow'. [33]

So on the 11th hour of the 11th day of the 11th month the so-called Great War of attrition finally ended in a decisive and absolute Allied victory.

At 11.00 hours Field Marshal Haig held a meeting at Cambrai with the five Army Commanders and General Kavanagh, Commanding Officer of the Cavalry Corps. Haig pointed out the importance of looking after the troops now that the war had ended. He informed the Commanding Officers it was as much the duty of all officers to keep their men amused as to train them for war.[34]

12 Nov. Work continued on the approaches to the Sambre Bridge and on the crater.

King George V sent Field Marshal Haig the following telegram:-

> 'I wish to express to you personally my grateful thanks. It is through your military knowledge and ability, combined with patient resolve, that you have led the British Armies to Victory'.

Field Marshal Haig replied:-

> 'I beg to offer my respectful and very grateful thanks for your Majesty's most kind and very generous message. No Commander has ever been so wholeheartedly supported by his troops as I have been. And to the many gallant and resolute officers, N.C.O.s and men of Your Majesty's Forces serving under my orders in France, I owe all. But I beg leave to say that the confidence which Your Majesty has been so graciously pleased to place in me during so many trying years of war did much to

strengthen and inspire me to do my duty so that I have been able to endure unto this victorious end'.[35]

13 Nov. Work continued on the Sambre Bridge and on the crater.

14 Nov. The battalion received Divisional Order 373 at 15.40 hours for the move of the 33rd Division to Montigny.

15 Nov. The battalion prepared to move camp.

Locquignol

16 Nov. The battalion route marched to Locquignol.

Forest

17 Nov. The battalion route marched to Forest.

Malincourt

18 Nov. The battalion route marched to Malincourt.

Private S.R.5153 Charles Chuck born in Holloway and enlisted in Mill Hill, Middlesex, died. He travelled to France on 9 October 1914 and joined the 4th Battalion Middlesex Regiment in the field.

The 4th Middlesex, stationed at Devonport, received their mobilisation orders at 5.25pm on the 4 August 1914 5 hours and 35 minutes before the British declaration of war against Germany. They embarked for France from Southampton aboard S.S. Mombasa on 13 August and arrived at Boulogne at midday on 14 August. Private Chuck's arrival in France saw him immediately engaged with the British Expeditionary Force in the Battle of La Bassée.

He was the son of Mr C. Chuck who lived at 55 Chalfont Road, Edmonton, London. He is buried in the Étaples Military Cemetery.[36]

19 to 27 Nov. The battalion cleaned billets and started training.

On the 27 November an explosion occurred at the salvage dump in Malincourt at 14.45 hours killing three members and wounding one member of the 33rd Battalion Machine Gun Corps. The explosion also killed three members and wounded one member of the 18th Battalion Middlesex Regiment.

A Court of Inquiry was held to investigate the explosion. The Court was told by Bombardier 39525 Alfred Charles Balm of Royal Field Artillery No. 2 Section 33rd Divisional Ammunition Column that he had been detailed 'to examine and make safe any shells on the dump and to mark dangerous any shells when this could not be done. At 13.00 hours I left the dump having made safe all the shells except such as were marked dangerous. The latter were placed fifty yards away from the main dump. I noticed during the morning about twenty mines which I believe to be anti-tank. After the explosion had occurred I returned to the dump and found that it was these mines which had exploded. No shells were affected'.[37] Bombardier Balm died on 15 February 1919 aged 33. He was the husband of Mrs Rose Balm of 70 Surrey Road, Peckham Rye. By 1911 they had 2 children Lillian Rosetta born in 1909 and Elsie born in 1910. He his buried in the Nunshead 'All Saints' Cemetery, London.[38]

2nd Lieut. Reginald Arthur Morrison Hughman of the 18th Battalion Middlesex Regiment told the Inquiry that he 'was the officer in charge of the dump at Malincourt. At 14.45 hours I heard the sound of an explosion and on going down to the dump found that an explosion had taken place. No. 201244 Pte. Smith J. of 18th Battalion Middlesex Regiment who was acting as policeman on the dump had been killed. This man had been posted at 13.00 hours and his instructions were to keep off the dump men without authorisation'. At the same time No. 12736 Pte. E.D. Hills and No. 3344 Pte. R.J. Powis were killed and No. 53254 Pte G.A. Vintin was wounded.

The Inquiry was told that the body of No. 159610 Pte. C. Gascoyne 33rd Battalion M.G.C. was found 70 yards from the dump, No. 172623 Pte. C.L. Unsworth 33rd Battalion M.G.C. had died on admission to 101st Field Ambulance and the remains of No. 39672 Pte. W. Burgess 33rd Battalion Machine Gun Corps were identified outside the aid post.

Captain H.V. Clarke of the 33rd Battalion Machine Gun Corps told the Inquiry that 'whilst acting Adjutant he issued an order on the authority of the O.C. 33rd Battalion M.G.C. that all leather equipment had to be replaced by webbing equipment and that this could be done from local dumps. The order was issued in accordance with V Corps letter No V.Q. 488 of 23rd November 1918'.

Captain G. Harrison M.C. Adjutant 33rd Battalion M.G.C. told the Inquiry

that he went to the dump immediately after hearing the explosion and took a statement from No. 137578 L/Cpl. P. Woodward who had been wounded in the incident. L/Cpl. Woodward told Captain Harrison 'On the 27th November 1918 about 2.45 in the afternoon I was on the dump at Malincourt salvaging webbing equipment. There were about 4 Machine Gunners and 3 Pioneers on the dump at the time. A Chinese Labour man came to the dump wheeling a barrow full of bricks. When he arrived at the shell dump he left his barrow and picked up one of the shells. I then heard a hissing sound come from the shell. The Chinaman then threw the shell down and it immediately exploded. I was blown up into the air and fell on some tins. About 5 explosions succeeded the first explosion. Several men were killed and some wounded. A soon as I recovered myself I went to the spot where the explosion occurred. I saw 2 men lying dead and others wounded. I then noticed that I was wounded in the hand myself. I immediately went for assistance'.

The Inquiry faced a difficulty because there was no dead or injured Chinaman at the scene of the explosions. No. 443322 Company Sergeant Major J. Walker 25th Company Chinese Labour Corps told the Inquiry that '70 Chinese were working on the dump at Malincourt. At 18.00 hours of the same afternoon I called the roll of the Company and there were no absentees'.

No. 179187 Corporal G. Crowder 23rd Company Chinese Labour Corps told the Inquiry 'I was in charge of a party of Chinese working in the vicinity of the dump. About 14.40 hours I marched the party back to camp. Five minutes later the explosion occurred. None of the Chinese were left near the camp'.

The Court of Inquiry found that the deaths of Private Burgess, Private Gascoyne, Private Unsworth and the wounding of Lance Corporal Woodward 'were occasioned whilst on duty by the explosion which took place at Malincourt dump on 27th November 1918 and that the cause of the explosion cannot be definitely established'.[39]

The following three soldiers are buried side by side in the Honnechy British Cemetery – Nord.

Private G/12736 Ernest Gilbert Dunstann Hills was born on 28 November 1892 in Chile, South America. Private Hills was an engineer by trade, single, 5′ 5½″ tall and attested at the Liverpool Walker Art Gallery on 1 March 1916.

He joined the Middlesex Regiment on 3 March at Mill Hill and was posted to the 5th Middlesex on 6 March. He transferred to the 16th Middlesex on 15 June 1916 and joined them in the field at Acheux Wood on 27 June where preparations for the coming Battle of the Somme were underway. The day after arriving in

France Private Hills was admitted to hospital suffering from P.U.O. No sooner was he back in action when on 28 July he experienced a sudden strain in the trenches causing an inguinal hernia and was hospitalised again. He rejoined his battalion on 2 August but recurring trouble with his hernia saw him back in hospital on 7 September and back in England on 16 September.

On 17 September Hills was admitted to 3 Southern General Hospital, Oxford which was a Territorial Forces hospital. He underwent surgery for his hernia which his doctor said achieved a good result. He transferred to the Milton Hill Section Hospital in Oxfordshire on 11 October and was discharged on 15 January 1917. Hills returned to France on 20 May 1917 and rejoined the 16th Middlesex in the field on 8 June. He spent most of July, August and September in various hospitals suffering from pyrexia and myalgia. He rejoined the 16th Middlesex on 18 October and managed to stay out of hospital for the rest of year.

On 10 January 1918 Hills suffered another bout of P.U.O. and was again admitted to hospital. He was discharged from hospital and transferred to the 18th Middlesex on 8 February 1918. On 26 March he suffered another bout of myalgia which was followed by a bout of measles and readmission to hospital on 28 May 1918. He rejoined the 18th Middlesex on 15 July. He was granted two weeks home leave from 7 to 21 October and he rejoined his battalion on 22 October for the final push. He was the son of Edward Dunstann Hills. His brother Private G.12737 L.W. Hills survived the war and by 23 March 1919 was stationed at the Middlesex Regiment Depot at Mill Hill. Private Ernest Hills was killed in the dump accident a day before his 26th Birthday.[40]

Private G/3344 Robert James Powis, born in Nine Elms, Battersea in July 1888 died of his wounds. He lived in Battersea and attested in Clifton Street, Middlesex on 2 September 1914. He joined up for three years with the proviso that if the war was over in less than three years he would be discharged at convenient speed. He was single and a carpenter by trade. He had a flower tattoo on his left forearm and a scroll of flowers tattoo on his right forearm.

Private Powis was posted to the 12th Middlesex on 25 September 1914. The 12th Middlesex embarked for France from Southampton on 25 July 1915 and joined the 18th Division, Third Army and proceeded to assemble at Fesselles. On 31 March 1916 Powis qualified as a machine gunner. He suffered gunshot wounds to his right shoulder and right hand on 13 April 1916. He passed through the 55th Field Ambulance, the 21 Casualty Clearing Station and was taken by the 19 Ambulance train to the 10 General Hospital at Rouen on 17 April. He was taken back to England on H.M.H.S. Asturias on 2 May.

Powis transferred to the 14th Middlesex on 6 July 1916 whilst stationed in England. He moved to the Middlesex Base Depot and to the 41st Infantry Base Depot before being posted to the 11th Middlesex on 4 October 1916 and travelling back to France to join the British Expeditionary Force. The 11th Middlesex, 11th Division were engaged in the Battle of the Transloy Ridge. He was made unpaid Lance Corporal on 9 March 1917. On 9 April he suffered a shrapnel wound to the back and was taken back to England on 16 April aboard H.M.H.S. Brighton. He was admitted to 4 Northern General Hospital at Lincoln on 19 April and discharged on 12 May. He was then given 9 days home leave. Powis rejoined the 16th Middlesex on the 8 June 1917 and returned to the British Expeditionary Force joining them in the field on 29 June. He suffered a bout of P.U.O. and was admitted to hospital on 11 July. He rejoined his battalion 23 July. On the 12 August he suffered a mild gunshot wound to his eye. He passed through the 89th Field Ambulance and the 61 Casualty Clearing Station and was admitted to the 83 General Hospital, Étaples on 17 August. He was discharged and posted to the 12th Middlesex on 13 September and joined them in the field on 14 September in Flanders.

Powis was made Acting Sergeant on 12 February 1918, he was attached to 18th Division Headquarters on 13 April and posted to the 18th Middlesex on 6 June. He then went on attachment to the 10th Battalion Essex Regiment and was wounded whilst on firing range duty on 30 July. He was hit by a ricochet bullet which caused a slight abrasion to his left shoulder. He returned to duty on 3 August. The Official Report into the accident found that the shooting was accidental and no one was to blame. Powis rejoined the 18th Middlesex on 14 August and reverted to the rank of Private.

He was the son of Sarah and William James Powis. His father's death was registered in the 1st quarter of 1912. His mother lived at 18 Ruskin Street, Battersea. On 25 April 1919, as his next of kin, Mrs Powis received the personal effects of her late son which comprised of a pipe, metal ring, whistle, note book, cigarette case, razor in case, photos, belt and letters. She was sent his identity disc on 5 March 1923. She received a Separation Allowance of 9 shillings and 3 pence.

Robert James Powis had 2 brothers who also served in the war. Private 234161 Sydney John Powis served with the 2/2nd Battalion London Regiment. He lived at 10 Chalmers Street, Wandsworth Road, Clapham. He survived the war being discharged from service on 4 December 1917 due to the gunshot wounds he received to his left thigh and right hand on 16 June 1917.

Private 3957 John Edward Powis of 1/23rd Battalion London Regiment was

killed in action on 26 October 1915 aged 20. His name is on the Loos Memorial.[41]

Private T.F.201244 James Smith lived in Hornsey Vale and enlisted in Hornsey, Middlesex, died of wounds.[42]

Lieut. R.A.M. Hughman was born on 10 December 1881 in Camberwell, Surrey. He went to Merchant Taylor School. He was married and was a submarine cable operator. His father was a Captain in the Territorials (Reserve) and lived at 120 Sinclair Road, West Kensington, London, W.14.

Reginald Hughman served with the Legion of Frontiersmen from 1912 and reached the rank of Lieutenant and was the organising officer for Cape Verde Islands until the outbreak of war. He applied for a commission in the British Army on 4 April 1917.

As an N.C.O. he attended an officer training course with the Signal Service but was deemed unsuitable for a commission with them because he failed in the technical knowledge part of the course at the training centre at Woburn, Bedfordshire. He was however considered suitable to be an officer in another branch of the service.[43]

He was appointed 2nd Lieutenant with seniority from 30 January 1918.[44] He was promoted to Temporary Lieutenant 30 July 1919 with precedence next below A.H. Twyman.[45] Temporary Lieutenant Hughman relinquished his commission on completion of service on 13 June 1920 and retained the rank of Lieutenant.[46]

28 Nov – 30 Nov. Training and cleaning up the billets.

Malincourt

1 December 1918. A parade service was held in the battalion theatre at 11am.

2 Dec. The whole battalion was employed on salvaging work.

3 Dec. The battalion continued salvaging and did some training.

4 Dec. At 10.15am the battalion paraded and marched to Iris Farm to cheer His Majesty King George V as he passed. King George was a regular visitor to the Western Front during World War One.

2nd Lieut. G.S. Ridout reported for duty.

5 Dec. Salvaging continued.

2nd Lieut. G.S. Ridout did not last long. He returned to base.

8 Dec. At 11.15am the battalion paraded for divine service.

9 Dec. The battalion finally finished clearing salvage.

10 Dec. The battalion rested and prepared for the move the following day.

Masnières

11 Dec. At 8am the battalion marched from Malincourt to Masnières under the orders of the 19th Infantry Brigade. It rained during the whole march and the men got absolutely drenched but no one fell out.

Hermies

12 Dec. The battalion marched from Masnières to Hermies. The head of the column was supposed to pass the brigade starting point at 09.33 hours but were unable to do so until 09.48 hours. No one fell out.

Lt.-Col. Crookshank rejoined from leave and took over command of the battalion from Major Hinman.

2nd Lieut. Scammel reported sick and went to hospital.

Sergeant P.W.1039 John Bean went on leave to Boulogne on 7 December when he was taken ill. He returned to England and was admitted to 2 Western General Hospital Manchester on 10 December 1918. He died of influenza during the night on 12 December aged 43. He was the husband of Sarah Bean (nee Wardle) of 6 Hanover Street, North Audenshaw, Manchester. He had enlisting on 3 April 1915 and he was a Collier by trade. He is buried in the Audenshaw Cemetery – Lancashire.[47]

Favreuil

13 Dec. The battalion marched from Hermies to Favreuil. The head of the

column passed the brigade starting point at 09.24 hours, stopped for dinner at 11.50 hours and set off again at 13.00 hours. The battalion arrived at Favreuil at 14.45 hours and was billeted. Again no one fell out.

Albert

14 Dec. The battalion marched to a camp west of Albert. The head of the column passed the brigade starting point at 08.37 hours, stopped for dinner at 11.50 hours and set off again at 13.00 hours. Again, no one fell out.

Bussy-lès-Daours

15 Dec. The march continued to Bussy-lès-Daours. The battalion lead the brigade passing the starting point at 09.00 hours. One man fell out on the march.

Argœuves

16 Dec. The battalion marched to Argœuves and St. Sauveur leaving at 09.05 hours. 'B' 'C' and 'H.Q.' Companies stopped at Argœuves. 'A' Company and the transport stopped at St. Sauveur.

Fricamps

17 Dec. 'A' and 'H.Q.' Companies marched to billets in Fricamps. 'B' and 'C' Companies marched to billets in Bussy-lès-Poix.

In six days solid marching the battalion covered nearly ninety miles, an average of sixteen miles a day. They certainly saw a great deal of the French countryside.

18 Dec. The battalion rested and engaged in the usual activity when arriving at a new set of billets of cleaning and improving the accommodation and equipment.

19 Dec. Work continued improving the billets.

20 Dec. Work continued on billets and started training again.
2nd Lieut. Yoxall reported sick and was admitted to hospital.

21 Dec. A voluntary church service was held in Fricamps at 09.00 hours.
There was a voluntary service in Bussy-lès-Poix at 11.00 hours.

22 Dec. Billet improvements and training continued. Major-General Pinney visited battalion H.Q.

23 Dec. Billet improvements and training continued.

24 Dec. Training and billet improvements continued.

25 Dec. A church service was held for the battalion at Fricamps at 09.00 hours. The battalion spent the rest of the day enjoying the Christmas celebrations. At last, it was Christmas and this time the bloody war was finally over.

26 to the 29 Dec. The battalion continued to train and improve the billets. On 29 December Mrs Sarah Bean received a letter from the War Office. It said, 'In order that I may be enabled to dispose of the plaque and scroll in commemoration of the soldier's name overleaf in accordance with the wishes of His Majesty the King, I have to request that the requisite information regarding the soldier's relatives now living may be furnished on the form overleaf in strict accordance with the instructions printed thereon.

The declaration thereon should be signed in your own handwriting and the form should be returned to me when certified by a minister or magistrate'.

Sarah Bean listed herself, three non-dependent children, and four dependent children including Dorothy aged 14, Eva aged 13, Henry aged 8 and Howard aged 3. She also listed seven other relatives of her late husband.[48]

30 Dec. A priority wire was received ordering the battalion to Abancourt on 31st. This destination was later changed to Haudicourt.

Private Thomas McBride got the news that he was to be demobilised from the 19th Middlesex.

Major-General Pinney inspected the 18th Middlesex at 11.30 hours near Bussy-lès-Poix.

1 January 1919. McBride left the Die Hards behind him. The War Office Dispersal Unit in Oswestry issued him with his 'PROTECTION CERTIFICATE AND CERTIFICATE OF IDENTITY (SOLDIER NOT REMAINING WITH THE COLOURS).

He was given an advance of £2 and told he had twenty-eight days furlough (leave of absence) during which he could wear his uniform. After the twenty-eight days were up he would only be allowed to wear his uniform on occasions authorised by Army Orders.

He was informed that his pay and discharge papers would be sent to his home address at 13 Jermyn Street, Ashton-under-Lyne. He was also told that he could be asked to rejoin the army in case of emergency.[47]

2 Jan. Private Thomas McBride finally made it home to Ashton and to his wife Martha Jane and baby Martha who was then six years old. For him the war was finally over. He was back in the bosom of his family. However there were ten million service men and six million civilians who had died in this World War, from both sides of the conflict, who did not return to their families. And there were millions more who were wounded and had their lives shattered by disability and trauma.

The devastation caused by this conflict was beyond belief and beyond comprehension from start to finish. Collective insanity prevailed allowing the war to start in the first place, it continued during the prosecution of the war with industrial scale slaughter as the Allied leaders continuously threw their best soldiers at the enemy's most strongly defended positions. When the deadlock was finally broken in the summer of 1918 the insanity delayed the advent of peace. When peace finally came the severely punitive terms of the armistice and subsequent conditions imposed on Germany at the Versailles Peace Conference insanely put in place the conditions which led directly to another bloody conflict on a world wide scale – World War Two.

One hundred years on and the study and interest in WWI has not diminished. The tragedy of those who lost their lives and the imperative of keeping the promise made to honour and remember them still passionately remains.

Middlesex Regiment Public Works Battalion Cap Badge

For The Fallen

'They shall grow not old, as we that are left grow old; age shall not weary them, nor the years condemn. At the going down of the sun, and in the morning, we will remember them'.[50]

'They gave their today for our tomorrow. We will remember them'.

1 33rd Division War Diary
2 *Soldiers Died In The Great War 1914 -19*, p. 102; Commonwealth War Graves Commission casualty details
3 1st Battalion Middlesex Regiment War Diary
4 1/9th Battalion Highland Light Infantry (Glasgow Highlanders) War Diary, National Archives, WO 95/2431, Image Ref. 526
5 33rd Division War Diary
6 Lloyd George, *War Memoirs, Vol. 2*, p.1967
7 Private Papers of Lieutenant G. Cotton, p. 115
8 Commonwealth War Graves Commission casualty details; Private Fenn Army Service Record, National Archives, WO 363
9 Private Papers Lieutenant G. Cotton, p. 116
10 Commonwealth War Graves Commission casualty details
11 *The Times Diary & Index of The War 1914 – 1918*, p. 165
12 Private Papers of Lieutenant G. Cotton p. 116
13 *Soldiers Died In The Great War 1914 -19*, p. 104; Commonwealth War Graves

Commission casualty details; Private Morgan Army Service Record, National Archives, WO 363

14 Boraston (Editor), Sir *Douglas Haig's Despatches (December 1915 – April 1919),* p. 293

15 Ibid., p.p. 293-294

16 Commonwealth War Graves Commission casualty details

17 33rd Division War Diary

18 Boraston (Editor), Sir *Douglas Haig's Despatches (December 1915 – April 1919),* p. 294

19 Ibid., p. 294 & p. 296

20 Lloyd George, *War Memoirs, Vol. 2*, p.p.1979 -1980

21 33rd Division War Diary

22 Ibid.

23 Private Smith Army Service Record, National Archives, WO 363

24 *Soldiers Died In The Great War 1914 -19*, p. 102; Commonwealth War Graves Commission casualty details; Private Adams Army Service Records, National Archives, WO 363

25 33rd Division War Diary

26 Boraston (Editor), Sir *Douglas Haig's Despatches (December 1915 – April 1919),* p. 297

27 Commonwealth War Graves Commission casualty details

28 Boraston (Editor), Sir *Douglas Haig's Despatches (December 1915 – April 1919),* p. 297

29 Lloyd George, *War Memoirs, Vol. 2*, p.p.1980 -1981

30 Boraston (Editor), Sir *Douglas Haig's Despatches (December 1915 – April 1919),* p. 297

31 Lloyd George, *War Memoirs, Vol. 2*, p. 1981

32 Ibid., p. 1985

33 Wyrall, *The Die-Hards in the Great War, Vol. 2*, p. 291

34 Blake(Editor), *The Private Papers of Douglas Haig 1914 -1919*, p. 340

35 Ibid., p.p. 343-344

36 *Soldiers Died In The Great War 1914 -19*, p. 102; Commonwealth War Graves Commission casualty details; Wyrall, *The Die-Hards in the Great War, Vol.1*, p.p. 3-4 & p. 73; British Army Medal Rolls Index Cards, 1914-1920

37 Private W. Burgess, Army Service Record, National Archives, WO 363

38 1911 Census; Commonwealth War Graves Commission Casualty details

39 Private W. Burgess, Army Service Record

40 *Soldiers Died In The Great War 1914 -19*, p. 103; Commonwealth War Graves Commission casualty details; Private Hills Army Service Record, National Archives, WO 363; Wyrall, *The Die-Hards in the Great War, Vol. 2,* p. 237

41 *Soldiers Died In The Great War 1914 -19*, p. 104; Commonwealth War Graves Commission casualty details; Private R. Powis Army Service Record, National Archives, WO 363; Private S. Powis British Army Pension Records, National Archives, WO 364; Wyrall, *The Die-Hards in the Great War, Vol.1,* p. 207; & *Vol. 2,* p. 314

42 Ibid.

43 Lieut. R.A.M. Hughman Service Record, National Archives, WO 339/101597

44 Third Supplement to the London Gazette 21st June 1918, Published 24th June 1918,

Gazette Issue 30762, p. 7443

45 Fourth Supplement to the London Gazette 30th September 1919, Published 2nd October 1919, Gazette Issue 31578, p. 12122

46 Third Supplement to the London Gazette 13th July 1920, Published 15th July 1920, Gazette Issue 31981, p. 7568

47 Death Certificate, General Register Office, Application Number COL258777; British Army Service Record, National Archives, WO 363; Commonwealth War Graves Commission casualty records

48 Sergeant John Bean Army Service Record, National Archives, WO 95/363

49 Private Thomas McBride Army Service Record

50 Lawrence Binyon, *For the fallen*, 1914.

POST SCRIPT

The Supplement to the London Gazette 17 January 1919 carried an extensive list of awards of the Meritorious Service Medal for service in World War One. Sergeant P.W.489 George Clark, Sergeant P.W.1209 John Mee, Sergeant P.W.56 John Wilkinson and Private 33889 Leonard Francis Hynes were four members of the 18th Battalion Middlesex Regiment to receive the award.[1]

John Mee lived at 1 Wellington Street, Hooley Hill, Audenshaw. He married Susannah Robinson on 14 May 1902 at St. Mark's Dukinfield, Cheshire. They had six children Sarah Elizabeth dob 26 June 1904, Alice dob 27 March 1907, Susannah dob 18 June 1909, John James dob 12 October 1911, Mark dob 23 November 1913 and Henry dob 25 November 1918. Mee had a spell of home leave from 9 March 1918 to 23 March 1918.

He was 5´ 9½″ tall and weighed 151 lbs. Aged 32 he attested at the Ashton-under-Lyne Army Recruiting office in Warrington Street on 8 April 1915. He was posted to the 18th Battalion Middlesex Regiment. Whilst stationed at Forrest Town he overstayed his pass from 12 midnight on 18 July 1915 until reporting himself at 2pm on 19 July. Sergeant Scott reported the incident and Mee was admonished by Captain Steele. 2nd Lieutenant E.V. Flockhart, acting on behalf of the Battalion Captain and Adjutant, imposed a forfeit of a day's pay on Mee.

John Mee was made Corporal on 14 August 1915 and made Sergeant on 15 November 1915. On 26 August 1916 he was promoted to Company Sergeant Major and transferred to 'C' Company. On 5 August 1917 he was arrested for being drunk and held in confinement for 6 days and was tried and found guilty by a Field General Court Martial for 'when on active service drunkenness'. His punishment could have been execution however the Court reduced his rank to Sergeant instead. This punishment was confirmed by the Commanding Officer of the 98th Infantry Brigade, Brigadier-General J.D. Heriot-Haitland, C.M.G., Rifle Brigade.

On 31 May 1918 Mee suffered a shell wound to his right forearm but he returned to duty on 2 June 1918. On 14 December 1918, in preparation for his

return to civilian life, Mee was given 28 days furlough and an advance of £2. He also signed the 'Statement of Disability' confirming he 'did not claim to be suffering from a disability due to (his) military service'. By this time he and his family had moved to 16 Dale Street off Guide Lane, Audenshaw. On 11 January 1919 he transferred to Class "Z" of the Army Reserve and as a coal miner returned to work in the pit. Mee was kept on the Army Reserve list until he was finally demobilised and discharged on 31 March 1920.[2]

Sergeant Clark attested at Cockspur Street, London on 9 March 1915 aged 25 years. He was born in the Parish of St. George in the East, was single and lived at 87 Boylin Road (Boleyn Road), Dalston. He was a labourer by trade, 5′ 8″ tall and weighed 140 lbs. His parents were Mary Ann and Frederick Clark of 19 Brunswick Street, Hackney Road, Shoreditch. He listed his father as his next of kin. He went to France on 12 November 1915 with the battalion. He rose through the ranks and was made Company Quartermaster Sergeant on 14 February 1919. He transferred to the Class 'Z' Reserve on 26 May 1919 and was demobilised on 31 March 1920. On leaving the Army he applied for a disability pension due to a broken ankle suffered during the war. His claim was dismissed on the grounds that the injury had not caused any disability.[3]

The 18th Battalion Middlesex Regiment remained in France until 31 October 1919 when the battalion Colours were consecrated by Rev. Thursby Pelham and then presented by Colonel D'Avery M. Clarke M.B.E. The battalion then marched past in the park at Cambrai.

The last duty undertaken by the battalion was a football match against a French Army team which the battalion won.

On 2 Nov 1919 Lt.-Col. C.P. Hinman, Commanding Office 18th Middlesex Regiment (1st Public Works Battalion) Pioneers signed off the battalion war diary for the last time.

7 February 1919 Sergeant L/16418 Frederick Thomas Sillitoe, dob 12 January 1898, aged 21, died of his wounds. He was the son of Elizabeth May and Frederick James Sillitoe of 44 Shaftesbury Street, New North Road, Hoxton, London. He is buried in the Abney Park Cemetery – London.[4]

13 February 1919 Private G/57977 Thomas Edward Whitford Pewtress, aged 19, from Leyton, Essex, died of his wounds. He was son of Elizabeth Kate Pewtress (nee Whitford) and Thomas Edward Edgington Pewtress of 27

Sedgemoor Place, Camberwell, London. His father was an insurance clerk. His mother had died on 3 September 1918 from a tubercular ulcer of the throat and pulmonary tuberculosis.

Private Pewtress was born in Leyton, Essex. He was a cask cutter before joining the army. He enlisted in Camberwell on 22 January 1917 at the age of 17 years and 8 months. He was 5′ 5″ tall and weighed 119 pounds. After six months training he was posted to 102nd Training Reserve Battalion on 31 July 1917. On 20 November 1917 he transferred to 250th Infantry Brigade and on 5 April 1918 he was transferred to the 18th Battalion Middlesex Regiment.

On 7 June 1918 he contracted influenza and spent six weeks away from the front sick. He rejoined the battalion on 21 July 1918. He suffered a gunshot wound in his left thigh on 25 October whilst repairing roads close to the front line south of Englefontaine and was transported home. He was admitted to the London General Hospital in Camberwell on 11 January 1919. He died on 13 February from septicaemia, septic bronchial pneumonia and ulcerative endocarditis. He is buried in the Camberwell (Forest Hill Road) Cemetery – London.[5]

13 February 1919 Private 570374 (238134 & 514970) Percy Rendle, who transferred to the 93rd Prisoners of War Company, Labour Corps, died of his wounds. He is buried in the Les Baraques Military Cemetery, Sangatte – Pas de Calais.[6]

17 August 1919 Private P.W. 5 Frederick George Hathaway, aged 46, died of his wounds. He enlisted on 9 February 1915 and travelled to France with the battalion on 12 November 1915. He was discharged from the Army on 12 September 1918 due to sickness and he was awarded the Silver War Badge. He is buried in the Edmonton Cemetery – Middlesex.[7]

27 June 1920 Private 99123 Stanley Williams aged 20 died of wounds caused by gas. He was the son of Julia Anney (Annie) Rose and Stephen Henry Williams. His mother died in 1913. His father Stephen lived to the grand old age of 96 passing away in 1949. He lived at 224 High Street, Tooting, London. Private Williams is buried in the Wandsworth (Streatham) Cemetery – London.[8]

Private Williams was the last 18th Battalion (1st Public Works) Pioneers Middlesex Regiment casualty of the war. His death brought to 313 the total number of fatalities suffered by the battalion during World War One.

The Supplement to the London Gazette 31 December 1918 confirmed that His Majesty the King had awarded the Distinguished Conduct Medal to L/13977 Sergeant H.C. Beale 18th Battalion Middlesex Regiment, attached to the 36th Trench Mortar Battery (Wood Green N.).[9]

The Second Supplement to the London Gazette 2 September 1919 carried the citation for this award which reads 'For conspicuous gallantry and devotion to duty during forty months' service, and especially during the period 25 February to 16 September, 1918, as battery serjeant. He has commanded his section of guns in a most able manner in action, and has on many occasions on his own initiative brought his guns forward into action and given great assistance to the attacking infantry'.[10]

1 The Supplement to the London Gazette 17th January 1919, Published 18th January 1919, Gazette Issue 31133, p. 994

2 Sergeant John Mee Army Service Record, National Archives, WO 363

3 Sergeant Clark Army Service Record, National Archives, WO 363; British Army WW1 Pension Records 1914 -1920, National Archives, WO 364; 1911 Census

4 Commonwealth War Graves Commission casualty details; London Metropolitan Archives, London Birth and Baptisms 1813 -1906

5 Private Pewtress Army Service Record, National Archives, WO 363; *Soldier Died In The Great War 1914 -1919*, p. 104; Commonwealth War Graves Commission casualty details

6 Commonwealth War Graves Commission casualty details; British Army Medal Rolls Index Cards, 1914 -1920

7 Ibid., British Army Medal Rolls Index Cards, 1914-1920; Silver War Badge Records, 1914 -1920

8 Ibid.; London Metropolitan Archives, Marriages and Banns 1754 -1921; England & Wales Death Index 1837-1915 & 1916 -2006; 1911 Census

9 Supplement to the London Gazette 31st December 1918, Gazette Issue 31092, p. 36

10 Second Supplement to the London Gazette 2nd September 1919, Gazette Issue 31534, p. 11096

EPILOGUE

Thomas McBride was unable to return to work in the mines because of the damage to his health caused by the war. He was no longer able to work in underground confined spaces. He became an outdoor labourer.

On the 10 October 1919 Martha Jane McBride gave birth to a baby daughter Norah McBride. (On 10 October 1980 Thomas Hall, the great grandson of Martha Jane and Thomas McBride was born.)

On 12 August 1921 Martha Jane McBride gave birth to another daughter Veronica.

On the 25 July 1922 Norah McBride died of whooping cough and bronchial pneumonia.

On 23 February 1926 an Appeals Tribunal of the Ministry of Pensions awarded Thomas McBride a pension of eight shillings a week from November 1923 to 10 November 1925. He received this pension because he had a twenty percent disability caused by aggravated fibrositis.[1]

On 1 April 1933 Thomas McBride put down a deposit of five shillings with Ashton-under-Lyne Corporation Housing Department for the keys to 115 Kings Road, Ashton-under-Lyne.

In March 1937 Thomas McBride, wrote To the Officer in charge of Records o. c Charg Deps-

> 'Sir is it possible for you to let me have a copy of any medical record? I have lost my copy when I last moved house. I am on the waiting list to go in a nose and throat hospital for an operation and having a copy of Army Medical records might be useful to the Doctors there. I left the army on the 2/1/19 to return to work in the mines. However, I was unable to work underground because of ill health. I am now a casual outdoor labourer. As you will know I do not have a pension. If my records can be found or if there is any advice you can give me I shall be ever thankful. Please note my address when I served in the Army was 13 Jermyn Street A-u-L.

Thanking you in anticipation of a soon reply and I thank you for the trouble.

I remain yours truly

T. McBride M.M.'

On 15 March 1937 Thomas McBride received a reply:-

'Sir, with reference to your letter, undated, I am directed to state that all army medical records are confidential and privileged and that it is contrary to the general practice of the Department to make disclosures there from. In these circumstances it is regretted that the Department is unable to accede to your request.

In view, however, of the circumstances of the case, I am to state that the Department will be prepared to furnish information respecting your medical history whilst in the Army, direct to your doctor, in confidence, and for the sole purpose of assisting him in the medical treatment of the case, on receipt of an application from him.

I am, Sir your obedient Servant,

(Brigadier) L. Hammond'.[2]

There is no evidence that Thomas McBride's doctor contacted the Army to ask for his medical records.

Private PW443 Thomas McBride's Army Casualty Card shows that on 30.7.16 he was reported by D.a.G. as being wounded on 20.7.16 and he remained at duty. On 26.9.17 he was reported by 9 Lakeside U.S.A. Gen. Hos. Rouen with mild diarrhoea. On 11.10.17 War Hospital Bath he was reported as being sick.

In February 1938 Thomas McBride applied to the Regimental Association of the Middlesex Regiment (DUKE OF CAMBRIDGE'S OWN) for assistance. On 11.2.38 G. W. Kerswill for the Lt. Colonel, Secretary of the Association wrote to the War Office in Walworth advising them that Thomas McBride had applied for assistance and asking to be informed of his character on discharge and how long he had served in the Middlesex Regiment.[3]

At the outbreak of World War Two Thomas McBride applied to be the Air Raid Warden for Ashton-under-Lyne. On the 5 November 1939 a letter arrived confirming that he been successful and he was appointed as the Air Raid Warden. Thomas McBride never saw the letter. He died that day in Ashton District Infirmary of pulmonary embolism, partial gastrectomy and carcinoma of the stomach.[4]

The Reverend Father Kelly officiated at his funeral. The Requiem Mass was held at St. Mary's Church and the funeral service was held at Hurst Cemetery, Ashton-under-Lyne. Martha Jane McBride, his daughters Veronica McBride and Martha Doyle and son-in-law George Doyle were present. Other family members present were his brother John (also known as Jack) McBride and his wife, his sister Mrs Mary Pye, his brother Owen and his wife, Mr O. McCaul, Mrs A. Carpenter, Mr and Mrs S. Carpenter, and Miss M. Carpenter.

The bearers were John McBride, James McBride, D. Carpenter (nephews) F. Poulson and Speakman.

Floral tributes were from Martha Jane McBride and Veronica McBride, Martha and George Doyle, Brother Jack and family, Sister Mary and family (Stockport), niece Mary (Stockport), Brother Owen and family, sister Ellen and family; Arthur, Mary and family; Sam, Mary and family; cousin Maggie, Mary, Agnes and Josephine; May, Kitty, Arthur, Myra, Frank and Joan; Mr and Mrs Oldfield, Mrs Carter, Mr and Mrs J. L. Wood and family, Jennie, Mr and Mrs Speakman, D. Axon and family, Mrs Tobin and Margery, and friends at the Oddfellows Arms.

Mass cards were from Mrs Pye, Mrs J. McBride, Mrs A. Carpenter, Eileen, and Mr and Mrs J.W. Carpenter.

Mr Greaves, Unsworth Cottage, Penny Meadow carried out the arrangements.[5]

On the 8 April 1940 Mrs Martha Jane McBride ordered a terra cotta vase to go on her husband's grave. She bought this from James Knott and Sons, Monumental Sculptors of Mossley Road, Ashton-under-Lyne. It cost £3.2s.6d. She paid £1 on 8 April and £2.2s.6d. on the 3 May.

Veronica McBride married Thomas (Tommy) Hall in St. Mary's Church on 16 February 1952. They had two sons Michael Thomas Hall born 20 September 1952 and Terence John Hall, born "watching the television", on 31 December 1954.

The genesis of the story was our family mythology surrounding the reason my Grandfather Thomas McBride was awarded the Military Medal.

In 1970 I started to try to find out why my grandfather was awarded the Military Medal. I wrote to the Ministry of Defence on the 8 October 1970. The reply I received stated that the M.O.D. no longer held the citation explaining why Thomas McBride had been awarded the M.M., but they did tell me his name appeared in the Supplement to the London Gazette on the 18 July 1917.[6]

I suppose I really ought to thank the then Prime Minister Tony Blair for giving me the time and the inclination to take up the search in earnest in May 2001. I had served in the Government Whip's Office from 1998 to 2001. After the 2001 General Election the Prime Minister told me that I had done an excellent job as a Government Whip and 'he did not know how he was going to manage without me in Government but he was going to try'. He sacked me over the phone.

I decided then that I would need something to keep me busy and so I decided to take up the challenge of researching Thomas McBride's war record.

Events overtook me. In June 2001 I was appointed the Parliamentary Private Secretary (P.P.S.) to my good friend Alan Milburn, the Secretary of State for Health. I was privileged to become John Reid's P.P.S. when he took over as Secretary of State for Health when Alan, to my complete surprise, which was shared by many of my colleagues, left the Cabinet.

After the 2005 General Election I got the same phone call from John Reid as the one I got from the Prime Minister in 2001 giving me the sack. I then really got stuck into this project. But once again events overtook me in 2008 when I was appointed to be the P.P.S. to Jack Straw Secretary of State for Justice and Lord Chancellor. I retired from Parliament in 2010. I hope you have enjoyed the results of my quest as much as I have. In early 2014 I became an expectant grandparent and my grandson George William Michael Hall was born on 11 November. This, together with Lesley's insistence and the 100th Anniversary of the start of World War One, convinced me to publish this book.

1 McBride Army Service Record
2 Ibid.
3 Ibid.
4 Certified Copy of an Entry of Death Form JB 411922
5 Ashton-under-Lyne Reporter 10th November 1939, p. 7
6 Second Supplement to the London Gazette 17th July 1917, Published 18th July 1917, Gazette Issue 30188, p. 7282

APPENDIX A

Trenches And Features Map References

Chapter One

p. 2 3/7/17 Arquèves -Sheet 57d O.14.a.
p.2 4/7/17 Villers-Bocage – Sheet 62d A.2.a. & b.
p. 3 5/7/17 St. Sauveur
p. 3 6/7/17 le Mesge
p. 11 31/7/17 Liercourt
p. 12 1/8/17 Coudekerque – Sheet 19 N.W.4 I.31.a.
p. 13 7/8/17 La Panne Bains
p. 16 17/8/17 Brisbane Camp Witte Burg – Sheet 11.S.E.2 X.3.a.
p. 16 17/8/17 Groot Labeur Farm (Grote Labeur Farm) – Sheet 12 S.W. 3 S.7.b.8.7.
p. 17 17/8/17 West Cloet Farm – Sheet 12 S.W.1 M.32.a.4.6.
p. 17 17/8/17 bridges over Canal de Passchendaele and Crique de Nieuwendamme M.29.a. & c.
p. 17 21/8/17 Yellow Line and Western Nieuport Switch
p. 18 22/8/17 New Avenue M.25.d.4.6. – M.21.c.3.5
p. 18 22/8/17 No Bon Avenue M.32.a.O.1 – M.33.6.8.0
p. 18 22/8/17 Nieuport M.34.
p. 20 25/8/17 Pelican Bridge
p. 21 28/8/17 Coudekerque Branche – Sheet 19 H.18.c.
p. 23 3/9/17 Ridge Wood north of Vierstraat – Sheet 28 S.W.2 N.5.c.9.6.
p. 23 4/9/17 Zillebeke – Sheet 28 N.W.4 & N.E.3 I.22.b.
p. 23 4/9/17 Hellfire Corner Menin Road I.10.c.9.3.
p. 23 5/9/17 slab road from Knoll Road past Battersea Cottage to Valley Cottages I.29.a.4.9. to I.23.c.8.6.
p. 23 5/9/17 Verbranden Road I.28.a. & b.
p. 24 7/9/17 Slab road Armagh Wood along Observation Ridge I.23.c. an I.24.c. & d.
p. 26 13/9/17 Matawai Camp – Sheet 28 N.W. H.29.b.6.6.

Chapter Two

p. 29 18/9/17 Camp north-east of Boeschepe – Sheet 27 S.E.2 R.5.a.8.6.
p. 29 18/9/17 Berthen R.22.a. & c.
p. 29 19/9/17 site of Nissen hut construction R.17. central
p. 29 19/9/17 Bangle Farm R.17.b.5.5.
p. 29 19/9/17 Nissen hut site north of Steen Akker – Sheet 27 L.32.d.
p. 31 23/9/17 Railway Dugouts – Sheet 28 N.W.4 and N.E.3 I.20.b. & d.
p. 31 23/9/17 Burgomaster Farm – Sheet 28 N.W. 4 H.34.a.5.6.
p. 32 24/9/17 Camp south-west of Dickebusch – Sheet 28 N.W.3 H.33.c.5.6.
p. 32 24/9/17 Stirling Castle – Sheet 28 N.E.3 J.13.d.5.1.
p. 32 24/9/17 Jap Avenue J.13.d. – J.14. c. & d.
p. 32 24/9/17 Northampton Trench
p. 32 24/9/17 Veldhoek Trench – Sheet 28 N.W.4 &N.E.3 (parts of) J.21.b.40.40. – J.21.b.35.10. – junction of Polygon Road with the Menin Road
p. 34 25/9/17 The Culvert I.18.1.7.
p. 34 25/9/17 Inverness Copse – Sheet 28 N.E.3 I.14.c. & d.
p. 34 25/9/17 Hellfire Corner – Sheet 28 N.W. & N.E.3 (parts of) I.10.c.9.3.
p. 35 25/9/17 Polygon Wood J.9.a.,b., c. and d.
p. 37 26/9/17 Machine Gun north side of Menin Road J.21.b.9.1.
p. 38 26/9/17 Railway Dugouts I.20.d.8.8. – I.21.2.7.
p. 38 26/9/17 Café Belge – Sheet 28 N.W.4 H.30.a.1.4.
p. 38 26/9/17 Advanced Divisional Dump – Sheet 28 N.W.4 & N.E.3 (parts of) I.24.c.8.5.
p. 38 26/9/17 Bedford House I.26.b.3.3.
p. 39 26/9/17 Tor Top Tunnel I.24.d.7.3. –I.24.d. 8.4.
p. 40 27/9/17 Battersea Farm I.23.c.8.2.
p. 41 28/9/17 Valley Cottages I.23.c.8.6.
p. 41 28/9/17 Clapham Junction J.13.d.9.8.
p. 41 28/9/17 Verbeek Farm J.14.b.9.5
p. 41 28/9/17 Black Watch Corner J.15.b.00.65.
p. 41 29/9/17 front line wire east of Gheluvelt – Sheet 28 N.E.3 J.29.a.2.8. – J.23.a.4.0.
p. 44 30/9/17 Plumer's Drive J.13.d.5.9.
p. 44 30/9/17 Étang de Zillebeke – Sheet 28 N.W.4 & N.E.3 (parts of) I.21. & 22.
p. 44 1/10/17 Plumer's Drive – Sanctuary Wood to Ypres – Menin road I.24.b.central.
p. 45 2/10/17 X Corps Camp near Abeele – Sheet 27 N.E.4 R.20.c.
p. 45 3/10/17 Jargon Switch north of Surbiton Villas – Sheet 28 N.W.4. & N.E.3 (parts of) J.13.b.9.8.
p. 45 3/10/17 Glencorse Wood J.14.a. & b.
p. 45 3/10/17 north-west corner Polygon Wood J.9.a.5.3.

Chapter Three

p. 51 4/10/17 Dickebusch – Sheet 28 N.W. H.34.a
p. 51 4/10/17 Hooge Crater – Sheet 28 N.W.4 & N.E.3 (parts of) I.18.b.2.6.
p. 52 5/10/17 Sherwood Camp – Sheet 28 N.W.3 H.33.c.3.6.
p. 52 6/10/17 La Clytte Dump – Sheet 28 S.W.1 N.7.a.8.5.
p. 53 7/10/17 Withuis Cabaret – Sheet 28 N.W.4 I.19.d.3.2.
p. 53 7/10/17 Curragh Camp Westoutre – Sheet 28 S.W.1 M.17.a. & c.
p. 53 8/10/17 Gable Farm Wulverghem – Sheet 28 S.W.4 T.5.a.0.5.
p. 53 8/10/17 Neuve Église – Sheet 28 S.W.3 T.15.a.
p. 55 9/10/17 New Cross Communication Trench/Street – Sheet 28.S.W.4 U.4.c., d., & 5.c.
p. 55 10/10/17 Fanny's Avenue (Fanny Street) O.33.d – O.34.central.
p. 55 10/10/17 Owl Trench O.34.central.
p. 56 10/10/17 Undulating Trench and Undulating Support U.4.c.9.0. –U.4.b.2.0.
p. 56 10/10/17 Blauwepoortbeek Stream – Delpotre Farm – Sheet 28 S.W.2 O.34.b.
p. 56 12/10/17 New Cross C.T. from Pollard Support – Sheet 28 S.W.4 U.5.c.2.6.
p. 57 14/10/17 Duke of Connaught railway marshalling yard – Sheet 28 S.W.3 T.26.c.2.5.
p. 59 21/10/17 Duckboard track from Pollard Support – Sheet 28 S.W.4 U.5.c.2.7. – U.5.d.4.9.
p. 59 23/10/17 Gapaard Group O.35.c.6.8.
p. 59 23/10/17 Steignast Farm U.5.a.2.8.
p. 61 26/10/17 Bethléem Road (Bethlehem Road) U.3.d.8.0.
p. 61 26/10/17 La Petite Douve Farm U.8.a.9.5.
p. 61 26/10/17 Tilluel Farm U.10.c.5.6.
p. 61 28/10/17 Kiwi Farm O.36.c.5.5.
p. 63 1/11/17 Bethléem Farm U.3.d.6.5.
p. 64 5/11/17 drain to New Cross Street U.4.d.4.3.
p. 65 6/11/17 North Midland Farm T.6.c.6.8.

Chapter Four

p. 75 16/11/17 Bailleul – Sheet 28 S.W.3 S.14.a.
p. 75 17/11/17 Locre – Sheet 28 S.W.1 M.23.c.
p. 76 18/11/17 Saint Jean – Sheet 28 N.W.2 C.27.d.2.2.
p. 76 18/11/17 Goldfish Château – Sheet 28 N.W.4 H.11.a.8.2.
p. 76 19/11/17 Savile Road Camp I.3.d.1.3.
p. 77 20/11/17 Artillery Road – Sheet 28 N.E.1 D.16., D.21., D.22. and D.27.
p. 77 20/11/17 Seine D.16.d.3.4.
p. 77 20/11/17 Hamburg D.16.b.2.8.
p. 79 23/11/17 Devil's Crossing D.26.b.9.4.
p. 79 24/11/17 Godley Road – Sheet 28 N.W.2 C.24.a.7.0. – C.30.d.2.5.

p. 79 24/11/17 'H' Track from Godley Road to RAMC Track C.24.d.2.3. – C.30.a.9.9.
p. 79 26/11/17 Zonnebeke Station 28 N.E.1 D.21.d.6.3.
p. 79 26/11/17 Manx Corner – Sheet 28 N.E.2 E.10.c.17.73.
p. 80 28/11/17 Lewis Gun placements Gravenstafel – Sheet 28 N.E.1 D.9.c.75.10., Seine D.16.d.5.6., Seine D.16.d.0.8. and west of Zonnebeke Station D.21.c.95.45.
p. 81 30/11/17 'H' Track between Oxford Road and Godley Road – Sheet 28 N.W.2 C.29.c.5.0. – C.30.a.9.9.
p. 81 4/12/17 Kansas Cross – Sheet 28 N.E.1 D.14.a.2.1.
p. 82 4/12/17 Bavaria House – Sheet 28 N.W.2 C.30.c.6.3.
p. 82 4/12/17 Levi Cottages – Sheet 28 N.E.1 D.21.a.7.4.
p. 82 4/12/17 north of Hill 40 D.21.d.3.8.
p. 82 5/12/17 Abraham Heights D.16.a.2.8.
p. 82 5/12/17 Crest Farm D.12.a.3.9.

Chapter Five

p. 86 8/12/17 Tyne Cot D.17.a.6.2.
p. 87 13/12/17 Plank Road D.26.b.5.4.
p. 88 17/12/17 Windmill Cabaret D.21.central
p. 88 20/12/17 South Road
p. 91 31/12/17 Fascine Road – Sheet 28 N.W.2 C.30.c.6.4. – I.6.a.9.7.
p. 91 31/12/17 Ibex Avenue I.6.a.5.4. – I.6.a.9.7.
p. 94 3/1/18 Frost House – Sheet 28 N.E.1 D.25.a.7.1.
p. 99 14/1/18 Observation post D.12.a.
p. 102 27/1/18 Heine House D.11.c.7.2.
p. 102 27/1/18 Tilques Training Area Parts of – Sheets 27a S.E. and 36d N.E.

Chapter Six

p. 104 28/1/18 Wizernes – Sheet 36d N.E. F.4.a.5.1.
p. 113 6/2/18 Training ground Parts of – Sheet 27a S.E. and 36d N.E X.20.c.4.6.
p. 113 6/2/18 Gondardennes F.4.a.
p. 113 6/2/18 Poudrerie west Esquerdes E.4.d.
p. 113 6/2/18 Etréhem W.10d.
p. 114 15/2/18 Firing range north-east of Cormette Q.29.c.
p. 114 15/2/18 60 yard firing range F.5.c.
p. 114 15/2/18 Gas demonstration trench north-west of Tatinghem X.1.a.
p. 114 19/2/18 Renescure – Sheet 27 S.W. T.20.d.
p. 115 19/2/18 Tatinghem X.2.d. & X.7.central
p. 115 20/2/18 Oudezeele – Sheet 27 N.E. J.14.a.

p. 115 21/2/18 Sunderland Camp
p. 115 22/2/18 Middlesex Camp – Savile Road – Sheet 28 N.W.4 I.3.c.1.3.
p. 115 22/2/18 Crest Farm south-west of Passchendaele – Sheet 28 N.E.1 D.12.a.1.9.
p. 115 22/2/18 Pickering Junction (Light Rail Siding) – Sheet 28 N.W.2 I.2.b.4.9.
p. 115 22/2/18 Van Isackere Farm – Sheet 28 N.E.1 D.21.a.3.6.
p. 115 22/2/18 Delva Farm D.20.a.0.3.
p. 116 24/2/18 Post S13 in Marne D.17.c.3.5.
p. 117 26/2/18 Dugout south-west of Passchendaele D.6.d.1.1.
p. 117 27/2/18 Trench through Passchendaele D.6.d.1.7. – D.6.d.4.9.

Chapter Seven

p. 119 1/3/18 Haalen Copse D.11.b.9.5.
p. 119 1/3/18 Manners Junction – Sheet 28 N.W.2 C.27.d.4.5.
p. 125 15/3/18 Tiber – Sheet 28 N.E.1 D.12.95.60.
p. 125 15/3/18 Grun D.12.d.35.95.
p. 128 20/3/18 Hillside Farm D.17.b.8.2.
p. 128 20/3/18 Tyne Cot Cemetery D.17.a.8.4.
p. 135 29/3/18 Waterfields D.10.d.8.9.
p. 136 30/3/18 Bellevue Switch (Track D.4.c.3.2. – D.5.c.2.4..
p. 136 30/3/18 Duckboard track connecting No. 5 Track and Crest Farm Track
p. 136 31/3/18 Grand-Rullecourt – Sheet 51c. S.W. O.9.central
p. 136 31/3/18 Abraham Heights Switch (Abraham Alley D.15.b3.6. – D.9.d.6.2.)
p. 136 1/4/18 Brick Kiln Road and F Track D.28.c.3.6.

Chapter Eight

p. 140 4/4/18 Camps 32 and 33 – Sheet 28.N.W. B.26.c.7.2.
p. 141 7/4/18 Lattre St. Quentin – Sheet 51c N.E. J.30.a.1.9.
p. 143 10/4/18 Adinfer – Sheet 51c S.E.4 X.21.b. & c.
p. 143 11/4/18 North of Méteren Veld – Sheet 27 X.16.d.8.9.
p. 143 11/4/18 La Crèche – Sheet 36 N.W.1 A.5.d.7.9.
p. 143 11/4/18 Méteren – Noote Boom Road – Sheet 27 S.E.4 X.15.d.5.7.
p. 143 11/4/18 Méteren – Fontaine Houck Road X.15.d.8.6. – X.4.c.1.6.
p. 145 12/4/18 La Barrière Calverdans X.23.a.8.4
p. 145 12/4/18 south on the road from Appetite Farm where it meets the Méteren to Armentières road X.18.c.8.2.
p. 145 12/4/18 Merville – Sheet 36a N.E.4 K.29.central
p. 145 12/4/18 Neuf Berquin L.14.c.
p. 145 12/4/18 Switch Line the Méteren – La Barrière Calverdans road to Blauvenlandt,

Scots Alley, Scots Trench, Rathfriland Support and Rally Support – Sheet 27 S.E.4 X.16.d.7.4. – X.10.b.7.6. – X.5.d.6.3.

p. 145 12/4/18 Strazeele W.30.d.5.1 – Steam Mill X.23.d.9.1.

p. 145 12/4/18 Halte Porte Farm X.10.b.2.4.

p. 146 13/4/18 Fontaine Houck X.4.c.4.5.

p. 150 14/4/18 Bailleul – Sheet 28 S.W.3 S.13., 14., 19., & 20.

p. 150 14/4/18 Appetite Farm – Sheet 27 S.E.4 X.17.b.9.2.

p. 150 14/4/18 four points of occupation south-west of Méteren X.20.d.1.1., X.20.d.4.7., X.20.d.5.5. and X.21.c.9.9.

p. 151 14/4/18 German gathering point on Strazeele to Bailleul road X.20.d.5.5. – X.21.c.9.9.

p. 151 14/4/18 18th Middlesex trench south from Les Ormes to the Strazeele to Bailleul road X.20.b.2.3. to X.20.b.8.2.

Chapter Nine

p. 159 15/4/18 Axe Mill Windmill Méteren X.16.a.3.8.

p. 159 15/4/18 Méteren Veld X.22.

p. 159 15/4/18 Blauvenlandt X.5.d.

p. 165 17/4/18 Mont des Cats – Sheet 27 R.19.b.8.6.

p. 166 17/4/18 Farm 'D' Company 4th Kings Headquarters – Sheet 27 S.E.4 X.15.c.2.9.

p. 168 20/4/18 Staple – Sheet 27.O.3.b.5.2.

Chapter Ten

p. 174 23/4/18 Camp on Eecke – Steenvorde Road – Sheet 27 S.E.1 Q.14.a.2.8.

p. 174 24/4/18 Caestre – Watou Line, Meulewalle – Sheet 27 Q.17.c.1.9. – Menham Cross Chapel K.35.c.9.4.

p. 174 26/4/18 Sainte-Marie-Cappel – Sheet 27 S.E.1 P.19.b.8.8.

p. 175 27/4/18 Reserve Line Baeck Houck – Sheet 27 Q.22.a.9.6. to west of Menham Cross Chapel K.35.c.1.3.

p. 176 29/4/17 Steen Akker Switch Godewaersvelde Q.6.d.4.6. to Steen Akker R.2.a.6.2. just outside the Belgium border.

p. 178 1/5/18 Abeele Switch Line – Sheet 27 N.E.4 K.29.c.1.7. – L.17.c.0.2.

p. 178 4/5/18 Camp west of Poperinghe L.9.c.3.5.

p. 178 4/5/18 Ouderdom Line Ottawa Camp – Sheet 28 N.W.3 G.24 to Red Horse Shoe Camp G.28.

p. 178 4/5/18 Front line East of Kruisstraathoek to Cheapside next to Godzonne Farm – Sheet 28 N.W.4 H.36.b.9.9. to 28 S.W.2 N.10.c.9.7.

p. 179 7/5/18 Butterfly Farm N.19.a.5.9. – Cheapside N.15.a.

p. 180 9/5/18 Waratah Camp south of Poperinghe – Sheet 28 N.W.3 G.15.c.0.7.
p. 181 15/5/18 East Poperinghe Line Condiment Cross G.32.d. – Ride Camp G.4.c.
p. 184 22/5/18 Dirty Bucket Camp – Sheet 28 N.W.1 A.30.a. & c.

Chapter Eleven

p. 196 7/6/18 Brandhoek – Sheet 28 N.W.3 G.12.b.6.3.
p. 196 8/6/18 Road Camp H.9.central
p. 196 8/6/18 Communication Trench H.22.d.7.1.
p. 196 8/6/18 Vijverhoek H.29.a.4.4.
p. 196 8/6/18 Communication Trench from Café Belge H.29.b.7.1. to Kruisstraathoek H.30.c.4.6.
p. 196 8/6/18 Dickebusch – Sheet 28 N.W. H.33.b. – Goldfish Château H.11.a. & b. – Brielen B.29.a.
p. 196 8/6/18 Goed Moet Mill Switch H.25.0.5. – H.15.b.8.8.
p. 196 8/6/18 Elverdinghe – Sheet 28 N.W.1 B.14.a. – Vlamertinghe – Sheet 28 N.W. H.9.a. – Ouderdom G.30.c.
p. 196 10/6/18 Moat Farm – Sheet 28 N.W.4 H.17.c.9.5.
p. 196 10/6/18 Kruisstraat H.18.d.9.6.
p. 196 10/6/18 White House (Withuis Cabaret H.19.d.4.2.)
p. 198 15/6/18 Query Camp – Sheet 28 N.W.3 G.11.a.3.2. – Oxley Farm G.9.b.6.4.
p. 198 16/6/18 Givenchy Camp – Sheet 28 N.W.3 H.8.d. & H.9.c.
p. 198 19/6/18 Manor Farm – Sheet 28 N.W.4 I.22.c.6.5.
p. 199 20/6/18 Winnipeg – Sheet 28 N.W.3 G.10.b.8.9.
p. 199 22/6/18 Lille Road Woodcote House/Three Kings Junction 28 N.W.4 I.20.c.4.4.
p. 199 22/6/18 Bedford House – I.26.b.2.8.
p. 199 22/6/18 Gas discharge frontage between Sandbag Track I.26.b.2.8. – east of Klietgatbeek I.20.d.9.4.
p. 199 22/6/18 Castle Siding I.19.d.6.8.
p. 200 22/6/18 Trois Rois Spur I.20.c.6.3.
p. 200 22/6/18 Frankton H.17.d.9.7. and Brisbane H.24.b.2.6.
p. 200 23/6/18 Bedford Junction I.26.b.2.8.
p. 202 28/6/18 Enemy post south bank of the Étang de Zillebeke I.21.d.95.95.
p. 203 1/7/18 Brandhoek – Sheet 28 N.W.3 G.12.b.6.6.
p. 203 1/7/18 Road repairs Den Groenen Jager Cabaret – Sheet 28 N.W.4 H.16.d.15.15. to Kruisstraat H.18.d.9.6. to north-east of Café Belge H.30.a.4.9.
p. 203 1/7/18 right flank defences Vijverhoek H.29.b.7.9. to Kruisstraathoek H.30.c.5.4.
p. 203 1/7/18 road repairs south of Vlamertinghe from Section Bend north of Givenchy Farm H.8.a.5.7. to one thousand yards north of Assam Farm H.16.a.1.1. and from Vlamertinghe Station H.9.a.7.5. to north of Assam Farm.
p. 206 5/7/18 communication trench north-west of Kruisstraathoek H.30. c.35.60.

p. 206 6/7/18 Front Line from east of Kruisstraatheok H.36.b.9.8. to Middlesex Wood H.36.a.20.25.
p. 206 6/7/18 Pigment Farm H.13.d.0.5.
p. 207 7/7/18 two wells west of Poperinghe – Sheet 27 N.E.4 L.8.c.1.3. and L.8.d.8.3.
p. 207 7/7/18 Rhodes Corner L.7.9.75.15.
p. 207 9/7/18 well west of Poperinghe south of Rhodes Corner L.13.b.central
p. 208 11/7/18 Maida Vale Trench – Sheet 28 N.W.4 H.29.d.7.9. – H.30.c.6.4.
p. 209 13/7/18 Halifax Camp – Sheet 28 N.W.3 H.14.c.52.85. – Vijverbeek Canal – Sheet 38 N.W.4 H.23.d.45.55.
p. 209 14/7/18 GHQI line Elzenwalle H.36.b. & c.
p. 209 14/7/18 Château Segard H.30.c.95.95. – Voormezeele H.36.b.95.95.

Chapter Twelve

p. 214 15/7/18 Pocklington H.11.a. & c.
p. 214 15/7/18 Stanley (Stanley Farm – Sheet 28 N.E.4 K.28.b.0.8.)
p. 215 19/7/18 Vauban Alley Communication Trench (Vauban Avenue – Sheet 28 N.W.4 H.30.c.95.95 – H.36.b.95.95
p. 219 26/7/18 Dawson south of Belgian Château H.23.b.9.1.
p. 220 1/8/18 Halifax – Dawson Track – Sheet 28 N.W.3 H.14.c.52.85. – Sheet 28 N.W.4 H.23.b.9.1.
p. 225 17/8/18 Strathcona Camp Proven – Sheet 27 N.E.2 F.7.b.2.3.
p. 225 19/8/18 Ouest Mont west of Watten crossroads D219 and D221 north-west of St. Omer – Sheet 27a N.E. K.26.b. & K.27.a.
p. 226 20/8/18 Holque F.25.d.
p. 227 23/8/18 Inglinghem (Inghem L.3.d. & L.4.c.)
p. 228 29/8/18 Sombrin – Sheet 51c O.23.central.

Chapter Thirteen

p. 234 4/9/18 Divisional Headquarters Château Lucheux T.16.b.0.1.
p. 235 8/9/18 Warlincourt – Sheet 57d N.E. C.6.a.
p. 237 14/9/18 Ginchy – Sheet 57c S.W.3 T.13.d.
p. 237 15/9/18 33rd Division H.Q. le Mesnil en Arrouaise – Sheet 57c S.W.4 U.4.b.
p. 239 18/9/18 Area between Équancourt and Fins – Sheet 57c S.E.3 V.11.
p. 239 18/9/18 Manancourt (Étricourt-Manancourt) V.13.central
p. 239 19/9/18 Équancourt Wood V.10.a., V.11.c. & V.16.b.
p. 239 19/9/18 Red Line Gloster Road to Lark Spur – Sheet 57c. S.E.4 X.15.d.9.9. – X.22.c.8.4.
p. 240 20/9/18 Meunier Trench X.9.c.0.0. to Kildare Avenue X.22.c.0.1.

p. 240 20/9/18 Lark Spur X.21.c.
p. 240 20/9/18 trenches west of sugar factory Heudicourt – Sheet 57c S.E.3 W.21.a. & b. and W.15.c. & d.
p. 240 20/9/18 Fives Trench – Sheet 57c S.E.4 X.7.d.7.3. to the Beet Factory X.14.b.5.2.
p. 241 22/9/18 Leith Walk X.16.c. – X.16.d.
p. 241 22/9/18 Targelle Valley X.22.a. – X.22.b.
p. 241 22/9/18 Tyhurst Quarry X.17.c.3.1.
p. 241 22/9/18 Pigeon Quarry X.17.c.2.5.
p. 247 24/9/18 Little Priel Farm – Sheet 57c S.E.4 X.28.d.8.1.
p. 247 24/9/18 Railton W.16.d.9.0.

Chapter Fourteen

p. 251 25/9/18 Étricourt – Heudicourt horse track – Sheet 57c S.E.3 V.8.c. – W.20.b.
p. 262 1/10/18 Tètard Wood – Sheet 62c N.E.2 F.2.a.
p. 262 1/10/18 Camp south-west of Villers-Guislain 57c S.E.4 X.13.b.8.8.
p. 263 3/10/18 Fir Support Thrush Valley X.26.a.2.5.
p. 263 5/10/18 Approaches to the heavy bridge over St Quentin Canal – Sheet 57b S.W.3 S.7.b.1.1.
p. 263 5/10/18 Ossus – Sheet 57b. S.W.3 S.19.d.
p. 263 5/10/18 Honnecourt S.7.b. & S.8.a.
p. 263 5/10/18 Kingston Quarry S.14.c.7.2.
p. 263 5/10/18 De La l'Eau S.26.a.
p. 264 5/10/18 la Terrière S.15.b. & S.16.a.
p. 264 5/10/18 Richmond Quarry S.28.a.
p. 264 5/10/18 Rancourt Farm S.4.c. & d., S.10.a. & b.
p. 264 5/10/18 Bonabus Farm S.5.d. & S.11.b.
p. 264 5/10/18 Mortho Wood T.1.c. & d. and T.7.a.
p. 264 5/10/18 Aubencheul-aux-Bois S.18.b. & d. and T.13.a. & c.
p. 264 5/10/18 West of la Terrière S.15.a.
p. 264 5/10/18 Franqueville S.7.b.

Chapter Fifteen

p. 267 6/10/18 Rag Trench – Sheet 57c S.E.4 X.17.a.9.7.
p. 267 6/10/18 Bosquet Farm X.18.a.8.3.
p. 267 6/10/18 Franque Wood – Sheet 57b S.W.3 S.8.c. & d.
p. 267 6/10/18 Honnecourt Wood – Sheet 57c S.E.4 X.11.a.
p. 267 6/10/18 Approach to bridges – Sheet 57b S.W.3 S.7.d.05.05

p. 267 6/10/18 Road repairs Cannon Gate to the bridge X.17.central to S.7.d.05.05.

p. 267 6/10/18 Road repairs from Pigeon Quarry to south of Noble Ville – Sheets parts of 57c N.E. & S.E. and 57b N.W. & S.W. X.12.b.9.9.

p. 267 6/10/18 Road repairs from north of Honnecourt Wood to Rancourt Farm X.5.d.0.0. to S.10.a.9.9.

p. 267 7/10/18 Battalion H.Q. Franque Wood – Sheet 57b S.W.3 S.8.c.6.8.

p. 267 7/10/18 Road from Franqueville to the south-east of la Terrière S.13.b.75.85 – S.16.a.9.6. and from the centre of la Terrière to the east of the village S.16.a.1.8. – S.16.a.9.9.

p. 267 7/10/18 Cross roads east of Franqueville through la Terrière to Rancourt Farm S.14.a.6.6., S.16.a.0.8. – S.10.a.9.9.

p. 268 7/10/18 Road along the west bank of the St. Quentin Canal – Sheets parts of 57c N.E. & S.E. and 57b N.W. & S.W. S.7.11. – X.17.b.9.9.

p. 268 7/10/18 road from the lock to the start of Cannon Gate road south of Les Tranchées S.7.b.8.7. – S.7.d.2.1.

p. 268 8/10/18 Road from western outskirts of la Terrière, through the village to the northern tip of Basket Wood – Sheet 57b S.W.3 S.15.b.6.9. – S.17.a.3.7.

p. 269 9/10/18 Road north of Rancourt Farm S.4.c.

p. 269 9/10/18 Angelus Orchard next Angelus Wood T.8.a.8.7.

p. 270 10/10/18 Iris Farm – Sheet 57b S.W.2 O.28.d.0.0.

p. 271 10/10/18 Malincourt – Sheet 57b S.W.4 T.5.central.

p. 271 10/10/18 Élincourt U.3.c.

p. 271 10/10/18 Clary – Sheet 57b S.W.2 O.17.d.

p. 272 11/10/18 Selvigny to Clary road O.13.d.3.6. – O.17.d.1.7.

p. 272 11/10/18 Pontoon bridges across the River Selle between Montay and Neuvilly – Sheet 57b K.15., K.16. & K.22.

p. 274 12/10/18 Bridges over River Selle K.16.c.5.0. – K.9.c.2.0.

p. 274 12/10/18 Clary – Bertry – Troisvilles road – Sheet 57b O.17.d. – P.8.d. – J.35.a.

p. 276 14/10/18 Hurtevent Farm – Clary road O.21.d.2.8. – O.23.c.3.9.

p. 276 14/10/18 Élincourt – Selvigny road U.3.c.3.1. – O.13.c.9.9.

p. 276 14/10/18 Élincourt – Walincourt road.U.3.c.3.1. – N.24.d.0.4.

p. 278 20/10/18 Bertry P.8.d.6.9.

p. 279 21/10/18 Montay to Reumont road K.28.a. – K.27.d.

p. 279 21/10/18 Demolished railway bridge on the Montay to Forest road K.22.d.8.8.

p. 279 22/10/18 Track for horsed transport over the River Selle K.16.c.1.4.

p. 279 23/10/18 Montay – Forest – Croix Road K.17.d.3.4.

p. 279 23/10/18 Forest K.12.b. and Croix L.1.b.

p. 279 23/10/18 H.Q. L'Évêque Wood camp L.23.a.5.8.

p. 280 23/10/18 Bousies Wood Farm F.22.b.9.8.

p. 281 24/10/18 Montay – Bavay main road from Vert Baudet to southern edge of Vendegies Wood north-east of Herpies Mill F.26.b.4.2. – F.21.central.

p. 281 24/10/18 Road from the church north-east of Croix to Vert Baudet L.2.a.3.7. –

F.26.b.4.2.
p. 281 24/10/18 Herpies Mill to Paul Jacques Farm F.21.c.5.4. – F.16.central.
p. 281 24/10/18 The advanced battalion H.Q. moved to the outskirts of Forest K.6.d.7.5.
p. 281 24/10/18 Englefontaine – Sheet 57b N.E. F.6.a.9.5. to Le Coupe Gorge – Sheet 51a X.24.c.9.9.
p. 281 24/10/18 Front line from Futoy into the Forêt du Mormal – Sheet 51 S.14.cenral – S.21 central – S.28.a.0.0.
p. 281 24/10/18 Line from Paul Jacques Farm between Vendegies-au-Bois and Wagnonville – Sheet 57b N.E. F.16.central – F.9.c. & d.
p. 281 24/10/18 Montay to Bavay road eight hundred yards west of Wagnonville F.11.b.
p. 281 24/10/18 Between Poix-du-Nord and Englefontaine F.5.central.
p. 281 24/10/18 98th Infantry Brigade held just short of the brewery F.11.
p. 281 24/10/18 high ground north of Les Tuileries – Sheet 51a X.29.d.
p. 281 24/10/18 19th Infantry Brigade position Wagnonville – Sheet 57d N.E. F.5.central and Les Tuileries – Sheet 51a X.29.d.
p. 282 24/10/18 Western outskirts of Englefontaine – Sheet 57d N.E. F.6.c. & a. and – Sheet 51a X.30c. & a. and X.24.c.

Chapter Sixteen

p. 287 26/10/18 Mont Carmel – Sheet 57a N.W. A.8.c.5.5.
p. 287 26/10/18 100th Infantry Brigade post south-eastern outskirts of Englefontaine A.2.c.2.8.
p. 289 30/10/18 Tank bridge over River Selle – Sheet 57b K.22.a.7.1.
p. 291 4/11/18 Route D'Hecq – Sheet 57a N.W. A.14.b.2.9. – B.1.d.4.9.
p. 291 5/11/18 Crater near Croisil Inn B.10.b.
p. 292 5/11/18 Tête Noire – Sheet 51 T.24.c.and Sarbaras T.30.d.
p. 292 5/11/18 Ribaumet – Sassegnies line (Sheet 57a C.2.b. – C.8.c.)
p. 292 5/11/18 Berlaimont – Sheet 51 U.20.d.
p. 292 5/11/18 Railway line triangle – Sheet 57a C.3.b.
p. 292 5/11/18 Factory – Sheet 51 U.27.d.
p. 292 5/11/18 Petit Maubeuge – Sheet 57a C.4.d.
p. 292 5/11/18 Avesnes to Maubeuge road – Sheet 57a E.7.b., E.1.d. & b. and Sheet 51 W.25.d. & b.
p. 292 6/11/18 Footbridge over River Sambre south of Mecrimont Farm – Sheet 57a C.3.c.5.4.
p. 292 6/11/18 Leval C.10.c.
p. 292 6/11/18 Transport Bridge on eastern outskirts of Berlaimont – Sheet 51 U.27.a.2.7.
p. 293 6/11/18 La Toque to Pot de Vin road – Sheet 51 U.30.c. – Sheet 57a D.9.a.
p. 293 6/11/18 Sassegnies Bridge – Sheet 57a C.14.b.3.7.
p. 293 6/11/18 Beaufort to Floursies line – Sheet 51 W.14.c. – Sheet 57a F.9.c.

p. 293 6/11/18 Croisil Inn – Sheet 57a N.W. B.10.b.
p. 294 7/11/18 Écuélin – Sheet 57a D.4.a.
p. 294 7/11/18 High ground south of Romeries (Sheet 51 W.27.)
p. 294 7/11/18 Limont-Fontaine – Sheet 51 V.23.a. & b.
p. 294 7/11/18 Bavay – Sheet 51 I.25.a. & b.
p. 297 14/11/18 Montigny – Sheet 57b S.W. O.12.a.
p. 297 16/11/18 Locquignol – Sheet 51 T.25.a. & b.
p. 297 18/11/18 Malincourt – Sheet 57b S.W. T.5.a. & b.
p. 298 27/11/18 salvage dump Malincourt – Sheet 57b S.W.4. T.5.d.5.6.

APPENDIX B

Lieutenant-Colonel Sir John Ward M.P.

Lieutenant-Colonel John Ward J.P., M.P. was born on 21 November 1866 in Oatlands Park, Surrey. His father Robert Ward, a journeyman plasterer, was married to Caroline Edmunds. Lieut.-Colonel Ward's father died when he was three years old. By 1871 Caroline Ward, her six year old daughter Mary, John and one year old son Tom had moved in to live with her father John Edmunds at 2nd Lodge, Penton Mewsey, Hampshire. John Ward's Uncle Thomas also lived in this household. Both his Uncle and Grandfather were agricultural labourers.

Ward had very little formal education and started work at the age of seven. At the age of 12 he lodged with a man in Weyhill village and started work as a navvy on the Andover and Weyhill railway. He was employed on many public works. In 1891 he had moved to live at 2 Bells Terrace, Barton upon Irwell as a lodger whilst working on the construction of the Manchester Ship Canal. In his youth a kind old lady taught him to read and he immediately started to buy books out of his five-pence an hour wages (this was pre-decimalisation old pence currency equivalent to 2 pence per hour in decimal currency).

He married Lillian Elizabeth Gibbs in 1892. They had five children, Madeline, Harold, Donald Barry and Larner Botha and a fifth child who died. By 1901 the Ward family were living at 4 Knoll Street, Wandsworth. By 1911 they had moved round the corner to 67 Herndon Road, Wandsworth.

In 1886 he joined the Social Democratic Federation. In 1889 he founded the Navvies' Union and also helped to establish the short lived National Federation of Labour Union. On the creation of the General Federation of Trade Unions in 1901 he was elected to the Management Committee and served until 1929. He was the Treasurer of the General Federation of Trade Unions from 1913 to 1929.

John Ward was one of the candidates who refused to sign the Labour Representation Committee constitution in 1903. Without the endorsement of

the L.R.C. Ward was elected to Parliament in 1906 and served as the Liberal/Labour Member for Stoke-on-Trent from 1906 to 1918. He was known as the 'Miners' M.P.

His military career started in 1885 when he volunteered and served as a civilian with the Suakin Force as part of Lord Wolseley's expedition to the Sudan. He was engaged in the construction of the abortive military railway from Suakin to Berber. He received the Khedive's Bronze Star and the Egyptian Medal and Clasp.

On 19 January 1915 John Ward M.P. was given a Temporary Commission as Captain with the 18th Battalion (1st Public Works Pioneers) The Duke of Cambridge's Own (Middlesex Regiment). On 15 April 1915 he was promoted to Temporary Lieutenant-Colonel and transferred to the 19th (2nd Public Works Pioneers) Battalion Middlesex Regiment and took command of that battalion. On 12 August 1915 he was transferred to 25th Reserve Battalion Middlesex Regiment and took command of that battalion.

He recruited five labour battalions for the Middlesex Regiment including the 18th Battalion and served for a time in France.

On 16 February 1917 the 25th Middlesex were on their way to the Far East onboard the troopship Tyndareus when it was mined off South Africa. Lt.-Col. Ward and his men were rescued, during which Ward greatly distinguished himself by his courage and resource. Later in 1917 Lieut.-Colonel Ward and the 25th Battalion Middlesex Regiment were deployed for a period of service in Hong Kong where Ward urged the Home Government, to no avail, to abolish the sale of Chinese women and children in the colony. The 25th Middlesex also served in the Straits Settlement.

During the campaign of intervention, after the Russian revolution, Allied armies sought contact with the Don Cossacks, who under General Kaledin and General Krasnov, had broken away from the Moscow government. In May 1918 a force of Czecho-Slovakian prisoners of war and volunteers, under Kerensky, initiated the first revolt against the Bolsheviks and threatened the Siberian railway from the Volga to the Urals.

The 25th Middlesex, though composed of 'B' category men, was ordered to Vladivostok for service in Siberia on garrison duty. Shortly after the battalion arrived in Russia the Allied Council in the Far East applied to the British Government for permission to deploy the 25th Middlesex in the field. The War Office referred the request to Lieut.-Colonel Ward who immediately agreed. The battalion, by railway, crossed six thousand miles from Vladivostok to Omsk amid the snow of the Siberian winter.

Ward and the 25th Middlesex assisted Kerensky's revolt against the Bolsheviks by joining Admiral Koltchak's uprising in Vladivostok. This saw the establishment of an anti-Bolshevik Government in the city and also in Omsk. These were later suppressed by the Lenin's Bolshevik Government.

Lt.-Col. Ward was the only left wing battalion commanding officer in the British Army during WW1. He was 'Mentioned in Despatches' twice. He received the British War Medal and Victory Medal with Oak Leaf Emblem in respect of being 'Mentioned in Despatches'.

He received the French, Italian and Czecho-Slovakian Croix de Guerre and the Japanese Order of the Sacred Treasure 3rd Class. He also received the high honour of being made a Cossack Ataman by his Tartar comrades.[1]

He was knighted for his service in the 1918 New Years Honours List being made a Companion of Saint Michael and Saint George.[2] He was appointed a Companion of the Order of the Bath on 22 March 1919.[3]

After the War there was a Parliamentary boundary change which came into effect for the 1918 General Election which took place on 14 December. By this time Lieut.-Colonel Ward had major policy differences with Labour particularly on national defence. He changed his political affiliations and stood as a Coalition Liberal. He was returned unopposed for the new seat of Stoke-on-Trent (Stoke Division). However, he did not take his seat in that Parliament immediately on account of being on active service in Russia.

Lieut.-Col. Ward only arrived back in Britain from Russia on 3 September 1919. The War Office wrote to him on 24 October 1919 informing him that he was to relinquish his Temporary Commission with effect from 1 November 1919. Ward replied protesting against the decision and the War Office amended the date of the relinquishment to 5 November 1919, the date when Ward swore his Parliamentary oath of allegiance to the King, his heirs and successors, took up his seat in the House of Commons and started to receive his Parliamentary salary.[4] The War Office wrote again to Ward on 11 November 1919 informing him of this decision and instructed him to contact the Officer Dispersal Unit London, Knaresborough House, Knaresborough Place, Earls Court, S.W.5 to complete the issue of his Protection Certificate.

The Protection Certificate served a dual purpose: 1) it provided a certificate for the Officer that he is released from military service; 2) it provided a notice for the agents of the Paymaster (Cox and Co. of London,) to stop his pay. Ward had the option of visiting the Officer Dispersal Unit in person or writing to

them. He did neither, his Protection Certificate was not issued and as a result he continued to receive his Army pay until 31 March 1920.

The War Office calculated that Lieut.-Col. Ward had been overpaid by £133. 2s. 6d. They spent a considerable amount time attempting to get Ward to repay the money. They made the point that Ward had received pay from public funds through two sources in respect of the same period and they requested him to repay an amount equivalent to the pay he received as a Member of Parliament for the period 6 November 1919 to 31 March 1920.

Lieut.-Col. Ward refused to repay the money on the grounds that he had not received notice of his demobilisation on the dates suggested by the War Office. He stressed that from the time he returned from Russia to March 1920 he was tidying up the affairs and accounts of his Battalion, his accounts from Hong Kong had not been squared until February 1920. He had been dealing with hundreds, if not thousands of letters from his men due to the failure to bring back their spare kit and belongings from Hong Kong to Mill Hill and those problems were still ongoing on 7 April 1920. He made the further point that he had received the money in good faith, it had been spent and he was not in a position to refund it and from that position he would not budge.

The War Office described Ward's attitude as 'somewhat contumacious' (insolent and disobedient) but 'not altogether unintelligible'. They considered asking the Fees Office, the House of Commons body responsible for paying M.P.s, to recover the overpayment in instalments from Ward's Parliamentary salary. They also considered asking Mr Speaker to sanction the same but decided against both. Instead the War Office asked the Treasury for permission to write off the overpayment. On 21 February 1921 the Lords Commissioners of His Majesty's Treasury sanctioned the write-off of the £133. 2s. 6d. to "Balances Irrecoverable and Claims Abandoned" .

The Supplement to the London Gazette of 1 April 1921 carried the notice that Lieut.-Col. J. Ward, C.B., C.M.G., relinquished his commission on completion of service on 6 November 1919 and he retained the rank of Lieutenant-Colonel.[5]

Whilst the dispute about the recovery of Ward's overpaid salary was under consideration Ward wrote to the War Office on 20 November 1919 confirming he had received notice of his demobilisation as from November 5. This clearly contradicts his claim on 7 April 1920 to Civil Servant Walter Waring, Parliamentary Private Secretary at the War Office, that he had not received notice from the War Office that he was to be demobilised in November 1919.

Likewise his protestation to the War Office about the originally proposed date of his demobilisation on 1 November 1919 contained in the War Office letter of 24 October 1919 confirms he received both letters.

In Ward's letter of 7 April 1920 he also lodged a claim with the War Office for compensation for an injury sustained in early 1915 whilst in command of the 19th Battalion Middlesex Regiment then stationed at Alexandra Palace. He was badly thrown by a restive charger falling on the right of the horse whilst his left leg was held in the stirrup. He prevented the horse from dragging him around the park by grasping the reins with both hands. He was badly shaken. A few days later a lump appeared in the left side of Lieut.-Col. Ward's groin. Dr. Shannon at the Middlesex Regimental Headquarters examined Ward. His diagnosis was that as a result of the riding accident Ward had suffered an inguinal rupture of the left side and some slight hernia on the right. He was advised by Dr. Shannon to wear a truss and had worn one ever since.

Ward informed the War Office that the truss was quite effective but at the age of 53 the injury had increased in severity and had by then stopped him from taking part in violent forms of exercise which he had previously enjoyed. He concluded his letter by requesting that his claim for compensation should not be barred by the lapse of time after relinquishing his commission.

By 1 January 1920 Ward had not received either an acknowledgement or substantive reply from the War Office to his claim for compensation for his war injury. He wrote again to the War Office raising his concerns telling the War Secretary 'if this is all the consideration that a demobilised officer's claim usually receives at the hands of your Department, there is no need to wonder at the discontent amongst Regimental officers at the treatment of their claims, and I promise to bring the matter to the attention of Parliament at the first suitable opportunity'.

On 7 January 1920 Mr B.B. Cubitt from the War Office replied to both of Ward's letters blaming a clerk's neglect for not acknowledging his first letter and reassuring him that his claim had been and was at present receiving attention.

The Lieut.-Col. Ward's impatience with the War Office grew and he used his Parliamentary position to try and get his claim resolved. On 19 February Sir Hamar Greenwood Bt. M.P., Secretary for Over Seas Trade wrote to Sir James Edward Masterton Smith, Assistant Secretary at the War Office asking him was it possible to give Colonel Ward what he was asking for.

The War Office had a problem with Ward's claim for an injury gratuity or pension. The War Office Medical Board confirmed that Lieut.-Col. Ward was

never off duty, did not report sick and continued to carry on all his duties from the date of the accident. Furthermore men with hernias were accepted for general service. However if they refused his claim on the basis that he was fit for general service all the time, they feared Ward would retort that he was not really fit but in spite of his injuries he carried on. The War Office speculated that had Ward been examined by a Medical Board at the time of his injury they would have found him unfit for general service. This begged the question whether Ward had really been unfit for general service ever since. The difficulty for the War Office was the fact that they were up against the Warrant in this case and had to judge Ward's claim accordingly and use sound reasoning.

On 19 February 1920 Mr B.B. Cubitt, on behalf of the Army Council, wrote to Ward. In his letter Cubitt acknowledged that Ward's injury in 1915 was of a severe character but after careful consideration the Army Council had decided that as he was not incapacitated for general service in consequence of the injury they were unable to award him an injury gratuity or pension. He further advised Ward that his case had been submitted to the Ministry of Pensions for consideration of compensation in the form of a Retired Pay for disability.

Lieut.-Col. Ward eventually received a disability pension of £90 per annum for malaria and a double inguinal hernia. On 6 July 1921 he had a Medical Board examination. As a result of the medical his disability was assessed at 20% and his pension was thus reduced to £60 per annum. Ward wrote to the Secretary of State for War on 2 September 1921 about his case. Ward did not dispute the findings of the Medical Board. He assumed that the reduction in pension was due either to the fact that the malaria had been cured or was no longer recognised on the ground of time since he contracted the disease and the 20% disability pension related to his hernia which was permanent in character.

The purpose of Ward's letter was, in view of his circumstances, to make another claim for an additional pension for special services as laid down in the Royal Warrant. Ward did not enumerate his services on the grounds that the War Office was aware of his contributions. Furthermore he did not want to appear boastful and was only proud to have had the opportunity to serve his country. In support of his claim for a special service pension Ward pointed out that a Lt.-Col., even though Temporary and retired, was expected to pay more attention and keep a better position than a mere private citizen and he had no private income beyond a few pounds a year. This claim was dealt with more promptly and on 22 September 1921 Ward was informed there was no regulation under which he could be granted retired pay or pension in respect of his service.

Lieut.-Col. John Ward was re-elected to Parliament in the 1922 General Election, this time as a National Liberal with a large majority over Labour. In the 1923 General Election he returned as Liberal but with a much reduced majority over Labour. In thc 1924 General Election Ward was returned to Parliament again but this time as a Constitutionalist with Liberal and Conservative support. In the 1929 General Election Ward was defeated by the Labour candidate Lady Cynthia Mosley, the first wife of Sir Oswald Mosley.

Also after the War Ward's health suffered. He was taken seriously ill in Geneva in 1922. In 1925 at conference of the General Federation of Trade Unions he denounced the 'hellish dictatorship of Moscow' and was then immediately seized with heart trouble. He was a determined opponent of 'direct action' at home and raised his voice in favour of conciliation in labour problems and the removal of workers' suspensions.

After his Parliamentary defeat in 1929 he retired to Hampshire where he was active in local affairs, already a Justice of the Peace he sat as a local magistrate and was president of the Andover branch of the British Legion.

Ward was exceptionally tall and retained his soldierly bearing throughout his life.

After an illness of some weeks John Ward died at his home Omsk, Weyhill near Andover on the 19 December 1934. He was buried on 22 December 1934 at Appleshaw. He left £5,234 and 5 shillings.[6]

1 Lt.-Col. Ward Army Service Record, National Archives, WO 339/22796; L.G. Wickham Legg, Dictionary of National Biography 1931-1940, Oxford University Press Reprint 1993, p.p. 889-890; The Times 20 December 1934; The Oxford Dictionary of National Biography, www.oxforddnb.com/view/article/36733?docPos=11

2 Supplement to the London Gazette, 28th December 1917, Published 1st January 1918, Gazette Issue 30450, p. 8

3 Second Supplement to the London Gazette, 21st March 1919, Published 22nd March 1919, Gazette Issue 31245, p. 3835

4 Hansard House of Commons, 5 November 1919, Vol. 120, Col. 1503

5 Supplement to the London Gazette, 1st April 1921, Published 1st April 1921, Gazette Issue 32276; p. 2627

6 Lt.-Col. Ward Army Service Record; L.G. Wickham Legg, Dictionary of National Biography 1931-1940, p.p. 889-890; The Times 20 December 1934; The Oxford Dictionary of National Biography; 1871, 1891,1901 and 1911 Censuses

Acknowledgements

The extensive source materials used in this book are fully referenced. The primary source for the daily activities of the 18th Battalion Middlesex Regiment is their War Diary held at the National Archives in Kew, reference number WO 95/2417. I have not individually referenced the activities of the 18th Middlesex. Whenever the activities of the 18th Middlesex are mentioned, unless otherwise stated, the source is my transcription of their War Diary.

The source for the daily activities of the 33rd Division is their War Diary also held at the National Archives. Their activities are individually referenced.

The front cover design is based on the 18th Middlesex Battalion flag held at the National Army Museum. The use of the flag in the design of the front cover is by "Courtesy of the Council of the National Army Museum, London".

The picture on p.184 of Private McFarlane's pardon is reproduced by courtesy of The National Archives, Kew, London from their file WO 71/644.

I have spent a considerable amount of time researching the book at the National Archives and the Imperial War Museum. My thanks go to all the staff at both institutions for their invaluable help and assistance.

I made extensive use of J. Edmonds, *Military Operations in France and Belgium 1914 – 1918* held at the University of Chester Reference Library. Again I thank the staff there for their help and assistance.

My wife Lesley must take the credit for this family history project turning into a published book. But for her insistence it would have remained an ever expanding piece of research that fascinated me but did not go any further. Since deciding to publish she has read and re-read this book many times. Undoubtedly without her help I would not have got through the painstaking, but necessary process involved in turning the manuscript into this book.

My good friend Dave Light proof read the original draft manuscript. His help, assistance and encouragement have contributed a great deal to getting this book into print.

I thank everyone at Troubador Publishing for their assistance at every stage of the printing and publishing process. Their enthusiasm and professionalism has been positively inspiring.

Finally, I proudly commend every service man and woman who engaged in the war effort during World War One. Their experience of the battlefield or associated activity was real and their contributions resulted in a victory that had to be won. The collective pledge to which we subscribe is 'We will remember them'. This book honours that tradition. We will remember their names with pride, honour them for their valour always, and never forget.

Index to Volume Two

Matador
9 Priory Business Park
Kibworth Beauchamp
Leicestershire LE8 0RX, UK
Tel: (+44) 116 279 2299
Fax: (+44) 116 279 2277
Email: books@troubador.co.uk
Web: www.troubador.co.uk/matador

ISBN 978 1784620 349

British Library Cataloguing in Publication Data.
A catalogue record for this book is available from the British Library.

Typeset in Aldine by Troubador Publishing Ltd
Printed and bound in the UK by TJ International, Padstow, Cornwall

Matador is an imprint of Troubador Publishing Ltd

A MINERS PALS BATTALION AT WAR

VOLUME TWO

THE HISTORY OF THE 18TH BATTALION MIDDLESEX REGIMENT (1ST PUBLIC WORKS) PIONEERS OF THE 33RD DIVISION – WORLD WAR ONE

MIKE HALL